EFFECTS OF ALCOHOL
ON THE INDIVIDUAL

A CRITICAL EXPOSITION OF
PRESENT KNOWLEDGE

VOLUME I

Alcohol Addiction and Chronic Alcoholism

*Edited on Behalf of the Scientific Committee of
The Research Council on Problems of Alcohol*

by

E. M. JELLINEK

NEW HAVEN
YALE UNIVERSITY PRESS
LONDON · HUMPHREY MILFORD · OXFORD UNIVERSITY PRESS
1942

The Printing-Office of the Yale University Press.

Contributors to Volume I

KARL M. BOWMAN, M.D.
  Professor of Psychiatry, University of California Medical School.
  Director, Langley Porter Clinic, San Francisco, California.

E. M. JELLINEK, Sc.D.
  Research Associate, Applied Physiology, Yale University.

NORMAN JOLLIFFE, M.D.
  Associate Professor of Medicine, New York University College of
    Medicine.
  Chief of the Medical Service, The Psychiatric Division, Bellevue
    Hospital, New York.

GIORGIO LOLLI, M.D.
  Research Assistant, Applied Physiology, Yale University.

MARTIN H. STEIN, M.D.
  Research Fellow in Medicine, Medical Service of the Psychiatric
    Division, Bellevue Hospital, New York.

HERMAN WORTIS, M.D.
  Assistant Clinical Professor of Psychiatry, New York University
    College of Medicine.
  Research Fellow in Psychiatry, Bellevue Hospital, New York.

Acknowledgments

THE Study of the Effects of Alcohol on the Individual, which gathered and analyzed the materials from which this book was prepared, was financed by a grant in aid from the Carnegie Corporation of New York.

The preparation of these reports for publication and the publication of this work were financed by the *Quarterly Journal of Studies on Alcohol* and the Laboratory of Applied Physiology, Yale University.

The survey of the vast literature on alcohol was greatly facilitated by the aid of the library of the New York Academy of Medicine, and special thanks are due to Dr. Archibald Malloch, the Chief Librarian, and his staff, for their valuable coöperation. Acknowledgment is also due to the Sterling Memorial Library and the Library of the School of Medicine of Yale University for facilities in aid of the preparation of these reports.

Dr. Merrill Moore generously placed at the disposal of the Study a large collection of titles of the alcohol literature which had been gathered under his direction by Works Projects Administration Projects Nos. 6148–1047 and 14667.

The Directors of the Study express their gratitude for the valuable work performed by Doctors Hedda Bolgar, Martin Gross and Anne Roe, and the Misses Vera Efron and Rose Street.

The conscientious checking of thousands of titles is a task which only the bibliographer can appreciate. This, as well as the onerous work of proofreading, was performed by Mr. Mark Keller, to whom also many cogent suggestions are due.

Preface

EVERY medical issue is, or ought to be, a social issue, too; and some social issues, regarded strictly as such, ought to become medical issues. The latter type of social issue usually becomes suitable for effective social handling only after medicine has adopted it, but only long after. This is due to the fact that when medicine first accepts a social issue as a medical one, the social affects tend to cling to it and temporarily to becloud the purely medical integration of the problem. Medicine can eliminate these encumbrances only gradually. When this has been accomplished, however, the quondam social issue emerges as a rigid medical problem. This stage, too, is not the most productive, for at this time society does not recognize the issue as its own but tends to accept the narrow view that it belongs in the restricted sphere of the medical scientist. Finally, the medical development of the problem reaches a stage when medicine can afford to drop the role of exclusiveness with respect to it. Medical science itself now reintegrates the desirable social aspects into the problem, and it becomes manifest in its correct proportions as a medico-social issue. Society is then ready to tackle it with the greatest promise of success. This process is operative with respect to the alcohol problem.

Although medical men have always treated alcoholic diseases, the alcohol problem was for centuries regarded as purely a social issue and its handling by society was encumbered by numerous emotional and political complexes. It is a relatively short time since medicine turned from the treatment of alcoholic diseases to the consideration of inebriety itself as a medical problem. This movement in medicine naturally had the effect of giving the problem a rigidly medical setting, and society was in a way alienated from the central issue. The time has come, however, when the medical purview of the alcohol problem has reached the stage of development in which exclusiveness is no longer necessary. Medicine is now able to reintegrate the social aspects of the problem and thus give it the completeness desirable for its proper handling. The sign that this stage has been reached and the promise that the alcohol problem can now be taken up and considered in its true aspect, as a medico-social issue, are the organization of the Research Council on Problems of Alcohol in the summer of 1937. The Council, which soon became an affiliated society of The American Association for the Advancement of Science, is made up primarily of scientists from every field who are seriously interested in the alcohol problem, but it includes in its membership representatives of religion, government, education, industry and business. The following quotations from statements of the purpose of the Council are indicative of its broad outlook.

"The Research Council on Problems of Alcohol is a wholly independent agency except for its connection with this Association [The American Association for the Advancement of Science]. While the Council, in its work [on alcoholism], has the moral and financial support of individuals and organizations representing various and different points of view in respect to the use of alcohol, it has no connection whatsoever with any prohibition or reform movement, or with any repeal agency or liquor organization. It is made up primarily of scientists whose sole purpose is to conduct an unbiased study of the relation of alcohol to the health of the individual and the welfare of society and to disseminate the results of its study in a socially useful manner. . .

"The alcohol problem has become one of the major perplexities of our civilization. On top of all the intrinsic difficulties of the situation, there have been superimposed emotional and political elements that have produced still further complications.

"It has become evident that nothing can be accomplished by the application of main force. If we are to find a way out, it can be only through the development of a complete factual basis on which can be built an intelligent, effective plan of action.

"The main and primary purpose of the Research Council on Problems of Alcohol is to ascertain the facts; the secondary objective is to make these facts available to the public in such a way that they will do the most good.

"Since the development of facts is essentially a scientific procedure, the personnel of the Council is predominantly made up of persons who are working in the field of science. To these are being added such others from the fields of education, business and public life as are competent to assist in carrying out the secondary objective."

The Council felt that in developing a program of research it was essential to avoid unnecessary repetition. On the other hand, it would be necessary to carry out again some investigations which had resulted only in controversy. These investigations, however, would have to be done under conditions which would resolve the conflicts by yielding scientifically valid answers to the doubtful issues. Furthermore, it seemed necessary to ascertain what gaps existed in research on inebriety and to determine whether these gaps were of an essential nature or merely of the character of curiosa. Since, moreover, research is limited by time and funds and appropriate personnel, a research program must, even if arbitrarily, center around a certain complex of problems, and all projects must be viewed in the light of their relevance and proximity to the central problems.

The first necessary step toward the formation of a research program complying with these requirements seemed to be an analysis of the existing scientific literature on problems of alcohol. Since this literature is of formidable proportions, it could be hoped to accomplish the goal in a reasonable time only through the work of a well-equipped staff. The Council therefore, in the spring of 1939, submitted plans for such a critical review of the literature to the Carnegie Corporation of New York. Considerable funds necessary for this project, called the Study of the Effects of Alcohol on the Individual, were granted by the Corporation. This was highly gratifying to the Council, as it not only afforded the means to carry out the proposed investigation but constituted a recognition of the value of the Council's program by one of the greatest American foundations supporting scientific research.

The funds for this study were assigned by the Council to the Department of Psychiatry of the New York University College of Medicine. A Committee was formed, including two Directors of the Study, to supervise the project. The Committee was constituted as follows:

Karl M. Bowman, Chairman; Hans T. Clarke; Irving Graef; E. M. Jellinek, Executive Director; Norman Jolliffe, Medical Director; A. T. Poffenberger; S. Bernard Wortis.

The Study was begun in September, 1939, with headquarters at the library of the New York Academy of Medicine. In the task of studying the vast literature of inebriety the Directors were aided by qualified personnel. The gathering and systematizing of the material was largely completed by December, 1940, but an extension of this work is still being carried on, an activity made possible through the *Quarterly Journal of Studies on Alcohol*.

The collected literature has been and in part is still being analyzed by the Directors of the Study in conjunction with other members of the Scientific Committee. Many of their reports have already been published in the *Quarterly Journal of Studies on Alcohol*. The Research Council has been utilizing the experience of this Study to a great extent and is now presenting the first volume of the analysis of the literature in book form. It is hoped that this volume will serve a large number of students of the problems of alcohol as an authoritative work of reference.

KARL M. BOWMAN

Scope and Method of the Study

BOOKS, pamphlets, and papers dealing with the effects of alcohol, the incidence, prevention, and cure of inebriety, and the statistics of alcohol consumption, may number roughly 100,000 titles. To review this literature would be a formidable task. Our object, however, is not to review it and report the contents of each paper but rather to make a critical exposition of the present knowledge about the effects of alcohol as revealed by the scientific literature.

Of the huge quantity of published material on alcohol, close to 80 per cent is of a propagandistic nature, against or for the use of alcoholic beverages. Many of these tendentious writings use, or rather abuse, scientific findings culled from the scientific literature in support of the condemnation or exculpation of alcohol. To a larger extent, however, they are moral philosophies or outright preachments. Some of the subjective writings are wise and cogent. Nevertheless, they do not constitute the kind of material that can serve the purpose of this work.

If it were the purpose of this study to analyze the problem of alcohol or to trace its history, most of this literature would have to be considered, irrespective of scientific merit. Our object, however, is to analyze the results of researches prompted by the alcohol problem. This limitation reduces the bulk of the literature to a possible 20,000 titles. Of these, about 30 per cent are compilations from scientific literature, without original opinions by the authors, and about 10 per cent are duplications by authors of their own publications, including popularizations, reformulations for publication in different journals, or republications in different form. This still leaves about 12,000 titles, and of these a large percentage deals with administrative problems; a part consists of medicolegal material of which only a small portion is relevant to our specific interest; and there is a fair number of statistical or sociologic writings which may be of great significance for the alcohol problem as a whole but not for the problem as delineated in the title of this work, namely, the effects of alcohol on the individual. We are left, thus, with about 6,000 titles. Some 500 of these are critical reanalyses of the results obtained by various investigators and are therefore valuable and must be taken into consideration. Nearly all of these reviews, however, are limited in scope to some specific problem, such as metabolism of alcohol, or experimental cirrhosis of the liver. The balance of some 5,500 titles consists of reports of original investigations on the psychiatric, physiologic, psychologic, biochemical, and pathologic aspects of the acute and chronic effects of alcohol. In this material, again, much has become obsolete, and the task before us requires the consideration of roughly 3,500 titles. Nevertheless, the selection of relevant literature has involved the reading or handling of a much larger number of papers.

The limitation of this study to the effects of alcohol on the individual implies that there is also an effect on society, which is to remain unconsidered in the present work. Admittedly this division is an arbitrary one. It is, indeed, not so much a policy based on reflection as a result of the financial limitations of the study. The arbitrariness of the division, moreover, is particularly manifest since on the one hand the process of habit formation in the addict and generally in the excessive drinker has its social determinants, and on the other hand the habit also has its social consequences. Owing to these interactions, the arbitrary line of division between effects of alcohol on the individual and on society cannot be observed consistently. It should be understood, also, that it is not the sociologic aspects of inebriety which are excluded but only the effects of inebriety on society. Thus, the effects of society on inebriety are given due consideration. Since the effects of alcohol cannot be dealt with abstractly, but the etiology of addiction and other forms of excessive drinking is implied in the effects—addiction itself may be considered as an effect—excursions must be made into other fields whenever required for comprehensive treatment of any subject.

Generally, the scope of this work is the etiology of abnormal drinking; the effects of such drinking on the bodily and mental functions of the individual; and the immediate effects of alcohol in any quantity on the organs and their functions and on psychologic behavior. These immediate effects, usually determined in laboratory experimentation, are considered either as throwing light on chronic processes or as bringing about, *per se*, significant temporary changes in the individual. Even within the limitations adopted, this work does not pretend to encyclopedic range. The aim is not to record every particle of information that is known about alcohol within the defined field but rather to consolidate that knowledge which may be of relevance in dealing with the alcohol problem, including prevention and treatment of inebriety and alcoholic disease, and in indicating the path of future research. The magnitude of the problem, however, also requires to be characterized. The incidence of various types of inebriety and chronic alcoholism, and indices of the incidence, are therefore also considered on the basis of critically reviewed reports.

Volume I is devoted entirely to the etiology and treatment of abnormal drinking and to the mental and bodily disorders of chronic alcoholism. It is largely restricted to clinical material. Experimental data have been drawn upon only insofar as they give direction to or aid in the interpretation of clinical investigations, or when they bear out or contradict hypotheses on the pathogenesis of bodily diseases of chronic alcoholism.

Volume II will deal largely with the experimental material. Thus the physiology of alcohol will be treated there as well as the absorption and metabolism of alcohol and the experimentally determined and chronic effects of alcohol on bodily organs and their functions and on psychologic functions. Just as the first volume must draw upon experimental material, the second volume will have to draw upon clinical material for the elucidation of experimental findings. There is even some clincial material which is best considered within the framework of the experimental part, such as the treatment of acute alcoholic intoxication. Volume II will also include the chapter on germ damage, the literature of which is partly statistical but to a considerable part experimental and flows from some of the experimental chapters included in that volume. The question of germ damage exceeds somewhat the line of effects on the individual. It is, however, so closely related to the discussion of physiologic effects on the individual that it cannot arbitrarily be excluded from this work.

Volume III will deal with the magnitude of the problem in terms of incidence and will analyze the statistics presented in the literature.

Excluded from this work, as related more particularly to effects on society, are effects on the family, on criminality, on poverty, and on industry. Nevertheless, some of these questions are dealt with to some extent inasmuch as they may be indices of inebriety.

For the subjects treated in Volume I the literature has been covered up to the year 1941, while for the subjects to be treated in the two following volumes the literature may be covered to a later date. As to how far back the literature has been reviewed, no general statement can be made. In the case of some subjects, particularly in the case of some of the mental disorders, it became evident that the older literature contained much description and theory which apparently had been forgotten or had not received sufficient attention in America. It was thought that a valuable service would be rendered by calling attention again to this material and by integrating it into what may be called the body of knowledge on those subjects. In other subjects the older literature seemed to be of historical interest only and was therefore dealt with briefly for that purpose. This was the case, for instance, in the question of the bodily diseases of chronic alcoholism, such as polyneuropathy. Generally, a few historical allusions are made on all topics, as these serve the purpose at least of gauging the degree of progress that has been made in each field. In a work which aims at contributing toward foundations of future research, such historical notes have a definite place when they tend to show the kind of obstacles which have been overcome or when they reveal a certain inertia which still seems to persist.

While the published reports of investigators of alcohol problems have been carefully analyzed and the findings of the various investigators are presented in the light of such analysis, it appeared essential to present also the data and opinions of these investigators free from superimposed analysis. For this purpose, throughout this work, not only experimental data but also etiologic theories and other theories or ideas are presented in tabular form whenever possible. The enumeration of these opinions and findings, however, does not imply acceptance by the contributors to this work. The critical attitude of the reviewers must be sought in the accompanying text. It has also been an editorial policy to go beyond analysis and to attempt a synthesis of the experience and thought of diverse students of inebriety. In this synthetic presentation the original authors have sometimes receded into the background. Since the experience of these various investigators has originated from consideration of different kinds of subject material, different methods of approach, and different interests, this type of synthesis has seemed to be particularly desirable in order to formulate the total picture of present knowledge.

In view of the aims of this work, namely, to clarify what is established fact, what is controversial, and what gaps exist in our knowledge, as well as to reconcile apparent contradictions and conflicts, it was necessary to reëvaluate the findings of various investigators on the basis of such raw data or averages as the literature affords; to attach less weight to those reports which did not give sufficient evidence for the basis of their conclusions; and to compare investigations of similar nature in the light of their techniques and methods and of critical examination of the material utilized.

In the course of such analysis it has become evident that many conclusions reached by investigators have been accepted on authority. It has been tacitly assumed that the investigator who is a competent biologist or biochemist, for instance, is necessarily a competent logician, and that his analysis of data is as valid as his analysis of chemical substances. This is not always a safe assumption. In the course of our readings we have come across investigations devised with such foresight as only the most competent scientist can accomplish and carried out with accuracy reflecting the finest workmanship. But the conclusions drawn from these excellently devised and performed experiments have sometimes been in direct, though surely unconscious, contradiction of the experimental data. Instances of such miscarriages of scientific intent will be seen particularly in the chapters on the experimental studies. It is worth while, however, to cite here one or two examples of this nature, and thus to illustrate how such material has been analyzed and treated in this work.

One investigator studied the reaction time of moderate and heavy drinkers before and after alcohol intake. All the measurements on each subject were reported but no consolidation of the hundreds of observations was attempted; and the conclusion was reached that after alcohol intake alcoholics return faster to their preëxperimental values than moderate drinkers. The reviewers* of this report for the present study, upon consolidating the data and analyzing it, found that there was actually no difference between the heavy and moderate drinkers, as all values could be matched in the two groups, and there was only one extreme value which apparently had caught the investigator's eye and impressed him unduly. Thus a conclusion differing from that of the investigator, but based entirely on his own data, was reached by the reviewers.

A more surprising finding has been that investigators sometimes, after carefully tabulating and averaging their material, come to conclusions which do not flow at all from their own data. Thus, one investigator presented the percentage difference between the number of errors in a test of steadiness of aim before and after taking various kinds of alcoholic beverages and stated as his conclusion that "the more concentrated the beverage the less is generally its effect on the steadiness of aim." Examination of the investigator's tabulated data, however, revealed that actually beer and cognac, the beverages of lowest and highest alcoholic concentration used in the experiment, consistently showed the smallest percentage differences in all the series of experiments. However, not even this interpretation could be considered legitimate since the experiment was invalidated by failure to control interfering factors. Thus, again, the reviewers† were justified in ignoring the verbalized conclusion of the investigator.

Some accepted conclusions have come from poorly devised experiments or from numerically inadequate material, and in some instances have been based on a misapplication of statistical methods to laboratory data. The most extraordinary example of this is the conclusion about the effect of alcohol on performance on an intelligence test, which was found by the reviewers‡ to have been drawn on the basis of an arithmetical artifact.

While iconoclasm was not the purpose of the analysis, it has seemed to be essential to demonstrate these points and thus to make possible the elimination from the category of accepted knowledge of those

*Jellinek, E. M. and McFarland, R. A. Reported in *Quart. J. Stud. Alc.*, I, 300, 1942.
†*Op. cit.*, p. 301.
‡*Op. cit.*, p. 360.

conclusions which had their origins in faults of procedure or inter-pretation.

The results of the analysis of the alcohol literature will be found in the following volumes. One may, however, attempt here a characteri-zation of the status of research itself, of its credits and debits.

There is a considerably greater fund of knowledge relating to the problems of alcohol than is usually admitted. The picture of the extent of progress in actual knowledge in this field has been obscured by several factors, among which is that epigrammatic wisdom which seems to be attracted by the problems of alcohol. More seriously, valuable findings have been damaged by extending their meaning beyond the legitimate limits of their inherent significance. The so-called conflicting results of alcohol research have been greatly exag-gerated by giving weight to numerous investigations which, although originating in honest interest, did not have the benefit of the pre-requisite experience, comprehension of the total problem, and the necessary logical equipment. Under the sign of fair-and-square dealing it has become a habit to accredit all reports in the literature on an equal basis. Insecurity is artificially created by giving the appearance of indefiniteness to the results of a first-class investigation when a reviewer cites the failure of "another investigator" to confirm these results, although the apparent disagreement may be due to the fact that the "other investigator" has ignored good experimental procedure, or shows no understanding of the problem or of its meaning. Unfor-tunately, some kind of scientific Bushido seems to compel us to con-cede the respectability of everything which gets published in a scientific journal, instead of permanently ignoring certain of these contributions. Naturally, the exclusion of any report from further consideration must be based on careful analysis of the material itself and not on the obscurity of the author's name or on any other irrelevant grounds.

A further impression of conflicting and contradictory research is frequently created by placing in contraposition investigations which are by no means mutually exclusive but rather complementary. Thus, an investigation on the occurrence of epilepsy among the offspring of alcoholic patients may be contrasted with the occurrence of inebriates in the ascendants of epileptics, and the fact that the two investigations show entirely different results is submitted as evidence of lack of knowledge around this problem, while actually there is only a want of the critical discernment that the two investigations were studying different issues which should not be expected to yield like results.

When careful analysis segregates the chaff, there undoubtedly remains a valuable residue of knowledge. And while this residue is far from enough to provide a solution of the total problem, it furnishes a sufficient basis for tackling in the future much more complex investigations than we usually admit being prepared for, and for abandoning the compulsion of eternal repetition dictated by the fear that we still lack a foundation for progress.

More research has been performed by investigators who have been brought into contact with some isolated aspect of the problems of alcohol than by investigators interested in the total problem. This has led to a preponderance of researches on interesting side issues over researches primarily relevant to the central problem of alcohol, which is the problem of the origins and development of addiction and of other forms of abnormal drinking. But even this problem of origins and development is central only inasmuch as it is prerequisite to the prevention and cure of abnormal alcoholic habits.

A list of publications on matters relating to alcohol would give the impression that the main problems are the effects of alcohol immediately following its ingestion. Of next greatest importance, by the number of publications, would appear to be the description and the cure of the bodily diseases consequent to the prolonged excessive indulgence in alcoholic beverages. The formation of the habit from which the grave consequences flow has received much less experimental and clinical attention, and its explanation has been left largely to intellectual efforts. It must be admitted that some of these intellectual efforts are the products of penetrating insight and logic. Without these we would be much less prepared for entering on an experimental phase of research in the central problems.

The preponderance of research on the immediate effects of alcohol may be traced to the historic origins of alcohol research. At one time the most urgent question was whether or not alcohol is a quick restorative of muscular strength, whether it is a stimulant or not. This was when it was thought that workmen employed in heavy labor should be allowed to have their drink in the factory. At that time the question of immediate effects had to take precedence over the question of the origin of addiction and excessive drinking. The first great impetus to alcohol research, particularly to psychologic experiments with alcohol, came from the industrial problems. The course of research once set was not overcome sufficiently when the original motivation of that type of research became obsolete. Today the question of the immediate effects of alcohol exists practically only in relation to automobile driving. Naturally, there are important theoretical questions which can be answered only by studying immediate effects.

Much of the physiologic research has been carried out by clinicians who, quite naturally, have not dealt with the problems in truly physiologic terms. Some outstanding physiologists have been attracted by important problems of alcohol but have not taken their lead from clinical medicine, although this would have been the most desirable setting. Physiologists have performed fundamental researches in the absorption and metabolism of alcohol; but since they came to these problems from the theoretical frame of reference of physiology, longitudinal studies, which are prerequisite to the understanding of the process of addiction and the development of chronic alcoholism, have been relatively rather rare.

The bulk of longitudinal studies reported in the literature had the object of studying brain pathology, or liver pathology, in animals exposed to prolonged alcoholization, without studying other processes which were going on during the development of that pathology. Also, a great deal of experimentation with continuously alcoholized animals was carried out with the object of studying germ damage.

The study of changes in absorption and metabolism of alcohol and in the general metabolism as well as of nutritional and behavioral aspects, has not been done sufficiently in longitudinal investigations. Experimental psychology has devoted its attention entirely to the immediate effects of alcohol on psychomotor functions, sensations, memory, and the associative functions. These studies have been of definite value in establishing the modus and sequence of the effect of alcohol on the nervous system. On the other hand, the psychology of motivation in alcohol addiction has not been considered experimentally, nor the emotional or personality changes.

Generally, all experimental research has shied away from the essential problems and has rationalized this by pleading insufficient knowledge of fundamental facts. Actually, the lack of this essential experimentation is due to the unfamiliarity of the experimentalists with the total problem of inebriety, while those familiar with it have rarely been experimentalists. It may be added that some rather trivial experiments have been given the appearance of delving to the depths.

Many inferences relative to processes in chronic alcoholism have been made from the known immediate effects of alcohol merely because of the existence of the large store of data on the latter aspect of the problem. As research leads, such inferences are valuable. They have, however, not been utilized as leads, but in the course of frequent repetition have come to be regarded as known facts.

The clinical study of bodily diseases of chronic alcoholism has led to the important discovery of the role of vitamin deficiencies in inebriety. On the other hand, this discovery which in itself does not explain the behavioral changes in inebriety, has led to extending the theory of the indirect effects of alcohol from the bodily diseases to the mental disturbances. Even previous to the discovery of the vitamin deficiencies in inebriety, direct effects of alcohol on the nervous system were denied and hypothetic metabolic processes were postulated. The denial of a direct permanent effect of the excessive intake of alcohol on the nervous system is not based on evidence but rather on the failure to demonstrate the direct causation.

Research on the etiology of the diseases of chronic alcoholism has neglected to exploit certain leads offered by precipitating and presumably predisposing factors. There has also been some complacency with reiterating certain suggestions relative to etiology rather than investigating them. Psychiatry has produced some highly valuable working hypotheses on alcohol addiction and inebriety in general, more on the basis of an accumulation of clinical experience than through systematic research. Occasionally clinical psychology has been drawn in by psychiatry for the study of the personality of inebriates, but largely psychiatry has not made its findings sufficiently palatable to other students of the alcohol question to stimulate research to take some leads from psychiatry.

On the whole, physiology, experimental psychology, and clinical medicine have produced basic data, and psychiatry has furnished the necessary insight and working hypotheses, sufficient to warrant application of the existing knowledge to the investigation of the essential and complex problems of the origins of inebriety and addiction, their prevention and treatment.

E. M. JELLINEK

Contents

Part I

CHAPTER I

Alcohol Addiction and Its Treatment*

KARL M. BOWMAN *and* E. M. JELLINEK

INTRODUCTION

IN the problems of alcohol, alcohol addiction and other forms of abnormal drinking occupy the central position and all other issues, except the immediate effect, emanate from these. Not that the other issues of alcohol are less important, but they cannot be divorced from the phenomena of abnormal drinking. Problems relating to the immediate effects of alcohol, however, would obtain even if abnormal drinking were nonexistent. On the other hand, while the study of the immediate effects sheds some light on certain aspects of all forms of drinking and of chronic alcoholism, it is really a secondary consideration. Acute intoxication and even the manifestations of sub-clinical intoxication, through their impairment of judgment, coördination, perception and other functions, may play a considerable role in all types of accidents, in delinquency and in the lowering of industrial efficiency. Nevertheless, the medical and the social problems of the immediate effects of alcohol are incomparably smaller than the problems of abnormal drinking and chronic alcoholism.

Despite its crucial significance and the considerable speculation which it has provoked, alcohol addiction has received much less attention from research than either the various manifestations of chronic alcoholism, or the immediate effects of alcohol. It is important to state this fact, since it bears on the planning of future research activities. One of the many reasons for this anomaly is the elusive nature of addiction, which makes its course difficult to trace.

That the study of addiction itself should be particularly difficult is rather paradoxical, since almost no disorder develops as overtly as this one. The patient is actually active in bringing it about and this is true in a much stricter sense than it is of the person who acquires an occupational disease. Theoretically, it should be possible to follow each step in the development of alcohol addiction. Actually, however, only the

*The combined bibliography of Chapters I and II appears at the end of Chapter II, pp. 152–169.

act of incorporating varying amounts of the intoxicating substance into the organism, and some of the immediate effects of this substance on the organism, are accessible to immediate observation. The drives behind this merely physical act of drinking are largely open only to reflective observation, although this does not exclude their being experimentally demonstrable.

The term "reflective observation" need not be defined beyond pointing out that it implies that every observation made on addiction is directed by a theory instead of being the element of a theory. Nevertheless, many of these reflective observations were made by men of great experience and that is a factor whose scientific merit cannot be denied. It is thus not a vain undertaking to analyze the ideas of the observers of addiction. An attempt will be made to summarize the present status of knowledge of, and of opinion on, the nature and etiology of addiction. The least that may be expected from such an analysis is direction for future researches.

Some examination of definitions and of terminology is needed before the question of the etiology of addiction can be discussed.

I. DEFINITIONS OF CHRONIC ALCOHOLISM AND ALCOHOL ADDICTION

The status of definitions in the pertinent literature is not as confused as some writers would make it appear; neither is it as clear-cut as would be desirable. The various definitions are not particularly original. Nevertheless, in our opinion, many of them are sufficient. Definitions relating to chronic alcoholism and to alcohol addiction lack that esoteric and frequently involved character which usually attaches to definitions in social biology. It may be this unimpressiveness of the definitions which has given rise, in some minds, to the idea that they are insufficient.

Generally in the scientific literature there is fairly good agreement on the diagnosis of alcohol addiction and chronic alcoholism and these two conditions are practically never confused with social drinking. It is only outside of the strictly scientific literature that disagreement on the criteria becomes obtrusive. Thus, in the emotionally colored propagandistic literature, one can find a man who once got drunk on his birthday termed an alcoholic. Since we are concerned here with the scientific literature only, the task of clarifying the question of definitions should not be too arduous.

In general, such confusion as one does encounter is due less to differences in criteria than to differences in terminology and in particular to the common practice of equating the terms chronic alcoholism* and alcohol addiction, or of using them interchangeably. This is not an insuperable difficulty, since it is usually clear from the context which condition is meant.

Perhaps the earliest definition of what may be called inebriety implies that addiction is a disease which gives rise ultimately to physical diseases. The author of this definition was Thomas Trotter. In other words, a distinction was made between what is now called alcohol addiction and what is now known as chronic alcoholism. After Trotter, this distinction was lost sight of until relatively recent years. The expression, chronic alcoholism, is followed in parentheses by the words, alcohol addiction, in the works of Krafft-Ebing, but even at present alcohol addiction and chronic alcoholism are not always distinguished; e.g., Rosanoff (b) speaks of "pathologic alcoholism," which includes both. Bleuler (b), however, found that in theory it was necessary to distinguish between chronic alcoholism and alcohol addiction, but admitted that in practice the distinction cannot be made consistently, because the addiction usually turns into chronic alcoholism, or it may become secondarily a symptom of chronic alcoholism. Bumke and Kant, too, felt that the concepts of chronic alcoholism and of alcohol addiction do not overlap completely, and that a separation between them was essential. Kürz and Kraepelin also made this distinction, although they did not formulate it. Sometimes an author defines only one or the other of these conditions, because his interest at the time is limited. We believe that this theoretical distinction is fundamental to clarity of discussion and should be adhered to with as much consistency as is possible.

Reflective students of inebriety have always stressed that the amount consumed by the individual cannot form a basis for judging whether or not he is intemperate. Thus, Dresel said, "From the nature and quantity of drink one cannot say that a man is a 'drinker.' Any conclusion as to this must be based on the consequences and manifestations of his drinking habits." A similar idea is expressed by Waddell and Haag: "We should always, in any attempt at classifying drinkers, employ the effect produced as the basis of subdivisions." The principle of using the effect as a criterion is a good one, but it must be stressed

* It may be remarked that Dittmer pointed out that the expression chronic alcoholism is a tautology since the termination "ism" implies a persistent state. This remark has its merits but is not so essential as to warrant breaking with the old established term.

that mere drunkenness is not regarded in the scientific literature as evidence of either addiction or chronic alcoholism [e.g., Silkworth (*a*)], while in the nonscientific literature, inebriety, addiction and chronic alcoholism are inextricably mingled.

We are listing below some definitions, usually paraphrased, which clearly refer to chronic alcoholism (Table 1).

TABLE I

Definitions of Chronic Alcoholism

Author	*Definitions*
Lancereaux	The word alcoholism created by Magnus Huss describes the complex of phenomena resulting from the action of the excessive use of distilled drinks on the organism.
Schroeder	Drinking of large amounts without any signs of chronic poisoning does not constitute chronic alcoholism in the clinical sense.
Crothers	Alcoholism is literally a condition of poisoning from spirits, the prominent symptoms of which are toxemia and paralysis.
Schultze	Chronic alcoholism is the totality of lasting physical and mental impairments resulting from continued abuse of alcohol.
Bogen (*b*)	Chronic alcoholism is the totality of effects brought about by habitual abuse of alcohol.
Rosenfeld	One should speak of chronic alcoholism only if signs of chronic intoxication are present.
Bumke and Kant	One speaks of chronic alcoholism only when permanent physical or psychic alterations are observed which are directly due to the action of alcohol.
Bleuler (*b*)	The chronic alcoholic is one who has been marked by drink, bodily or psychologically.
Stefan	Diagnosis of chronic alcoholism must only be made in the presence of diseases of the internal organs.
Waddell and Haag	Alcoholism may be defined as any change in the condition of the body or in its physical or mental activities caused by alcohol or the alcoholic beverages.

Among all these definitions there is close agreement: they all regard chronic alcoholism as determined by mental or physiological changes following the prolonged use of alcoholic beverages, but not by drinking itself. As Silkworth (*a*) has expressed it, "Alcoholism is not a habit." In spite of the general practice of defining alcoholism as a diseased state and not as an activity, the word alcoholism, not preceded by *chronic*, is commonly used to denote excessive drinking and even by those who are responsible for the strict definition of chronic alcoholism in terms of definite bodily and mental changes. We wish to avoid the use of the word alcoholism in the sense of excessive drinking since that would imply, in spite of all definitions, that chronic alcoholism is permanent or habitual excessive drinking. It seems that such discrepancies as are found in the use of the words chronic alcoholism may be largely attributed to the use of the term alcoholism in the sense of excessive drinking. As convenient as the word alcoholism may be, we shall use instead the terms inebriety and abnormal drinking, without implying that personality abnormalities must always be present.

It may seem that the brief definitions which are given in Table 1 do not say much, but the fact that they all insist on organic or mental changes makes it quite possible to recognize chronic alcoholism by objective criteria, since these changes are well known, e.g., polyneuropathy, pellagra, amblyopia, Korsakoff's disease, delirium tremens. The only condition is that these changes must have occurred in a person with a history or other evidence of drinking.

Rosanoff (b) gives much more detailed criteria, but in his term "pathologic alcoholism" he includes both chronic alcoholism and alcohol addiction. "One is justified in speaking of pathologic alcoholism in cases in which, by reason of resulting disability or illness, the drinking gives rise to serious social maladjustments: neglecting work, losing jobs, getting into accidents, getting arrested in disturbing the peace, committing impulsive crimes, drifting into domestic trouble, having to be hospitalized for a psychotic breakdown, becoming involved in social scandals, etc. However, even in the absence of such maladjustments and illnesses, habitual drinking must be considered pathologic if the drinker has urgent craving for alcohol and has lost control of the situation to such an extent that he is no longer able to give it up even in the presence of a sincere desire to do so and following a definitely declared resolution." While he gives some very useful criteria, the placing of these two conditions into one category is not helpful. It may be remarked that the term pathologic alcoholism is not felicitous, since, while one can distinguish between normal and pathological drinking, alcoholism is always a pathological state.

Some definitions of alcohol addiction are listed in Table 2. In some of these entries the terms used by the authors relate to chronic alcoholism, but it is evident that they refer to alcohol addiction. This is presumably due to the fact that these authors were interested in addiction and not in the alcoholic diseases and therefore did not feel the necessity for making a distinction between chronic alcoholism and alcohol addiction.

TABLE 2

Definitions of Alcohol Addiction

Author	Definition
Kürz and Kraepelin	The person who is designated as an addict does not have the resistance to give up alcohol even when serious economic, social and somatic damage results. Thus in the definition of an alcohol addict, emphasis must be laid on the lack of will power. In this respect he resembles the drug addict.
Cimbal	It is not the habit of using alcoholic drinks which makes for alcohol addiction, but rather the craving for intoxication, i.e., the inability to achieve the psychological contents necessary for harmonic living through anything else but intoxicants.
Ernst	Alcohol addicts are those who cannot stop drinking; and alcoholics are those who get damaged through chronic alcohol consumption.
Adams	Addiction is a state of bondage to a masterful drug, usually but not always of the narcotic class and is manifested by craving, tolerance, intense discomfort of a specialized type on withdrawal of the drug and tendency to relapse.
Bumke and Kant	The alcohol addict has no possibility of resisting his craving for alcohol. He is an addict in the sense of a morphinist.
Gabriel and Kratzmann	Addiction is the urgent desire to remove by external means a permanent, tormenting disturbance of psychic equilibrium inherent in the personality.
Bleuler (*b*)	By alcohol addiction we mean all those cases in whom because of habit or some kind of disposition, and in spite of insight, alcohol indulgence cannot be given up or cannot be reduced, but where the symptoms of chronic alcoholism have not yet appeared.
Menninger, K. A.	"Alcohol addiction can be thought of not as a disease but as a suicidal *flight from* disease, a disastrous attempt at the self-cure of an unseen inner conflict, aggravated but not primarily caused (as many think) by external conflict."
Fleming (*c*)	True alcohol addiction is characterized by specific craving and associated with real habituation.
Durfee (*b*)	An individual becomes an alcoholic or "problem drinker" when drinking gets beyond his control.
Anon.	The true test of whether or not a person is an alcohol addict is whether he can, after an evening of drinking, go without another drink until the end of the following day.
Moore	Addicts: constant steady drinkers who drink not only to relieve psychologic distress but also to overcome symptoms resulting from the previous day's alcoholic intake.
Janet (cit. Lewis)	An alcoholic is an individual who needs alcohol in order to be normal. A drunken man is a person whose mental condition was normal but who, under the influence of alcohol, rapidly enters an abnormal state.

Author	*Definition*
Peabody	To the chronic alcoholic a night's sleep does not represent the end of an alcoholic occasion but rather an unusually long period of abstention; morning drinkers are chronic alcoholics.
Meyer, A.	Chronic alcoholism is a state in which craving makes it impossible to stop drinking and in which continuation is the only resource.
Strecker	The borderline between normal and abnormal drinking is crossed when alcohol is used as an aid to adjust oneself to reality. True alcoholism is a neurosis.
Tokarsky	The differential diagnosis of whether or not a person is a chronic alcoholic is made on the basis of whether or not the patient wants to give up alcohol and cannot.
Williams, T. A.	Inebriety is not a disease itself but merely a habit of psychic reaction. It eventually becomes a craving.

Craving and the inability to resist it are contained in all of these definitions and, although only Cimbal and Strecker include in their definition that alcohol serves in these people as a means of social adjustment, most of the others do consider the aspect of adjustment in their discussions. The factor of habituation or acquired tolerance is considered by some, but only as one of the criteria of addiction [e.g., Adams; Fleming (b, c)]. Such definitions as that given by an anonymous author are too narrow, since they do not embrace the addict who uses intoxication as a means of adjustment.

On the whole, all these definitions show great agreement, but nevertheless, they are much less satisfactory than the definitions of chronic alcoholism. Actually, they are of value in theoretical discussion only, and there they are indispensable. While, however, the definition of chronic alcoholism enables one to recognize by examination any given chronic alcoholic, the definition of alcohol addiction does not permit of an immediate diagnosis.

In the problem of alcohol we are concerned not only with those drinkers who are unable to give up alcohol, i.e., the addicts, but also with the much more numerous abnormal drinkers all of whom are potential secondary addicts. We must have some definition for abnormal drinking and this can be formulated as habitual indulgence in alcoholic beverages beyond the limits of merely satisfying thirst, or of using the alcoholic beverages in the sense in which a condiment is used, or in its formal social use, or as an *occasional* stimulant. The words drinking, drinking habits, drinker, unless accompanied by the qualifying adjective moderate, will be used here in the sense of drinking beyond those limits. This broader formulation is necessary since—in anticipation of the results of this analysis—it may be stated that addiction does not necessarily originate in the desire for the psychological or physiological effects of alcohol, but may develop as a secondary result of drinking habits.

The basic formulations for further discussion are:

1. Chronic alcoholism and alcohol addiction must be distinguished for theoretical purposes, although in practice the distinction is frequently neither feasible nor important.

2. Chronic alcoholism is defined in the scientific literature with great agreement as physical and psychological changes following the prolonged use of alcoholic beverages. These changes are known and can be diagnosed in any individual case.

3. Alcohol addiction may be defined as an uncontrollable craving for alcohol. The outstanding criterion is the inability to break with the habit. In primary addiction, this craving serves the purpose of artificial social adjustment. In secondary addiction, the purpose is that of counteracting the physical effects of a preceding bout.

4. Chronic alcoholism may exist with or without addiction and addiction may exist without chronic alcoholism.

5. Not every abnormal drinker is an addict in the true sense of the word, but he is a potential secondary addict.

6. The entire population of chronic alcoholics, alcohol addicts and abnormal drinkers may be designated as inebriates, and this expression may be used also when a distinction between various types is not possible.

II. THE ETIOLOGY OF ALCOHOL ADDICTION

Strictly, by etiology of alcohol addiction, the causes leading to an irresistible craving for alcohol, or rather for its effects, should be understood. However, the question is usually formulated in a much broader sense to examine the causes which lie behind habitual indulgence in alcoholic beverages beyond the limits of what may be called normal drinking.

Etiological theories usually consider one or more of the following: personality, heredity, constitution, psychotic or psychopathic tendencies, the emotional situation, environmental factors, such as occupation and the drinking mores of the community, tolerance and the physiological processes. The effect of alcohol on the total person, i.e., the molar effect, is also an element to be considered in the etiology of the drinking habit.

The Function of Alcohol

Many writers on alcoholism and alcohol addiction enumerate "reasons" for drinking. These "reasons" generally describe the functions of alcohol, i.e., what the drinker expects to receive from it. We may begin by discussing the motives of the moderate, or, as he is sometimes called, the normal drinker. What constitutes normal drinking is largely a matter of the customs of the country. In this country, the regular use of one or two glasses of wine (2 to 4 oz.) or a glass of beer with a meal is encountered only in limited circles. Generally this is strange to Americans and, therefore, the American literature often neglects all consideration of this aspect of normal drinking. Actually, the person who indulges in this habit uses the alcoholic beverage as he would use a condiment. He does not expect, nor does he get from these small amounts, complete pacification of his troubles, elation, or the release of inhibitions. He takes the alcoholic beverage for its taste, just as he would eat cheese, and for its mild comfort. As Pohlisch (b) said, in Latin and German countries, beer and wine are often taken without any desire for intoxication and also without a psychological readiness for addiction. Outside of this type of normal drinking, which is fairly restricted geographically, the moderate drinker will use alcoholic beverages for relaxation and recreation and in compliance with social forms and "to overcome fatigue," especially in hard manual labor (Meggendorfer). Naturally an *occasional* recourse to alcohol for its expected stimulating effects, or for its power of dispelling anxiety, is still within the range of the normal. The reasons for drinking enumerated by Myerson (b) are largely within the scope of normal drinking but may go beyond that: "Men drink in celebration as well as for relief. They drink to lend ceremony, color, and fellowship to life, just as surely as to banish anxiety, dread, and frustration. They drink out of recklessness and abandon which is not at all necessarily a compensation for an inherent caution and fatigue of spirit. They drink, too, because the inhibitions of life seem at times ridiculous and often alcohol represents not an *escape* but a *revolt* against the overstressed, perhaps necessary caution, decorum, and orderliness of existence." Karl A. Menninger sees a fairly wide function of alcohol within the normal limits. "There is much to indicate that in our civilization alcohol has a very useful function to perform, and may be a source of increased happiness and decreased hostilities."

Alcohol as a stimulus to artistic and literary creation is frequently mentioned and undoubtedly in many persons this is a motive, in spite of the fact that the scientific literature does not uphold such a theory. As Scharpff has put it: the majority of drinking geniuses have created their masterpieces, not on account of, but in spite of alcohol.

Turning now to the reasons for drinking, other than normal drinking, we are listing below some statements from various authors.

All these statements pertain only to the effect of alcohol and, although the expected effect to some degree reflects the motivation, the deepest motives are not expressed and writers on inebriety usually deal with them under another designation. These same kinds of "reasons" will again appear in a somewhat different formulation in some of the classifications of "drinker types," while in the sense of precipitating factors, driving forces, etc., they will be dealt with under various headings. The formulations as given in Table 3 all include the release of inhibitions, the compensations (wish-fulfilment, daydreaming) and generally the means of escape from conflict and anxiety which alcohol affords. Actually each and any of the formulations could be expressed in terms of escape. This function of drinking was recognized rather early and has been referred to under the less technical designation of "drinking to forget." This was very clearly expressed at the end of the 18th century by Immanuel Kant. England's famous Doctor Johnson said, "In the bottle, discontent seeks for comfort, cowardice for courage, and bashfulness for confidence." Thus, practically all of the

TABLE 3

"Reasons" for Drinking

Author	Statement
Lamb	Alcoholic drinks are frequently taken to overcome shyness and awkwardness. Some individuals take alcohol because the tavern offers company and comfort otherwise unobtainable for a large group of people.
Seliger (c)	To escape from life situations which the patient cannot face; because of maladjusted personality including sexual maladjustment; as a means of relieving incurable physical pain.
Henderson, J. L.	1. To be a "he man." 2. To find a way of rebelling and allowing relief of destructive impulses. 3. To obtain pleasure.
Davidson	1. Alcohol serves as "pacifier" for physiological and psychological tensions. 2. Alcohol is taken to increase function; it promotes compensation.

Author	*Statement*
Plottke	Adler's individual psychology provides a clue as to why people drink, i.e., they are unable to overcome their sense of inferiority in a socially useful way and so escape to alcohol.
Crichton-Miller	In the broadest sense it may be said that alcohol is taken in order to modify the feeling tone. Alcohol may be taken in order to modify emotional experience such as fear or inferiority.
Mapother (*a*)	Normal drinkers drink to get pleasure; morbid drinkers to evade pain.
Ferenczi (*b*)	The neurotic person drinks to make up for inability to produce endogenic pleasure and thus to silence depressive effects.
Carver (*a*)	Alcohol, by producing euphoria, blunting the critical power and progressively relaxing inhibitions, permits a flight from reality.
Morris	1. Cenesthetic discomfort. 2. Desire for liberation of that part of the personality which is kept in check by convention.
Trotter, W.	In the tragic conflict between what he has been taught to desire and what he has been allowed to get, man has found in alcohol, as he has found in certain other drugs, a sinister but effective peacemaker, a means of securing for however short a time some way out of the prison house of reality back to the Golden Age.
Strecker	Alcohol is utilized as an escape from the responsibility and burden of mature emotional life and its decisions. It provides wish-fulfilment.
Tait	Alcohol is a means for realizing day dreams. Its popularity is due to the compensation it affords for desired but unattained things in life.
Hart	Drink in some cases seems a definite substitute for sexual satisfaction because of the diminished libido which results.
Knight (*a*)	Alcohol is used as pacifier for disappointment and rage, as a potent means of carrying out hostile impulses to spite his parents and friends, as a method of securing masochistic debasement and as a symbolic gratification of the need for affection.
Barnes	Heredity no doubt gives some people neurotic tendencies and such patients find that excessive nervous manifestations are controlled to a degree by alcohol.
Read	Alcohol is taken to promote the social instincts and alleviate and narcotize the many mental conflicts to which we must all to some extent be victims. It thus constitutes itself a psychological necessity in modern civilization.
Wilson	The function of narcosis is "to inflate the ego or depress the veneer of culture and civilization."
Wall (*a*)	Alcohol offers an escape to the blissful state of infantile omnipotence.

"reasons" given here refer to the true addict rather than to abnormal drinkers in general, except the aspect of relief from physical pain which may be an etiological factor in abnormal drinking in some persons who are not primarily addicts. Generally these formulations are rudimentary etiological theories which are usually elaborated in greater detail.

Physiological Views

Numerous publications on the physiological effects of alcohol imply by their titles that they are dealing with etiology of addiction or of chronic alcoholism, but instead describe and explain the physiological processes of the release of inhibitions through alcohol. In justice to these physiologists, it must be said that perhaps none of them believes that these explanations are actually etiological explanations, but rather that they are a contribution to the understanding of the function of alcohol. As a matter of fact, these are important contributions, but unfortunately they often give the impression that the writer actually considers them as the full etiology. This impression is responsible for much pessimism with regard to the possibilities of a physiological explanation of alcohol addiction. This pessimism is the more deplorable as it not only discourages physiological investigations on addiction, but also belittles the actual accomplishments which are important for certain aspects of the matter. Words, unfortunately, have magical contents and the choice of a title is not a minor matter of consideration.

There are, however, physiological theories which may be called etiological, although not in the strictest sense of the word, i.e., they do not deal with the initial factors which start the process, but rather explain the genesis of one of its stages. These physiological theories relate to the factors which, after years of excessive drinking, lead to a physical dependence upon alcohol. This physical dependence is regarded by many as the criterion of addiction. However, such a theory does not explain *why* the person had been drinking to excess for years; any theory of the etiology of addiction must answer this question, i.e., must show the driving forces, psychological or physiological, which cause this drinking. Furthermore, addiction in the sense of physical dependence is, as we have explained before, a criterion of secondary addiction. In the primary addict, the dependence upon alcohol is practically immediate and is psychologically motivated although not necessarily without any physiological component: his inability to give up alcohol is to all intents an initial phenomenon. The secondary addict is initially not dependent upon alcohol and simply does not give it up because he does not seem to have any reason to do so. In the course of years, habituation develops; this makes him physically dependent and this physical dependence may then be rationalized into psychological dependence. The fact remains, however, that he now is an addict and, as far as medicine and society are concerned, he presents the same problem as the primary addict. This, and the fact that secondary addicts are probably much more numerous than primary addicts, lends importance to physiological theories of the genesis of such dependence. The importance of such theories, however, should not obscure the fact that they do not touch upon the initial causes. What these theories do explain is the physiological process of habituation, but not the necessary conditions for such a habituation.

The physiological theories relating to the etiology of secondary addiction are discussed in the physiological chapters* of this work and hence only a few examples will be mentioned here. In one of his papers Baldie (a) spoke of the "origin of craving" in terms of the chemical influence exerted by alcohol on the metabolism. From another of his papers (b), however, it is evident that he recognized this as a secondary addiction and he discussed separately the etiology of the drinking habit for which he gave chiefly sociological explanations. Ladrague thought that in the course of excessive drinking an accumulation of toxins occurred which then led to the pathological drive for drink (evidently secondary addiction). Apparently he believed that the need for alcohol was caused by "cellular paresis." T. A. Williams also spoke of metabolic poisoning as the cause for dependence upon alcohol and described as the main results of this poisoning, irritability, increased blood pressure and fibrosis of the tissues.

The allergic theory of addiction obviously also refers to the habituation process, i.e., to secondary addiction only. Silkworth (a) said that the allergic state was the result of an increasing sensitization to alcohol over a more or less extended period. This is only a new name for the concept of physiological habituation. The formulations of Seliger (c) and of Strasser do not differ essentially from Silkworth's. Thus the allergic theory does not contribute to understanding of the initiation of the drinking habit.

The investigations of Richter† on the taste threshold in rats promise to make an approach at least to some aspects of the establishment of the drink habit, but these investigations have not reached a stage which would permit a final interpretation.

*To be published in a later volume.

†These investigations will be described in detail in the physiological chapter in a later volume of this work.

In discussing physiological theories of the etiology of addiction the postulation of predisposing physiological constitutional types must also be mentioned. This view is represented by Crichton-Miller who described the hypopietic and the subthyroid types of drinkers. No reason, however, was given by him why these types should be predisposed to alcohol addiction. Carroll postulates a poor hematoencephalic barrier which is part of the constitutional inheritance of the addict. This "second-class" barrier, as he calls it, permits the easy passage of toxic substances into the cerebrospinal fluid, "thus causing erratic and underactive synapse functions."

As early as 1868, Marcet suggested the predisposing role of tobacco for habitual drinking and this idea has found a few believers. However, it has more commonly been observed that excessive drinkers develop excessive indulgence in tobacco; this may be partly determined by their poor nutritional habits.

On the whole, then, while there may be satisfactory explanations of the process of habituation, one cannot speak of a physiological theory of the factors which determine excessive drinking in the first place. Nevertheless, it does not seem unreasonable to expect illuminating facts from purposive physiological research. Suggestions relative to such research are made in the physiological and in the psychological chapters.

Personality Factors

In view of the present status of the physiologically oriented etiological theories of alcohol addiction one must concede that the psychological views are much more satisfactory and this in spite of their incompleteness, indefiniteness and other failings. Theories which stress the hereditary factors belong strictly neither to the physiological nor to the psychological viewpoints. Since, however, the exponents of the hereditary factors generally offer an explanation based on genetically determined personality deviations, it is appropriate to deal with their etiological theories within the frame of the psychological discussions.

The psychological theories of alcohol addiction operate practically entirely with concepts of personality. The majority of investigators are interested in personality in terms of structure, others—particularly psychoanalysts—place the emphasis on developmental elements of the personality. There is hardly a paper on addiction or its treatment which does not at least mention the etiological significance of personality. The personality factor has been, perhaps, somewhat overvalued. We do not wish to minimize the role of personality in the genesis of addiction; as a matter of fact, we would predict that even if a physiological basis of addiction should be found, personality would still remain an important factor. Overvaluation is to be understood in the sense that frequently it has not been recognized that personality furnishes the terrain on which alcohol addiction may or may not grow and that, in itself, it is not a sufficient cause of addiction. No personality constellation leads of necessity to addiction. Certain forces must act on the terrain to bring about addiction or abnormal drinking.

Some students of the personality of drinkers have been interested not only in the analysis of personality in its relation to abnormal drinking, but also in the question of a more or less unitary personality type of alcohol addicts. It may be stated in anticipation of the analysis that the quest for the "alcoholic personality" has been a vain one. While, however, the seekers of the unitary personality type have resigned themselves to failure, they have by no means confused the issue with the significance of personality factors in alcohol addiction. They grant the personality a decisive role even in the absence of a unitary type.

The personality studies encountered are of varying nature and scope. Some investigators have carried out formal psychometric studies with the aid of personality inventories. These studies were made mostly on patients with alcoholic psychoses, but a few studies had addicts or abnormal drinkers without psychoses as their subjects. In this chapter, only the latter will be considered. Other investigators, although they have not employed formal personality inventories, have proceeded largely on the same statistical principles as the psychometricians, namely, they counted the presence or absence of certain selected structural and developmental traits of personality as well as some characteristics not strictly related to personality in groups of abnormal drinkers. Another type of statistical personality studies is the determination of the incidence of such broad personality types as introverts and extroverts, or cyclothymic and schizothymic personalities among drinkers.

More frequent are what may be called naturalistic personality studies. Observers of wide experience and varying degrees of insight have made generalizations based on their impressions and have given word pictures of certain personality types encountered in their practice. Others, who do not seem to have had confidence in their generalizing ability, have merely given case histories of addicts and have sought to indicate types by the order of presentation of the histories.

Many statements on personality are hardly more than epigrams, but are nevertheless the epitomization of total views on the etiology of alcohol addiction. Some writers on addiction restrict their remarks to reasons for drinking, but such a remark as that alcohol is used to evade mature facing of sex and its emotional and social responsibilities, postulates a personality which has this need.

Psychoanalytic studies are also not lacking. These studies develop the personality description on the basis of interview material which is interpreted in terms of analytic theorems.

Many personality descriptions have resulted incidentally from efforts to classify alcohol addicts. While not all classifications are based on personality types, the two questions are closely associated.

Lastly there are numerous studies whose interest in the personality of the drinker is restricted to the incidence of psychopathies. The majority of these studies is based on hereditary aspects of constitution.

In order to clear the ground for an analysis of the literature on personality in alcohol addiction the best course seems to be to consider the studies on heredity first.

Constitution and heredity. Apart from the psychoanalysts, perhaps the majority of writers mean by personality factors, constitutional disposition, although this may be only implicitly expressed. Furthermore, the most frequent standpoint is that the constitutional disposition is a psychopathic one and there are probably more writers who postulate a nonspecific hereditary factor in the constitution than there are those who regard it as a matter of congenital constitution. It may be stated here that, at least in the scientific literature, there are nowadays no representatives of the view that alcohol addiction itself can be directly inherited.

There are only a few who explicitly state that the whole question of alcohol addiction is reducible to hereditary constitution; Kolle (*b*), for instance, goes so far as to state that "the essential thing is to realize that the inherited disposition is the decisive factor." Juliusburger stated that addiction is innate; Stefan is of the same conviction.

Most numerous are those writers who, after listing various factors in the genesis of alcohol addiction, proceed to forget most of these and to develop a theory in which constitution, either hereditary or congenital, is practically the only factor [Rosenfeld; Meggendorfer; D. K. Henderson (*b*); Brugger (*b*)].

There are some authors who, in general, overemphasize the role of heredity in alcohol addiction, but who concede that in one or a few forms this factor plays no part, for instance, Pohlisch (*d, g, h*); Gabriel and Kratzmann; Dresel. On the other hand, Legrain considers a hereditary factor important in only one small group, a certain type of dipsomania. There is, however, no lack of writers who assign to hereditary constitution a role which is reasonably proportional to that of the numerous other factors which enter into the situation [e.g., Bleuler (*b*); Graf; Baldie (*b*); Strecker and Chambers].

The extreme of denying the role of heredity entirely is hardly represented in the literature, although Tokarsky does deny it entirely and assigns the decisive role to congenital constitution. There are, of course, many who discuss personality factors with no mention of constitutional disposition and hence imply that it is of no importance. Varying as is the treatment accorded the problem by different authors, the impression received from a perusal of all of the literature is that the questions of psychopathic disposition and hereditary constitution are very prominent. These questions are treated in great detail in the chapter entitled "Alcohol, Germ Damage and Heredity," to which the reader is referred,* and hence we shall limit ourselves here to a brief statement.

Two ideas underlie the discussions of psychopathic constitution: (*a*) The most common idea is that addiction grows on the ground of a weak personality organization which may be purely congenital or may be the expression of a nonspecific heredity. (*b*) Tolerance is widely regarded as being an element of constitutional disposition, e.g., Bleuler (*b*) considers this one of the two elements of congenital disposition. He spoke of a disposition of smaller resistance to the ingested quantities and stressed the special psychiatric importance of the resistance of the brain. The hereditary basis of tolerance has also been upheld; for instance, Dent (*a, b*) said that addiction can be produced in anybody given sufficient drink, but the individual's heredity determines how much drink is sufficient. This factor of tolerance is often vaguely referred to as a susceptibility of the nervous system to drugs.

The strong stress on psychopathic disposition and on hereditary liability in alcohol addiction seems to be a gross exaggeration when one scans the quantitative evidence pertaining to the question (see the chapter on heredity*). Particularly, exception must be taken to estimates of hereditary liability which take into account, among others, traumatic disorders, other uninheritable mental disorders, migraine and petty deviations occurring in the families of alcoholic patients.

*To be published in a later volume of this work.

Conclusions in this discussion are based on investigations not suffering from this defect. Some investigations have been based entirely on the heredity or on the prepsychotic psychopathies of patients with alcoholic psychoses, including all those types of psychoses which are, in the modern view, not of alcoholic origin but in which drinking is incidental. It is quite natural that in a group of psychotics a high degree of hereditary liability should be found. Several investigators reported in this group over 70 per cent of hereditary liability. The findings themselves are quite valid, but the fault is that conclusions from these findings, which were established on patients with the so-called alcoholic psychoses, were then taken to apply to alcohol addiction in general. The psychotics form, however, only a part of the population of excessive drinkers and since many of them are symptomatic drinkers they need not have much in common with the true addict or with other types of abnormal drinkers.

Investigations which were carried out on cross sections of the inebriate population, i.e., on alcoholic patients admitted to general hospitals, show, with high consistency, an incidence of 35 to 40 per cent hereditary liability and an incidence of psychopathic dispositions in the patients of about the same degree. In view of the fact that, in the majority of the patients, neither hereditary nor psychopathic disposition is found, it is rather surprising to see the factor of the hereditary and psychopathic disposition stressed practically to a degree of exclusiveness. Actually, psychopathic disposition, and perhaps hereditary liability, may be expected in the symptomatic drinkers, who are probably the farthest removed from the problem of addiction and the group which we have designated as true addicts and who form, although the most interesting, a relatively small part of the inebriate population. That large group which furnishes the secondary addict is generally free from hereditary liability, as well as from psychopathic disposition, according to the evidence available. The untenable position that alcohol addiction is generally an expression of psychopathy has been pointed out from time to time by the greatest authorities on addiction but in spite of this, the idea of the decisive role of hereditary liability or of psychopathic disposition has prevailed. Bleuler (b) said that simple craving for drink is not necessarily connected with the psychopathic disposition and that the variation of the normal human personality is large enough to furnish the multiplicity of psychological premises for this craving. (He concedes, of course, that psychopathic disposition probably exists in most patients with alcoholic psychoses.)

The fact that women and Jews have as much psychopathic disposition as others, but nevertheless show a very low incidence of alcohol addiction, has been cited as proof that psychopathic disposition does not lead necessarily to alcohol addiction. This has been formulated by Wlassak (*a*), and recently more emphatically and convincingly by Myerson (*b*).

The available evidence shows that the incidence of hereditary liability as well as of psychopathic disposition in the population of excessive drinkers is greater than in the general population. But this is all. The incidence is not so high that a general statement could be made of it nor has any evidence been produced to show that psychopathic disposition or a nonspecific hereditary factor necessarily leads to addiction. All one can say is that persons with such hereditary liability or with such dispositions have a greater probability of succumbing to the risks of addiction. A full realization of this is important from the standpoint of therapy and mental hygiene. As Norman Kerr said, "The idea of hereditary disease is gratifying to the patient but makes for fatalism which stultifies all effort to overcome it."

Personality studies. The study of the personality of abnormal drinkers has been obscured by several factors. The most important of these are enumerated below:

1. In the study of the personality of alcohol addicts, reasons for drinking, personality traits and manifestations of drunkenness have not been kept sufficiently apart. Naturally, personality traits are involved, but many of the reasons can apply to a variety of personalities. The different types of drunkenness may or may not be related to different personality types. It is apparent that these three questions are related, but their distinction must be kept in mind. To interchange them within a discussion necessarily leads to confusion and contradiction.

2. Frequently personality studies carried out on patients with alcoholic psychoses have been used to describe the personality of the alcohol addict. First, patients with alcoholic psychoses represent no more than a fraction of the population of abnormal drinkers. Second, these patients constitute a highly selected group of this population. Third, these studies either reveal the personality as modified by psychosis and alcoholism, or, at best, reflect the prepsychotic personality as ascertained from inadequate case histories. The personality of the psychotic alcoholic can be used as a supplement to the study of the alcohol addict, but not as a basis for such a study.

3. While every student of inebriety recognizes that there are in general two types of addicts—those whose addiction is incidental to social drinking over a long period and those whose addiction is entrenched in the deeper layers of the personality—these two groups have not been kept separate in personality studies and the resulting heterogeneity has probably obscured the results. Neither group is likely to be a purely homogeneous one so far as personality factors are concerned, but it is highly probable that there is some underlying homogeneity in each group, which has been completely obscured by combining them.

4. The adequacy of the methods of personality study may frequently be questioned. This criticism is, naturally, not specific to personality studies in inebriety. The study of personality is still an art and the attempts at scientific methods have been made without well-formulated basic concepts and have involved oversimplification and many irrelevancies. For the present we may place better reliance on the naturalistic descriptions of the empathic psychologist than on statistically oriented attempts to "measure personality."

As mentioned before, most of the formal personality studies were carried out on patients with alcoholic psychosis. There are only a few psychometric and clinical-statistical personality studies on abnormal drinkers without psychosis. These studies will be discussed now.

Phyllis Wittman made perhaps the most thorough investigation in this field. She studied 100 "chronic alcoholic patients without psychosis" at the Elgin State Hospital and compared them with 100 normal controls who were equated with the patients' age and education. In a study of the "temperament" of these groups [Wittman (*a*)] she used Humm and Wadsworth's temperament scale based on Rosanoff's theory of personality. The findings were that "chronic alcoholics" are not a homogeneous group as far as temperament is concerned; they are distinguished from normal controls only roughly with many exceptions. A more or less characteristic picture of the chronic alcoholic was found to be: He has a comparatively weak degree of restraint, mental poise and stability; he has difficulty in controlling his moods and desires, as well as their overt expression. He is slightly more selfish, conceited, and hence more antisocial, than the average individual. He has relatively strong cycloid tendencies, pronounced swings in mood and activity, together with distractibility and lack of attention. His moods alternate between the extremes of euphoria and optimism with heightened activity on the one hand, and irritability, with a gloomy, sad, apprehensive mental state with lessened psychomotor activity on the other. He is not particularly shy, sensitive, or given to daydreaming. The characteristic which definitely distinguishes him from the average is his strong paranoid tendency. He is consequently suspicious, self-conceited, stubborn, scornful of the ideas of others, and steadfast in adherence to his own ideas.

The investigator pointed out that no conclusion may be drawn as to whether the obtained picture is characteristic of fundamental personality traits of the abnormal drinker or of temperament modified by alcoholic excess. We may add that even if the traits were primary they would contribute little to the understanding of the etiology of addiction.

In another study [Wittman (b)] patients and normal controls were rated for "adjustment" ("Experience Variable Scale," Parts II to XV). The maximum score on this test is 300. A score below 190 is considered as "poor" and above 220 as "excellent." The average adjustment score for the patients was 190 and for the normal controls 211. On some items the patients showed higher scores than the controls, but the differences in these cases were not marked. These items were sibling relationship, intellectual development and, most surprisingly, social adjustment. Even if this should indicate no more than that social adjustment is no worse in the abnormal drinkers than in the normal controls, one must wonder about the meaningfulness of the test. The most interesting finding was that the need for religious security and standards rated so highly that they indicated an interference with rather than a contribution to good adjustment.

The developmental and personality characteristics of "chronic alcoholics" were investigated in a third study [Wittman (c)]. The investigator found the following outstanding traits in the patient group:

1. A domineering but idealized mother and a stern, autocratic father whom the patient feared as a child.

2. A marked degree of strict, unquestioning obedience demanded in family life, with little freedom allowed.

3. A feeling of insecurity as evidenced by an insistent feeling of need for religious security and a strong feeling of sin and guilt.

4. Marked interest in opposite sex with many love affairs but poor marital adjustment.

5. Lack of self-consciousness with marked ability to get along with and be socially acceptable to others.

6. Occasional depression and periods of marked unhappiness.

7. A keyed-up emotional level—work done under high nervous tension.

8. A definitely expressed and disproportionately greater love for the maternal parent.

Generally, Wittman's studies are interesting contributions to the knowledge of the abnormal drinker as he appears after years of indulgence in alcoholic drinks. Whether or not any of the fundamental traits of the prealcoholic period have been gauged in these studies must remain in doubt. Evidently, however, all these traits which have been uncovered are indicative of general personality deviations rather than of deviations specific to the person who may become an addict or abnormal drinker.

Fleming and Tillotson used their wide clinical observations rather than psychometric devices but proceeded statistically, i.e., on the basis of the frequency of occurrence of isolated traits. They found no one personality pattern typically alcoholic. On the other hand, secondary traits of alcohol addiction, such as sociability, inferiority and emotional instability, were found characteristic of the group. In an earlier paper (Tillotson and Fleming), they found that in male patients maternal attachment was twice as frequent as paternal. This latter point is in agreement with Wittman's findings and may be a primary characteristic. Since, however, this trait is common to many behavior disturbances not much importance attaches to it relative to the etiology of alcohol addiction. Furthermore, little is known about the balance between maternal and paternal attachment in normal persons.

The descriptions of Miles definitely refer to the secondary traits of addiction only. In a small group of abnormal drinkers he found fair ability, but lack of persistence in motivation and ambition for accomplishment. The drinkers admitted fewer neurotic tendencies than normal controls. They tended to emphasize extrovert behavior patterns and were inclined to react more to social pressure than to well-defined and adequate personal goals. They also were more self-conscious than average and deficient in independence.

Wall's (a, b) studies on chronic alcoholics included too great a proportion of patients with psychosis to be considered here. His studies will be discussed in Chapter II.

On the whole statistical studies on isolated personality traits have not tended to illuminate either the problem of etiology of addiction or the question of personality types. Although the studies showed that a unitary personality type did not seem to obtain among abnormal drinkers, the question of a variety of different but well-defined types was not broached.

Another type of statistically oriented personality studies operates with broad labels rather than with isolated traits. The determination of the incidence of cyclothymia and schizothymia or of introversion and extroversion, however, has been carried out, with the exception of the study by Pohlisch (*d*), on patients with alcoholic psychoses.

Pohlisch (*d*) found in 75 chronic alcoholics without psychosis 64 per cent cyclothymic personalities, 5 per cent epileptoids and 3 per cent schizothymic personalities. The remaining 28 per cent of the subjects were unclassifiable. These findings are particularly interesting when contrasted with findings on abnormal drinkers with psychoses. Hoch studied introversion and extroversion in 102 patients with alcoholic psychoses and found 47 per cent introverts and 53 per cent extroverts. Introversion roughly corresponds to schizothymia and extroversion to cyclothymia. The distribution of these types thus appears to be entirely different among nonpsychotic and psychotic abnormal drinkers. It would appear that schizothymia is a characteristic largely of symptomatic drinkers and probably also of the group of primary or true addicts. The abnormal drinkers who are potential secondary addicts, however, belong largely to the cyclothymic group. It is evident from this that the personality type of the addict cannot be derived from the psychotic chronic alcoholic, nor can a trait study be carried out effectively on a mixed sample.

Lewis expressed the view that in spite of wide divergencies "it may be possible eventually to find some fundamental similarities in the personality of the alcoholic group." This seems to be a warrantable expectation, but the fundamental similarities need not be of any great importance. It seems that the recognition and sharp delimitation of different types would contribute more toward theory as well as therapy than the finding of some common traits. Parenthetically it is interesting to note that many writers who state that no unitary type exists in the same breath speak of the universal occurrence of "weak will power," homosexual tendencies and suicidal drive among abnormal drinkers. The first step toward clarity in this type of study is the realization that abnormal drinkers are not necessarily addicts and that what is learned about addicts cannot be applied to habitual excessive drinking in general. The study of isolated traits will never throw light on this question. Generalizations must be obtained from biographical approaches rather than from cross sectional studies.

The formulations of Cimbal originate in biographical studies of "drinkers." He did not rely on the "run of the mill" case histories, but delved into the histories of the families of his patients and into the life of the patient with the outlook of the true biographer rather than of the clinician. The following formulations are the result of hundreds of individual studies:

In families in which pampering and mating with like partners have been going on for generations, the driving forces become extinct, and an *Erlebnislehre* results, which parallel with bodily degeneration—asthenia—continuously requires stimuli in order to maintain a mood equilibrium. In this group the more robust ones become decadent drinkers (*Entartungstrinker*), the more sensitive ones become gamblers, adventurers, cocainists, and complicated sexual perverts, since they are too tired for the finer forms of experience. They go into a stage of senium without having had a phase of youth and maturation.

Another group is that of the "impassioned" drinker, which is diametrically opposed to the decadent group. Here we find the passionate, discordant drinker whose lacking or belated mental or emotional maturation is not fit to withstand the storms of instinctual life. These discordant passionates remain unduly long in a youth period. If the maturation, and thus the harmonizing of conflicting dispositions, does not succeed, a craving for intoxication and habituation to intoxicants may develop out of the need for temporary relief of the tension which results from this conflict. The number of these embittered and discordant drinkers is at least as great as that of the decadent drinkers. These impassioned drinkers not infrequently develop into dipsomaniacs. The impassioned drinkers are the best risks for therapy, because in their case one often succeeds in extinguishing not only the drink habit but the discordance itself. These discordant, intoxicant-craving characters furnish the most enthusiastic leaders against addiction.

The third group are the spineless (*Haltlose*) who succumb to each and every temptation. Their disposition comes from an oligophrenia. In this group, which includes many vagrants and criminals, liquor is a customary part of social forms simply because it is the cheapest and lowest form of gregariousness that can be obtained. All other forms of enjoyment involve at least to some extent a mental or cultural activity and even the most degenerate forms of sex intercourse involve the burden of wooing. Thus these intoxicants are an entirely passive form of enjoyment. This third group may be best characterized as the type of the stupid drinker (*Stumpfsinntrinker*). The stupid drinkers develop into the dangerous and criminal drinkers, because in them the dormant primitive drives are whipped up by drink, and because in their personality structure the trained inhibitions which can withstand even intoxication have never come to full development. Intoxication is the touchstone between the trained and habitual inhibitions on the one hand and the conscious and deliberate inhibitions on the other hand.

Lastly, we may talk of the self-aggrandizing drinker (*Selbstwertungstrinker*). This is a form of ambition without energy. There are drinkers who on analysis of their personality do not reveal any other cause for their addiction than craving for power and ascendance in a very primitive, undeveloped form, characterized by weak will power. Here we find the weak-charactered professionals who in some subordinate position give themselves to the building of aircastles, and at the *Stammtisch* find an outlet for boasting. This type is usually incapable of wooing, or camaraderie with the opposite sex. The tavern life, so opposed to the domestic setting, helps him over his sexual inferiority feeling and lends him courage to play the tyrant at home. It is this type of drinker who has the most harassing influence on wife and children. His only salvation is if the family has enough strength to make themselves economically independent of him, and so put themselves in a position to cow him. True inner change in these characters does not occur.

These descriptions, although incomplete relative to the number of types, give much more insight into the genesis of alcohol addiction than any psychometric study could yield. Cimbal's types are theoretically and clinically relevant. The descriptions are brief and thus do not reveal the variation which may take place within any of the given types. The most important implication of these types is that the understanding of abnormal drinking does not require necessarily the discovery of unitary personality traits.

Another illuminating contribution of naturalistic observation comes from Pohlisch's (*f*) comparison of morphinists and alcohol addicts. He points out that the main characteristic of the morphinist is a need of self-assertion which is out of proportion to the actual accomplishments. This is not due to lack of intelligence but to incapability for steady work and goal and frequent indulgence in organ sensations. In contrast to this is the psychological and bodily robustness of the drinker. Morphine quiets the need for self-assertion, but alcohol increases the ego feeling. The morphinist does not seek gregariousness as the drinker does. Furthermore morphinists are not concerned about the waning of libido and potency, while the abnormal drinker feels this keenly and manifests it in his jealousies.

The generalizations here are somewhat too sweeping. The psychological and bodily robustness apply only to a certain type of abnormal drinker—surely not to the primary addict—but nevertheless the differences pointed out by Pohlisch constitute a lead for research. Similar differences between morphinists and alcohol addicts have been pointed out by Möllenhoff and there is rather great agreement among observers of addicts that the different kinds of addictions are generally mutually exclusive. Occasionally, however, the opinion is expressed that abnormal drinking is a source of other drug addictions (e.g., Mapother).

Generally, the study of the similarities and differences between alcohol addiction and other drug addictions may tend to bring greater clarity into the discussion of these problems. Gabriel and Kratzmann's monograph on this subject, however, has not contributed much to clarity because of a type of argument which William James has appropriately called "vicious intellectualism." Many psychoanalysts claim that all addictions must be studied as one entity. Rado (*b*) stated that all types of drug craving are one single disease: pharmacothymia. Drugs have two effects: (*a*) to prevent pain; (*b*) to give pleasure. These constitute the pharmacogenic pleasure effect. Ego frustration creates depression, drugs create elation followed by worse depression. This statement sounds plausible but it contains a fallacy, namely, not all drugs in question create elation, nor do all addicts seek it. Pohlisch (*f*) has pointed out that the enforced abstinence during the war did not make morphinists or cocainists of former alcohol addicts. Furthermore, Bleuler (*b*) found that the psychopathic disposition in alcohol addiction has no affinity with the one in morphinism and that there is no general disposition for addictions. Alcohol addiction and morphine addiction are different genotypes. Bleuler also found that in the families of abnormal drinkers morphinism occurs only in the same proportion as in the general population.

White (*a*) denied that alcohol is a habit-forming drug and Diethelm was in doubt whether one should speak of addiction in the case of abnormal drinking. He remarked that although the chronic alcoholic develops a certain tolerance, he then remains on a certain level and does not react with increased physiological craving.

It must be granted that the tissue physiology is not the same following the habitual indulgence in alcohol and that in morphine or cocaine. If addiction is viewed in terms of tissue conditioning only, it is not justified to speak of alcohol addiction. The fact remains, however, that a not inconsiderable number of persons after experiencing the relief of conflicts through alcohol become dependent upon it for their conduct of life. In view of this it seems neither necessary nor—from the standpoint of mental hygiene—advisable to deny the phenomenon of alcohol addiction. On the other hand, it must be repeated that abnormal drinking cannot be equated without qualification with alcohol addiction.

In the comparison of addictions the personality is treated as an important, probably the most important, feature but without much elaboration. This is true in general of the discussion of personality in the alcohol literature. There is much more of implied theory from case histories without comment and even more in the form of brief statement than in the nature of elaborate descriptions of type. Many valuable observations on personality are contained in classificatory systems of drinkers and will be mentioned in the discussion of these systems.

The least that any writer on alcohol addiction will say about personality is a reference to "weakness of will." This term has often been exposed to criticism. Glover said ". . . terms such as 'weakness of will' combine diagnosis with moral judgement in much the same way that the phrase 'obstinate constipation' combines an accurate psycho-physiological diagnosis with an expression of the diagnostician's annoyance." This remark is more amusing than appropriate and the cogency of Glover's explanation of "weakness of will" is not apparent. "What is generally called weakness of will in the chronic alcoholic can be described in psycho-pathological terminology as the gratification of previously inhibited impulse."

We are inclined to think that while psychiatrists have used the colloquial term "weakness of will," they have not meant by this the naïve concept of volition, but rather the control of inhibitions.

In whatever sense "weakness of will" may be used, it seems to be an epiphenomenon of alcohol addiction rather than an etiological personality factor.

Psychoanalytic studies. The psychoanalytic technique affords the deepest insight into the personality make-up of a person and particularly into developmental factors of the personality structure. On the other hand, the experience of the analyst with abnormal drinkers is limited by number and by the type of drinkers who come within his ken. The analyst is more likely to see the true neurotic, primary addict rather than the abnormal drinker who develops his habits under the influence of predominantly exogenous factors. The primary addict constitutes only a fraction of the population of abnormal drinkers, but the analyst generalizes from his experience with true addicts and gives a psychological picture of excessive drinking which applies most likely to the true addict only. No doubt, some of the psychological elements operative in alcohol addiction enter also in a less fundamental way into all forms of abnormal and even normal drinking. Pohlisch (*b*) pointed out that the one-sided approach of the Freudian and Adlerian schools and the cliché-like use of terms such as "neurotic addict" miss the variety of conditions which lead to addiction. We believe that the fault is inherent not so much in the one-sided approach as in the one-sided experience of the analyst.

Crowley's review of the psychoanalytic literature on the addictions reveals a rather wide divergence of the etiological views of analysts. However, this is hardly surprising, since many of the views are based on the analysis of one or two patients only or are interpretations of data of other analysts.

The same elements of personality development in the addict are found by all analysts; the difference lies in the singling out of those elements to which the particular analyst assigns the true etiological importance. Thus, we encounter the main emphasis placed on the oral erotic aspects, or on mother fixation or a repressed homosexuality, a castration fear and other elements.

The oral erotic aspects of alcohol addiction were first pointed out by Freud in 1905 and have been considered as a more or less important etiological factor by Rado (*a*); Glover; Wall (*a, b*); Knight (*b, c*); Simmel; and Robbins. Most of these analysts, however, have treated this aspect as a contributory but not the basic element in alcohol addiction. Simmel assigned to it a more important role. According to him in patients with morbid cravings onanism has succumbed to a threat of castration and the subject is compelled to regress to pregenital positions of the libido. The form of cravings is determined by phantasies and drinking corresponds to an oral-sadistic phantasy.* Schilder (*b*), however, thought the emphasis on oral and anal libidinous trends had been misplaced. "It seems more or less accidental that the alcoholic ingests the alcohol by mouth and the satisfaction received from drinking has no deeper relation to the oral gratification of eating."

Drinking has also been equated with sexual activity in a perverted form in which forepleasure becomes the end. This has been stressed by Abraham; Tausk; Sachs; Rado (*a, b*); and Davidson. Davidson has explained the mechanism of addiction on the principle of forepleasure; ". . . alcohol which causes physiological imbalance of stimulation and depression of the integrated nervous system, will also result in a

---

*In this connection it is of interest to note that according to English folk belief a person who often has his hand in his mouth becomes a drunkard (Rolleston).

continuous urge for repetition of the excitation due to the mediated pleasure and necessity for discharge. Since the pleasure derived from alcohol is diffuse, it is akin to forepleasure. Not finding discharge it will try again and again."

The most widely known psychoanalytic theory of alcohol addiction is its interpretation in terms of repressed homosexuality. The fact that drinking usually goes on in groups of the same sex led to the first surmises in this direction, although the psychoanalytic views are based on much more weighty considerations. This analytic theory has been accepted also outside of analytic circles, although it also has been frequently rejected. Most analysts give the homosexual trend a place in the general etiological picture of alcohol addiction but some of them see it as the crucial element. Thus Read; Juliusburger; and Tabori have assigned the decisive role to homosexuality. The latter said: "The psychic reason for alcohol addiction is the incompletely repressed homosexuality which the individual cannot sublimate." On the other hand, Glover distinctly stated that the homosexual phantasy system has no direct etiological bearing on alcohol addiction. Abraham has found the significance of alcohol relative to homosexuality in its property of dispelling the disgust which results from homosexual repression. He also pointed out that modesty, which is the repression of scotophilia and exhibitionism, gives way to alcohol. The obscenity of drinking songs (La Barre) is witness to this.

Another prominent psychoanalytic theory explains alcohol addiction in terms of suicide. This theory, too, has found wide acceptance outside of psychoanalytic circles. The chief exponent of this theory is K. A. Menninger. He considers alcohol addiction as one of the "chronic and attenuated forms of self-destruction," and he relates the motives discovered in them to "those of direct undisguised suicide which have been discussed heretofore, namely, an externally directed aggressive component; a punitive drive, that is, submission to punishment from a sense of guilt; an erotic motive (achievement of pleasure, the essentially sexual nature of which is cloaked in elaborate disguise); and finally, a self-destructive impulse whose sole aim is the extinction of the individual." In summary Menninger says: "Alcohol addiction, then, can be considered a form of self-destruction used to avert a greater self-destruction, deriving from elements of aggressiveness, excited by thwarting, ungratified eroticism, and the feeling of a need for punishment from a sense of guilt related to aggressiveness. Its further quality is that in a practical sense the self-destruction is accomplished *in spite of* and at the same time *by means of* the very device used by the sufferer to relieve his pain and avert this feared destruction." Rado (*b*) has a different evaluation of the role of suicide in alcohol addiction. According to him, a pharmacothymic crisis arises when the pharmacothymic regime (instead of realistic regime) fails to provide elation. There are three ways out of this crisis: (*a*) a free interval to rehabilitate the depreciated value of the drug; (*b*) suicide; (*c*) psychosis. Suicide is not self-destructive masochism, not punishment, but a means to dispel the depression for good. Schilder (*b*) thought that the stress on the self-destructive tendencies of alcoholism "overlooks the deep striving of the alcoholic to be loved and appreciated by society, which would grant to him the integrity of his body and his sex parts. . . . It is true, however, that in the deeper layers the alcoholic experiences the striving for prestige as a struggle for life and death. He may feel that by incapacitating himself by alcohol he may gain a greater claim for mercy."

The aspect of castration anxiety, as discussed by Simmel; Rado (*a*); and especially by Bromberg and Schilder, hardly leaves any difference between alcohol addiction and schizophrenia. It may be said of all the psychoanalytic studies discussed here that they do not reveal any of the sufficient conditions of alcohol addiction. All the developmental elements which have been invoked as etiological factors enter generally into behavior deviations of very different nature. Fundamentally, only the necessary conditions of abnormal behavior are touched upon. The psychoanalytic studies are by no means unimportant contributions. They contribute to the knowledge of the terrain on which alcohol addiction grows but not to the knowledge of the decisive factors.

The Classification of Abnormal Drinkers

We have repeatedly pointed out that the various etiological studies in personality and its development touched upon the terrain only. We did not mean to imply, however, that this knowledge is of minor importance. As a matter of fact the importance of the terrain is so great that a clear exposition of it seems essential to the discussion of alcohol addiction. The analysis and synthesis of classifications should serve the purpose of clarification. Also, as has been mentioned before, the classificatory attempts contain much material on the personality of addicts. In Table 4 the main classifications by various writers are given. From this table emanates a discussion of classificatory systems and a synthesis is attempted in Figure 1. It may be noted that only the classification of drinkers but not the classification of types of drunkenness is considered here.

A large variety of classifications is found in the accompanying table and the impression may be derived that there is confusion and conflict. However, these different classifications are not mutually exclusive. Each of them has a definite meaning and utility and they can be integrated into a system of subordination and coördination. The experience and thought of the many writers on this subject can be synthesized.

If one investigator classifies drinkers as intermittent and steady drinkers, and the other as endogenous and exogenous types, it does not follow that the literature is confused and conflicting on this point. Such, however, has been the nuncupatory verdict of the perusers of the literature. While it may be asked whether one or the other of these two

TABLE 4

Classifications of Abnormal Drinkers

Author	*Classification*
Dittmer	*1.* Occasionally and irregularly recurring drunkenness without pathological reaction. *2.* Fairly frequently recurring drunkenness on exogenous basis; pathological reactions and inclination to violence. *3.* Endogenous addicts, drinking without interruption.
Wingfield	*1.* Pseudodipsomania: craving is absent unless alcohol be first taken; the patient drinks in great excess. *2.* Chronic sober alcoholism: patient drinks regularly to excess for a long period; usually not intoxicated. *3.* Chronic inebriate alcoholism: resembles above but patient is never sober. *4.* True dipsomania: craving spontaneously.
Brühl-Cramer (cit. Gaupp)	Distinction between constant, temporary and mixed alcoholism. Within temporary type there are the (*a*) *nachlassende Trunksucht* in which craving varies from one time of the day to another, (*b*) *intermittierende Trunksucht* in which alcoholic excesses return after short intervals—several times in one month—and last 1 to 3 days; and (*c*) *periodische Trunksucht* or *Quartalsuff*, which lasts 3 to 21 days and is preceded by prodromal depressive state.
Carver (*b*)	It is clinically convenient to classify alcoholics as *1.* Intermittent; *2.* Regular (*a*) with intermittent exacerbation; (*b*) sober; *3.* Paroxysmal dipsomania.
Coriat (*a*)	*1.* The steady tippler. *2.* The periodic drinker (*a*) due to depression; (*b*) epileptic equivalent, the genuine dipsomaniac; (*c*) cyclothymic; (*d*) as a psychasthenic impulsion.

Author	*Classification*
Allen	*1.* The psychopathic alcoholic who is inadequate from youth, who starts drinking at puberty and never accomplishes anything worthwhile. *2.* The neurotic alcoholic who may show underlying inadequacies in youth but generally can find overcompensations to sustain him for a while.
Gabriel (*b*)	*1.* Genuine addicted drinker whose addiction is constitutional and who might have to be institutionalized. Alcohol by chance; might be some other drug. *2.* Those who develop drinking habit without being forced to drink.
Wuth (*b*)	Exogenic and endogenic etiology. Monotrope and heterotrope drug addicts.
Fleming (*c*)	*1.* Symptomatic drinking due to underlying physical or mental pathologic condition for which alcohol provides relief. *2.* True alcohol addiction associated with real habituation and characterized mainly by specific craving.
Dent (*a*)	"Active" drink to drown some sorrow, trying to commit mental suicide. "Habitual" drinker wants to, but thinks he cannot give up alcohol.
Stevenson	Normal, social drinker and problem drinker.
Grotjan (cit. Meggendorfer)	*1.* Intemperate drinkers (exceed the damaging amounts but are still masters of their drinking). *2.* Addicts (without resistance to craving).
Kehrer and Kretschmer	*1.* Pyknic, cyclothymic type. Mere drinking develops on the basis of a gregarious disposition. (These are the *Stammtisch* inebriates.) *2.* Schizoid types, difficult and nervous people who strive to find relief in alcohol from their internal strains and stresses.
Stockert	*1. Stammtisch* inebriates. *2.* Alcohol addicts: (*a*) mainly schizoids and mentally deficient who drink to escape unpleasantness; (*b*) psychopaths who fight against addiction but relapse.
Mangold	*1.* The one time normal individual who becomes inebriate through "degrading social customs or institutions" or other environmental factors. *2.* Persons who are naturally weak, neurotic, feebleminded or defective characters.
Legrain	*1.* Amoral individuals who do everything to excess except think. *2.* The escapists and those who enjoy the mental effects. *3.* Dipsomaniacs.
Gabriel and Kratzmann	Individuals are divided into two principal groups: the positivistic and the negativistic. Each of those is subdivided into active and passive. Roughly the negativistic individual corresponds to Kretschmer's schizothymic, the positivistic to the cyclothymic type. All types are to be found among chronic alcoholics as well as among dipsomaniacs, but very active types are naturally less frequent than the passive ones. (The phenomenon of periodicity is explained by the struggle between the depressive and the activistic elements. Physically dipsomaniacs are frequently mixed types.)

Author	*Classification*

Möllenhoff
1. The exuberant reckless drinker.
2. The *gemütlich* drinker.
3. The "misery" drinker.

Crichton-Miller
1. Steady drinkers: (*a*) hypopietic; (*b*) subthyroidic; (*c*) sensorial type (these seek modification in sensory experience); (*d*) rebels (e.g., sons of temperance reformers).
2. Intermittent drinkers: (*a*) epileptic; (*b*) dual personality; (*c*) manic depressive.

Pohlisch (*f*)
1. Hyperthymic and depressive psychopaths.
2. Schizoid drinkers (Binswanger's type).
3. The excitable, irritable, explosive drinkers. (These are largely temporary drinkers in whom there is an accumulation of excesses but not true habituation.)
4. The remainder though large is so varied that it can be described only individually.

Knight (*c*)
1. The "essential type" includes those in whom the maladjustment has been conspicuous since childhood or adolescence and usually the first alcoholic episodes occur in their teens. There is a continuous demand for pleasure; little regard for reality.
2. The "reactive type" includes those in whom alcohol addiction is a response to an attempted adjustment to overtaxing situation. There is usually a history of achievement prior to addiction which may occur only late in life.
3. Symptomatic inebriates, who drink only incidentally.

Menninger, W. C.
1. "Essential type." See Knight.
2. "Reactive type." See Knight.
3. "Neurotic characters" (named by Alexander) whose excessive drinking is only one evidence of maladjustment.
4. This group are psychotic personalities. In these individuals alcohol represents only a symptom in a paranoid or a schizoid or otherwise psychotic system.

White (*b*)
1. Drinking, the expression of a psychosis and in no wise its cause. Especially early paresis and mild manic depressive.
2. Those who drink to drown their troubles. Escape phenomenon chiefly hysterics and psychoneurotics. Dipsomaniacs here.
3. The highly susceptible group, especially posttraumatic constitution.
4. Inebriety complicating other psychoses.
5. Purely alcoholic psychoses.

Cimbal
1. Decadent drinkers.*
2. Impassioned drinkers.*
3. Self-aggrandizing drinkers.*
4. Stupid drinkers.*

classificatory systems is of greater value, and while the answer will probably favor the latter, this does not imply that the former, being of

*The labels are not self-explanatory, but Cimbal's terms are discussed in detail in this chapter.

lesser utility, should be discarded. The evaluation here is of a different nature than, for example, in choosing between two materials for construction purposes. In the latter case, if one material is of greater value and is therefore selected, the other material cannot be used. In the case of these classificatory systems, however, in spite of differences in degree of utility, both can and should be used.

The subordination and coördination of the various classifications will be attempted here. In order to facilitate this, the different classificatory principles must first be examined relative to their contents and merits. The simplest forms of classification of drinkers are dichotomous. The first desideratum in the categories of a dichotomy is that they should be all-inclusive. The greater the heterogeneity in any of the classes, the less, generally, is its utility. Heterogeneity has its quantitative as well as its qualitative aspects and in spite of great diversity the different elements of a category may have something in common which justifies gathering them into one collective. Naturally, this common element cannot be trivial. The relevance of a classification that goes beyond mere pigeonholing is determined by its predictive value. Classification of abnormal drinkers into steady and intermittent drinkers is based only on a pattern of drinking; overtly it does not give any information about origins. Predictive classifications, however, must be genetic. Nevertheless there is a certain superficial relationship between the forms of drinking and the origins. This relationship is sufficient to base a first or initial prediction on it. Thus the knowledge that an individual belongs in the intermittent group practically assures that he is not a true addict and this prediction is unquestionably of some value. It does not exclude the possibility that the person is a periodic dipsomaniac. In classification by the forms of drinking, however, the intermittent drinker may be further classified into irregular and periodic drinkers. The class "irregular" then excludes all true addicts as well as dipsomaniacs. An initial classification is justified when it delimits the territory remaining to be explored. In this sense the classification by the steadiness or intermittency of the drinking habit may be regarded as a useful initial classification. Since in either of its classes, however, the heterogeneity is very great, as we shall see later, it cannot stand as a sole classificatory system. Its utility obtains only within the framework of an elaborate classification.

Another dichotomous system classifies the abnormal drinkers according to whether or not the drinking develops on an endogenous or

an exogenous basis. In using this terminology we must point out immediately that these terms are tacitly qualified as principally endogenous
and principally exogenous. There are very few who do not agree that,
on the one hand, in spite of inner drives, certain environmental elements must be operative to make a drinker, and that, on the other
hand, environment can act only as a determining factor when there is
at least a minimum of psychological readiness. While this classification
has greater predictive properties than a classification by the criterion
of continuity, the two classes are still too heterogeneous to permit of
far reaching valid generalizations in either group. The endogenous
group, for example, includes, among others, true addicts as well as
symptomatic drinkers; and the difference between these two, from the
theoretical as well as from the practical therapeutic standpoint, is of a
fundamental nature. Furthermore, physiological conditions, such as
the hypothetical disturbance of the midbrain in dipsomania must be
classed as an endogenous cause although it differs greatly from endogenous psychological conflicts. Thus one sees that the heterogeneity
in either category of these classifications is considerable. Nevertheless,
it is of a lesser degree than in the categories based on the criterion of
continuity. Combining the two classificatory systems discussed so far,
results in a system which has greater predictive value than either alone
and which serves as an efficient scheme for the orderly grouping of
ultimate types.

A mere division into the groups (a) true addicts and (b) all other
abnormal drinkers is less efficient than either of the classifications
which have been discussed, since group (b), because of its merely negative character, is much more heterogeneous than any of the categories
in either of the other two classifications. In view of the excessive
tendency to regard all abnormal drinkers as addicts, however, this
classification at least recognizes one of the essentials of clear discussion.
As a classificatory system we may disregard this group; but the investigators who have used it, explicitly or implicitly, have in some instances
characterized the "other" group by describing one of its prominent
types and have incidentally recorded some clear and useful descriptions.

A dichotomy into addicts and symptomatic drinkers implies either
that the proponent believes that all abnormal drinkers who are not true
addicts are symptomatic drinkers, or that he is disregarding all drinkers who are neither addicts nor symptomatic drinkers. Neither of these

standpoints can be accepted. Division into true addicts and symptomatic drinkers is a necessary subclassification within a certain group, but cannot serve as a major system of classification.

Many writers on alcohol addiction have not used dichotomous systems or even tried to develop all-inclusive classifications, but have rather described three or more etiological types, either because they thought these the most important ones in the entire population of abnormal drinkers, or because of their special, personal interests, or because of not recognizing that they were not all-inclusive. [For example, Knight (*c*) classifying into essential type, reactive type and symptomatic drinkers, presents three types, each of which is distinct from the others and important; but he leaves out of consideration all abnormal drinkers on a principally exogenous basis. This omission may reflect the limitations of the author's interest and experience.]

Various investigators who were not interested in classifying described just one type of drinker that appealed to them for some reason. Inasmuch as some of these are relevant members of our synthesis of classifications, they also will be taken into consideration although they do not appear in Table 4.

True addicts. This is actually not a type but a group of types with the common characteristic that alcohol is a definite need for them, that it has a definite function in their scheme of things and that their dependence on the intoxicant and their inability to give it up are not determined by habit and physiological processes. This distinguishes them from the secondary addicts who have developed a physiological and ultimately also a psychological need, in the process of habituation, but in whose management of life alcohol has not played an essentially dominant role. These secondary addicts do not form a group in the sense that the true addicts form one, since their addiction is only a developmental stage which may be reached by any habitual drinker. The true addicts all come to their addiction on an endogenous basis and they are steady drinkers. Within the group of true addicts belong the following types: (*1*) the decadent; (*2*) the discordant personality (one type of schizoid drinker); (*3*) the compensating drinker; (*4*) the poverty drinker. Finer classifications may be made, but from the existing literature these seem to emerge as relevant types. The same remark applies also to the types enumerated as symptomatic drinkers, as well as to the entire classificatory system developed here.

1. The decadent drinker. This type was fully described, following Cimbal, at the beginning of this chapter. It only remains to point out that Cimbal's decadent drinker and the essential type as described by Knight (c), and W. C. Menninger, are very much the same. He is also practically the same as Legrain's immoral individual who does everything to excess except think, or Benon's (b) "perverted drinker." This type, which is essentially blasé and needs constant stimulation in order to escape emptiness, may be especially prone to commit suicide.

2. The discordant or impassioned drinker (Cimbal) was also described above. This type corresponds in some degree to Knight's reactive type and, as it has been pointed out variously, is identical with K. Binswanger's schizoid drinker. Cimbal's discordant drinker, however, is only one group of the schizoids described by Binswanger. It does not seem advantageous to refer to this type as schizoid drinkers since among the latter there are symptomatic drinkers as well as true addicts. The discordant type is definitely a schizoid personality for whom alcohol is the only means of temporary relief from conflict. There is, however, a schizoid type whose only difficulty is his seclusiveness and whom alcohol assists in jumping this barrier. Alcohol is not indispensable in his life; he is usually an intermittent drinker and may be classed among the symptomatic drinkers. The discordant type drinker may also have suicidal tendencies.

3. The compensating drinker. By compensating drinker we shall designate the type called self-aggrandizing by Cimbal and described above under this term. While inferiority feeling may be present to some degree in all drinker-types, it is the basic characteristic of Cimbal's self-aggrandizing type and is the mainspring of their drinking. The term compensating drinker is chosen here in preference to Cimbal's term because the latter is rarely used. There are two groups whose drinking is fundamentally motivated by feelings of inferiority. In one, these feelings are very deep-seated and largely unconscious; this type belongs with true addicts. The other is the man, frequently gifted, whose feelings of inferiority are more or less conscious and are likely to be largely in the social sphere. He belongs with the *Stammtisch* type and will be referred to as the predominantly social type of drinker.

4. The poverty drinker. This is a somewhat anomalous type of drinker, in many respects very like the type of the compensating drinker, but differing from it in that some exogenous precipitating factor, usually unemployment, is present, although endogenic readiness plays a considerable role. Now seen infrequently, it occurred in the past as a mass phenomenon at about the time of the industrial revolution. That the recent depression did not bring about a recurrence of this type in large numbers may be due to the present relatively high cost of alcoholic beverages as a result of high taxation. The German literature refers to it as *Elendstrinker*, or "misery" drinker, but as this English term has been applied to all those who drink to drown their sorrow, the term poverty drinker is adopted here. Poverty drinkers are true addicts, because drinking is essential to them and is for them a sufficient solution of the problem presented by their unemployment. Although the type is relatively uncommon now, it is included in the classification because it may recur.

Symptomatic drinkers. Another group whose drinking is endogenously conditioned may be termed the symptomatic drinkers. In the sense that his drinking is evidence of a deep-seated maladjustment the true addict may also be thought of as a symptomatic drinker, but there is a clear distinction between these groups. For the addict, drinking is not only an essential in life, but also, however undesirable from a social point of view, a sufficient means of dealing with his problem. In the symptomatic drinker, however, the drinking does not solve the problem and the underlying cause breaks through, usually in the form of some clearly defined clinical entity, such as schizophrenia, manic-depressive psychosis or epilepsy. The drinking is only one of many symptoms. It may also be quite superficial and in some cases nothing more than a manifestation of exhibitionism. Types 5 to 10 belong in this category.

5. The symptomatic schizoid drinker. In discussing the discordant drinker, who is essentially schizoid and a true addict, we mentioned another type of schizoid drinker who uses alcohol only as a means of breaking his seclusiveness. This type will be referred to as the symptomatic schizoid drinker, since his drinking is incidental to his personality difficulties rather than a solution of them.

6. The schizophrenic drinker. Witless, continuous drinking frequently occurs at the onset stage of schizophrenia, particularly of the so-called simple and hebephrenic types. This is so well recognized that one may be suspicious of schizophrenia when violent drinking occurs in persons below the age of 20. The drinking is here, generally, a result of bewilderment at the lack of emotional reactions. Violent drinking is, in these cases, only one of many symptoms. When such patients are hospitalized there is usually no craving for alcohol.

7. Early general paresis. In these persons wild, continuous drinking

is probably nothing more than one of the expressions of the changes toward a grandiose personality.

8. The manic-depressive drinker. Manic depressives frequently drink to excess either in the manic or in the depressed phase. Drinking in both phases does not, however, occur in the same person, so that periodic drinking results with, usually, entirely abstemious intervals. The drinking in the manic phase is probably merely an exhibitionistic manifestation, while in the depressive phase it may be a symbolic suicide. In both phases, naturally, the drinking is just one of many symptoms. It should be noted that we mean here the clinical entity of manic-depressive psychosis and not the normal cyclothymic personality. Due to this periodicity of drinking, manic-depressive drinkers have been frequently described as dipsomaniacs but those who postulate an organic dipsomania usually refer to the manic-depressive periodic drinkers as pseudodipsomaniacs.

9. Epileptic and epileptoid drinkers. The well-known dysphorias of epileptics and of epileptoid personalities frequently lead to temporary wild drinking bouts. The frequency of periodic drinking in epileptics has led some investigators to believe that dipsomania is a form of epilepsy. This question, as well as those of alcoholic causation of epilepsy and epileptic origins of abnormal drinking, will be treated in the chapters on the alcoholic mental disorders and on heredity and germ damage.

10. True dipsomania? The question of a true dipsomania. If a true dipsomania, i.e., a periodic drinking originating in neurological and biochemical changes, exists, and we must say that this has not been definitely established, the drinking must be regarded as a symptom of an organic disease. Views about true dipsomania as well as pseudo-dipsomanias will be discussed in the chapters on alcoholic mental disorders. Tentatively we shall include true dipsomania in the final classification. According to numerous observers, dipsomaniacs may develop into steady drinkers. This would have to be attributed to physiological habituation processes and thus, even at that stage, they could be regarded as secondary addicts only.

There remain a few types of drinkers who cannot be regarded either as addicts or as symptomatic drinkers. These will be described below:

11. The stupid drinker. The stupid drinker has been described as one of Cimbal's types and does not require further elaboration. Inasmuch as his excessive drinking is, in part, determined by a lack of resistance inherent in the feeble-minded constitution, he may be regarded as belonging to the endogenous group. He is, however, not a true addict since alcohol has no other function than to supply brute pleasure and it is not so much inner motivations as temptations that lead to his drinking. Thus he is also not a symptomatic drinker.

12. The exuberant drinker. This is the type who avails himself of any special occasion to go into excess. His excessive drinking is thus irregular but not periodic. He is hypomanic in the normal sense and some tension is present; he may be exhibitionistic or just bubbling over. The jolly student drinker is of this type. It is a type which is very unlikely to become a secondary addict or even a chronic alcoholic but with maturity will probably calm down and become a moderate drinker, or even abstinent.

13. The *Stammtisch* drinker. Although various English terms, such as excessive social drinker, gregarious drinker, good-fellow drinker, could be substituted for the German term, none of them covers the entire variety that gather around the *Stammtisch*, i.e., around the table which sees the same drinking companions practically every night. These drinkers go to excess at irregular intervals only. Between such excesses they drink fairly large amounts, but not in such quantity as would be outside the limits of their psychological and physiological tolerance. Various types may be distinguished among them:

(*a*) Predominantly social compensating drinkers. This is the type whose inferiority feelings are fairly conscious and chiefly with regard to social life. He recognizes them somewhat wistfully, and perhaps humorously, and intermittently drinks deliberately to overcome his social inadequacy; he may, and often does, become a secondary addict. He is obviously in great danger of doing so, since he will have both physiological habituation and psychological motivation to that end. He is neither schizothymic nor cyclothymic.

(*b*) The easy-going drinker. This is a robust, good-natured, burgher type, but unlike (*a*) he is rather unsophisticated and drinking is for him a form of relaxation. He is usually of a cyclothymic personality.

(*c*) The promotional drinker. Typical of this group is the salesman who utilizes the camaraderie of drinking to promote his business. He is the professional treater—an American specialty. He often falls a victim to his own methods.

While the *Stammtisch* drinker may only rarely become a secondary addict he is likely, on account of his tolerance, to develop alcoholic diseases, among them delirium tremens. Since the drinking of these people is mainly in conformity with their cultural group, it may be considered as principally exogenous. There are other subtypes whose occurrence is too sporadic to consider in detail.

14. The occupational drinker. This is the exogenously determined drinker *par excellence.* It has been pointed out by observers of all nationalities that brewery and distillery employees, waiters and barmen, through their constant exposure to alcoholic beverages, frequently become excessive drinkers. Among the occupational drinkers belongs, also, the man who engages in heavy manual labor. The frequent occurrence of heavy drinkers in these occupational groups is well-documented (see the chapter on statistical sidelights on alcohol). Drinking among these people is continuous; but only irregularly excessive. Secondary addiction and chronic alcoholism are common in this group.

The *Stammtisch* drinker and the occupational drinker numerically form a very large part of the drinking population, while the true addicts are probably a comparatively small group, perhaps exceeded even by the symptomatic drinkers. The types outside of the true addicts and the symptomatic drinkers are of significance, inasmuch as they are all potentially secondary addicts and chronic alcoholics.

It may seem strange that no special type of the neurotic drinker, and of those who drink for relief from pain, has been mentioned. The chronic invalid who uses alcohol for assuaging pain is perhaps a true addict, but the occurrence of this type is so infrequent that it need not be included in the classification. The neurotic has been classified under various designations. The term neurosis covers so many conditions that it does not seem to be a useful classification in itself. The discordant drinker, for instance, may be a neurotic.

These types will now be brought into a classification, as shown by the diagram in Figure 1, in which they can be coördinated and subordinated within broader categories.

If this diagram does nothing but impress the wide variety of origins of abnormal drinking, it has served its purpose. It is evident that generalizations based on observations made on the endogenic types cannot be extended to the exogenic types. Neither is it permissible, within the endogenic types, to generalize from the true addicts to the symptomatic drinkers. Briefly, while valid generalizations may be made relative to the drinking in a given type, no statements can be made about abnormal drinking in general save for some generalizations of little

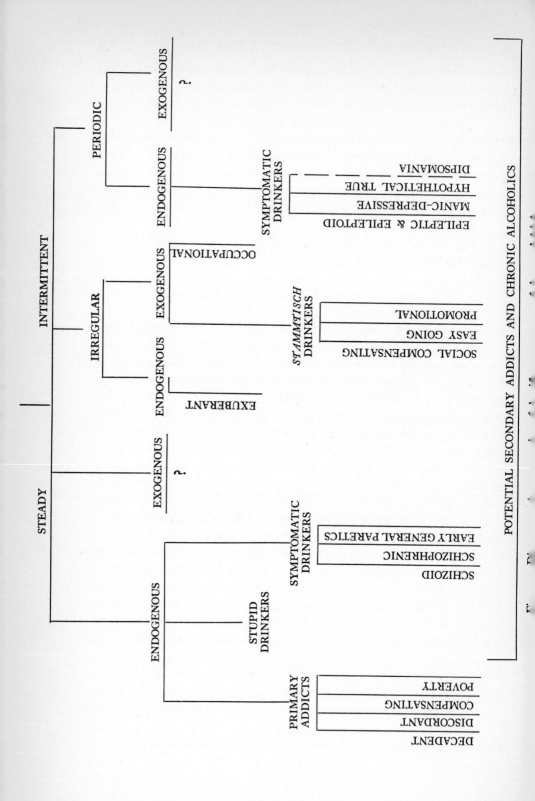

POTENTIAL SECONDARY ADDICTS AND CHRONIC ALCOHOLICS

explanatory value. The unity of the problem of abnormal drinking is an apparent one which arises from the fact that all abnormal drinkers are potential secondary addicts as well as potential chronic alcoholics.

As has been pointed out before, all this was exploration of the terrain on which abnormal drinking grows. None of the types necessarily becomes addicted or turns to abnormal drinking. There must be forces acting on this terrain before alcohol addiction arises. Nevertheless, as far as mental hygiene is concerned, the knowledge of the terrain is of great importance for it shows where efforts must be concentrated.

*The Tolerance Factor**

Among the etiological elements of alcohol addiction, tolerance is mentioned not infrequently. Thus, it is said that individuals with a low alcohol tolerance are not likely to become addicts [e.g., Myerson (b)]. Dent (b) said that anyone can be made an addict, but that the amount required for this depends on the constitutionally inherited tolerance. The word tolerance is used as if it were evident what the meaning of the word is and as if only one kind of tolerance exists. However, scanning of the literature shows that ideas about tolerance are not uniform and that various kinds of tolerance may be distinguished. If tolerance is considered as an etiological factor, it is necessary to have clearly in mind which kind of tolerance is meant. We are not thinking merely of the usual distinction between tissue tolerance and consumption tolerance. Although formally it may be irrelevant, operationally it seems to be necessary to distinguish between physiological and psychological tolerance to alcohol. Within the physiological tolerance, further distinctions must be made. Thus, it would appear to be useful to consider gastric tolerance to alcohol separately. Relative to psychological tolerance, it might be advantageous to relegate the functions on a physiological level, such as reaction time, perception and psychomotor functions, to the concept of physiological tolerance and to restrict the concept of psychological tolerance more to the molar manifestations. Gastric tolerance does not require any definition. On the other hand, psychological tolerance must be defined here. By this is meant the ability of the individual to withstand the disintegrating effects of the impact of alcohol on the total behavior. Some individuals lose control through the slightest stress caused by some misadventure or, as one would say in the vernacular, they become upset while others

* The mechanisms of tolerance are discussed in detail in the physiological chapters. Here only aspects of immediate interest to the subject of addiction are considered.

are able to take these things in their stride. The ability to integrate stresses into the total behavior is a function of the organization of the personality. It may be assumed that the well-organized personality is also better equipped to withstand stresses of a physiological nature. One may say that the well-organized person is alert to factors which may upset his equilibrium and is immediately aware of them and compensates for them through volitional control, or even partially unconsciously. The psychological ability to counteract the effects may develop through familiarity with the nature of these effects. Thus, what is termed habituation or acquired tolerance may be largely a psychological process, unaccompanied by any physiological adaptation.

Hence, the role of tolerance in the development of addiction is not a simple one. A person with a low gastric tolerance is not likely to become an addict, since he is not likely to expose himself to such inevitable discomfort. It must also be considered that this gastric intolerance may be a psychological defense mechanism in some cases. While, however, the gastric intolerance may be practically always preventive of the development of addiction, psychological intolerance may actually foster it. The person whose inhibitions are easily released through alcohol, and who is thus easily divorced from reality, may be more liable to addiction. On the other hand, high psychological tolerance, i.e., the facility for managing the stresses set up by alcohol, may lead to heavy drinking and ultimately to secondary addiction.

Initial or inherent tolerance in all its aspects must play a prominent role in the origins of addiction. In any given personality type alcohol tolerance may at least codetermine whether or not the person will become an addict. The experimental study of factors determining inherent tolerance offers a first approximation to the systematic exploration of the etiology of addiction. A brief outline of an experimental investigation of tolerance is presented in the chapter on the psychological effects of alcohol (Jellinek and McFarland).*

Social Factors

While all writers on alcohol addiction at least enumerate social factors among the etiological elements, there are few who have recognized these factors as the principal ones and who have given the matter adequate consideration. The role of social factors has been particularly stressed by Myerson (b); Cimbal; Pohlisch (g); and Mapother (a). The latter goes so far as to exclude individual psychological factors from

*To be published in another volume of this work.

serious consideration. More commonly, however, the discussion of social influences is limited to a paragraph enumerating a few possible social factors. Thus, Mangold merely mentioned that among the social factors which may foster alcohol addiction are child labor, unemployment, long hours, low wages, unsanitary living conditions and uncertain opportunities for recreation and leisure. Undoubtedly, these factors are of importance, but their consideration does not constitute a social theory of addiction.

Poverty is one of the social factors which has been discussed by many writers as an important source of addiction and, in connection with this, the easy accessibility and cheapness of alcoholic beverages has usually been mentioned. The latter two are factors which make abnormal drinking as a mass phenomenon at all possible. These factors are taken so much for granted that, with few exceptions [e.g., D. K. Henderson (b, c)], they hardly receive sufficient consideration in the scientific literature, although they are prominently discussed in propagandistically oriented writings.

The question of poverty as an etiological factor in addiction is a rather complex one and the role of poverty has probably been greatly overrated. The poverty theory originated in the wave of alcohol addiction which followed in the wake of the rapid industrialization of Europe and the consequent impoverishment in the classes of skilled trades. Pohlisch (f), however, has pointed out that impoverishment is followed by alcohol addiction under certain conditions only. He showed that, in general, in the last 50 years the consumption of alcoholic beverages and also the incidence of inebriety has decreased in times of economic depression and unemployment and increased in times of prosperity.

The impression that is obtained from many descriptions is that alcohol addiction is a poverty disease and its occurrence in high economic levels is sporadic only. As far as the alcoholic psychoses go, this has been definitely stated by Faris and Dunham.

This erroneous impression is obtained from the rather one-sided source from which knowledge about alcohol addiction is derived. Statistical studies are based largely on state hospital populations and on admissions to general hospitals which draw their patients from the lower income levels. The alcoholic population of the private institutions remains uninvestigated. However, these latter institutions absorb a considerable proportion of all first admissions with alcoholic psychoses. Since the minimum rate in these institutions is approximately

$30 per week, and since patients with alcoholic psychoses are usually hospitalized for a considerable time, it is evident that, for the greater part, patients from the higher economic levels come to the private institutions.

In 1937, there was a total of 5,639 first admissions for alcoholic psychoses to all mental institutions of this country; of these 1,157 were admitted to private mental institutions (Bureau of the Census). Thus, the latter institutions received 20.5 per cent of all first admissions for alcoholic psychoses. Evidently the incidence of abnormal drinking is considerable in the higher income levels. On the whole, poverty may account for addiction in a certain part of the addicted population, but the idea of addiction as a "poverty disease" must be rejected. Unless addiction in the higher economic strata is studied, and this is imperative, a biased picture of alcohol addiction will be obtained.

Occupation, as one of the extraneous factors of abnormal drinking, is also mentioned routinely in papers on alcohol addiction. This matter has received consideration from a statistical standpoint only. There is no question but that employees of breweries and distilleries, as well as bar attendants and waiters, contribute more than their share to chronic alcoholism. This may be inferred from occupational mortality studies (e.g., Whitney; Reploh), as well as from occupational statistics of admissions to mental hospitals [e.g., Roch; Pohlisch (g)].* Little is known, however, about the factors which differentiate between those members of these occupations who become abnormal drinkers and those who do not. An investigation of these factors may be well worth while.

Of deeper social meaning are reflections on the role which our social customs play in fostering alcohol addiction. This has been pointed out, by Herttell, as early as 1819, and has been elaborated among others by Mapother (a) as well as Baldie (b). Recently Shalloo has stated: "With so many various forms of culturally approved drinking, the amazing result is that we have so few persons emotionally dependent upon alcohol in some form. The teetotaler is, after all, equally as abnormal from the cultural standpoint as is the habitual drinker."

Nothing indicates better the influence of social mores on alcohol addiction than the variation of the male–female ratio of inebriety from country to country. In the United States, the ratio is approximately 6 men to 1 woman; in England, the ratio is 2 to 1; in Switzerland, 12 to 1; and in Norway, 23 to 1 [Wlassak (b)]. The relative scarceness of alcohol addiction among women has been interpreted, also, by Myerson as

*This question will be dealt with in detail in Vol. III of this work.

an indication of social forces at play in the genesis of alcohol addiction. Myerson (*b*) sees the main social factor in what he calls "social ambivalence." He points out how society on the one hand praises drinking in song, incorporates it in social and religious customs, regards it as the sign of good fellowship and on the other hand regards with contempt —sometimes mixed with amusement—the man who succumbs to drinking. This social ambivalence is one of the greatest obstacles to purposeful education in moderation.

A primary cultural theory of alcohol addiction is that of Cimbal. "In the individual it [alcohol addiction] arises from disposition and influences of the surroundings, and in the people as a whole as a consequence of insufficient balance between culture and civilization. It is the fault of epochs in which a lack of culture does not offer sufficient compensation for the arbitrariness of living, as determined by technical and economic conditions." Unfortunately Cimbal's theory remained fragmentary. This interesting theory calls for a history of addiction. Not a history of drinking customs, of which there is an abundance, but a history of alcohol addiction as a mass phenomenon.

There are many allusions in the literature to the social factors in alcohol addiction, some of a routine nature, some of great originality, but there is little that goes beyond the stage of suggestions. All indications are that an ecological study of alcohol addiction and of chronic alcoholism is one of the primary needs of research on the etiology of addiction. Such an ecological study will be of value only if it also includes the higher economic and educational strata. A follow-up study of discharged alcoholic patients, such as outlined in the following chapter, may also elucidate some of the social factors at play.

The terrain on which alcohol addiction grows has been well explored; the forces which are necessary to act on it to bring addiction about are more or less a matter of surmise. It remains for future research to explore these forces: physiological, psychological and social.

III. THE TREATMENT OF ALCOHOL ADDICTION

Introduction

There are a vast number of papers entitled "Treatment of Alcoholism." Many of these deal only with the treatment of the manifestations of chronic alcoholism. Many others under this title discuss exclusively the question of the legal status of inebriates and their handling by public institutions and still others deal with the question of prohibition. Hence, papers actually dealing with the treatment of addiction are much less numerous than would be inferred from scanning a list of titles.

Important as is the question of the management of the alcoholic, that is, the governmental or municipal or civil policy covering the care of inebriates, it cannot be dealt with in the context of this book, although some allusions to the question cannot be avoided. The treatment of the alcoholic psychoses will be dealt with in connection with the discussion of the alcoholic mental disorders. The joint discussion of the treatment of alcohol addiction and the treatment of the alcoholic psychoses has led in the past to great lack of clarity and has introduced an entirely unnecessary element of conflict into this already controversial material.

The question of the treatment of alcohol addiction has been obfuscated to no small degree by failure to differentiate between addiction and symptomatic inebriety. When drinking is incidental to feeble-mindedness, to psychosis, or to some severe psychopathy, the treatment must refer primarily to the basic condition, not to the symptom. It has been noted in a previous section that not more than 60 per cent of abnormal drinkers are neurotics, social drinkers, etc. and that some 40 per cent are psychotics, psychopaths or feeble-minded. In the absence of limiting criteria, the discussion of the treatment of alcohol addiction cannot attain either to an agreement on principles or to an evaluation of results.

In our discussion we shall not be able to adhere consistently to such limitations, since the various factors are inextricably mixed in the existing literature. The best we can do under the circumstances is to keep these criteria in mind when we are interpreting and evaluating the results.

Abnormal drinking as a mass phenomenon has occurred at various times and in various countries since recorded history and in proportions which have caused apprehension. Nevertheless, the medical nature of the problem was not recognized, or only by a very few, and the medical treatment of alcohol addiction was not thought of, although there was some medical as well as lay prescribing to counteract its unpleasant effects. Whenever inebriety became a public nuisance, the remedy was punitive rather than curative. Ulpian, a Roman jurist of the second century, urged treating inebriates as sick and diseased persons (Masters), but there is no evidence of any resulting medical efforts. In the thirteenth century, the kings of Spain enacted laws recognizing inebriety as a disease (Masters), but this had legal rather than medical repercussions. Although some attempts at the treatment of alcohol addiction on the basis of psychiatric considerations and insight seem to have been made sporadically (Thomas Trotter), the impetus to systematic treatment was given in 1849 by Magnus Huss when he described the disease *Alcoholismus chronicus*. The first attempts embraced principles which, in a different form, are still operative in the treatment of addiction. Thus, Nasse, in the first half of the nineteenth century, stressed the necessity of bringing about disgust for alcohol in the person suffering from alcohol addiction. This he achieved by adding alcohol to the soup, beef, vegetables and dessert of his patients. It is claimed that some dipsomaniacs were cured completely, but that in most patients the cure was not of long duration. C. O. G. Napier of England "cured" by vegetarianism (McConnell).

With few exceptions, however, the treatment of alcohol addiction was of a punitive nature up to the end of the nineteenth century and the punitive attitude still persists, not only in the legislation of some of the states of this country, but also in the minds of some modern physicians. Thus, Benon (*b*) says that to call the alcoholic pervert mentally sick, or to regard drunkenness as a mitigating circumstance, is a social danger; the inebriate's place is in prison, not in the hospital. McClellan claimed excellent results with two patients, one of whom he put in the back wards in a state hospital to clean up the soiled patients, while the other one he put in restraint. This attitude is surely a reactionary one and although it bears a superficial resemblance to, it must be clearly distinguished from, the attitude that persons in whom inebriety is only an accompaniment of psychopathy or feeble-mindedness should be segregated in an institution for the protection of society. This latter attitude is not a punitive one although it, too, demands the removal of the individual's freedom. Salinger pointed out that 6 inebriate hobos cost the state 70,000 marks because of repeated admissions to a hospital and that they should have been placed in the workhouse in the first instance. In the opinion of Seliger (*a*), feeble-minded inebriates with a history of repeated commitments should be handled by the penal system. Some writers on the treatment of alcohol addiction refer to any intramural therapy as punitive. Since, however, the majority of treatments requiring isolation do not involve any punitive element, and since isolation is carried out only for facilitation of the treatment, the designation of these therapies as punitive seems to be a misnomer which tends to create confusion.

Persuasion, religious and moral arguments and threatening or sympathetic suggestions must always have been used by the fathers, wives, husbands or friends of inebriates, but when the treatment of alcohol addiction was attempted systematically, recourse was first taken to drugs, backed by various rationales, and the psychotherapeutic approach developed only later. As mentioned before, psychotherapy had been practiced sporadically by physicians before this. In the modern treatment of addiction, however, psychological methods have begun to predominate, but drug therapies are still widely used. The main issue today is drug treatment versus psychotherapy, although almost no drug treatment entirely lacks a psychological element. Within each school, differences center around the specific methods, around the question of whether the patient should be treated in his own home or in institutions, and around the type of institution.

Therapists generally agree on the difficulties and the limited applicability of all methods. Stevenson says there is no "guaranteed" or easy cure for alcohol addiction and D. K. Henderson (a) says "Frankly we know of no specific, specialized form of treatment for chronic alcoholism which we can wholeheartedly recommend."

A basic difficulty has been pointed out by Hart, who said that alcohol addiction cannot be regarded as a disease which runs its course and from which the patient is glad to recover. Another fundamental difficulty has been indicated by Künkel who stated that in the treatment of alcohol addiction the whole person must be changed. This is profoundly true and therefore all treatment which does not have as its goal a change of the total personality must necessarily be either approximate or substitutive.

One of the immediate difficulties is that part of the alcohol addict's trouble is his environment and a doctor can do very little to alter that. All that can usually be done is to help the patient to live in his given environment [Dent (b)].

Barham considered that the difficulties encountered are of four types: (a) those of the patient consisting mainly of fear of being confined in a place which is more or less a prison, of sudden withdrawal of alcohol, of still more diminished sleep by withdrawal of sedatives, of the stigma of meeting someone in the institution whom he wants to avoid, of admitting being a drunkard, of the treatment failing; (b) those of the patient's friends who cannot forgive what they consider to be a vice rather than a disease; (c) those of the doctor who wants to persuade the patient to submit to institutional treatment and tries to integrate administrative technicalities and the patient's varying moods; (*d*) those of the management of the institution in keeping the patient (who does not enter under legal commitment but voluntarily) from procuring alcohol and in imprinting on the patient's mind that he must become a total abstainer.

Intramural versus Extramural Treatment

The effect of institutional confinement must be a matter of serious consideration and opinions show wide divergence. Arguments both for and against intramural treatment have been cogent. J. L. Henderson expressed the belief that inebriates, even if voluntarily seeking treatment, need restriction from alcohol under enforced detention. The impracticability of home treatment and the greater suitability of nursing homes and hospitals for treatment of these patients has been emphasized by Dent (*a*); Fleming (*c*); Masters; Praetorius; I. D. Williams; and Wolff.

Knight stated that the best choice was combined hospital treatment and psychoanalysis, as first instituted by Simmel.

Diethelm, as well as W. C. Menninger, would carry out the first phase of treatment in a closed and the second phase in an open institution.

Tilliss expressed a preference for treatment in closed institutions, since his impression was that success was no greater in the open ones. Although his statistics actually showed a considerably higher success rate in the open institutions, he explained this away on the basis that the open institutions had voluntary patients almost entirely, while the closed institutions had many enforced commitments. This distinction in patient populations is probably correct, but no conclusion as to comparative rates of success in open and closed institutions can be made on this basis alone.

The most cogent arguments in favor of institutional treatment have been presented by Carver (*b*). He pointed out that at home the attitude of mutual resentment is too great and that, furthermore, "Wherever we mass individuals together, certain regulations become inevitable and under such conditions special restrictions become less obtrusive and less objected to than they would be if applied to individuals." This does not imply a stereotyped regimen, but rather the advantage that can be taken of numbers in an institution. Carver also considered the type of institution in which the alcohol addict should be treated. Such an institution should be situated in the country with opportunity for sport and outdoor work. This is a principle which Durfee (*a*, *b*) has also strongly advocated. According to him a small farm is the best place where the alcohol addict can find the way to psychological freedom and can learn to live without drink.

Graf, and also Reynell, would generally favor home treatment, but prefer hospitalization for the first phase.

On the other hand, Lee contended that long periods of even semi-hospitalization lead to mental and physical lethargy and place the patient in danger of becoming the "chronic boarder type." According to Tokarsky, the patients who voluntarily seek help should feel that the physician is sure of his own methods and that he trusts the patient; only relapsed patients and those who have no home life at all should be treated in institutions. Strasser would limit institutionalization to those who are too dangerous to society. Strong advocated institutionalization only for cases requiring continuous hospital care and only when temperance organizations had tried their heavy schedule treatment and had failed.

Arguments on both sides are well considered and the only conclusion one can reach is that the matter must be handled individually. The personality and the circumstances of the patient should be considered when deciding upon intramural or extramural treatment. These considerations have been formulated by Seliger (*a*) as follows:

1. Psychotherapy in office practice. The patient who wishes to abstain but cannot; life habits and contacts not too bad; good intelligence and some maturity.

2. Rest-home farm with psychotherapy. The patient who wishes to abstain but cannot; poor habits and contacts; good intelligence and some maturity.

3. Commitment to alcohol farm, sanitarium or hospital under the Inebriate Act, for a definite length of time. The patient without desire to abstain; good intelligence but rather immature make-up.

4. Handling by penal system. The feeble-minded with a history of repeated commitment.

Even more criteria of selection among the various methods of handling alcohol addicts are desirable, and a more careful choice of treatment in the individual case, based on such criteria, would eliminate many failures.

The Problem of Withdrawal of Alcohol

One of the arguments for intramural treatment of the alcohol addict is the necessity for keeping the patient effectively away from alcohol.

There is unanimity among therapists that in the course of treatment absolute abstinence must be maintained and, with very few exceptions, therapists also agree that the patient must become a total abstainer and that he cannot be trained to become a social drinker. There are, however, differing opinions on the question whether or not alcohol should be withdrawn immediately at the beginning of the treatment or whether alcohol should be tapered off gradually.

Immediate withdrawal proves to the patient that there is no medical necessity for the use of alcohol (Tillotson and Fleming). The opinion that the immediate withdrawal of alcohol is essential is shared by Brown; Diethelm; Gabriel (c); Howard and Hurdum; McConnell; Seliger (a, b); and Tokarsky.

On the other hand, some therapists would taper off alcohol gradually, usually within the course of 5 to 10 days, either for psychological reasons which are, however, not explained, or because of the imminent danger of delirium tremens, e.g., Bostock; Durfee (a); Lee; Masters; and Wills. One even encounters such statements as that "Immediate and complete withholding of alcoholic beverages . . . is the real reason for alcoholic insanity" (Towns). Some writers recognized long ago that the fear of the ill effects of sudden withdrawal were unfounded. Thus, Thomas Trotter at the opening of the nineteenth century stated: "With drunkards therefore my opinion is, and confirmed by much experience, that wine, malt liquor, and spirits, in every form, ought *at once* to be taken from them. . . . That dangerous degree of debility which has been said to follow the subtraction of vinous stimulous, I have never met with, however universal the cry has been in its favour; it is the war-whoop of alarmists; the idle cant of arch theorists." Benjamin Rush, also, had a similar opinion, though not formulated so felicitously.

The delirium tremens argument may be regarded as disproved. In American state hospitals, where thousands of alcoholics are admitted annually, not a drop of alcohol is given and the development of delirium tremens in these institutions is a rarity. Statistics relative to withdrawal of alcohol and delirium tremens are discussed in Chapter II, in the section on delirium tremens; it can be said, at least, that immediate withdrawal is not contraindicated for this reason. In the public institutions for alcohol addicts in Sweden, the old Austria and Switzerland, alcohol is cut off immediately, while in England (no public institutions, only private voluntary ones) tapering off is practiced [Fleming (b)].

Another question is whether or not alcohol should be kept out of sight of the patient. This question is answered in the affirmative by most therapists, but there are some cogent dissenting opinions. Durfee (a) does not remove alcohol from the environment of the patient, who has to learn how to get along without it even where it is available. Patients are invited to cocktail parties at his house where they learn to adjust to the fact that they cannot take alcohol and to lose self-consciousness. Seliger, too, inclines toward this procedure.

In some of the drug treatments, especially in those based on conditioning, the giving of alcohol is naturally a part of the treatment, but is usually not continued for any length of time.

Treatment by Means of Drugs

There are several rationales in support of drug treatments although not all of them are rational. The oldest idea, perhaps, is that of creating disgust toward alcohol by adding nauseants to the drinks. This principle in its modern scientific elaboration is known as the conditioned reflex treatment.

The idea of immunization to the effects of alcohol was advanced at the end of the nineteenth century by Toulouse. Two of his followers gradually alcoholized horses and then injected their serum into alcohol addicts. Since, in alcoholic intoxication, no antibodies are formed, the immunization idea naturally did not work.

A frequently used principle is that of detoxication which may be based on scientific concepts of metabolic changes in chronic alcoholic intoxication, but which is all too frequently derived from some vague, naïve idea of speculative physiology. Some assume that the craving for drink is a result of the toxic state of tissues and that the craving can be broken "by removing all traces of the toxin from the cells," e.g., Towns. Others want to rid the body of "gouty impurities" (Wingfield), and Lee thinks that whatever form of treatment is used, it must be a rapidly detoxicating and eliminating one. This school is convinced that with the completion of detoxication the craving for alcohol vanishes, but admits it can be reactivated. As Keeley somewhat obscurely stated, "The primary causes which lead a person to drink are the causes which bring about a relapse." Also, "I claim to destroy only the craving for drink and this I have never failed to do, unless a barrier is presented by reason of antecedent physical or mental conditions, whereby the system will not tolerate the absence of accustomed alcoholic stimulation." Keeley's undisclosed remedies* were supposed to

---

*It has been repeatedly asserted that apomorphine or emetine were at least part of the treatment. According to a personal communication from Doctor A. J. McGee of the Keeley Institute, this is not the case.

"antagonize this effect of alcohol upon the nerve cells and break up the rhythmical automatic craving for liquor."

The various "gold cures" are all devised with a view toward some hypothetical physiological changes in the alcoholic. According to Silkworth (b), orthocolloidal iodine and orthocolloidal gold serve the purpose of physical normalization and cell revitalization. Silkworth uses these substances only as a supplementary treatment with psychotherapy and Bostock, too, advocates such supplementary treatment. The idea of nervous reconditioning underlies Schwarte's treatment. He gave cerebrin to 21 patients but did not obtain complete abstinence in any of them.

Naturally, a good many nostrums for breaking the alcohol habit have been in circulation and probably never will be entirely removed. Masters described a few of these; perhaps the most curious among them was the "Teetolia Treatment" which contained 30 per cent by volume of alcohol. There has also been a search for nonintoxicating alcoholic beverages and a recent product of this group was marketed under the name of "Prescription Brand Whisky," which the producer claimed to be nonintoxicating and therefore useful in the treatment of alcoholism. As the commentator of the Journal of the American Medical Association remarked: "The only way to fix whisky so that it does not produce drunkenness is to remove the alcohol, and then it is not whisky."

Insulin treatment in shock dosages as well as in subshock dosages has been practiced with appealing rationales in acute intoxication as well as in delirium tremens and the Korsakoff psychosis, but, to our knowledge, has not been used in the treatment of alcohol addiction. On the other hand, metrazol, which also has been used in the treatment of acute intoxication, has been tried in the treatment of alcohol addiction, but on 1 or 2 patients only and without success (Hill).

The old idea of creating disgust for alcohol has been put on a more scientific basis with the application of Pavlov's concepts of the conditioned reflex. For the establishment of a conditioned reflex, Kantorovich, in 1930, reported the use of a pain stimulus. Even this seems to have had its early forerunners. Benjamin Rush, early in the nineteenth century, wrote that "the association of the idea of ardent spirits with a painful or disagreeable impression upon some part of the body has sometimes cured the love of strong drink."* Generally, nauseant drugs,

*This statement does not appear in Rush's An Inquiry into the Effects of Spirituous Liquors on the Human Body, published in 1790, but appears in the edition cited in our bibliography.

notably apomorphine, are used at present. The technique of Galant
(*b*) is given as an example of the less exact and earlier form of conditioned reflex therapy. He started his treatments with strychnine injections, pretending that this created aversion against alcohol. After
a few days of this, he gave apomorphine injections together with a glass
of vodka and made the patient believe that the vomiting was due to
the drink. This was repeated 10 to 20 times, but intermittently
strychnine without vodka was given. Out of 22 patients, only 2 remained abstinent while the others relapsed from within a few days to
6 months. As a result, Galant expressed the opinion that the conditioned reflex treatment should be combined with psychotherapy. Dent
(*b*) attempted to utilize a painful situation as the unconditioned
stimulus, but later employed apomorphine. His results (4 patients
only) were not encouraging. He raised several questions: (*a*) Does
stimulation of the vomiting and other centers in the floor of the fourth
ventricle by apomorphine replace stimulation indirectly caused by
alcohol? (*b*) Is there a physiological need for this stimulation in certain
individuals? (*c*) Does this stimulation assist reorientation of habits?
Conditioning with apomorphine was also carried out by Fleming (*c*);
Markovnikov; Sluchevsky and Friken; and by Wingfield. None of
these had notable success. Fleming felt that those 25 per cent of his
patients who remained abstinent were patients who were anxious to
stop drinking and other methods would have produced the same
results. Lévy-Valensi, in 1939, summarizing the results of the conditioned reflex treatment, said that none of the tried methods had proved
useful. Voegtlin, Lemere and Broz, however, claimed that the failure
of earlier studies was due in part to the wrong choice of nauseant and
in part to insufficiently elaborated techniques. With carefully worked
out procedures and with emetine instead of apomorphine, Voegtlin
obtained 64 per cent of "cures" in 685 unselected patients by a criterion of a minimum of 4 years of abstinence following treatment.

As a result of their experience, Voegtlin and his associates insist upon
the following: The necessity for an exact technique, which includes a
treatment room in which extraneous stimuli in all sensory modalities
are reduced to an absolute minimum, and in which adequate attention
is given to the comfort of the patient; the use of all types of beverages
for conditioned stimuli; development of the ability to discriminate
between noxious and innoxious beverages, cultivated by serving soft
drinks freely between seances; particular attention to the technical
points of the time of the first administration of liquor and the deter-

mination of the optimum number of treatments for the individual case; the institution of a reinforcement program to anticipate and avoid the spontaneous extinction of the conditioned reflex.

Gabriel (d), a thorough connoisseur of alcohol addicts, does not believe in any special medication against alcohol addiction. According to him, most treatments which are temporarily successful are based on suggestion and on producing nausea, but as soon as a patient discovers that his dislike of alcohol depends on a drug, the effect is lost. Myerson (c) attributes some usefulness to benzedrine in combating the depression and lowered mood of the alcoholic. He believes that "its use will relate prophylactically to a relatively few cases."

There have also been attempts to promote in patients, through the use of drugs, a general feeling of well being which would make the use of alcohol to this end unnecessary. The drug which has been employed for this purpose is amphetamine (benzedrine) sulfate. Bloomberg gave his 21 patients one 10 mg. tablet on rising and one at noon; the dosage was increased in most patients. The patients had no desire to drink; they felt alert, energetic and did not require the support of alcohol. Bloomberg thinks that the fact that the patient is able to stop drinking gives him confidence which may allow the institution of more fundamental psychotherapeutic approaches. Diminished craving was noticed also in 3 patients who had been given benzedrine by Wilbur, MacLean and Allen. Encouraging results were reported by Miller, whose experience, however, did not extend to more than 4 patients who received 10 mg. twice daily. Reifenstein and Davidoff (b) gave 20 to 30 mg. of amphetamine sulfate to various groups of alcoholic patients. In acute alcoholism they obtained good results, but they had no success with alcohol addicts. They observed, however, that the depression following continuous daily imbibing responds to the drug during institutionalization. Moore gives benzedrine incidentally in his general scheme of treatment. That this drug per se cannot bring about cure of alcohol addiction is evident, but it may be a valuable accessory in psychotherapy. Experience with this treatment, however, has not advanced sufficiently for definite conclusions to have been reached.

The Psychotherapeutic Approach

The therapist who relies entirely on drug treatment assumes that the problem of the alcohol addict is alcohol and nothing else; hence, he directs his treatment toward the alcoholic habit, but not toward the emotional and intellectual difficulties which are in back of that habit.

If the habit is broken, there still remains a maladjusted person, and the maladjustment will manifest itself somehow, even though it takes a different form. Perhaps this new form will be less obtrusive, and therefore more acceptable to society, but, as far as the patient is concerned, it may be just as detrimental as the old one.

This is theoretically the case. Actually, it may happen that some patients, who have been enabled to get along fairly well physically for a considerable time without alcohol, have had a chance to make a psychological readjustment also. They also may have become more accessible to the influence of sympathetic and wise relatives and friends if they are fortunate enough to have them. But, in fact, it is practically inconceivable that in the case of prolonged drug treatment the therapist and his assistants should not have exerted some psychological influence, deliberately or not. The surroundings in which the drug treatment takes place, and the attention which the patient receives, have their psychological aspects, but not necessarily favorable ones, and the same conditions may be favorable to one patient and unfavorable to another. Thus it is possible that in some patients recovery from alcohol addiction may be brought about indirectly by those psychological factors which are incidental to drug treatments, but theoretically these treatments are symptomatic and actually misjudge the main issue. As Wexberg (a) said, it is no use getting a patient over a physical predicament without taking care of underlying mental conditions. The weakness of drug treatments has been best expressed by Carver (b): to achieve success, the specific "would have to change the patient's mentality in the direction of enabling him to face the situations which he shirks by taking alcohol." No such drug exists, but Carver added that, although medicine can never take the place of measures aimed at readaptation, certain drugs may be powerful auxiliaries.

As discussed in the section on the etiology of addiction, there are some chronic alcoholic patients whose inebriety is not rooted in alcohol addiction but who have become addicts through alcoholism. Hypothetically, one might assume that in these persons the problem is really alcohol and nothing else and that, therefore, a drug treatment which breaks the habit may be perfectly adequate, but this assumption can be verified or disproved only by carefully kept case histories.

One would expect from psychotherapy, therefore, that it attack the total personality with all of its conflicts and disabilities. Some of the psychotherapies, however, are not broader in their scope than drug treatments. To this group belong those which rely upon various forms of suggestion and hypnosis. A second group may be termed the emotional treatments and these are largely substitutive, although no implication of inferiority is meant by this term. In a third group are the treatments which are designed to uncover the true motives behind the addiction and to give the patient the basis for readjustment through insight into his motives.

Suggestion and hypnosis. Hypnosis has been used not infrequently in the treatment of alcohol addiction, not for the purpose of revealing unconscious conflicts but for what may be called the influencing of the will power. For Tokarsky, psychotherapy is equated with hypnosis, and insofar as he concedes other treatments, he cannot think of them without the reinforcement of hypnotic suggestion. He believes the treatment to be especially suitable for alcohol addicts, since they are more susceptible to hypnosis than other patients. According to him, however, only sober patients should be hypnotized, as it may have harmful effects in the intoxicated. He does not think that collective hypnosis, as suggested by Bechterev, is successful. Bostock has used suggestion under light or deep hypnosis. He advocated positive suggestion, i.e., repeating over and over to the patient that his personality is improving and that he is mastering himself. He also advocated the exploitation of the fear complex through the medium of the sphygmomanometer, the stethoscope and pleximeter. Wingfield was also convinced that drug treatments, as well as moral encouragement, gave permanent results only when combined with light hypnosis. Kallenberg reported favorable results by hypnotic treatment of "a few patients." Dent (*a*) would carry out hypnosis to a stage of "complete anesthesia" when a patient refused apomorphine treatment because of the total abstinence demanded. Nicolle stated that the "cures" obtained by hypnosis were surprising, but that the results were only temporary. Cotlier said that hypnosis is important, but is not sufficient by itself as it does not affect the causes; the effective treatment is reeducation.

For Carver (*b*), a drawback to hypnosis lies in the fact that the patient's reason is abrogated in this process, while in a persuasive treatment the patient comes to stand by himself, rather than to acquire dependence upon the suggester. In our view, hypnosis, inasmuch as it is not used for probing but only for influencing, has no wider aims and, therefore, no deeper effect than most of the drug treatments.

Substitutive treatment. The fostering of hobbies and recreational and occupational therapies are all forms of substitutive treatment but they are perhaps never used alone, but rather as integral parts of treatments of wider scope. The true substitutive treatment goes much deeper than merely creating new interests or building up the assets of the patient. It is largely directed at new emotional experiences. According to Masters, there is nothing more effective in the eradication of alcohol addiction than the "expulsive power of a new affection." As such a new affection, he regards religious conversion; religion is concerned with the whole man and reaches deep seated troubles. In the course of the religious treatment, he would use restraint as well as freedom, rewards as well as restrictions.

This emotional rebirth is the medium which has been used rather successfully by temperance societies. Graf pointed out that alcohol gives content to the life of the addict, that withdrawal takes this content away and that, therefore, some substitute must be given him. As he phrased it, the primitive and sometimes repulsive methods of temperance societies are very effective; their songs and speeches must not be judged from the aesthetic or artistic standpoint but from the standpoint of the emotions which they stimulate. While the methods of these societies harp on the sinfulness of drinking, they always leave room for hope. Graf thought that whenever a spark of sensitivity remains in the patient, religious treatment is worth while. Gabriel (c) saw a great deal of usefulness in the heavy schedule of activity which these societies impose on their converts and it seemed to Praetorius, also, that there was greatest hope for recovery when the coöperation of these societies was obtained. Fleming (c) has expressed a preference for substitution for alcohol of some socially acceptable source of satisfaction. The choice of the substitute must depend on the individuality of the patient, but he has found religious conversion often very successful, since it provides companionship, spiritual exaltation and a follow-up system through life. According to Lamb, the effective cure is change of environment accompanied by suitable work and "salvation." And Baldie (b), although inclined toward Adlerian methods, admits the value of religious emotion in certain cases.

Religious conversion without the aid of "preaching" and of the "holier-than-thou" attitude is the fundamental idea of the Fellowship of Alcoholics Anonymous (Alcoholics Anonymous). Although they insist that alcohol addiction is also a physical disease, probably of an allergic nature, they consider the main cause to be emotional maladjustment. Their solution is a deep and effective spiritual experience which revolutionizes the whole attitude toward life. They believe that human aid is insufficient and that the defense against the "first" drink can only be from a higher power. In their view, the ex-addict is better equipped than anyone else to win the addict's confidence. Their program of recovery is stated as follows:

1. We admitted we were powerless over alcohol—that our lives had become unmanageable.
2. Came to believe that a Power greater than ourselves could restore us to sanity.
3. Made a decision to turn our will and our lives over to the care of God *as we understood Him*.
4. Made a searching and fearless moral inventory of ourselves.
5. Admitted to God, to ourselves and to another human being the exact nature of our wrongs.
6. Were entirely ready to have God remove all these defects of character.
7. Humbly asked Him to remove our shortcomings.
8. Made a list of all persons we had harmed and became willing to make amends to them all.
9. Made direct amends to such people wherever possible, except when to do so would injure them or others.
10. Continued to take personal inventory and when we were wrong promptly admitted it.
11. Sought through prayer and meditation to improve our conscious contact with God *as we understood Him* praying only for knowledge of His will for us and the power to carry that out.
12. Having had a spiritual experience as the result of these steps, we tried to carry this message to alcoholics, and to practice these principles in all our affairs.

It is interesting that they recommend hospital treatment before their psychological measures can be applied. Silkworth (*d*) has stated that he has found no emotionalism in this group and thinks that the movement will spread and recoveries will be permanent ones.

With regard to emotionally based substitutive treatment in general, Strecker and Chambers have expressed the opinion that "unfortunately 'cures' on an emotional basis are not common enough to make it a satisfactory source of treatment reliance." It appears to us that a therapist's concepts of the applicability of various forms of treatment will be largely influenced by the type of patient whom he sees in his practice and that those who draw their patients from the higher educational levels are likely to encounter relatively few with whom an emotional appeal would be possible.

While the substitutive emotional treatments do not approach the theoretical ideal, they must be regarded as fully legitimate and useful therapeutic media. The difficulties, the long duration and the costliness of causative treatments make them out of the question for a large number of alcohol addicts.

Causative treatment. All causative treatment of alcohol addiction starts from the assumption that, for the addict, alcoholic indulgence is the solution of his emotional conflicts, of his inability to make normal adjustments and of his unwillingness to face reality. Whatever the method of the individual psychotherapist may be, the aim is to make the patient realize the true, instead of the apparent, cause of his drinking and to give him the means by which he may make his adjustments without the aid of the artifacts of intoxication and, occasionally, to eradicate the sources of conflict. As to how these aims can best be achieved, therapists have differing convictions. The methods differ chiefly in the depth to which they probe and in the factors on which they place emphasis. Generally, the therapist does not stop with the uncovering of true causes, but assists the patient to reorganize his life through planned activities. This whole system of activities is best designated as reeducation, and whether the therapist calls it so or not, with few exceptions it plays a part in the general scheme. Strasser has expressed the process of psychotherapy in three words: Insight, knowledge, action.

There is a group of abnormal drinkers to whom this "understanding" treatment does not apply. We have made reference to that group whose alcohol habits originate more in social circumstances than in inherent conflicts. Brown pointed out that these patients cannot be treated "as if running away from something" and he advocated simply the training of will power and control of imagination for them.

Evidently causative treatments require an intimate knowledge of the patient and therefore involve more difficulties and more resistance on his part; they require more coöperation from the relatives, generally demand a higher intellectual level in the patient than other treatments and are naturally of much longer duration. All of these difficulties necessarily result in compromise and the value of the treatment in any individual case depends on how felicitous this compromise is and where the emphasis is placed. Durfee (a) has attributed many therapeutic failures to too much emphasis on the overcoming of the drinking habit, instead of trying to solve personality difficulties and to the lack of sufficient understanding of the psychological mechanisms in habit formation.

Extrinsic as well as intrinsic factors place difficulties in the path of causative treatment. The usual lack of understanding and consequent lack of coöperation on the part of the patient's relatives have been pointed out by many therapists, e.g., Knight (c); and Carver (b). Not only must interference on the part of relatives be eliminated, but they must be integrated into the therapeutic scheme. Thus, W. C. Menninger found it necessary that the patient's relatives should be made familiar with the theory and technique of therapy. Bostock stressed that the transference must include the family. Gabriel (c) always included the family of the patient in the treatment and required them to abstain completely from alcohol. Practically every paper on the psychotherapy of alcohol addiction makes some mention of the part of the relatives in the general scheme.

One of the intrinsic difficulties of these treatment methods is the necessity for establishing a transference between therapist and patient. This was recognized as early as the beginning of the nineteenth century. Thus Thomas Trotter says, "When the physician has once gained the full confidence of his patient, he will find little difficulty in beginning his plan of cure." While different therapists may allude to the relationship under different names and differing formulations, it all comes down to what has become generally known by its psychoanalytic designation, namely transference. In the psychoanalytic treatment, the transference assumes, however, a much greater significance than in other psychotherapies. There it is not merely a question of good rapport, but the transference is evaluated at its various stages and the treatment is modified according to the forms which the transference takes. The aspect of transference naturally injects a wholly subjective element into the therapy and makes success largely dependent upon personalities and their interactions.

Obviously not every therapist can establish transference with every patient. The Fellowship of Alcoholics Anonymous maintains that only an ex-addict can effectively establish transference with an alcohol addict. This is a principle to which some therapists subscribe [e.g., Silkworth (c)]. There are others who feel that while transference can be effected by a nonalcoholic, it is best and most easily accomplished by an ex-addict; thus, Forel admitted that the old shoemaker Boshardt, an ex-addict and the founder of Elikon, had better results than he (Graf). It may be questioned whether this is based on greater insight in the ex-addict. It is probable that it is not so much a question of insight as of the feeling on the part of the alcohol addict that the ex-

addict cannot look down on him and must surely understand his difficulties without condemnation. Some, e.g., Seliger (a), take the position
that confidence in the good faith of the therapist is best established if
the therapist is a total abstainer. It is perhaps due to an inclination
toward the idea that an ex-addict is more likely to be successful in
this work that lay therapists are accorded a greater role by medical
men in the treatment of alcohol addiction than in any other behavior
disorder.

The greatest intrinsic difficulty, however, lies in the patient's attitude toward his own problems, or rather in his misjudging of his
problems. Strecker and Chambers have made one of the most illuminating and important observations on the fundamental problems.
They said that most alcohol addicts want to become normal, but that
"normality is synonymous in the mind of the alcoholic with only one
thing—drinking normally." . . . "He who essays to treat alcoholic
patients and does not recognize that there is a definite psychic tie-up
between 'normality' and the desire to drink normally is defeated before
he begins. He must recognize that this perverted normality complex
about drinking exists, and until it is dispelled by understanding and reeducation, no permanent curative measures can be expected."

Furthermore, it is usually the case that the alcohol addict desires dependence and Künkel has stressed, as have others, that one of the
necessities of treatment is to train the patient to take responsibility
and to make him stand on his own; this often leads to a crisis since the
patient feels that he is being let down.

The uncovering of the true psychological causes of the patient's
behavior deviations varies from a superficial interview of the patient's
relatives and friends, through intimate conversations with the patient,
up to the tedious but deep searching, free association methods of psychoanalysis. The exact techniques used in this probing are varied and
need not be discussed here in detail, but we shall give some consideration to the general principles and aims involved in the various psychotherapeutic schemes. The basic principle underlying all variations of
these procedures was admirably formulated by Thomas Trotter, in
1804, who speaks of "the necessity of studying the patient's temper
and character, that we may acquire his confidence. These will lead us
to the particular cause, time and place of his love of the bottle. The
danger of continuing his career may then calmly be argued with him,
and something proposed that will effectually wean his affections from
it, and strenuously engage his attention. This may be varied according

to circumstances, and must be left to the discretion of the physician."

In this country, Peabody has probably exerted more influence than anyone else on the psychotherapy of alcohol addiction. His reeducational program proceeded in nine steps as follows: *1*. A mental analysis and removal of doubts, fears, conflicts, created in the past. *2*. Permanent removal of tension, which is only temporarily released by alcohol, by formal relaxation and suggestion. *3*. Influencing the unconscious mind by suggestion "so that it coöperates with the conscious to bring about a consistent intelligent course of action." *4*. Control of thoughts and actions. *5*. Hygiene. *6*. Daily routine of self-imposed schedule to keep the patient occupied, to train his will power and efficiency and to give him the feeling that he is doing something about his problem. *7*. Warning the patient against unexpected pitfalls. *8*. Providing the patient with some means of self-expression. *9*. Realization that the same force which drove the patient to disintegration will, under conditions of sobriety, carry him beyond the level of average attainment.

Outside of psychoanalysis, most of the psychotherapies are either weaker or modified or reinforced forms of the above and, as mentioned before, different therapists shift the emphasis to different aspects. Durfee (*a*, *b*) stresses the process of emotional reeducation, since emotional immaturity is the outstanding characteristic of the alcohol addict. His discussions with the patient are mainly concerned with the emotional maladjustment, rarely with the question of alcohol itself. The main objective of Strecker and Chambers as well as of Carroll is also to develop emotional maturity, as well as to produce abstinence. Künkel felt that the essential point is to increase the frustration tolerance of the patient. Wexberg (*a*) thought the most important thing is to make the patient understand what he tries to gain by drinking and Nossen's standpoint is similar. For Diethelm, the only effective treatment combines personality analysis and adjustment with the training of healthy habits. Incidentally, he warned that the insight shown by patients at the beginning of treatment is not due to true understanding but rather to alcoholic euphoria; this period is followed by a revolt of a few weeks and only after that can coöperation be expected. Reynell, who leans toward Adlerian psychology, is not satisfied with the mere elucidation of the causes of addiction and the training of habits, but insists on treatment of the causes and resolution of the conflicts. Strong, on the basis of a thorough study of the patient, endeavors to replace his weakness with whatever assets he may possess. The building up of self-respect is never neglected in psychotherapeutic procedures but Lambert makes it the central issue. There are, however, treatments such as Weiss uses which are merely mild forms of psychiatric social work. In view of the great variety of patients and in view of limiting conditions, such simple treatments, too, may have their place.

Evidently, in large institutions, effective psychotherapy is not readily feasible. In Sweden and in Austria, however, the institutions, in addition to their occupational, recreational and medical therapies, have found that psychotherapy can be reinforced through contact with temperance societies and the Salvation Army [Fleming (b)].

Psychoanalytic treatment is aimed at the deepest levels of human motivation and theoretically should give the best results in the treatment of alcohol addiction. Actually, the majority of abnormal drinkers are not suitable for this treatment for various reasons: intellectual and educational handicaps, the advanced age at which the alcohol addict usually presents himself, financial restrictions. Nevertheless, there has been some psychoanalytic activity in the treatment of alcohol addiction even in institutions. As a matter of fact, Simmel as well as W. C. Menninger and Knight (c) have utilized some features of institutions for the specific requirements of the treatment of alcohol addicts. Simmel found that the putting to bed of the patient and the circumstances attendant on it are a gratification of the unconscious desires of the victim of morbid cravings, namely, to be a child again, and to have a kind mother feed him and be present whenever anxiety seizes him. This situation is transformed back into the analytic situation as the treatment progresses and the infantile phase spontaneously disappears. The value of the hospital personnel as father and mother substitutes has also been stressed by I. D. Williams. Institutional treatment based on psychoanalytic principles adapts the patient's activities to his unconscious needs; outlets for aggressive drives are provided, anxieties are made endurable, praise and affection are given at appropriate times [Knight (c)]. However, both Menninger and Knight have admitted that psychoanalysis in these cases must be modified. Knight (c) felt that the addict cannot withstand the passive withdrawn attitude of the analyst and that unorthodox anamnestic interviews must be used to help rapport. Throughout the analysis, concentration should not be focused on drinking *per se*. The addict's great need for affection must be met rather than simply analyzed and interpreted. The emotional relationship with the analyst acts as partial substitute for drinking. Knight (c) thought it important that the analyst should make no initial demands, that he should suggest substitutes for alcohol and that homosexuality should not be mentioned too early. Relative to the success of this institutional psychoanalytic treatment, there is not much information. In 1938, Knight (c) reported on the treatment of 11 patients. At that time, 2 were still in analysis. The treatment of 4 patients had been stopped by relatives: 1 of these remained slightly improved, 1 relapsed in reaction to the interference and 2 remained moderately improved. The other 5 patients stopped treatment for various reasons: of these, 1 had improved, and 3 were moderately improved. This is not all too encouraging. Fleming (c) considered the results by psychoanalytic methods disappointing.

There has probably been more extramural than intramural psychoanalysis of alcohol addicts, but while there are some 80 psychoanalytic papers dealing with the question of inebriety, only 16* of these mention treatment of particular addicts. The authors of the other papers may have based their discussions on case material of their own, but this is not definite. Since the interest of the analyst is directed mainly toward the implications of the uncovered material, we learn little, if anything, about the results of these analytic treatments and cannot compare them with the results of the institutional analytic procedures.

Carver (b), while not seeing much scope for the psychoanalytic treatment of alcohol addiction, has expressed the opinion that it is highly desirable that the physician in charge should have a thorough knowledge of psychoanalysis. "Without actually analyzing the patient as that term would be allowed by the psychoanalysts, the physician experienced in it is able to explain to a patient the significance of various details in his history as they are disclosed from time to time in general discussion."

As we have mentioned before, there is a large variety of types of abnormal drinkers and a large variety of circumstances from which they come. It would seem that the alcohol addict who is a neurotic character, who has a sufficiently high intellectual level and who can afford the time and cost, will be, in all probability, much benefited by extramural psychoanalytic treatment. For the large majority, however, we must agree with Carver's attitude.

Unfortunately, causative treatments require long periods of time. Seliger (a) says that psychotherapy must be continued over years, possibly at 6 month intervals. Diethelm has also emphasized the necessity

* Clark; Coriat (a); Daniels; Ferenczi (a); Glover; Juliusburger; Kielholz (a); Knight (c); Oberndorf; Riggall; Robbins; Sadger; Schilder (a); Wall (a); Wholey.

for long treatment periods. Chambers estimated the time necessary at 80 to 100 hours over a period of a year and according to Knight (c) effective combined institutional and psychoanalytic treatment should last from 18 months to 3 or 4 years. In the opinion of Wolff, it takes 5 years before an alcohol addict must be given up as incurable. Such prolonged treatment can naturally be carried out only in private institutions at considerable expense or, at the other extreme, by temperance societies. Public institutions, however, usually have to rely on a less elaborate and less time consuming treatment.

Graf has pointed out that too little attention has been given to bringing the patient back into the community. This must be regarded as a definite phase of the treatment and contact with the patient in this phase should be maintained for considerable time. Graf believed that this was best accomplished by temperance societies. In the Austrian public institutions, clubs of ex-addicts were formed to carry out this function [Fleming (b)].

So far we have dealt with isolated aspects of the treatment of alcohol addiction. The general scheme of treatments will now be considered briefly. Modern therapies, even the most psychologically oriented ones, never neglect the physical aspects of chronic alcoholism. The treatment of concomitant "alcoholic diseases" as well as building up of the physique, which in these patients is usually impaired by nutritional involvements, is usually instituted routinely. Lévy-Valensi suggested that in the first phase, all symptoms must be treated as if they were cardiac, gastrointestinal or other disturbances and that treatment of behavior and mental disturbances should follow in the second phase. Wilson, whose main reliance is on psychotherapy, regards it as essential that this should be preceded by the injection of colloidal calcium and dextrose, "for the purpose of obtaining an improvement in glycogenesis, combating hypoglycemia, with the prevention of the accumulation of lactic acid in the tissues." Tillotson and Fleming recommend that in the treatment of alcohol addiction a thorough physical examination be included, that the hepatic and gastrointestinal changes be given special attention and that there should be supportive treatment in the form of baths, physiotherapy and dietary regimen. In view of the widely spread vitamin deficiencies among alcoholics, dietary measures and supplementary vitamins seem to be indicated as a routine adjunct to all psychotherapeutic schemes. As Meyerson (b) has pointed out, however, vitamin administration cannot form the basis of the therapy of alcohol addiction.

The use of sedatives is incidental to practically every form of treatment, although some therapists wish to avoid them as far as possible (e.g., Tillotson and Fleming). It is generally agreed that morphine is contraindicated in chronic alcoholism; nevertheless it is still given at times. The barbiturates are widely used at present, although Damrau regards them as more toxic than alcohol; Lee has pointed out that the prevailing tendency to give large doses of barbitals may make the use of any kind of additional sedative fatal. Bromides are also much used, but caution relative to their use is being voiced [Curran (b)]. Paraldehyde, which has been found the most appropriate sedative in delirium tremens, has been suggested in the treatment of alcohol addiction, although its habit forming properties must be considered [Carver (b)].

Moore has a comprehensive scheme for the treatment of alcohol addiction which we will summarize briefly. He excludes patients with psychopathic personalities from treatment. The patient must first be made alcohol free and gotten into good physical condition; to this end a diet well balanced in minerals and vitamins is provided and supplemented with 5 to 10 mg. of thiamin chloride daily. Fifteen grains of sodium bromide or 0.5 to 1.0 gr. of phenobarbital are given 3 to 4 times daily and 10 mg. of benzedrine twice daily. Eventually there is a psychiatric examination, and in patients with deep-rooted, unconscious difficulties, psychoanalysis is instituted. Important elements in the success of the treatment are the sincerity of the patient and the effectiveness of the transference. A trial period of treatment is usually advisable, during which the patient's veracity can be checked by information from others. The treatment includes analysis of the patient's life and an endeavor to make him recognize his own psychological mechanisms; the development of a rational program of mental hygiene; the achievement of a normal family life, for which some training of the family is also necessary; and the use of sports, dancing and physical activities to develop relaxation without the use of alcohol. No moral pressure is put on the patient.

Psychotherapeutic methods show quite a variation of principles and this may create the impression that there is considerable conflict in this field, but the conflict is much more apparent than real.

First, the fact that abnormal drinkers form a heterogeneous population embracing different and even antagonistic personality types with different origins of their addiction, actually demands a certain range of treatments.

Second, a therapist—and we are talking now of the therapist of addiction, but not of the alcoholic diseases—rarely sees in his practice a cross section of alcoholics, but draws his patients generally from restricted strata of that population. Consequently, he molds his therapeutic system according to his experience with the type which he most frequently encounters in his practice. Thus, the therapist who is likely to see mainly hobos and morons will differ markedly in his therapeutic principles and in his attitude toward the possibilities of therapy from the principles and attitudes of a therapist who draws his patients mainly from persons with a neurotic character and even more from the ideas of the therapist whose patients have become addicts by way of social drinking. A variety of treatment is, therefore, compatible with basic soundness.

The fact that the therapist forms his ideas according to the type of patient he most often sees may account for some failures, since a therapy designed for and successfully applied to such a limited group, and hence the technique upon which the therapist relies, may easily fail when applied to patients who do not fall into just this pattern. There are, of course, differences even among therapists who deal with much the same type of patient in much the same way. These differences are largely the result of the different personalities of the therapists themselves, and that they exist is not a cause for misgiving or for condemnation of any or all of the therapies, since certainly any man does best with the method in which he has greatest faith. The one really unfortunate aspect of the matter is that this subjectivity in methods makes their extension difficult, since they are not readily taught. No single prescription for the psychotherapy of the alcohol addict can be given, for the personal touch remains the vital element in the situation.

Prognostic Criteria and Estimates of Therapeutic Success

In discussing the prognosis of addiction and in evaluating therapies, we must state again that the patients with alcoholic psychoses are not considered here in order not to obscure the issues.

It is a useless undertaking to talk about the prognosis of abnormal drinkers in general. As mentioned repeatedly in our discussion, there is a considerable group of chronic alcoholics who are not true alcohol addicts, but in whom drinking is symptomatic of psychopathy or of moronism. As Knight (c) pointed out, the prognosis in this group is dependent on the basic condition and it is not legitimate to include it in evaluation of the prognosis of addiction. Even after the elimination of this group, the population of alcoholics which remains is etiologically heterogeneous and the prognosis is in part dependent upon the genesis of the addiction. Wlassak (b) enumerated several other factors which diminish the prospects of therapeutic success. He regarded as poor therapeutic risks: (a) Those who were already heavy drinkers at the age of 20; (b) infantile inebriates of higher age; (c) inebriates over 50; (d) lonely, artistic drinkers; (e) schizoid drinkers; (f) inebriates with organic brain changes; (g) inebriates with disordered home conditions; (h) divorced inebriates; (i) drinkers in alcoholic professions who remain in the profession.

Wlassak's age criteria are borne out by Künzler who was most successful with patients between 40 and 50 and least with patients under 25 and over 50. Voegtlin also mentioned that he had no success with patients below the age of 28. The most probable explanation for this situation is that these very heavy drinkers at early ages are really not addicts, but symptomatic drinkers in whom the onset of psychosis is manifested by heavy drinking.

That drinkers with psychopathic personalities have a poor prognosis has been pointed out by many (e.g., Moore; Stevenson). As stated before, this, too, is not true addiction and it is not this condition which requires treatment.

Poor heredity is also frequently mentioned as an indicator of poor prognosis [e.g., Graf; Pohlisch (f)], but Tillotson and Fleming do not regard heredity as a prognostic criterion.

It is the general opinion that women addicts are more difficult to treat than men, but Masters believes that they respond somewhat quicker to treatments involving religious conversion.

Dent (a) found that the "habitual drinker" who wants to give up, but thinks he cannot, has good prospects, but that the "active drinker" who drinks to drown his sorrows has a poor prognosis. Inasmuch as the "active" inebriate is not a symptomatic drinker, he is the one around whom the problem of the treatment of alcohol addiction is actually centered.

As Durfee (a) has stated, the extent and duration of drinking are not indications of whether or not a patient will be a difficult case.

Not much optimism prevails among therapists relative to permanent recovery from alcohol addiction, but there are a few exceptions. Nossen claims that among his patients, "the percentage of failures is hearteningly small." Ten of the 12 patients discussed in his book are designated as recovered, but there is no indication of the length of time after the treatment during which no relapses had occurred.

It is rather difficult to obtain an estimate of the degree of success of various therapies and it is even more difficult to judge the relative merits of different therapies since the description of the patient material is usually insufficient to form an idea of whether or not the type of patients was the same in the different treatments employed and therapeutic reports frequently have inadequate or no standards of success. Any standards must necessarily be arbitrary. In no instance is it possible to follow through all of the patients from the time of discharge to death, and as Carver (b) has pointed out, if the patient died soon after treatment, there is no assurance that he would not have relapsed had he lived longer. Thus, it is preferable not to talk of permanent cures, but rather to gauge success in terms of the incidence of patients who remain abstinent for a certain number of years after the completion of treatment. Usually an observation period of 2 to 4 years is available.

The evaluation of therapeutic success is hampered by the frequent lack of detailed case histories, by vague information relative to the duration of treatment and by the omission of many other pertinent data. In the past, much conflict has been introduced into the comparison of treatments and into the estimation of success by the inclusion of procedures which can hardly be designated as treatment, but which are in essence, simple custodial care. The success of therapy has probably been greatly underestimated by such inclusions.

In order to obtain a half-way meaningful estimate of therapeutic success we have listed in Table 5 only those reports which are based on large samples and which unquestionably relate to procedures with definite therapeutic rationales.* The requirement of large samples naturally reduces the number of utilizable reports to a minimum. The first four items of Table 5 are comparable inasmuch as they involve, on broad principles, the same type of treatment and perhaps largely the same type of patients. The estimates for total abstinence of 2 to 4 years after discharge are rather consistent and range from 25 to 30 per cent. Some estimates which are apparently based only on impressions, but presumably acquired as the result of extensive experience, are in good agreement with the figures mentioned above. Thus, Masters believes that 35 per cent of those who are under treatment for at least one year are permanently restored, and Reynell puts this at 20 per cent. Tilliss gives 2 estimates (see Table 5): one of 24.7 per cent and one of

---

*A number of investigators have made reference to the treatment of large numbers of addicts but unfortunately have not given any data relative to success except for indefinite qualitative statements, e.g., Rupp and Puckett; Wyrsch (b); Schwarz.

TABLE 5

Some Reports on the Success of Treatments of Alcohol Addiction
Based on Large Samples

Author	Date of Report and Country	Type of Institution	No. of* Patients	Treatment	Time since Discharge	Criteria of Success Totally Abstinent Per cent	Criteria of Success Improved Per cent	Remarks
Künzler	1930 Switzerland	Public	354	Character analysis, persuasion, occupational therapy. Medicinal adjuvants.	At least 4 years	30.5	7.6	
Wolff	1933 Germany	Public homes for inebriates	1082	Character analysis, persuasion, occupational therapy. Medicinal adjuvants.	At least 2 years	25.0	28.0	
Tilliss	1933 Germany	Public, open	1000	In general, same as above.	At least 2 years	24.7	27.4	
		Public, closed	398	In general, same as above.	At least 2 years	7.0	38.7	
Gabriel (d)	1935 Austria	Public homes for inebriates	1109	Character analysis, persuasion, occupational therapy. Medicinal adjuvants.	Not given	28.0	14.2	
Kruse	1932 Germany	Private sanitaria	1104	"Psychotherapy"; no description.	2 years	24.7	28.0	
Tokarsky	1938 Russia	Public	523	Hypnosis. Medicinal adjuvants.	Not given	13.0	—	
Voegtlin	1940 United States	Sanitarium, private	538	Conditioning by emetine.	At least 4 years	64.0	—	84.7 per cent stopped treatment. 2.3 per cent relapsed.

* Only those patients for whom follow-up data were given are included in the table.

7 per cent. The 7 per cent estimate pertains, however, to a highly selected population, namely, court commitments and therefore it may be assumed that a very large percentage of hobos and psychopaths is included in this sample. Thus it seems safe to estimate that with fairly elaborate psychotherapy, a minimum of 25 per cent success may be expected in public institutions. It must be kept in mind that none of these treatments really had a "fair break." As pointed out before, they are each devised for a certain type of patient, but in a public institution with a rather heterogeneous population, they are carried out on patients to whom they actually do not apply. Thus these estimates do not really characterize the potency of the treatment, but only express the average success obtainable without the necessary selection.

In contrast to the estimates obtained with broad psychotherapy is the 13 per cent success with hypnosis, as reported by Tokarsky. He gives no time criterion and it is possible that the estimate for this treatment should be even lower.

At the other end of the range, we find 64 per cent success in the conditioning treatment reported on by Voegtlin. His time standard of 4 years of abstinence is strict in comparison with the others. It may be questioned, however, whether the high success ratio should be attributed to the type of treatment or to the type of patients treated. Voegtlin's experience derives from a private sanitarium, while the other reports pertain to experience in public institutions. It is not unreasonable to assume that in a private sanitarium there would be a high incidence of the type of patient who goes from social drinking to excessive drinking, i.e., who is not a true addict and in whom the problem, therefore, is a comparatively simple one.

Unfortunately no data are available for an estimate of spontaneous remissions in alcohol addiction. For the alcoholic psychoses, such an estimate could be obtained, but would be of no relevance to this question, especially since recovery from the psychosis does not necessarily involve recovery from the addiction. The general opinion of students of inebriety, however, is that the spontaneous recovery rate is rather low. Thus, one could infer that if the indiscriminate application of psychotherapeutic methods results in 25 per cent success, variation of treatment based on selective principles would bring a considerably better result.

Outlook

What may be expected, then, of the future of the treatment of alcohol addiction? One possibility is that systematic research may reveal psychosomatic relations in the genesis of abnormal drinking which at present are unknown. Much research has centered around the physiological changes brought about by addiction, but few attempts have been made to learn whether the addict—and we exclude the symptomatic drinker—has characteristically a specific psychosomatic deviation. Fleming (b) has suggested, "If there could be created an Institute for the Study of Alcoholism where the biochemist, the internist, the psychologist, the anthropologist, the psychiatrist, and, possibly, the theologian, working coöperatively could each bring to a common focus, on the manifold problems of alcoholism, his own special knowledge, then it should be possible to remove from this field some of the ignorance, prejudice and charlatanry that characterize it today. Such an institute would provide a place where, under standardized conditions, the different methods of handling drunkards could be tested and compared."

Unless a psychosomatic basis of addiction, and consequently of its treatment, is found, the only possibility is to bring greater order into psychotherapeutic procedures. By this we mean that a definite effort has to be made to establish criteria for the suitability of any given method to a given patient; the criteria so far established are definitely superficial.* A method for determining these criteria may be found in follow-up studies far outside the routine techniques and aims of the run-of-the-mill follow-up study. It is doubtful whether any such study could be carried out with the aid of such case histories as are now available. In order to establish whether or not any correlation obtains, and of what nature, among success, type of treatment, type of personality and origin of addiction, personality studies and life histories are required of a type which will go far beyond those currently made. It would appear much more profitable to lay now the foundations of such a study, which can be evaluated only after several years, than to

---

* In the preface to his book, *What Price Alcohol?* Carroll says: "The sincere scientific study of recent years makes evident that successful therapy for the ordinary alcoholic demands a catholicity of approach quite beyond the average psychiatrist's interests and complexity of treatment not available in the typical institution." The necessity for great variation in treatment methods, though its general recognition may be of "recent years," had already been pointed out by Thomas Trotter, who said: "The perfect knowledge of those remote causes which first induced the propensity to vinous liquors, whether they sprung from situation in life, or depended on any peculiar temperament of body, is also necessary for conducting the cure. A due acquaintance with the human character will afford much assistance; for the objects of our care are as diversified as the varieties of corporeal structure. . . . In treating these various descriptions of persons and characters, it will readily appear to a discerning physician, that very different methods will be required."

attempt immediately an evaluation on the basis of existing ineffectual data. On the whole, we feel that the practical possibilities of prevention are greater than those of cure and that efforts should be centered around the selection of those who have to be guarded and around the best methods of guarding them.

Pending the outcome of such researches, certain immediate measures may be suggested:

1. In the general hospitals where patients suffering from delirium tremens, polyneuropathy, etc., are sent, some treatment of addiction should also be undertaken. Lange pointed out that there is no such thing as treatment of an alcoholic disease. Treatment must be directed at inebriety itself. Bowman, Wortis and Keiser have made a start in the case of delirium tremens patients at the Bellevue Hospital. Naturally the general hospital is not in a position to retain patients for the time required for such treatment and all that can be done there is to start the patient on his way to therapy and perhaps put temperance or welfare societies in touch with him.

2. Another measure should be to make effective psychotherapy available to much broader masses than is the case at present. The vast majority of inebriates are not in a position to go into private sanitariums, or to have recourse to private therapists. Adequate public provision is made in this country only for the treatment of patients with alcoholic psychoses. For the nonpsychotic addict, however, only a few states have made provision and in these instances it is more a question of segregation than of actual treatment.

Recapitulation

1. The psychotic, the severe psychopathic and the feeble-minded inebriates cannot be subjects of treatment for alcohol addiction. In their case the treatment must be directed at the basic condition. The place for the psychotic and many of the psychopaths is the mental hospital. Some of the feeble-minded drinkers belong in institutions for the feeble-minded and some should be handled by the penal system. The inclusion of these types in the treatment of alcohol addiction only obscures the issues and makes it impossible ever to arrive at a unitary theory of treatment.

2. The question of the treatment environment (open or closed institution or outside of an institution) cannot be decided in a general way, but must be reconsidered in each individual case.

3. Arguments against immediate withdrawal of alcohol are not substantiated by facts; on the other hand, a quick tapering off, rather than immediate withdrawal, seems to do no harm. The question must be regarded as a minor one as long as the object of the treatment is total abstinence and this is actually the case in all treatments.

4. All types of drug treatment, including conditioning, imply that the only problem of the alcohol addict is alcohol. Therefore, even if successful in eliminating the symptom, they leave the patient with the same basic difficulties that he had before.

Drug treatment may, however, be useful and even the treatment of choice in the case of those drinkers who have come to their addiction by way of environmental factors rather than by way of basic conflicts.

5. Hypnosis, inasmuch as it is not used for the uncovering of hidden conflicts but only for the training of will power, is no wider in its aims and scope than drug treatments.

6. Substitutive treatments, mainly religious conversion, are being increasingly favored. Although these treatments do not reach the underlying personality conflicts they afford a radical reorientation of the personality and therefore achieve a certain amount of success. For a large group of alcohol addicts this treatment is more feasible than causative therapies with their many difficulties and restrictions.

7. Causative treatments, while theoretically most desirable, encounter such great difficulties, intrinsically and extrinsically, that only compromise treatments are actually possible. They are best applied to the drinker of a neurotic character.

8. The diversity of the psychotherapies is actually not a sign of conflict, but reflects the fact that the various forms of psychotherapy have been largely individually developed to meet the requirements of the most frequently occurring type of patient in the therapist's practice. Since psychotherapy is a highly subjectively colored procedure, it also must be expected that every therapist will succeed best with the method in which he has the most faith, assuming that the method is actually adapted to the patient.

9. Psychotherapies, as they are applied at present without many selective criteria, may have an average success of 25 to 30 per cent in terms of 2 to 4 years of total abstinence.

10. Unless a psychosomatic basis of addiction, and consequently for its treatment, is found, the improvement of the treatment of alcohol addiction must depend on the development of valid criteria for the selection of the suitability of any given method. This may be achieved by follow-up studies based on case histories which go far beyond the

scope of routine records. It would appear much more profitable to lay now the foundations of such a study, which can be evaluated only after several years, than to attempt immediately an evaluation on the basis of existing ineffectual data.

Selective criteria should also be established with a view to prevention, which may have greater prospects than the cure of addiction.

General hospitals, although not suitable for the treatment of addiction, should initiate such treatment in their patients and establish contact between the patient and welfare or temperance societies.

Effective psychotherapy must be made available to much larger numbers than is the case at present. Public provision is made in this country only for the treatment of patients with alcoholic psychoses.

CHAPTER II

Alcoholic Mental Disorders*

KARL M. BOWMAN *and* E. M. JELLINEK

INTRODUCTION

ACUTE alcoholic intoxication produces changes in behavior which present a picture of mental derangement of some degree. It is therefore quite natural that speculation should have led to the idea of mental disorder developing from an accumulation of such episodes. The belief that heavy habitual drinking may cause a "crazed mind" is reflected in the ancient oriental literature and in the Greco-Roman classics. This belief is also expressed in many proverbs and legends of European and American folklore.

With the beginning of psychiatry as a medical discipline the role of alcohol in mental disorders received systematic consideration. There was at first a tendency to exaggerate the etiological importance of alcohol, as well as a tendency to distinguish a large variety of alcoholic mental disorders. Initially a strict causal nexus was seen between drinking and any psychosis which the drinker may have developed. This has given place to the modern standpoint that the connection between heavy drinking and many of the so-called alcoholic mental disorders is not causative but that the drinking itself is the symptom of a psychosis. The term "modern standpoint" is not intended to imply that this is a discovery of recent date, but to denote the contemporaneous adoption of this viewpoint by a majority. In the 1830's Esquirol said, "Whenever delirium or insanity are preceded by the abuse of fermented drinks, and especially drunkenness, we are disposed to charge this abuse with being the primitive cause of the cerebral disorders, though in many cases it is only the first, and sometimes the characteristic, symptom of a commencing monomania." While he recognized that alcohol addiction may be a symptom, Esquirol did not regard all abnormal drinking as symptomatic and thought that it could be the direct cause of some mental diseases. Although the idea reappeared in the literature since Esquirol, it is only recently that it has

*The statistical aspects of the alcoholic psychoses are not dealt with in the present chapter but will be presented in a later volume of this work.

found general acceptance. Actually agreement is even more widespread than appears from the explicit statements, for this view is implicit in all discussions of constitutional factors in these disorders. The postulation of the relation of alcohol addiction and alcoholic mental disorders to schizophrenia or to manic-depressive psychosis also assumes this concept.

Bonhoeffer (*c*), in 1901, concluded as follows:

Alcohol addiction is in the first place a symptom of a mental disease. It may, however, exaggerate stationary epilepsy, chronic mania, etc., which hitherto were latent and perhaps would remain still latent without alcohol abuses and it may lead to a sudden outbreak of turbulent disease manifestations. It may also give these diseases peculiar traits or peculiar coloring for some time, which above all may appear as the most striking phenomena and thus cover up the symptoms of the fundamental disorder. Furthermore it may also on the basis of this constitutional disease give rise to independent clinical pictures.

In discussing the problem whether abnormal drinking is a symptom or a disease we must distinguish between two questions: (*a*) Is alcohol addiction (without psychosis) itself a symptom of an underlying personality disorder; (*b*) in the case of alcoholic mental disorders is drinking itself etiological or symptomatic?

The first question has been treated in Chapter I. Relative to the second question, we have pointed out before that the symptomatic nature of drinking was suggested as early as in the 1830's, and that this idea has been expressed sporadically since then until its general adoption. Thus, it was expressed by Bonhoeffer (*c*) in 1901, Ferenczi (*a*) in 1911, Wlassak (*a*) and Schroeder, both in 1912, White (*a*) and Williams, both in 1916, and Read in 1920.

The concept of alcohol addiction as symptomatic of disease rather than as a primary disease led to attempts to assign the so-called alcoholic mental disorders to some definite group of psychoses. Thus Graeter, in 1909, classified alcoholic dementia with dementia praecox and in the same year Stoecker thought it possible to classify all the alcoholic psychoses either with epilepsy, manic-depressive psychoses, or dementia praecox. His statements were so sweeping that they created antagonism which made it difficult to accept even what was true in them and thus retarded its recognition. The recognition, however, of certain alcoholic mental disorders as schizophrenia or some other psychosis has been established in the past 20 years. K. Binswanger and Bleuler (*b*) were particularly instrumental in bringing this about.

In order to characterize the present status of the question of heavy drinking as a symptom of psychosis, statements of students of inebriety in the past 10 years are presented in Table 1. It should be borne in mind that while many of these statements refer to "alcoholism" they relate definitely to alcohol addiction.

TABLE I

Recent Views (1930–1940) on the Role of Alcohol in the So-called Alcoholic Psychoses

Author	*Statement*
Bowman (a)	In many cases the use of alcohol is symptomatic of an underlying mental disorder.
Ernst	Alcoholism is not an isolated unitary disease, but is the expression or symptom of the general disturbance of the total personality; and not only of the personality as a single being but as a member of the social community, a symptom of social disturbance.
Henderson, D. K. (b)	Alcohol is responsible (a) for producing certain specific types of mental disorder; (b) it is a complicating factor in many other types of nervous and mental illnesses; (c) it is a symptom or index of an underlying nervous constitution and instability which may be determined at various levels of development—hereditary, congenital, environmental.
Henderson and Gillespie	The role of alcohol in the production of mental disease has been greatly exaggerated. Alcoholism is more commonly a symptom than a cause of mental disorders of a serious and long-standing kind. . . . It is the neuropathic or psychopathic tendency which determines whether a person will become insane, and not the amount of alcohol.
Jelliffe and White	Indulgence in alcohol is often the expression of a neurosis or psychosis.
Knight (b)	In alcohol addiction there are always neurotic trends or paranoid or schizoid features.
Knight (c)	No excessive drinker is normal and well-adjusted even when he is sober.
Kolle (b)	Severe alcoholism is a symptom and this, from the medical standpoint, is not an entity.
Menninger, W. C.	Alcohol addiction is only the symptom, and not the diagnosis, of a personality disorder. It always implies presence of many other disturbances within the personality.
Minski	Alcoholics are not actually suffering from a particular form of mental disorder resulting from alcohol but they present the same symptoms for which other patients are admitted.
Möllenhoff	Alcoholism is often a secondary symptom of another disease.
Noyes	Alcoholism may be the expression of another psychosis.

Author	*Statement*
Stefan	Alcoholism is a symptom, not a disease, and as such not directly hereditary.
Strecker and Chambers	Abnormal drinking constitutes a psychoneurotic reaction type.
Strecker and Ebaugh	Alcoholism may be a symptom of other psychoses but in itself it accounts for from 5 to 10 per cent of all mental diseases.
Strong	Very few patients appear to be "pure" alcoholics. The great majority are alcoholics because of some pre-existing psychobiological or psychopathological inadequacy.
White (*a*)	"That the psychoses produced as the result of the abuse of alcohol are dependent, in the last analysis, upon something besides the alcohol, namely, upon some peculiarity of make-up of the individual, is well shown by the fact that, while the history of abuse of alcohol is frequent in cases admitted to hospitals for the insane, it is very rare to find at autopsy, what in general hospitals is considered so typical of alcoholism, namely, cirrhosis of the liver."
Wolfensberger	At least in a large majority of all cases alcoholic hallucinosis may only be considered a symptom, i.e., the reaction of "a schizophrenic brain" for a certain kind of alcoholic intoxication.
Zehner	Certain symptoms and the course of chronic alcoholic psychosis resemble schizophrenia which makes the alcoholic etiology seem doubtful.

It will be apparent from this table that there is a great agreement among present-day psychiatrists on the question of alcohol addiction as symptomatic of many psychoses rather than as their primary cause. Although it may appear that these statements include all the so-called alcoholic psychoses it is tacitly understood that they do not apply to delirium tremens and Korsakoff's psychosis. This will be more clearly seen in the development of the classifications.

While distinctions are made between true alcoholic mental disorders and those psychoses in which heavy drinking and addiction are incidental, the question of a nonalcoholic psychosis being precipitated by alcohol has also been considered. Such an opinion is expressed, for example, by Ruggles, who says that if we could control the excessive use of alcohol and drugs we would have prevented at least another 10 per cent of the psychoses.

To venture on distinguishing between drinking merely incidental to the psychosis and drinking as a precipitating factor of the nonalcoholic psychosis, although desirable, is not altogether feasible at the present stage of knowledge. Only a vague suggestion can be offered, mainly that when a psychosis of a schizophrenic type develops at an early age coincidental with drinking, the drinking might be regarded as purely symptomatic and of no etiological importance, while if the same disorder appears at a later age in drinkers, the precipitating role of alcohol should be considered. Abnormal drinking in early general paresis is, naturally, always merely symptomatic. In the manic-depressive psychoses abnormal drinking may be occasionally a precipitating factor.*

Classification

At the beginning of the nineteenth century the position of the alcoholic mental disorders among the psychoses was somewhat uncertain. The term dipsomania, now used practically exclusively to designate pathological periodic drinking, was used at that time to denote any mental disorder of supposedly alcoholic origin. In 1817 Salvatore and in 1818 Hufeland (both cit. May), referred to dipsomania as a disorder due to inebriety. The classification later became more and more elaborate, with a tendency toward simplification in more recent times, although even at present elaborate systems of classification are occasionally found.

In 1844 Flemming distinguished *ferocitas et morositas ebriosorum, anoesia e potu, anoesia semisomnis*, delirium tremens and *mania a potu*. Clouston, in 1898, described *mania a potu*, dipsomania, alcoholic dementia and degeneration. Krafft-Ebing, in 1897, enumerated hallucinations of the inebriate, delirium tremens, alcoholic melancholia, *mania gravis potatorum*, hallucinatory insanity, alcoholic paranoia, alcoholic paralysis and epilepsy.

Mott, in 1910, made the distinction between true alcoholic psychoses and those in which the drinking was symptomatic. In his first group are the psychoses which result from the direct or indirect action of alcohol on a previously healthy brain over a considerable period of time. In this group he mentions only delirium tremens and Korsakoff's psychosis. The second group consists of psychoses resulting from inebriety occurring in an individual who is either potentially psychotic or possesses a morbid temperament.

Bonhoeffer (c), as well as Schroeder, eliminated from the classification of alcoholic mental disorder the inebriates with delusions, the so-called *wahnkranke Trinker*, but alcoholic jealousy states have maintained their status as a distinct alcoholic mental disorder for a

---

*Symptomatic drinking in the manic-depressive psychoses has been discussed in Chapter I.

much longer time, and have been disappearing from classificatory systems since Kolle's (*a*) investigations of 1932.

White (*b*), in 1932, discussed pathological intoxication, delirium tremens, chronic alcoholism, alcoholic pseudoparesis, alcoholic epilepsy, alcoholic hallucinosis, alcoholic pseudoparanoia, Korsakoff's psychosis, dream states and dipsomania.

In his recent textbook Billings distinguishes ten personality reactions produced by alcohol. More representative, however, of the present position of the classification of alcoholic mental disorders are the following:

Strecker and Ebaugh differentiate between pathological intoxication, delirium tremens, Korsakoff's psychosis, acute hallucinosis, chronic hallucinosis, acute paranoid type, chronic paranoid type and alcoholic deterioration. Chronic hallucinosis and the two paranoid types, however, are now included by only a few psychiatrists in the classification of alcoholic mental disorders. Parenthetically it may be pointed out that alcoholic deterioration is referred to by some writers on the subject as chronic alcoholic psychosis.

Henderson and Gillespie recognize only three main clinical types of alcoholic psychosis, namely, delirium tremens, Korsakoff's psychosis and chronic alcoholism. According to them, alcoholic hallucinosis and alcoholic paranoia are misnomers, since drinking is, in these cases, a symptom of underlying instability rather than a cause of the latter. Relative to epileptiform episodes in inebriates they believe that these do not constitute a monosymptomatic disorder and that there is no reason why they should be placed in a separate category of "alcoholic epilepsy."

Henry recognizes periodic intoxication, delirium tremens, acute alcoholic hallucinosis, chronic delusional alcoholic psychosis and Korsakoff's psychosis, while Noyes enumerates pathological intoxication, delirium tremens, acute alcoholic hallucinosis and alcoholic deterioration.

Bumke and Kant discuss only dipsomania, alcoholic epilepsy, delirium tremens, Korsakoff's psychosis, alcoholic hallucinosis and Wernicke's pseudoencephalopathy.

Most representative of the present trend in classification of alcoholic mental disorders is Bleuler's (*b*) scheme as given below.

Bleuler's relegation of dipsomania and alcoholic epilepsy into the epileptic, manic-depressive and schizophrenic groups is today fairly generally accepted. Nevertheless the role of alcohol in these two dis-

Cyclothymic group	Schizophrenic group	Epileptic group	Specific group
Dipsomania	Pathological intoxication		Delirium tremens
Alcoholic melan-	Dipsomania	Dipsomania	Korsakoff's
cholia	Alcoholic dementia	Alcoholic epilepsy	psychosis
	Chronic jealousy	Epileptiform	Alcoholic pseudo-
	state of drinkers	seizures of	paralysis
	Alcoholic paranoia	drinkers	Polioencephalitis
	Acute alcoholic		superior
	hallucinosis		

orders is so essential that they must be included in the discussion of alcoholic mental disorders. Relative to acute alcoholic hallucinosis Bleuler's standpoint has not met with general acceptance, although great caution is emphasized by most writers in making a definite diagnosis of acute alcoholic hallucinosis.

How well the modern views are established is reflected in the statistical manual for the use of hospitals for mental disease prepared by the Committee on Statistics of the American Psychiatric Association and published by the National Committee for Mental Hygiene. Under the heading *Alcoholic Psychoses* we find:

The diagnosis of alcoholic psychosis should be restricted to those mental disorders arising, with few exceptions, in connection with *chronic* drinking and presenting fairly well-defined symptom-pictures. One must guard against making the alcoholic group too inclusive. Overindulgence in alcohol is often found to be merely a symptom of another psychosis, or at any rate may be incidental to another psychosis, such as general paralysis, manic-depressive psychoses, dementia praecox, epilepsy, etc. The cases to be regarded as alcoholic psychoses which do not result from chronic drinking are the episodic attacks in some psychopathic personalities, the dipsomaniacs (the true periodic drinkers) and pathological intoxication, any one of which may develop as the result of a single imbibition or a relatively short spree.

The following alcoholic reactions usually present symptoms distinctive enough to allow of clinical differentiation and should be specified in the statistical report.

(*a*) *Delirium tremens:* An hallucinatory delirium with marked general tremor and toxic symptoms.

(*b*) *Korsakoff's psychosis:* This occurs with or without polyneuritis. The delirious type is not readily differentiated in the early stages from severe delirium tremens, but is more protracted. The non-delirious type presents a characteristic retention defect with disorientation, fabrication, suggestibility and tendency to misidentify persons. Hallucinations are infrequent after the acute phase.

(*c*) *Acute hallucinosis:* This is chiefly an auditory hallucinosis of rapid development with clearness of the sensorium, marked fears, and a more or less systematized persecutory trend.

(*d*) *Other types, acute or chronic* (to be specified).

Wernicke's syndrome and the related encephalopathies definitely belong with the alcoholic mental disorders but are rarely dealt with in psychiatric papers as they are of greater interest to neuropathologists and nutritionists. Since these disorders are dealt with in Chapter IV of this volume we shall not touch upon them any further here.

I. ACUTE ALCOHOLIC INTOXICATION

"That acute alcohol intoxication is not designated as a mental disorder is simply due to a tacit agreement because of the consequences which such a designation would involve. In reality the acute alcoholic intoxication is a poisoning of the brain and can be placed side by side with the severest mental disturbances which are known to us." (Meggendorfer). Kraepelin said, "The *Rausch* is under the rules of our drinking habits such a frequent form of mental disturbance that it is regarded as a natural accompaniment of our social life." It is therefore appropriate to discuss acute alcoholic intoxication in reviewing alcoholic mental disorders.

While the state of acute intoxication may be regarded as a mental disorder it is distinguished fundamentally in two aspects from the now recognized alcoholic psychoses. The latter, with the exception of pathological intoxication, never result from any one alcoholic bout, no matter how great a quantity is consumed. Furthermore, they are not regarded as being caused by direct action of alcohol on the nervous system, but rather through secondary metabolic and toxic processes contingent upon prolonged excessive drinking. On the other hand, acute intoxication, as Schultze points out, "is the somatic and psychic reaction to one occasion of alcohol consumption," and the intoxication is the direct consequence of the alcohol ingested. The second distinction is that the alcoholic psychoses, even in the most acute form, such as pathological intoxication, do not, in their symptomatology, resemble acute intoxication.

The discussion of acute intoxication (state of drunkenness) is sometimes obscured by not distinguishing this state from what may be called "being under the influence of liquor." The latter condition may mean any slight impairment of faculties which renders a person unable to execute safely any given occupation. This question of being under the influence* of liquor need not be dealt with in discussing the psychiatric aspects of drunkenness. Unfortunately there is no English equivalent for the German word *Rausch* which would facilitate the discussion of this question. While there may be great difficulties in determining when a man is "under the influence" of liquor, there is little difference among observers in recognizing *Rausch*, and this in spite of the varied symptomatology of this condition.

Bumke and Kant give the following picture of acute alcoholic intoxication.

In the mild state of intoxication there are unnecessary vocal efforts, pathos which is incongruent in view of the unessential content of conversation, exaggerated expressions of affect, laughter and exaggerated motorics. With this comes an increase in the subjective feeling of well-being. After larger alcohol intake there is impairment of sensory function, the thought processes become superficial and conversation becomes flatter. There is a tendency toward flight of ideas. Judgment is clouded and self-criticism, especially in reference to condition, vanishes. There is a grotesque disproportion between the increased ego feeling and the objective ability to produce. This contrast is sometimes vaguely felt by the intoxicated person and results in a feeling of insecurity. On the basis of this mood tone then develop the symptoms of irritability and readiness to paranoid reactions. In the severest states of intoxication there is ataxia, staggering gait, slurred speech and, finally, severe impairment of perception. The intoxicated person becomes apathetic and falls into deep sleep. Although some personality characteristics break through into the picture of intoxication it is not possible to construct a law of relation between type of alcohol reaction and personality, especially as the picture may change on different occasions in the same person. The degree of drunkenness is related to the alcohol concentration in the blood only in a very broad way.

Binder describes simple intoxication as the average human reaction to acute alcoholic excess. The first state is one of slight, subcortical "vital-psychic" excitation. This is followed by a state of drowsiness, functional paralysis beginning in the cortex and spreading slowly, hence the release of more primitive functions which, however, does not

---

*The physiological and psychological aspects of being under the influence of liquor and the question of the correlation between alcohol concentration in the blood and degree of intoxication have been treated in part (Jellinek and McFarland) in a paper which will constitute a chapter to be published in a later volume of this work, and will be considered in other aspects in another chapter.

go very far and soon disappears. Normal mental connections and orientation are conserved until the intoxicated individual falls asleep. There are no delusions or hallucinations. Such intoxication represents only a slight change of personality. Will power is maintained and influences behavior so that no actions arise which are not in accordance with the normal personality. There is usually no amnesia for the period of intoxication.

The essence of the state of drunkenness has hardly ever been more clearly and concisely expressed than by Immanuel Kant: "Drunkenness is the unnatural state of inability to organize sense impressions according to the laws of experience."

The physiological effects of acute alcoholic intoxication are muscular incoördination, increase in pulse and blood pressure, according to McCormick, and decrease in blood pressure according to Piker (a), dilatation of the peripheral vessels, increased radiation of heat with consequent fall of internal body temperature, diplopia, nystagmus, conjunctivitis of the eyes, stimulation of mucous membranes and vomiting. In severe intoxication heart damage and lung edema may become dangerous. Respiratory paralysis may also ensue.*

That the picture of acute intoxication varies from man to man, and may vary even from occasion to occasion in the same individual, has been pointed out by so many writers and is of such common knowledge that there is no need to cite sources. According to Fleming (a) the varied symptomatology of acute alcoholic intoxication depends upon the interplay of two main factors: The pharmacological action of alcohol on the physiological systems and the personality of the individual with its constitutional and acquired components. The pharmacological action may be modified by the dose of alcohol, the nature of the beverage and the physiological state of the organism, but ultimately it is dependent upon the concentration of alcohol in the tissues. The study of the elements contributed by the personality to the clinical picture of drunkenness has been neglected but offers a promising field for modern psychiatric investigation. Schroeder, however, believed that in spite of the variation in symptoms the basic processes in acute alcoholic intoxication are largely the same in every individual, and that the main differences are in the level of affect and in the type of motor reactions.

It should be remembered that while for the same amount of alcohol

---

*The physiological processes underlying acute intoxication will be discussed in a chapter to be published in a later volume of this work. They have also been touched upon in Chapter I.

ingested the degree and nature of drunkenness may vary considerably from person to person, there are certain limiting amounts. Any quantity of any alcoholic beverage that will bring about an alcohol concentration of 4 to 5 mg. per cubic centimeter of urine will result in any individual in narcosis and stupor, as Bogen (*a*) has shown.

That type of drunkenness and personality structure are related has been postulated since ancient times. In his famous *Anatomy of Drunkenness* MacNish distinguished seven varieties of intoxication which corresponded to the then recognized personality, or rather temperament, types. Although the question of type of personality and type of drunkenness is mentioned again and again in the psychiatric literature, an experimental approach to the problem is still lacking. Furthermore, although the typology of drunkenness is very old, as Fleming (*a*) points out, its scientific classification is nonexistent and it is contained mainly in belletristic literature. It may be noted also that studies of the relationship between personality and type of drunkenness may prove to have still another value, as they may reveal a possible correlation between the type of syndrome developed in acute intoxication and type of psychosis developed after chronic alcohol abuse.

The effect of the kind of beverage, that is, whether there is a different type of drunkenness from wine, beer and distilled liquor, is entirely a matter of surmise, but would lend itself to experimental investigation. For obvious reasons there has been much more psychological and physiological investigation at levels of subclinical intoxication than frank drunkenness. From a psychiatric standpoint, however, the latter type of experiment would appear to be of greater value.

II. PATHOLOGICAL INTOXICATION

There is a form of acute reaction to alcohol which is usually designated as pathological intoxication. This condition is distinguished from the ordinary alcoholic intoxication not quantitatively but rather qualitatively. In spite of various objections, such as Meggendorfer's point that this term assumes a "normal" intoxication, the designation "pathological intoxication" has maintained itself. Ziehen preferred the term "complicated intoxication" and Pontoppidan called it "atypical intoxication." The term "pathologic alcohol reaction" proposed by Krafft-Ebing seems to us to be of more classificatory relevance, as the condition commonly referred to as pathological intoxication largely lacks the characteristic toxic symptoms. Thus motor incoördination, slurred speech and diplopia are usually absent [Bing and Schönberg;

Bleuler (*b*); Schroeder], although in some persons the pathologic reaction sets in after objective signs of drunkenness have developed (H. Binswanger). It should be noted that the designation "pathological intoxication" originates in forensic considerations. It is a concession to the general opinion that all intoxications do not constitute mental disturbances in the sense of the responsibility concept of criminal law (Schroeder).

Before discussing pathologic alcohol reactions, it is necessary to make a negative definition. It is true, of course, that it has been frequently reported that pathological intoxication occurred after ingestion of such small quantities of alcohol as two glasses of beer, and H. Binswanger found in his patients blood alcohol concentrations ranging from 3.9 to 26.4 mg. per cent. But Bleuler (*b*) has emphasized that this condition should not be confused with alcohol intolerance, in which small quantities bring about disproportionately strong reactions without qualitatively abnormal features. This warning is especially important since some textbooks, in the endeavor to make concise statements, have defined pathological intoxication as intoxication following the ingestion of small quantities of alcohol.

The frequency of pathological intoxication is difficult to estimate. Abortive delirium tremens is often diagnosed as pathological intoxication and this error tends to produce an overestimate. On the other hand, the pathologic reaction is oftentimes of such brief duration that the subject never reaches a hospital, especially a mental hospital. This factor tends to create a negative bias in the estimate. It can only be said that reported cases of pathological intoxication are probably less than 1 per cent of all admissions for acute and chronic alcoholism to any type of hospital.*

The average age of patients with pathological intoxication in H. Binswanger's sample was 31 years. This is more than 10 years below the average age of all alcoholic admissions and the difference is related to the fact that pathological intoxication is not a manifestation of chronic alcoholism.

Clinical Picture

From the works of Strecker and Ebaugh; Bleuler (*b*); White (*b*);

---

*From Pollock's (*b*) data on first admissions for pathological intoxication to the New York State Hospitals for 1920–1923 and 1936–1937 we have computed that pathological intoxication constituted 8 to 9 per cent of all first admissions for alcoholic psychoses and consequently less than 1 per cent of all cases of alcoholism.

Schroeder; Binder; and H. Binswanger it is apparent that the outstanding characteristics of the pathologic reaction to alcohol are blind rage and confusion, with usually complete amnesia for the condition. This is all independent of the amount of alcohol consumed. Occasionally the reaction manifests itself, not as a fit of rage, but as an ecstatic state. It must be emphasized that neither ecstasy nor furor is a symptom of the ordinary acute alcoholic intoxication, and further, that in the pathologic reaction there is usually absence of the motor incoördination, slurred speech and diplopia which characterize ordinary drunkenness. Hallucinosis also is mentioned in the symptomatology but as this occurs only in chronic alcoholics this manifestation should not be classified with pathological intoxication.

It is pointed out repeatedly that the pathologic reaction lasts for short periods varying from a few minutes to a few hours. Schroeder states that in these cases the symptoms of intoxication may be transitory or even absent, and that occasionally the condition is accompanied by ideas of ownership of the world and omnipotence. These expansive ideas are most likely to occur in what Schroeder has called the epileptic form of pathological intoxication. Frequently this condition is followed by exhaustion and anorexia.

Binder points out that the behavior of the individual thus intoxicated often cannot be understood by the observer; it seems fantastic, unreal and marked by complete misunderstanding of the situation. Either it does not reveal much of the anxiety or it manifests itself in wild rages with delusions of persecution.

In the state of rage, anxiety and paranoia which characterizes the pathologic reaction it is not surprising that crimes of violence are frequently attempted. H. Binswanger found that of 174 patients with this disorder 26 (15 per cent) had been charged with offenses or crimes such as threats, manslaughter, attempted murder, arson, burglary and sex offenses. In these cases we have a true nexus between alcohol and crime, although there may be no criminal disposition, whereas in other "alcoholic" crimes there is a question whether it is a case of crime caused by alcohol or alcohol consumed by criminals. It is possible also that suicidal tendencies are more frequent in this group than in any other alcoholic psychosis.

The chief neurologic manifestation of the pathologic reaction to alcohol is reflex rigidity of the pupils, although swaying and weak tendon reflexes have also been reported. This change in the pathological intoxication is therefore of considerable diagnostic importance, since it lasts much longer than the mental symptoms and is thus, in view of the short duration of the attack, frequently the only sign which the physician can observe. The same importance will apply to the other neurologic manifestations when present. In spite of the agreement of Binder; Bonhoeffer (c); Gudden; and Stapel that reflex rigidity of the pupils is almost universal in pathological intoxication, H. Binswanger reported observing it in only 6 of 135 patients examined, while 24 showed a sluggish reaction and 105 had normal pupillary reflexes.

The diagnosis of pathological intoxication, according to H. Binswanger, is more difficult in women than in men, since in the former, symptoms of hysteria tend to overlap. Cramer, as well as Heilbronner, considers the individual's neuropathic disposition, affect, normal motor behavior, pupillary reactions, presence of delusions, terminal sleep and total or partial amnesia as important criteria in the diagnosis of pathological intoxication. Bing and Schönberg believe the chief distinguishing factor between pathological intoxication and ordinary intoxication to be the absence of ataxia and speech disturbances in the former. H. Binswanger was not satisfied that reliable diagnostic criteria had been established. This, of course, does not refer to acute intoxication, from which the pathological form is easily differentiated, but to other acute alcoholic psychoses which are often erroneously diagnosed as pathological intoxication. This is due to the fact that he included many forms of pathological intoxication which have been generally rejected from this classification. Mönkemöller (b) regarded the fact that pathological intoxication is a twilight state while ordinary intoxication does not have this character as the outstanding differentiating factor; in addition he emphasized the characteristic anxiety or fear. Siebert (a) considered the diagnosis to be greatly validated if the patient's history showed previous pathological intoxications and also, especially, if there had been head trauma or syphilis.

Classification of Pathological Intoxication

Various forms of pathological intoxication have been described by different authors and numerous classifications of this disorder have been proposed, but only the form designated originally as "epileptoid pathological intoxication" is regarded at present by a majority of psychiatrists as genuine pathological intoxication.

Heilbronner, as well as Bonhoeffer (c), distinguished an epileptoid and a delirant form of pathological intoxication. The latter type, however, has been found only in chronic alcoholics and as an abortive form of delirium tremens by Schultze; Bleuler (b); Schroeder; and others. H. Binswanger, however, still recognized it in 1935 and also included the protracted form of pathological intoxication. Benon (a) classified delirant, hallucinatory, confused, and maniacal pathological intoxication. Schroeder pointed out that the "protracted pathological intoxication" is actually a transitory alcoholic psychosis such as hysteriform twilight states in which Ganser's syndrome is characteristic. Such states have been described by Kutner, by Heilbronner, and by Voss.

Etiology

Originally it was thought that pathological intoxication occurred only in psychopathic personalities. Later it was found that it occurred also in other conditions and recently the role of hypoglycemia in this reaction has been emphasized. Exclusive views are not held at present by any investigator. The tendency is rather to recognize several etiological factors. On the whole, however, the greater role is still assigned to psychopathies. This seems to be justified since H. Binswanger reported that among his 194 patients with pathological intoxication 90 per cent were also diagnosed as psychopathic, namely, hysteric, feeble-minded, unstable, schizoid, epileptic, etc. This standpoint is expressed among others by Schroeder; Schultze; Meggendorfer; Bleuler (b); Bumke and Kant; Binder; H. Binswanger; White (b); and Noyes.

Meggendorfer said that for pathological intoxication there must always be a personal disposition. This may be a transitory or a lasting one and if lasting it is largely an hereditary one. Bleuler (b), too, wrote of permanent and accidental disposing moments. Among the former he recognized especially epilepsy, schizophrenia, hysteria and brain traumata. Among the passing dispositions he discussed exhaustion, extreme heat or cold, affective excitement and sexual exhaustion. It should not be supposed, however, that the presence of permanent predisposing factors means that an individual will always react to alcohol by pathological intoxication. Neither Bonhoeffer (c) nor H. Binswanger was able to provoke pathological intoxication experimentally in persons who had previously shown this reaction. It must be assumed, therefore, that psychopathic personalities will show these reactions only on the occasion of temporary dysphorias.

Among the acquired dispositions brain lesions are mentioned especially (Schultze; Busch). In this case, too, however, the pathologic reaction to alcohol is not constant. Busch found no pathologic reaction in 400 patients with brain injuries, although many of them complained that since the injury even smaller amounts of alcohol "went to their heads" and that they got severe headache from drinking. In these cases, too, an additional factor, besides that of disposition, must enter before the pathologic reaction to alcohol is provoked.

A vague reference to organically determined twilight conditions in pathological intoxication was made by Jahrreiss. Much more definite is the suggestion of Seelert that one of the specific factors involved in the production of pathological intoxication is a temporary hypoglycemia or a related process. He pointed out that both hypoglycemia and pathological intoxication may be brought about by hunger, great bodily exertion and illness. In connection with this it may be mentioned that Bumke and Kant pointed out the frequent occurrence of pathological intoxication on the battlefield. It may also be worth noting that Wuth (a) suggested that close connections exist between epileptoid states and the hypoglycemic syndrome. Seelert did not state definitely that hypoglycemia causes pathological intoxication but believed that in this condition, as well as in hypoglycemia, there are acute changes in the blood composition which are related to regulatory processes in the vegetative hormonal functions. The suggestion of hypoglycemia receives renewed interest through the recent finding of Haggard and Greenberg who showed that the lethal dosage of alcohol for rats was increased as the sugar concentration in the blood attained higher levels.

In recapitulation it may be stated that pathological intoxication, or preferably the pathologic reaction to alcohol, in contrast to other alcoholic psychoses is not a disturbance of chronic alcoholism but occurs as a direct effect of drinking—frequently of very small quantities of alcohol—and is distinguished from acute intoxication qualitatively rather than quantitatively. Predominantly this disturbance occurs in psychopathic personalities who, even in the absence of drinking, show unprovoked fits of rage. It is not, however, a constant reaction in these personalities, but requires special conditions, such as temporary dysphorias and perhaps temporary hypoglycemic states, which may be occasioned by exhaustion or illness. In these states it may also occur in nonpsychopathic personalities. The occurrence of pathological intoxication in persons suffering from brain injury is also dependent on temporary specific conditions.

The pathologic reaction to alcohol is one of the less known alcoholic psychoses and, in view of its possible relation to the problem of tolerance and to the genesis of alcoholic psychosis, merits systematic investigation. Although the diagnosis of pathological intoxication seems to be made in this country routinely, it has received little consideration from American psychiatrists.

III. DELIRIUM TREMENS

The disorder to which Thomas Sutton gave the name delirium tremens in 1813 was first recognized as a distinct entity by Samuel Burton Pearson. There are some earlier descriptions of the condition, e.g., Lettsom (1787), but without recognizing it as a specific disorder. In the first quarter of the nineteenth century delirium tremens was not regarded as a mental disorder, but beginning with 1830 it has been classified as a psychosis. Medicolegally, it is regarded in some states as relieving from criminal responsibility to the same extent as any other insanity, but in other states, e.g., California, the contrary has been held (Hertzog) and puzzling questions have arisen relative to responsibility for crimes committed after the delirious episode is over [Benon (b)].

While the onset of this psychosis is by no means insidious, prodromal symptoms frequently occur days, or even several weeks, before the outbreak. The average duration of the delirium itself is 3 to 4 days and most of the symptoms disappear after the so-called terminal sleep. Abstinence for protracted periods often occurs after delirium. Its recurrence depends largely on the resumption of the drinking habit but there are some reports that there are relapses in periods of abstinence [Bonhoeffer (c)]. The outcome of the disease depends largely upon the concomitant conditions.

Relative to the incidence of delirium tremens among chronic alcoholics there are numerous statistics.* These are not quite comparable since the incidence figures vary greatly according to whether the information comes from a general hospital, a mental hospital, or an outpatient clinic. Naturally the time factor enters into the picture and there are also geographic variations, perhaps according to the nature of the chief alcoholic beverage consumed in different regions. Moore and Gray (c) give the delirium tremens admissions to Boston City Hospital from 1915–1935. From 1916–1919 the percentage of de-

---

*Pollock (a); Richardson and Blankenhorn; Heron; Lyathaud; Moore and Gray (a, b, c); Steck; Beninde, Bonhoeffer and Partsch; Wortis (b); and Ladame.

lirium tremens admissions of all alcoholic admissions varied between 10 and 15 per cent; from 1920–1933, between 3 and 7 per cent; and during 1934 and 1935 it was 11 per cent. In 1939 the delirium tremens admissions to Bellevue Hospital, in a sample of 12,114 alcoholics, did not amount to more than 2.6 per cent [Wortis (*b*)]. Diagnostic error greatly invalidates delirium tremens statistics. There is a tendency in some hospitals to diagnose many cases of delirium tremens as acute alcoholic hallucinosis or as a "protracted" form of pathological intoxication. Taking all the available material, the average of delirium tremens patients among chronic alcoholics with and without psychosis is perhaps 4 to 5 per cent.

It has been frequently pointed out that delirium tremens is much rarer among women than among men, but alcoholism in general is rarer among women. Certainly in the large Bellevue Hospital sample the per cent of female delirium tremens patients to total female alcoholic admissions was practically the same as the per cent of male delirium tremens patients to total male alcoholic admissions. Regional differences, however, must be considered as possible.

Clinical Picture

The colorful mental picture of delirium tremens has given rise to some classic descriptions in the psychiatric literature, such as those of Magnan (*b*); Bonhoeffer (*c*); Kraepelin; Adolf Meyer; Meggendorfer; and Bumke and Kant. Schematically, the mental symptoms may be presented as follows:

The prodromal signs are anxiety, restlessness, fear, insomnia, nightmares, sensitivity of sense organs, occasional hallucinations, tendency to perspiration, headaches, vertigo, convulsions. Signs appear mostly at night. Actual onset of disease sudden, mostly at night, occasionally with epileptic or epileptiform attack. Predominantly visual hallucinations, few illusions. Objects seem in movement, change in size, number, form, color. Also tactile and auditory and combined hallucinations. Suggestibility. Impaired learning ability. Consciousness dimmed; attention and perception decreased. Spatial and temporal disorientation. Motor excitation and hyperactivity (Schultze).

The objects of the hallucinations are largely animals and predominantly fast-moving animals such as small rodents, members of the feline family, etc. Bumke and Kant point out the curious fact that, since the introduction of continuous baths in the treatment of delirium tremens, the popular white mice have been replaced by fishes and lobsters. Dynes reported actual statistics of the animals occurring in the hallucinations of 113 delirium tremens patients. The most frequently occurring animals were dogs, insects and snakes. Rodents occurred only once and so did the famous "pink" elephant. Cats and birds were slightly more frequent. The fast-moving character of the animals has been attributed, by Kraepelin, to the extraordinary motor restlessness of the patients. He also points out that the patients usually see a large number of the same category of objects which may be of a rather trivial nature; thus, the rooms may be filled with pants buttons or slippers. The pictures change with great rapidity and Adolf Meyer has compared this effect to cinematic projection. The dreamlike character of the pictures has been stressed by many authors.

Kraepelin believed that the hallucinations are brought about by falsification of perception due to a blending of endogenous and exogenous stimulation. Morel (a, b), however, stated that scotomata, which he found in all cases of visual hallucinations in inebriates, gave rise to these pictures. Since scotomata are rather frequently reported in chronic alcoholics without any hallucinations, Morel's argument does not seem particularly potent. Bürger-Prinz was also of the opinion that, although a change of all perceiving organs must be expected in delirium tremens, these changes do not explain the hallucinations. Epstein explained the sensory illusions of alcoholic delirium on the basis of disturbances of the vestibular apparatus. He stated that the nearer the stage of psychosis the greater the vestibular disturbance.

According to Bumke and Kant, auditory illusions and hallucinations are not half so frequent as the visual ones. The patients hear murmurs, the noise of running water, shooting, bells, or music. Voices, however, are practically always the accompaniment of optic experiences and are in the form of conversation. The visions and voices are generally of a threatening nature and express the fear which is the characteristic affect of delirium tremens. The anxiety is manifested typically in the occupational hallucinations in which endless tasks of the patient's routine work must be performed. There are also, however, some pleasant visions, of which the most common are those of Lilliputian figures. The differences between the Lilliputian hallucinations of delirium tremens and those of schizophrenia have been pointed out by Angyal, i.e., in delirium tremens the hallucinations are referred to the environment, while in schizophrenia the objects seem to come from the body of the patient.

A commonly described characteristic of delirium tremens is spatial and temporal disorientation. Schroeder said that the delirants are not merely disoriented but they are wrongly oriented. They believe the hospital to be a tavern, a palace, a schoolhouse or a church; they believe that they are in an entirely different country, at some past time, and they recognize the doctors and nursing personnel as old friends or take them to be government officials, priests or well-known politicians.

The suggestibility of delirium tremens patients is notorious. They can be made to read from empty sheets of paper, they readily interpret spots on the wall according to the suggestions of the examiner and generally can be made to see almost any picture that is suggested to them. Liepmann (a) has produced a succession of visions in delirium tremens patients by pressure on the eyeballs. Kraepelin pointed out one fact which is of very great significance in the evaluation of the changes occurring in delirium tremens patients, and that is, that in spite of their great suggestibility, their ideas of their own identity cannot be influenced. Quite generally the personality structure is not impaired by this psychosis.

The immediate memory and learning ability, according to Bonhoeffer's (a) investigations, are greatly impaired but remote memory does not seem to suffer. While Bonhoeffer's determinations were quantitative, naturalistic observations of this phenomenon are given by practically every investigator of delirium tremens.

Clouding of the consciousness in delirium tremens is mentioned, practically routinely, in descriptions of this disease. Bonhoeffer (c), however, believed that this is simply an impression caused through the blending of sensory illusions, impairment of attention and immediate memory and incoherent thought and confabulation, to which the disorientation gives a peculiar color. He emphasized that thought processes are not slowed down and that when the patients are spoken to energetically they can be kept, for a time, at one topic and the apperception is fair. The perception is less impaired than could be inferred from the lacking orientation. He believed that these points show that it is not a question of clouding of consciousness. Kraepelin, too, pointed out that, in spite of the disturbing and exciting illusions and hallucinations, the patients still retain a certain feeling for the unreality of these illusions and occasionally view them with a tinge of whimsical humor. In connection with this, Kraepelin again emphasized that there are no changes in the consciousness of personality. Bürger-Prinz expressed similar opinions and, among others, Cosack and Richards have presented convincing case histories of delirium tremens patients with full insight into the hallucinatory character of their visions. In view of the differences of opinion prevailing in the literature relative to the meaning of "clouding of consciousness" this argument cannot be accepted without reservation.

Personality and constitution. The question whether or not delirium tremens occurs in persons differing in their personality make-up from other chronic alcoholics has interested investigators for a considerable time. Mott early indicated that delirium tremens was a disease of psychologically normal persons. He divided the alcoholic psychoses into two groups: *1*. Psychoses which are the result of the direct or indirect action of alcohol upon a previously healthy brain for a considerable period of time. *2*. Psychoses resulting from inebriety occurring in an individual who is either potentially insane or possesses a morbid temperament. In the first group he placed only delirium tremens and Korsakoff's disease.

Similar to this, but somewhat more elaborate, is the classification of Gabriel (*a*). He divided inebriates into two groups: *1*. The genuine addicts (who cannot give up drinking voluntarily), whose addiction is constitutional and who have to be institutionalized. Their addiction need not be specifically alcohol addiction—to what drug they become addicted is rather a matter of chance. *2*. Those who develop the drinking habit without being constitutionally forced to drink. They are "normal" drinkers even if the various organic symptoms which occur on the basis of long alcohol abuse increase the alcohol consumption and create a resemblance between their drinking and addiction. In this second group, organic impairments are more frequent than psychic ones. With the exception of delirium tremens, alcoholic psychoses occur very rarely in these patients.

This problem was most exhaustively treated by Pohlisch (*c, d, f*). He found, among 75 delirium tremens patients, 64 per cent cyclothymics, 5 per cent epileptoids, 3 per cent schizoids and 27 per cent partly constitutional inferiors and partly persons without typical characteristics. He believes that the frequent cyclothymic disposition is not a disposition to delirium tremens but to habitual drinking, and does not believe in a specifically poor cerebral disposition in delirium tremens patients. His later investigations led to the following statement:

In their adaptation to large quantities of alcohol, the delirants produce through many years most astonishing feats. Only after great accumulation of metabolic disturbances do pathological intoxication, epileptic seizures, febrile and other new diseases occur, which then give the last impetus to the delirium. If one compares with this long-lasting resistance, the early failure of drinkers with demonstrable anomalous disposition of the brain and other organs, one must concede that there is much in favor of the idea that delirium tremens is the reaction form of the basically sound brain to a certain degree of continual alcoholic poisoning.

In the most recent study on this subject, Hoch found considerably more extroverts among delirium tremens patients than among other alcoholic psychoses. His interesting findings are given in Table 2.

TABLE 2

The Occurrences of Introversion and Extroversion in Various Alcoholic Psychoses (Adapted from Hoch)

Psychosis	Introverted No.	Introverted Per cent	Extroverted No.	Extroverted Per cent	Total No.	Total Per cent
Delirium tremens	3	12.5	21	87.5	24	100
Korsakoff's psychosis	7	41.1	10	58.9	17	100
Alcoholic hallucinosis	26	60.5	17	39.5	43	100
Other alcoholic psychoses	12	66.7	6	33.3	18	100

Stanojewitsch found, in Jugoslavia, mainly cyclothymic individuals with pyknic body build among the delirium tremens patients.

Bigelow, Lehrmann and Palmer, however, do not believe that delirium tremens may be regarded as a reaction of the so-called normal individual to excessive alcohol intake. They consider that the impression of "normality" is created by the oral traits which are characteristic of manics who approach the normal more closely than other psychotics.

Another side to the question of normal or abnormal psyche in delirium tremens patients is that of hereditary liability. Myerson (a) remarked that while not every chronic drinker is a candidate, to assume that some have a neuropathic liability to delirium tremens is like assuming that every patient with delirium in diseases, such as pneumonia, has such a liability. This statement implies that no one would make such an assumption about pneumonia delirium, but just this assumption was made 8 years later by Curtius and Wallenberg. They stated that delirium in pneumonia is not dependent on the bacteriological processes nor upon the degree of fever, but originates in a neuropathic disposition. This hypothesis does not appear to have made any considerable impression.

Modern studies in heredity tend to show a nonspecific hereditary liability among alcohol addicts, but Brugger (a) believed that he found a tendency for symptomatic deliria among the siblings of delirium tremens patients. This has not been borne out by the investigations of either Gabriel (*b*) or Boeters. On the other hand, Brugger (*a*) had good evidence that the parents and siblings of 116 delirium tremens patients showed, for schizophrenia, manic-depressive psychosis, epilepsy and mental deficiency, an incidence as low as in the general population, while among the relatives of other chronic alcoholics there is a drastic excess of this liability. "Queer" individuals were also rarer among delirium tremens patients and their relatives than among inebriates generally and their relatives. Ostmann's material shows similar characteristics. Benon (*a*) confirmed these findings on French patients. Most important of these investigations, because of its excellent methods and unquestionable material, is that of Pohlisch (*e*). The contrast between the occurrence of psychoses and psychopathies among the parents, siblings and descendants of delirium tremens patients and of other chronic alcoholics, as shown by Pohlisch, is striking. In the former, it is of the same magnitude as in the general population, while in the latter it is significantly higher. These data have been regarded, in Germany at least, as so significant that the commentaries to the German sterilization laws exempt delirium tremens patients from sterilization, while other chronic alcoholics are subject to it. The absence in delirium tremens patients of that nonspecific psychotic and psychopathic liability that so greatly characterizes other chronic alcoholics strengthens the assumption that this psychosis occurs largely in psychologically normal drinkers.

The physical picture. The most obtrusive physical symptom is the coarse arrhythmic tremor of the tongue, face, fingers, legs, and even the trunk, for which this disease was named by Sutton. Great restlessness and hyperactivity, as well as insomnia, have been widely described. In other respects the physical signs of delirium tremens are greatly obscured through concomitant conditions, especially through simultaneous polyneuropathy, and possibly through lacking distinction from severe encephalopathies.

Bonhoeffer (*a*) reported marked disturbances of equilibrium. Many delirium tremens patients cannot sit up but want to remain on their backs. Their bodily orientation in space is disturbed. If this actually occurs in delirium tremens, uncomplicated by severe encephalopathies, it would be of definite significance for tracing the pathogenetic processes.

It has been reported that there is no loss of pain sensitivity [Bonhoeffer (*a*)]. Bürger-Prinz, however, found that when successive touch and pain stimulation of the same spot had elicited positive reactions, there came a sudden cessation of pain response. Beringer and Ruffin found disturbances of cutaneous sensations, particularly lability of threshold. Rose [cit. Bonhoeffer (c)], however, rightly pointed out that the agitated condition of delirium tremens patients does not permit of clean experimentation in the field of sensations, and therefore no conclusions should be drawn. Since polyneuropathy may or may not be present in delirium tremens patients, one may expect great variation in the reports on cutaneous sensations in these patients.

Nausea and vomiting, the paucity of urine, profuse perspiration and the occurrence of constipation, have been so commonly described that there is no need for reference. Bowman and Keiser emphasized the high degree of dehydration in their patients.

Wassermeyer, after eliminating all cases in which complications were present, found slightly increased temperatures in 80 to 90 per cent of delirium tremens patients. This has been confirmed by many other investigators, who generally agree that Magnan's (b) "delirium tremens febrille" is only a quantitative deviation. Alzheimer believed that this rise in temperature in delirium tremens, free of accompanying disease, is of great importance since it can be attributed only to cerebral causes.

Changes in blood pressure and pulse have also been described. According to Döllken the blood pressure rises, on an average, 30 per cent on the third or fourth day of delirium. At this time the pulse may average 125 beats per minute and the temperature may reach 38.5° C. Kraepelin quotes numerous investigators who confirmed Döllken's findings. The circulatory conditions and myocardial changes are not infrequently rather severe and require immediate attention in the treatment of delirium tremens.

Accompanying diseases and conditions, some of which may be precipitating factors, which will be discussed more fully later, are surgical conditions, pneumonia, erysipelas, polyneuropathy and various forms of encephalopathy. Naturally, one also encounters the malnutrition which is so common in alcoholism.

Biochemical findings. The study of the urine chemistry of delirium tremens dates back to the 1870's and has since been taken up fairly frequently but in recent years there has been little activity in this field. On the other hand, the blood chemistry of this psychosis has been investigated only recently and is certainly gaining in interest.

Unfortunately, quite a number of investigations have been carried out on groups of "chronic alcoholics" composed of patients with greatly differing diseases and the results have not been stated for each of the disease groups but only as averages for the entire heterogeneous group of "chronic alcoholics." Some of these results have been claimed by one author to be characteristic of alcoholic pellagra because 5 or 6 such patients were included in a sample of perhaps 60 chronic alcoholics, while the same findings are claimed by another author to be characteristic of alcoholic paranoid psychosis or delirium tremens because there are also 7 or 8 of that type represented in the sample. Such procedures make it difficult to arrive at specific findings in any one of the alcoholic diseases and are the source of unnecessarily "conflicting" evidence.

In Tables 3A and 3B, findings on the urine and blood chemistry of

TABLE 3 A

Biochemical Findings in Delirium Tremens — Urine

Author	Finding
Arndt	In 72 of 106 D.T. patients (68 per cent) marked albuminuria at some phase of the delirium. Glycosuria in 30 per cent of 99 D.T. patients, but 30 per cent of alcoholic new admissions without delirium also showed glycosuria.
Bonhoeffer (*c*)	Albuminuria in 68 per cent of 22 D.T. patients.
Bostroem	Urobiligenuria in all of 26 D.T. patients.
Döllken	Albuminuria in 30 per cent of 120 male D.T. patients. Glycosuria in only 3 patients.
Fürstner (cit. Döllken)	Albuminuria in 40 per cent of D.T. patients.
Jacobsen (cit. Döllken)	Albuminuria in 60 per cent of D.T. patients.
Kauffmann	Pathological values of acetone, indican and oxalic acid in urine of 4 D.T. patients.
Liepmann (*b*)	Albuminuria in 76 per cent of 111 D.T. patients.
Montmolin	Urobilinuria in most of 24 D.T. patients.
Näcke (cit. Döllken)	Albuminuria in 82 per cent of D.T. patients.
Sceleth and Beifeld	Albumin and some sugar in urine of D.T. patients.
Truche	In 21 cases: urea, no changes; urobiligen, urobilin and biliary pigments always increased. Albuminuria and slight glycosuria in 1 case only.
Weinberg (cit. Döllken)	Albuminuria in 30 per cent of D.T. patients.

delirium tremens are given and only investigations carried out on un-mixed samples of delirium tremens patients are considered. The entries in these tables require little comment. They are suggestive of dis-turbances of protein metabolism which, however, cannot be closely defined. There are also definite indications of loss of the detoxicating function of the liver and of disturbed fat metabolism and mineral metabolism.

The findings on albuminuria in terms of percentage of occurrence among delirium tremens patients show a rather wide range. Since the albuminuria becomes most marked at the height of the delirium and ebbs off with it, the discrepant findings are perhaps due to different investigators having made their determinations at different stages of the delirium.

As to the specificity of biochemical findings in delirium tremens it is

TABLE 3 B

Biochemical Findings in Delirium Tremens — Blood

Author	*Finding*
Achard, Lévy and Wellisch	In 3 D.T. patients, potassium increased during crisis on an average 18 per cent; calcium decreased 15 per cent and sodium decreased 5 per cent.
Keeser and Keeser	In 5 D.T. patients, cholesterol increased from 148 to 382 mg. per 100 cc. Albumin increased 18 per cent but did not increase in other chronic alcoholics. Indican increased several hundred per cent but not in other alcoholics and the same was true with bile pigments. Phosphatides and soaps decreased 40 per cent.
Thomas, Semrad and Schwab (*a*)	In 12 of 22 D.T. patients, blood albumin was lower at time of dis-charge than on admission. Changes in the serum globulin were in-significant.
Toulouse, Courtois and Russell	Twenty-eight D.T. patients. At the beginning of crisis, urea, sugar and cholesterol normal or slightly increased. During crisis urea rises markedly. Bile pigments increased from the beginning of crisis, decreased swiftly afterwards.
Truche	Urea increased in 20 of 21 cases 0.60 to 1.0 g. Residual nitrogen in-creased slightly in half of the cases. Chlorides, slight variation. pH noticeably increased in 80 per cent of the cases.
Euziere, Vidal and Zakhamm	Marked increase of urea.
Wortis, Wortis and Marsh	Fourteen D.T. patients. Vitamin C in blood, 62 per cent below normal value. (In spinal fluid, vitamin C values were, on the aver-age, 66 per cent below normal.)
Wortis, Wortis, Frank, *et al.*	In D.T. patients, blood chlorides are low. Chlorides are always excreted as sodium chloride.

difficult to come to conclusions. Thomas does not believe that any specific findings have been produced as yet in the biological sphere. Bostroem stated that while chronic alcoholics with liver cirrhosis have constant urobilinuria, in delirium tremens a spontaneous urobilinogenuria occurs.

In relation to serum albumin, Thomas, Semrad and Schwab (a) remarked that all their patients gave a history of inadequate diet before the onset of the delirium and it is possible that dietary deficiency is responsible for the reduction in serum albumin. They considered, however, that liver damage, too, might cause such findings.

In their investigations of blood chemistry in delirium tremens, Keeser and Keeser used 5 normal controls to whom they gave intoxicating dosages of alcohol. The blood constituents were determined on these controls before alcohol administration and at various times after administration. In these controls there were no changes in indican or acetone bodies. There were also no changes in the serum albumin. Acute intoxication, however, did produce a 75 per cent rise in the total cholesterol but no changes in the other lipids. The fact that in delirium tremens patients there was a 40 per cent loss in phosphatides and soaps is interpreted by the Keesers as an expression of inhibited oxidation, since, with Bloor, they regard the phosphatides as intermediary changes in the oxidation of fats.

On the whole, the biochemical approach to the problem of delirium tremens is promising, but very much remains to be done in this field.

Differential diagnosis. The differential diagnosis of delirium tremens in relation to febrile deliria, and the delirium of epilepsy, as well as of paraldehyde delirium, is fairly easy and will not be discussed here. A more controversial issue is the relation of delirium tremens to acute hallucinosis. This is discussed in detail in the section on acute alcoholic hallucinosis.

The question of a personality differential in hallucinosis and delirium tremens has been broached by Bonhoeffer (c), von Speyr (cit. Tetz), and also Pohlisch (c), but Bigelow, Lehrmann and Palmer do not believe that a differential diagnosis between delirium tremens and hallucinosis can be based on personality factors.

A neurological differential criterion has been suggested by Tramer. According to this investigator the tibialis anterior reflex occurs almost exclusively in delirium tremens. Schabelitz, as well as Stiefel, regards it as pathognostically important. Except for these authors this criterion is never mentioned.

Pathology

That "morbid anatomy has thrown little light upon the nature of that particular affection of the brain and central nervous system which gives rise to the distinctive symptoms of delirium tremens" has recently been pointed out by Wortis (b). He adds that "the pathology is further complicated by the frequent failure to differentiate the changes in delirium tremens from those occurring in chronic alcoholism which is a necessary precursor."

Many investigators of delirium tremens have complained that it is difficult to find satisfactory pathological reports on delirium tremens, since most of the autopsy studies are made on a miscellaneous group of chronic alcoholics and the results are generalized for this group. There are, however, a few studies which have been made on delirium tremens patients only, although it is by no means certain that these do not include material from severe encephalopathies. Nevertheless, it seems desirable to give here some of the pathological evidence reported in the literature.

Generally, it may be said that all autopsy reports on delirium tremens patients mention brain edema, and almost since the first description of delirium tremens this has been regarded as an outstanding and significant characteristic. The first large scale investigation of the central nervous system in delirium tremens cases was published by Bonhoeffer (b) in 1899. He had autopsy material on some 20 delirium tremens patients but based his report chiefly on 5 patients who, to his best knowledge, had no complicating diseases. It would appear, however, that the condition of nicotinic acid deficiency encephalopathy was included in the sample. On the basis of his autopsy material, Bonhoeffer (b) thought he had found a relationship between delirium tremens and polioencephalitis hemorrhagica superior. This is of great interest since, although the relation of delirium tremens to the encephalopathies was overlooked for many years, it has been brought to the fore again in recent discussions [Bender (a); and Toulouse, Marchand and Courtois]. It is quite possible that Bonhoeffer, as well as Toulouse and his associates, included unrecognized encephalopathies other than delirium tremens in their material.

Marchand gives the following description of the central nervous system in 14 fatal cases of delirium tremens:

1. Macroscopically. Congestion of pia mater. No atheroma of cerebral arteria was found in spite of the fact that some of these alcoholics were 50 years of age. No cerebral atrophy. Hemorrhagic encephalitis in one case.

2. Microscopically. Chronic meningitis lesions. Pia mater thickened. No lymphatic reaction of the blood vessels in the cortex and in other parts of the brain. Changes in the pyramidal cells of the cortex as atrophy, hyalinization and granulation, frequent pigmentation of cortex and *couche optique*. No demyelinization around the vessels. Mononuclear cells along the capillaries; veins and capillaries are distended with perivascular blood. Hyperplasia of the neuroglia in the molecular layer (*couche moleculaire*) of the cortex. No changes in microglia. Cerebellum less involved. In the cerebral peduncles and the medullary bulb chronic atrophy and fatty degeneration of the nuclei of cranial and peripheral nerves are found. The inferior olives show acute disintegration. Here, too, the inclusion of conditions other than delirium tremens must be considered.

This same material has been used by Toulouse, Marchand and Courtois and on the basis of these findings they grouped delirium tremens with the encephalopathies and, as a matter of fact, gave it the name *encéphalite psychosique des alcooliques*, and described it as an encephalopathy in which the mental symptoms predominated over the neurological ones.

Bender (*a*) has pointed out that "in the more prolonged deliria there are nearly always present one or more signs which suggest encephalo-pathic lesions in the brain stem." She also noted a specific finding, although she considers that delirium tremens patients rarely die of this alcoholic condition but rather of head traumas, pneumonia and other associated conditions: "In such cases we commonly find an ependymal proliferation with underlying glial and vascular disturbances. In such cases the involvement of the mammillary body is highly diagnostic."

Stevenson, Allen and McGowan studied a group of 44 chronic alcoholics who came to autopsy and reported that "the severity of the clinical features was out of all proportion to the slight microscopic changes found in the brain." This group included 6 cases of delirium tremens but the statement is made for the group as a whole.

Liver pathology as well as endocrine pathology in delirium tremens patients is mentioned in most reports on delirium tremens but these are so obviously nonspecific changes that discussion is not necessary. It may be mentioned, however, that Marchand found in 14 cases of delirium tremens, only 1 Laënnec cirrhosis while the other 13 all represented fatty hypertrophic cirrhosis.

The blood picture was first investigated by Elsholz (cit. Bumke and Kant) and by Suckow (*a*). Both reported a neutrophilic leucocytosis, aneosinophilia and lymphopenia. According to Suckow, the severity of the delirium corresponds to the degree of the shift in the white blood count toward the granulocytes. In other chronic alcoholics who did not show deliria, only a lymphocytosis was found. Streltschuk believed that the blood count in alcoholism is so characteristic that sometimes the form of the illness can be judged by it. He attributed conflicting results of other investigators to the fact that the blood examinations were performed for an insufficient period of time.

Etiology and Pathogenesis

In the narrowest sense of the term, the etiology of delirium tremens is inebriety. The full-fledged syndrome occurs only in chronic alcoholics, although deliria resembling delirium tremens but not including all of its symptoms occur also in nonalcoholics. Since, on the other hand, delirium tremens occurs in only a small percentage of inebriates, alcoholism must be regarded as a necessary, but not as a sufficient, condition for the origin of this disease. The question, therefore, is one of determining the sufficient condition or conditions. While no satisfactory etiological explanation has emerged as yet, there has been considerable advance in the recognition of the possible underlying processes and an initial oversimplification of the problem has been largely abandoned. There are, however, at least leads for future research and tentative hypotheses have even advanced the treatment of delirium tremens.

At practically no time has delirium tremens been regarded as a form of acute intoxication; rather its distinction from these forms has been accentuated. There has always been agreement that it is a phenomenon brought about by alcohol abuse over many years—6 to 10 years of heavy drinking according to the survey of the literature by Bumke and Kant. Chronic intoxication is assumed in all etiologies of delirium tremens but there are great differences in opinions relative to the direct or indirect toxic effects of alcohol.

Apparently not all alcoholic beverages are of etiological importance in the production of delirium tremens, at least not to the same extent. Magnan (*b*) believed that only absinthe drinkers developed delirium tremens. High proof liquors are regarded by some authorities as the only agents. Bumke and Kant cite in favor of this view the great frequency of delirium tremens in liquor-drinking North and East Germany and the relative rarity in beer-drinking Bavaria. They admit, however, that the psychosis may occur in exclusive wine drinkers. Neither these authors nor Bonhoeffer (c) found it among exclusive beer drinkers, and Sceleth and Beifeld did not see it among beer-drinking Americans. On the other hand, Kraepelin found 15 per cent beer drinkers among delirium tremens patients and his findings were confirmed by Siemerling (cit. Bumke and Kant). Among the 51 delirium tremens patients of Drobnes 42 per cent consumed brandy as well as wine, 34 per cent wine only (average 3 liters per day) and 24 per cent wine and beer. Pollock (b) has analyzed the drinking habits of 61 delirium tremens patients admitted between 1921 and 1923 and of 252 such patients admitted in 1936 and 1937 to the New York State mental hospitals. In the first sample he found 11 (18 per cent) and in the second sample 15 (6 per cent) exclusive beer drinkers. Dougnac stated that in France delirium tremens rarely occurs among exclusive wine drinkers in spite of the consumption of 5, 10 and even 15 liters (sic!) of wine a day. Dougnac, however, belongs to that group of French physicians who do not recognize wine as an alcoholic drink.

Naturally, all these statistics are based, to a large extent, on the statements of the patients themselves and these are notoriously unreliable. It would appear then, on the whole, that there is some occurrence of delirium tremens among exclusive beer drinkers, but that most probably it is rather rare. There may even be some correlation between the severity of the delirium and the kind of alcoholic beverage consumed. Meggendorfer, in 1928, stated that in the preceding years delirium tremens in Germany was of a milder nature, and in his opinion this was due to a decrease in exclusive liquor consumption with an increase in mixed drinking—liquor, wine and beer.

All investigators of delirium tremens agree that edema of the brain practically always occurs, but the affirmation or negation of its etiological significance depends on whether or not the investigator connected this with the concomitance of intracranial pressure. The theory of intracranial pressure contingent upon edema of the brain has dominated etiologies, and consequently treatment, for a long period of time. Recently, however, it has become increasingly evident that intracranial pressure is not a necessary resultant of edema and may be entirely normal in these cases [Thomas, Semrad and Schwab (b); and Wortis (b)].

The simple explanation in terms of a withdrawal phenomenon has maintained itself for a long time in spite of early protests (e.g., both

Benjamin Rush and Thomas Trotter, early in the nineteenth century, and Döllken in 1901), and has been virtually discarded only in this country. In Europe, particularly in France, it still has some unquestioning adherents. The withdrawal theory was greatly strengthened through Bonhoeffer's (c) authority. He had observed that vagrants frequently developed delirium tremens 2 or 3 days after imprisonment. Pohlisch (d) found similar conditions in soldiers a few days after mobilization. Bumke and Kant, however, pointed out that these older statistical investigations do not stand the test of critique. Modern statistics are contrary to the withdrawal etiology. Bostock stated that in English prisons only 264 of 63,000 inebriates, i.e., less than 0.5 per cent, developed delirium tremens; and Bowman, Wortis and Keiser found that of the annual average of 10,000 alcoholic patients admitted to Bellevue Hospital only a very few developed delirium tremens after admission. Interesting statistics on the time which elapsed between drinking and the onset of delirium tremens have been presented by Piker (a). In 275 patients investigated by him 205, that is, 74.5 per cent, had their delirium start during drinking. The fallacy involved in the withdrawal theory has been pointed out by Bumke and Kant in their statement that "abstinence is in itself an expression of the beginning of delirium." Noyes states that the cessation of drinking may be "indicative of an oncoming delirium, during the prodromal period of which the patient may be so nauseated and experience such a disgust for liquor that he does not drink." This standpoint has been elaborated by Bowman, Wortis and Keiser as follows: "In the prodromal period of delirium tremens, the patient often experiences a disgust for alcohol sufficient to cause abstinence for several days. The acute gastritis and hepatitis which so many patients have, often makes it impossible for them to retain anything by mouth, including alcohol. It is this type of abstinence which has often been mistaken as a cause rather than a result of delirium tremens." Another factor which must be considered is the fact that the outbreak of delirium tremens in hospitals is frequently precipitated by the disease for which the patient has been admitted. In spite of the significant arguments against the withdrawal theory, some investigators of the past 3 or 4 years still regard it as the sole or at least the most important etiology [Baonville and Titeca; Bruel; Drobnes; Dent (c)].

It has been noticed quite recently that delirium tremens usually develops in inebriates who have been admitted to hospitals for injuries and acute infections. Statistics on this aspect have been gathered by some investigators. Pohlisch (*b*) found that of his 162 delirium tremens patients 44 (27 per cent) had had an epileptic attack shortly before the delirium (some of these also had injuries); 23 (14 per cent) had pneumonia* and 38 (23 per cent) had injuries only. This means that not more than 36 per cent of the delirium tremens patients had no illness or injury immediately preceding the delirium. Bonhoeffer's (*c*) figure for this is 30 per cent, rather good agreement. It is not unreasonable to surmise that among these 30 or 36 per cent there may have been quite a few cases of other encephalopathies which were not recognized owing to the lack of familiarity with that disease complex at that time. Practically every investigator of delirium tremens regards these injuries or infections as precipitating or predisposing factors. Schultze also includes in these factors neurosyphilis and arteriosclerosis; and Wortis (*b*) adds nicotinic acid deficiency encephalopathy. Generally it is regarded that the injuries and infections bring about a lowered resistance to the toxic processes going on in the inebriate individual and release the reaction in the form of delirium tremens. Bumke and Kant pointed out that one may say that the injuries are consequences, but not causes, of the psychosis. Nevertheless, they were inclined to agree with Pohlisch (*b*) that although the susceptibility to infection and delirium have chronic alcoholism as a parent factor, the intercurrent diseases give the last impetus to the delirium. The infectious precipitating diseases in delirium tremens are so conspicuous that delirium tremens itself has been occasionally regarded as an infectious process [e.g., Damaye (*b*)].

In relation to the predisposing factors Pohlisch (*b*) has made a suggestion which should receive careful attention in future research on delirium tremens. He proposed that the object of investigation should be, not merely the acute diseases which may or may not lead to the onset of delirium tremens, but also the conditions which lead to the development of those acute illnesses and their ability to produce delirium tremens. Not every epileptic attack in a chronic alcoholic is followed by delirium tremens, nor every pneumonia or other acute infectious

---

*There is quite some variation in reports on the occurrence of pneumonia among delirium tremens patients. This, however, is attributable to the selectivity of samples rather than to the variability of the phenomenon. Thus Dynes reports that among 103 patients with delirium tremens admitted to the Boston Psychopathic Hospital there were only 5 patients with pneumonia. Naturally, the tendency may be to take patients with pneumonia, even if they had delirium tremens, to the Boston City Hospital rather than to the Psychopathic Hospital. Samples from mental hospitals will generally tend to show a lower incidence of pneumonia.

disease. Apparently a special state of chronic alcoholism must be reached. The question therefore is: "Which pathogenic conditions lead to those acute processes which so frequently precede delirium tremens?" One must agree with Pohlisch that this is an important step in delirium tremens research but it appears even more promising to connect this with the investigation of the person in whom the process occurs.

The processes to which delirium tremens is supposed to be a reaction, released by precipitating factors, have been generally conceived as metabolic disturbances. The chief bases for the various theories are the biochemical changes discussed in a preceding section. According to the predilections of the investigators, the stress in the metabolic disturbance is placed on different factors. There has also been reconciliation of the withdrawal and metabolic theories. Of this Wagner von Jauregg has been the chief representative. The following quotation gives the essence of his views:

If alcohol removes disturbances in chronic alcoholism, it acts somewhat like an antitoxin. The disturbances which are removed by alcohol cannot be caused by it. Therefore, we must assume that in chronic alcoholism under the influence of alcohol a toxic agent is formed in the body which produces certain disturbances like tremor, vomiting and occasionally delirium; a toxic agent which depends upon the supply of alcohol but cannot be alcohol itself as alcohol nullifies its effect. We may add this: a toxic agent which is eliminated more slowly than alcohol, for its effects only take place after the alcohol has left the body.

Kraepelin, too, negated the direct toxic effect of alcohol in delirium tremens, which he attributed to such an extent to metabolic processes that he called it a "metalcoholic disease" and compared it with the mental disturbances of uremia or with a *coma diabeticum*.

Bonhoeffer (*c*) postulated the formation of a poison in the intestinal tract. In contrast to older ideas, however, he did not regard this toxin as the result of the summation of a rapid sequence of effects of alcohol but rather as a secondary disease form. He and many followers believed that this secondary toxin appeared shortly before the onset of the delirium. Pohlisch (*b*), however, generally following Bonhoeffer's ideas, believed that the secondary toxin involved is the result of a slow accumulation present long before the delirium.

All these theories involve a generalized, somewhat obscure metabolic disturbance, although Pohlisch (*a*), on the basis of the investigations of Keeser and Keeser, assumed serious disturbances of the protein metabolism. Such an assumption had been made before him by Kauffmann. Metabolic disturbances of hepatic origin had been postulated for delirium tremens by Bostroem, later by de Crinis and some others, as has been seen in the section on biochemical findings. More recent views (1930–40) on the nature and etiology of delirium tremens are listed in Table 4.

TABLE 4

Recent Views on the Nature and Etiology of Delirium Tremens, 1930–1940

Date	Author	Delirium Tremens
1930	de Crinis	A toxic condition created by the impairment of hepatic function.
1932	Marchand	Conditioned by a diffuse inflammatory and degenerative encephalitis without tendency to demyelinization. Ultimate etiology: toxic agent.
1932	Meyer, A.	A member of the group of disorders coming largely from disturbances of the integrative functions through poisons or metabolic or circulatory disorders involving the brain.
1933	Curtius and Wallenberg	D.T., as well as delirium of pneumonia, originates in a neuropathic disposition.
1933	Mignot	Based on a predisposition, created by certain conditions which are often unrecognized, such as malaria or cranial trauma.
1933	Pohlisch (*f*)	(Following Bonhoeffer.) A secondary new disturbance rather than the summation of a series of alcoholic intoxications. It develops largely in the nonpathological drinker.
1933	Toulouse, Marchand and Courtois	An encephalopathy in which the mental manifestations predominate over the neurological ones.
1934	Brugger (*a*)	A specific constitutional factor is involved.
1934	Martin and Martin	Intoxication through hepatorenal insufficiency.
1935	Cosack	A direct consequence of serious physical trauma in the chronic alcoholic.
1935	Rosenfeld	A result of the impairment of the liver, vascular system and metabolism.
1936	Cline and Coleman	A disorder of obscure etiology, with no satisfactory explanation for its development. But it is generally a separate entity arising on the basis of changes in chronic alcoholism, with particular stress on increased intracranial pressure.
1936	Damaye (*b*)	An infectious disease, meningo-encephalitis, probably due to an ultravirus.
1936	Drobnes	A withdrawal phenomenon.

Date	Author	Delirium Tremens
1937	Baonville and Titeca	A withdrawal phenomenon.
1937	Gabriel (*c*)	Not a withdrawal phenomenon but the result of serious, chronic damage, especially to the liver, by alcohol.
1937	Heringa	Chronic impairment of the central nervous system is the predisposing factor; temporary reduction of use of alcohol the releasing factor.
1938	Brodsky	A deficiency of the vitamin B complex is at least one of the factors involved.
1938	Kloster	A vitamin B_1 deficiency is one of the factors involved.
1938	Rosanoff (*b*)	Probably a combination of psychogenic and avitaminotic factors.
1939	Bowman and Keiser	Emphasis on disturbance of water metabolism.
1939	Bowman, Wortis and Keiser	Emphasis on gastric and hepatic damage, on chloride and lactic acid metabolism, with attention to psychogenic factors.
1939	Bruel	A withdrawal phenomenon.
1939	Erwin	Anoxia.
1939	Mainzer and Krause	Nicotinic acid deficiency is a contributing factor.
1939	Noyes	Starvation acidosis may contribute to its development.
1939	Pagniez (*b*)	A possibility of involvement of a B complex avitaminosis.
1939	Säker	Dysfunction of endocrine glands, mainly hypofunction of the pituitary, adrenals and thyroid.
1939	Santesson	A vitamin B complex deficiency is one of the factors involved.
1940	Kiene, Streitwieser and Miller	The cause is a B_1 deficiency brought about by a sudden deficit in the maintenance requirements.
1940	Wortis (*b*)	Same as Bowman, Wortis and Keiser, with greater emphasis on the psychobiological aspects and relation to encephalopathies.

Disturbances of the water metabolism, as emphasized by Bowman and Keiser, form a link in the pathogenetic chain explaining part of the phenomenology of delirium tremens. Suboxidation as well as disturbances of the carbohydrate metabolism have been cited as etiological factors in delirium tremens on the basis of findings in chronic alcoholism in general and in animal experiments rather than on the basis of direct observation in delirium tremens.

The modern theories on the relationship of the avitaminoses to alcoholic diseases have been naturally extended to delirium tremens, although rather tentatively for the most part. Most of the exponents suggest that a vitamin B₁ or a nicotinic acid deficiency may be among the contributory factors. Only Kiene, Streitwieser and Miller go as far as to assign delirium tremens definitely, and it would seem exclusively, to vitamin B₁ deficiency. Rosanoff (*b*) believes that particularly a lack of the pellagra-preventive factor is likely to be involved in the etiology. Since delirium tremens occurs in chronic alcoholics it is only natural that it should appear in association with other alcoholic diseases, the avitaminotic nature of which is unquestionable. Consequently vitamin deficiencies are necessarily found in a large number of delirium tremens patients. Wortis (*b*) has made a masterly analysis of this question and came to the following conclusion:

It would therefore seem that deficiency of vitamin B₁ and nicotinic acid is not specific in the causation of delirium tremens, nor administration of these vitamins in the treatment of the disease. They are, however, invaluable for certain other syndromes which frequently complicate delirious episodes or develop during the delirium. Delirium tremens may, of course, be related to some as yet untried or undiscovered vitamin, but the evidence for vitamin B₁ and nicotinic acid is very meager indeed.

Lastly, the personality of the individuals suffering from delirium tremens belongs in the etiological picture. In a preceding section, evidence bearing on the question has been discussed and there appears to be some likelihood that delirium tremens develops in the psychologically normal drinker. Should this be confirmed the etiological quest would be narrowed down.

Working hypothesis. On the basis of the preceding discussions, one may form the following working hypothesis which may be discarded in part or *in toto* according to the indications of progressing clinical experience and of systematic research.

Delirium tremens is a psychosis of episodic nature which does not reach down to the personality structure. It is, in all probability, a form of encephalopathy which befalls only a fraction of chronic alcoholics. Its physical nature is greatly obscured by concomitant conditions, some of which may be precipitating factors. It apparently grows on the ground of metabolic disturbances in which loss of the detoxicating function of the liver, faulty carbohydrate metabolism, disturbed protein metabolism, acidosis, suboxidation of the brain and general nutritional deficiencies, as well as the anomalous water economy of the body, are in complex interaction. The much emphasized occurrence of edema of the brain may be largely an epiphenomenon of these disturbances, although as a link in the pathogenesis of delirium tremens it should not be entirely neglected. Since metabolic disturbances are common in all chronic alcoholics but delirium tremens only occurs in probably less than 5 per cent of them, one must postulate the following alternatives:

1. At least one component of the general metabolic disturbances of delirium tremens does not occur in other alcoholic conditions, or at least one component differs in its mechanism from the mechanism of that same component in other alcoholic diseases.

2. Generally one of the metabolic disorders occurs in the same form in all alcoholic diseases, but the different combinations result in different manifestations, and delirium tremens has its specific combination of such disorders.

3. Neither point 1 nor 2 holds, but in delirium tremens there is merely a lower intensity of metabolic disturbances which manifest themselves only when additional stress, such as certain infections or injuries, temporarily accentuates the disturbed metabolic processes.

4. Delirium tremens occurs only in psychologically unencumbered persons of high alcohol tolerance, when the stress of certain infections or injuries lowers their resistance to the metabolic disorders contingent on inebriety.

Suggestions for future researches. This survey of the literature shows that there has been no paucity of ideas in the etiological theories of delirium tremens, but they are rather vague and at their best scratch the surface only. The desiderata of future investigations in this field may be summarized as follows:

1. Biochemical investigations are needed to fill in the rather wide gaps in our knowledge. In particular, the blood chemistry must be better known. It is essential that parallel investigations should be carried out on nondelirant chronic alcoholics in order to determine whether or not there are specific biochemical findings in delirium tremens. It is also essential that brain chemistry, a much neglected field, should be studied, as the chemical changes in the brain may be more illuminating than the anatomopathological ones.

2. Much importance has been attributed to precipitating or predisposing factors, but there has been little serious analytic effort. In order that the concept of precipitating factors should attain true meaning, and contribute to the understanding of delirium tremens, these factors should be studied along the lines suggested by Pohlisch.

3. Some leads have come from the neurological side but have not been adequately followed up. The reported disturbances of equilibrium should be investigated further. If they can be confirmed they may lead to the localization of the brain involvement.

4. Should it be confirmed that delirium tremens occurs mainly in persons free of psychopathic heredity, and with a largely normal personality make-up, there would at once be a definite lead for further delirium tremens researches as well as a better understanding of abnormal drinking in general. Personality studies should, therefore, be fostered, but it must be pointed out that little may be expected from routine studies with the personality inventory methods. Studies must be made individually and must operate with humanly meaningful concepts such as, for instance, O. Kant's "personality-stratification."

5. Some of the preceding suggestions can only be carried out with the aid of purposeful, detailed records. It is desirable that at least one or two of the hospitals with the largest alcoholic admissions should keep records going beyond the scope of the present ones. It is futile at this time to attempt to answer far-reaching questions by a statistical survey of the existing records. Given adequate material, however, statistical studies may yield important side lights on the question of etiology.

6. Generally, therapeutic studies should not be hampered by research requirements. A few well controlled, comparative studies of methods, carried out on patients whose histories and personalities are well known, may contribute significantly, however, to the understanding of the problems of delirium tremens.

Treatment

The treatment of delirium tremens was, for a long period, dominated by two ideas: (*a*) that delirium tremens is a withdrawal phenomenon; and (*b*) that it is largely determined by edema of the brain and consequent increased intracranial pressure. (The pros and cons of this latter idea have been discussed in the section on etiology.) Strychnine, the early panacea for all alcoholic diseases, was naturally used in the treatment of delirium tremens, too, and its use is occasionally encountered in present day practice.

More modern treatment is based on the tentative metabolic etiologies and on the recognition of the importance of concomitant conditions. Bumke and Kant attributed the decrease in fatality in Germany, from 24 per cent to 5 per cent, largely to medical attention to the heart condition in delirium tremens. Ganser had only 0.88 per cent fatalities after introducing digitalis as an accessory treatment in delirium tremens. The importance of the concomitant conditions in relation to a prognosis *ad vitam* is illustrated by the experience of Pohlisch (*b*), who found 15 per cent mortality in delirium tremens in connection with other diseases, but only 3.5 per cent mortality in cases without concomitant diseases.* Probably in these 3.5 per cent, too, death was not due to delirium tremens itself but to cardiac conditions. It may be safely stated that uncomplicated delirium tremens—if the heart is taken care of—is never fatal.

Apart from the etiological treatment, or rather tentative etiological treatment, of the disease itself, supplementary treatments of several aspects of delirium tremens are required. Attention has already been drawn to the concomitant diseases, especially the heart conditions. Since the restlessness and hyperactivity of delirium tremens are of danger to the patient himself, and also increase the difficulty of handling him, the necessity for sedative treatment was recognized fairly early. Unfortunately physical restraint was commonly used, but the view that it should be avoided is now generally accepted. The danger in the use of morphine in delirium tremens has also been pointed out at different times, but has probably still not received sufficient attention. Generally, however, since Bumke's 1902 paper on the use of paraldehyde, this drug has been employed and its appropriateness in delirium tremens is still being emphasized. Another factor which is receiving more attention is the poor nutritional status of most delirium tremens patients. This is corrected by giving a high calory, high vitamin diet and occasionally also through the administration of supplementary vitamins.

The simple therapies, i.e., the presumably etiological ones, naturally vary greatly with the etiological convictions of the therapists. In recognition of liver dysfunctions and disturbances of the carbohydrate metabolism, de Crinis introduced the use of decholin and stated that in 17 patients the symptoms disappeared within 3 to 7 hours. Bancroft, Gutsell and Rutzler advocated the use of peptizing agents. Klemperer was the first to introduce an insulin treatment for delirium tremens and this has been used in small dosages by Kral, Pollak and Schirmer and by Hadlik, and in shock dosages by Kulcsár and Lajtavári. Robinson used insulin and glucose.

Among the modern treatments the vitamins have naturally ap-

*Mazel compiled reports of many observers on mortality in delirium tremens.

TABLE 5

Treatment of Delirium Tremens, 1936–1940

Author	Country	Date	No. of Patients	Basic Treatment	Dosage; Method	Other Treatment	Diet	Criteria of Success
Bargues and Grimal	France	1936	3	Sodium-butyl-ethyl-barbiturate.	1.5 mg. per kg. in 20 parts water. ½ dose may be repeated in 4–6 hrs.	Saline and liver extracts. Patient kept in quiet, warm room. Cardiotonics.		Patient sleeps as in slight general anesthesia. Results: No untoward effects.
Cline and Coleman	U.S.	1936	157	Cerebral dehydration.	Spinal drainage 50–75 cc. Intrav. dextrose 50–100 cc. 50% solution. Paraldehyde 7.8–15.0 g. Fluid intake limited to 1,000 cc. for 24 hrs. Sometimes repeated.			Most patients slept immediately. 6 deaths (3.8%), none from exhaustion.
Diethelm	U.S.	1936	—	Increased fluid intake; symptomatic treatment.		Continuous tub; withdrawal of alcohol. Cardiac stimulants, gastric lavage, etc.		
Baonville and Titeca	Belgium	1937	—	Small doses of alcohol.				
Kral, Pollak and Schirmer	Germany	1937	3	Insulin.	30–85 units total dosage.			Occupational fantasies ceased after 30 min. Delirium stopped after 2 days' treatment.

TABLE 5 (continued)

Author	Country	Date	No. of Patients	Basic Treatment	Dosage; Method	Other Treatment	Diet	Criteria of Success
de Ajuriaguerra and Neveu	France	1938	—	Etiologic, symptomatic and pathogenic.	Withdrawal. Sedatives. Acceleration of alcohol elimination.	Liver extracts. Restraint and small doses of alcohol if necessary. 1–2 cg. strychnine sulfate per day.		
Bell and Talkington	U.S.	1938	112	Withdrawal; hydrotherapy.	Wet packs; continuous baths, fan douche, etc.	Saline catharsis.	High caloric.	Av. duration of hallucinosis 3.2 days, of hospital stay 27.3 days. 5 (4.46%) deaths. Not definite for D.T.
Cossa, Bougeant, Puech and Sassi	France	1938	2	Strychnine sulfate.	Repeated injections of 5–10 mg. up to 30–50 mg. per day (sic!).			
Kloster	Germany	1938	2	Thiamin hydrochloride.	20–80 mg.			Excellent results.
Piker and Stern	U.S.	1938	300	150 given high fluids; 150 restricted. General symptomatic.	(a) 3,000–4,000 cc. fluid daily. (b) 1,000 cc. fluid daily.	Cardiac stimulants, lavage, purge, spinal drainage in severe cases, etc.	High caloric, soft liquid, supplemented with substances containing B complex.	Equally good results in both groups.
Reifenstein and Davidoff (a)	U.S.	1938	5	Benzedrine sulfate.	10–30 mg. per os or intravenously (in stupor).			At least as effective as spinal fluid drainage. Days needed for recovery 1–7, average 3.6.

TABLE 5 (continued)

Author	Country	Date	No. of Patients	Basic Treatment	Dosage; Method	Other Treatment	Diet	Criteria of Success
Bowman and Keiser	U.S.	1939	129	Rehydration.	Sodium chloride, 300 cc. by nasal tube, in connection with forcing fluids.			Many fell asleep at once. Delirium cleared in an average of 2.2 days. No deaths.
Erwin	U.S.	1939	3	Oxygen.	300 cc. by nasal tube.			Patients symptom-free in 28–35 hrs. Hospital stay 2.2 days (untreated cases 12.8).
Hadlik	Czechoslovakia	1939	17	Insulin.	Av. total dosage 68½ units in 5–15 units per dose.	Glucose when needed.	High carbohydrate. Fluids.	Reduction of duration of delirium.
Kulcsár and Lajtavári	Hungary	1939	5	Insulin and dextrose.	Intravenously 60–100 units insulin, up to 200 cc. dextrose.			D.T. stopped in 3–4 days.
Mainzer and Krause	Egypt	1939	1	Nicotinic acid.	0.6 g.	0.55 g. thiamin (ineffective). Scopolamine.		All symptoms disappeared within 12 hrs.
Säker	Germany	1939	2	Insulin and dextrose.	20–60 units at a dose.	B₁		Recovery in 5 and 9 days.
Santesson	Sweden	1939	2	"Betabion forte."	3 cc. intravenously in one; 50 mg. intravenously in other.	15 drops thebaicine later.		Patients slept and symptoms disappeared.

TABLE 5 (continued)

Author	Country	Date	No. of Patients	Basic Treatment	Dosage; Method	Other Treatment	Diet	Criteria of Success
Stungo	England	1939	—	Rossium	1 gr. every 4 hrs.	Nembutal. Immediate withdrawal for young, tapering off for old.		Shortens period of aberration.
Thomas, Semrad and Schwab (b)	U.S.	1939	A20	Paraldehyde: Dextrose:	Freely Intravenously 100 cc. 50% sol.		High caloric. Rich in B. Fluids up to 1,000 cc., afterwards at will.	Recovery in 1–3 days.
				Mag. sulfate: Lumbar puncture:	1 oz. per os. 10–40 cc.			
			B20	Paraldehyde: Dextrose: No puncture	Minimum to control restlessness. 1,500–2,000 cc. 5% in normal saline by hypodermoclysis.		High caloric. Rich in B. 2,000–3,000 cc. fluids.	Recovery in 1–3 days. Less tremulousness and fewer signs of exhaustion than Group A.
Krinsky	U.S.	1940	860	Symptomatic		Nursing care, no restraint, withdrawal, food, fluids, sleep.		
Reifenstein and Davidoff (b)	U.S.	1940	15 15	Amphetamine sulfate General	20–30 mg. per os or intravenously.			Av. days for recovery 3.1. Av. days for recovery 7.0.

TABLE 5 (*continued*)

Author	*Country*	*Date*	*No. of Patients*	*Basic Treatment*	*Dosage; Method*	*Other Treatment*	*Diet*	*Criteria of Success*
Robinson	U.S.	1940	24	Insulin	20 units at 3 hr. intervals.	Orange juice. Glucose solutions.		Average time for relief of delirium 2.4 days. 15 cases without complications: 1.5 days.
Rosenbaum, Piker and Lederer	U.S.	1940	142	Forced fluids				Average days in hospital, 4.75.
			142	Limited fluids				Average days in hospital, 4.65.
Sciclounoff and Flagg	Switzerland	1940	7	Vitamin B_1	10-100 mg. intravenously.			"Prompt" recovery in 4 cases of imminent D.T.; no success in 3 cases of frank D.T.

peared, particularly B$_1$ and nicotinic acid. (See section on etiology.) Success has also been attributed, recently, to the use of benzedrine sulfate. Reports on treatments of the past 5 years are given in Table 5 and do not require further discussion here. It need only be pointed out that cerebral dehydration through lumbar punctures is on the decrease since it is being recognized more and more that intracranial pressure is not associated with brain edema. Bowman, Wortis and Keiser have emphasized the general dehydration of delirium tremens patients with a concomitant dangerous mineral loss leading to serious disturbances of the acid-base equilibrium. This general dehydration is regarded as so central in the disease that the possible hydration of the brain may be neglected in the therapy. They practice, therefore, rehydration rather than dehydration.* The principles of their treatment are summarized as follows:

1. Withdraw alcohol abruptly.
2. Give sedative medication judiciously, paraldehyde being preferred, and morphine condemned.
3. Omit restraints unless absolutely necessary.
4. Give carbohydrate in large quantities.
5. Administer sodium chloride in an attempt to combat dehydration and to restore the normal acid-base equilibrium of the body.
6. Provide a high calory, high vitamin diet.
7. Force fluids.
8. Do lumbar punctures for diagnostic purposes only.
9. *Treat complicating or precipitating factors with specific therapy.*
10. Give individual psychotherapy according to the needs of the patient.

The administration of hypertonic solutions of sodium chloride has recently been found useful also by Silverman.† The rationale for the sodium chloride treatment has been stated by Bowman (*b*) as follows:

Closely related to the loss of fluid is the loss of salt. The kidney normally puts out 15 g. of salt every 24 hours when there is little salt loss through the sweat glands. If the patient is overactive and febrile, more salt is eliminated through the skin. The sweat glands are more permeable to salt at high temperatures so that the percentage of salt loss in the sweat increases. . . .
If the salts of the body are depleted as well as the fluids, giving fluid with-

*Hydration and the use of saline solutions were suggested by Brush in 1931.
†Although Rosenbaum, Piker and Lederer found no difference in results obtained by forcing fluids and limiting fluids, they recommend forcing fluids because they feel that the general toxic factors are important. This general conclusion is stated by them as follows: "Our results seem to us to indicate strongly that regardless of what sort of treatment procedure is used, and so long as no measures are instituted which are actually injurious, adequate general medical and psychiatric care should serve to keep the mortality rate in uncomplicated delirium tremens down to a minimum."

out salt results in further elimination of fluid because there is not the salt necessary to keep it in the body, or if it is retained in the body it may cause edema. The recognition of the first part of this statement has led some to advocate the restriction of fluids in certain conditions such as head injuries and delirium tremens, feeling that forcing fluids will result in edema of the brain, thus harming rather than benefiting the patient. If, however, salt is given with fluids the edema will not occur and a very beneficial effect will be obtained by forcing fluids. In attempting to force fluids one frequently finds patients who object to taking further fluids. The patients feel water-logged and have great difficulty in taking more fluid, and it becomes difficult to build up the fluid intake to the desired amount. If, however, salt is given as well, the patient develops a thirst and oftentimes will spontaneously request more fluids. . . . It is possible to make up a fluid which will have much the same mineral constituents as normal blood and thus supply the needs of the body. Not only does salt enable the individual to drink more fluids, prevent the development of edema, and replace the salt lost through elimination, but, if the kidneys are functioning in normal fashion, salt will restore the normal electrolyte pattern. If the body is in an acid condition, chlorides will be eliminated and the acidity of the body will be decreased. If the body is too alkaline, sodium will be eliminated and the alkalinity of the body decreased. The use of fluids and salt, therefore, will largely combat dehydration and acidosis.

The treatment of delirium tremens will advance with the recognition of the true underlying factors. This is naturally dependent upon research. On the other hand, research may be initiated by empirical therapeutic trials and it may be hoped that there will be a healthy interaction between these two vehicles of medical progress.

IV. KORSAKOFF'S PSYCHOSIS

In 1887 the Russian psychiatrist Korsakoff described* a psychosis which was apparently associated with polyneuropathy and which had as its central manifestation severe disturbances of the memory function. This subsequently became known as Korsakoff's psychosis or Korsakoff's syndrome.† Actually, this condition had been superficially described by Magnus Huss in 1852 as one of the manifestations of chronic alcoholism.

Kraepelin spoke of Korsakoff's psychosis as the severest form of chronic alcoholism, perhaps because of the great rarity of recovery from it; but this view is not generally held.

*The original description was published in Russian but an author's abstract as well as a full version appeared in German in 1890.

†The expressions "Korsakoff's psychosis" and "Korsakoff's syndrome" are frequently used interchangeably. In this paper the former will refer to the alcoholic form only, in accordance with Bonhoeffer's suggestion.

Although the psychosis is relatively infrequent, its interesting symptomatology has provoked a considerable literature. It is generally agreed that, in the large group of chronic alcoholics, this psychosis occurs rather rarely, but few statistics are available. Bonhoeffer (d) estimated its occurrence at 3 per cent of all chronic alcoholics, Meggendorfer at 1 to 2 per cent. Pollock has furnished data in two studies from which it would appear that approximately 10 per cent of first admissions in New York state for alcoholic psychosis had Korsakoff's psychosis. Since all alcoholic psychoses form about 10 per cent of all chronic alcoholics, it may be said that about one in every hundred chronic alcoholics develops Korsakoff's psychosis.

The Clinical Picture*

Schematically the symptoms forming the total complex are as follows:

Onset: Either sudden in delirious form, or fairly insidious in stuporous form. *Mental traits:* Anterograde amnesia, sometimes impairment of remote memory; impaired learning ability; disorientation in space and time; confabulation; occasionally illusions, stereotypy of speech, aphasia, agraphia.[†] *Mood:* Indifferent; sometimes euphoric. *Physical signs:* Polyneuropathy[‡] practically always present in the alcoholic form of Korsakoff's psychosis (Radu; Schultze).

Opinions on the frequency of delirium tremens as the form of onset of Korsakoff's psychosis show wide variation. A few important estimates derived from fairly large samples are given in Table 6.

Kraepelin suggested that the discrepancy between his and Bonhoef-

TABLE 6

Per Cent Occurrence of Delirium Tremens as Form of Onset of Korsakoff's Psychosis According to Various Investigators

Investigator	Per Cent Occurrence
Bonhoeffer (d)	75
Rosenbaum and Merritt	38
Kraepelin	25
Meggendorfer	25
Kauffmann (cit. Meggendorfer)	18
Anderson (cit. Bumke and Kant)	17

*In addition to papers to which direct reference is made in the text, important contributions to the knowledge of Korsakoff's syndrome were made by Mönkemöller (a); Knapp; Lapinsky; Steinthal; and Boedeker (the latter three cit. Schneider).

†Aphasia and agraphia would be indicative of focal brain pathology.

‡The symptomatology of polyneuropathy is discussed in Chapter III.

fer's estimate may be due to regional differences in the use of liquor and beer. Bumke and Kant believed that delirium tremens is the onset form when pronounced polyneuropathy is present. It has been variously pointed out that Korsakoff's psychosis seldom develops after a first delirium, but rather after second or third attacks of delirium tremens (e.g., Schroeder). Parenthetically it may be pointed out that delirium tremens contains the elements of amnesia [Bonhoeffer (c)].

The stuporous form of this psychosis may not involve true stupor. Bumke and Kant stated that this stupor is rather a stage of somnolence from which the patients can be awakened. They remain then, for awhile, quite attentive, but when left to themselves relapse into somnolence. These conditions are characterized by narcolepsy and disturbances of the eye muscles, the latter being symptomatic of Wernicke's syndrome. It may be noted that patients recovering from Wernicke's syndrome frequently develop Korsakoff's psychosis (Jolliffe, Wortis and Fein). The stuporous onset is more frequent in women [Bonhoeffer (d)].

In the initial stages of this psychosis the main symptoms are not obtrusive. The following description given by Korsakoff is illustrative of this aspect:

In the beginning it is difficult to notice any mental disturbance in conversation with this patient. He gives the impression of a person who has command of his mental capacity; he speaks with deliberation, draws the proper conclusions from given premises, plays chess or cards; in brief he comports himself as a mentally normal person. Only after a long conversation can one notice that the patient mixes up the events and does not keep in mind things which happen around him. He does not, for instance, remember whether he has eaten or whether he had gotten up from bed. Sometimes the patient forgets immediately what has happened. One may have visited him and left him for a minute, and on returning he has not the least idea that one had been there before. Such patients may look at one and the same page for hours because what they have read does not remain in their memory. They may repeat the same thing twenty times without being aware of the repetition and stereotypy of their speech. The patient does not remember persons with whom he is in continual contact. He does not remember his attending physician, the nurses, and assures one every time that it is the first meeting.

It is remarkable, however, that these patients who forget everything that has just happened are usually able to recall events which happened before their illness. Everything that happens during the illness or shortly before it vanishes from their memory. This, however, is the rule in the more typical cases only. In others remote memory is also lost.

Consciousness is unclouded, sometimes for a quite considerable time, but in some cases there is already a disturbance of consciousness in the first days.

The memory disturbance has been regarded as so marked and of such a central nature that Korsakoff's psychosis or syndrome has been frequently called an amnestic psychosis. Intricate analysis, based partly on psychometric findings and invoking philosophical concepts, has tended to show that the memory disturbances may be only an apparent manifestation of complicated processes. Early investigators tended to consider the memory disturbances purely *qua* disturbances of memory; later investigators have been so intent on analyzing the underlying mechanisms that the presenting memory disturbance has sometimes been, in effect, ignored.

There is still no agreement as to the precise nature of the mental symptoms. They have been generally considered as manifestations of a basic disorder, but this basic disorder has been variously designated as one of perception, fixation (in the sense of ability to form new associations), retention, reproduction, time-sense, and so forth. The views of numerous investigators are presented in condensed form in Table 7.

TABLE 7

*Views on the Nature of the Main Mental Symptoms
Manifested in Korsakoff's Psychosis*

Investigator	On Memory and Learning
Bonhoeffer (*d*)	The memory disturbance cannot be attributed fully to a lack of memory traces.
Brodman	Latent dispositions of relations persist, even after passing out of consciousness.
Bumke and Kant	The memory disturbance is not as deep-rooted as it would appear, but on the other hand it cannot be regarded as an epiphenomenon.
Bürger-Prinz and Kaila	The memory disturbances are secondary; they result from the interaction of such elements as disturbance of "set" and of perception, and nonutilization of knowledge and lack of need for correcting errors.
Gregor and Roemer	Acquisition of new associations is possible because economy in relearning can be shown.
Grünthal (*a*)	A primary memory disturbance is present, but "Der Fehler liegt in mangelnder Beziehungssetzung von gerade bestehenden Vorstellungen oder Gedachten zur Gesamterfahrung." Questionnaires relating to old experiential material were answered well.
Hartmann	There is a tendency to remember emotionally indifferent material and forget emotionally positive material.
van der Horst	Memory disturbances are a manifestation of a disturbance in the time-sense.

Investigator	*On Memory and Learning*
Köppen and Kutzinski	In delayed reproduction many details are recalled that were not recalled immediately.
Korsakoff	The memory disturbances are central. There is, however, not a complete lack of all memory traces.
Krauss	New associations are not formed, as there is no economy in relearning.
Schneider	True disturbance is not of memory but of comprehension and reproduction.
Weber	Postdelirious amnesia cannot be explained by deterioration only, but it has a definite tendency; emotionally toned responses, such as alcoholic, sexual and color shock responses, are forgotten.
Wechsler	The prime cause of the retention defect is the patient's inability to form new associations.

On Perception, Perception of Time, Gestalt Function

Bender (*b*)	Perceptive difficulties lead to incompletely perceived *Gestalten*.
Bender, Curran and Schilder	Changes in *Gestalt*-patterns represent reversion to a primitive type of organization in the perceptive field and are the expressions of strong field forces which have been liberated by the organic process.
Ehrenwald	Distinction between "primitive sense of time" and "gnostic perception of time"; the former is unimpaired in Korsakoff's psychosis, the latter disturbed.
Grünthal (*a*)	Responses to tachistoscopic tests are essentially normal.
van der Horst	The time concept is impaired.
Kraepelin	In one patient, perception decreased to one-sixth of normal.
Krauss	A peculiar action-time-memory disturbance; the development of formed "wholes" is difficult due to an amorphous emotional state.

On Association

Grünthal (*a*)	Responses on association test are qualitatively normal; no *Klang* associations. More than 70 per cent of the responses were not more than 1.0 to 1.8 seconds.
Pick	Frequent juxtaposition of unconnected ideas.

On Confabulation

Bonhoeffer (*d*)	A way out of embarrassment caused by memory lapses.
van der Horst	Due to lack of a one-dimensional time concept.
Körner	The result of increased suggestibility, response to outside mental stimulation and ability to react without self-criticism.
Wechsler	Results from a tendency to fill up gaps in memory with the readiest associates.

Any formulation is difficult, but on the whole it would appear that isolated functions are relatively intact and that integrative functions are impaired. There is a great loss of the ability to relate things to each other. The juxtaposition of unconnected ideas, shown by Pick, is another instance of this same disorder.

Consciousness may not be actually clouded in Korsakoff's psychosis. Indeed, A. Meyer speaks of entirely clear consciousness and Bender (b) remarks that in the alcoholic encephalopathies the deep clouding of consciousness leads to extremely marked perceptive difficulties, which are less in Korsakoff's psychosis because the clouding of consciousness is less.

Since there is a close relationship between the alcoholic Korsakoff's psychosis and delirium tremens one must expect that findings relative to the personality of patients having this disorder would be in accord with those in delirium tremens. This is actually the case. According to Siebert (b) amnestic polyneuritic psychosis should be considered almost exclusively as an exogenic syndrome in which endogenic factors of psychopathic constitution play a negligible part. Alexander has stated that Korsakoff's syndrome and delirium tremens develop without dependence on any constitutional factor. Mott placed this psychosis together with delirium tremens in that group of alcoholic psychoses which is recruited from individuals without psychopathic taint. As can be seen from Table 2 in Hoch's small sample there was a slight preponderance of extroverts (59 per cent) among Korsakoff patients.

All of this discussion has referred chiefly to the acute stages. When Korsakoff's psychosis becomes chronic, deterioration sets in, and the terminal phase is frequently paranoid. There is usually a single idea of outside influence which is not elaborated and which persists like an automatism (Chotzen).

Since we are dealing exclusively with the alcoholic form of Korsakoff's psychosis and not with Korsakoff's syndrome in general, the physical concomitants may be restricted to polyneuropathy, which will be dealt with for greater convenience in the section on etiology.

Biochemical changes have not been studied to any great extent in Korsakoff's psychosis. What there is, however, is much the same as in delirium tremens, namely, acetonuria and albuminuria (Bargues and Berton; Környey). It should be remembered, however, that delirium tremens is frequently the onset form of Korsakoff's psychosis and if, as cannot be determined from the material as presented, this were true in some or all of the patients studied by these investigators, it might well be that the physical findings should be related to the delirium tremens and not to the ensuing Korsakoff's psychosis. This applies also to the finding of Wortis, Wortis and Marsh that there is decreased vitamin C in the blood and spinal fluid of Korsakoff patients; they observed the same condition in delirium tremens and in other conditions of chronic alcoholism.

There is no difficulty in differentiating Korsakoff's psychosis from other alcoholic mental disorders. There is, however, the question of differentiating it from nonalcoholic forms of Korsakoff's syndrome and from certain mental disorders of the senium. Naturally age factors are to be taken into consideration. In these latter cases, also, polyneuropathy does not occur. Generally in the nonalcoholic forms of Korsakoff's syndrome there is little confabulation, limited to a few recurring fantasies, and there is also insight into the amnesia (Verstraeten). In the infectious form, according to Meggendorfer, the clouding of consciousness is more pronounced, the mood is lachrymose, and, naturally, the characteristic bodily signs of chronic alcoholism are lacking. Meggendorfer is the only observer who mentions the lachrymose mood in Korsakoff's syndrome of infectious etiology.

Pathology

As the alcoholic form of Korsakoff's psychosis is practically always associated with some degree of polyneuropathy, the usual degenerative changes of the peripheral nerves are found. These have been described by Jolliffe (see Chapter III). Relative to the brain changes in Korsakoff's psychosis Bumke and Kant point out that these correspond entirely to the changes in chronic alcoholism in general. The brain pathology does not seem to contribute to the understanding of the clinical picture. Nevertheless we shall present the older description of Mott and a few recent ones in Table 8.

Etiology and Treatment

This discussion of etiology deals solely with the alcoholic form. It has been frequently stated that Korsakoff's psychosis is more common among women than among men and this has been repeatedly misunderstood as meaning that there are more female than male Korsakoffs. This is not the case. According to both Kraepelin and Meggendorfer women constitute about one-third of all Korsakoffs. By actual count the men usually outnumber the women, but the relative incidence in inebriates is greater among women than among men. In the United States the ratio of male to female chronic alcoholics with and without psychosis is approximately 6:1. In the case of Korsakoff's psychosis Pollock's figures would give a male:female ratio of 1.7:1.0. Of

TABLE 8

Brain Changes in Alcoholic Korsakoff's Psychosis

Investigator	Description
Mott (1910)	"The brains are generally of good weight, of good convolutional pattern, and do not, as a rule, show much evidence of thickening of the pre-arachnoid membranes, increase of cerebrospinal fluid, or other obvious signs of cerebral wasting. "The ventricles are not granular, but there may be a few ependymal granulations in the lateral sacs of the fourth ventricle. Micro-scopical examination shows some wasting of the tangential fibers and subpial glial cell proliferation and felting but, as a rule, this is not marked. The fibre systems as a general rule are otherwise well preserved. There is no very marked glia cell proliferation in the cortex, and when sections are stained by the Nissl method the cells of the columns of Meynert are not distorted or poorly stained, their apical processes are not corkscrewed, and there is no marked coarse change of the cortical neurones as in general paralysis. There is no lymphocyte and plasma cell infiltration of the membranes and peri-vascular sheaths."
Carmichael and Stern (1931)	The lesions are almost always confined to the cerebral cortex; rarely there are slight changes in the thalamus; the lesions are entirely upon the cells—there is no tract degeneration. The outstanding finding is widespread deposit of lipochrome material in nerve and neuroglial cells in the cortex, especially in the Betz cells; this is also common around the blood vessels and in their walls. Lipochrome deposits are seen also in senile patients and those dying from "pro-longed exhausting diseases," but they are much greater in the Korsakoff patients. The only disease in which equally great lipo-chrome deposits are seen is pellagra.
Radu (1933)	Macroscopically the cerebrum shows a simple congestion, with edema and bloody extravasation into the pia mater; microscopically the lesions are abundant, especially in the frontal lobes of the cerebral cortex. The cellular lesions consist of a degenerative and a diffuse regenerative process.
Cobb and Coggeshall (1934)	The conspicuous lesion is nerve cell degeneration in the cerebral cortex; the changes are much like those in pellagra.
Guiraud, Ey and Bonnafous-Serieux (1938)	Destruction of many cortical cells; peripheral lysis of cytoplasm; areas of granular degeneration and disappearance of neurofibrils on the base and top of the great pyramidal cells; new formation of capillaries and hypertrophy of the walls of arterioles. Proliferation of oligodendroglia and Penfield degeneration in the white sub-stance; frequent hypertrophy and deformation of macroglia nuclei. Thick pia mater. In the putamen cytoplasmal lysis of many nerve cells, homogenization of nucleus, hyperpigmentation of macroglia; in the pallidus, cellular lysis and satellitosis. The thalamus less in-volved. Hypopigmentation of the substantia nigra cells. The two corpora mammillaria are fragile, with intense gliosis, increase of capillaries and lysis of nerve cells. On the level of the bulbus, diffuse gliosis and involvement of the olive cells.
Grünthal (b) (1939)	Circumscribed destruction of the corpora mammillaria.
Stevenson, McGowan and Allen (1941)	Increase of lipochrome in and about the nerve cells.

the references listed in this paper only about half of those in which the number of patients is stated specify the sex of the patients. From these it appears that the sex ratio is probably about 1:1. This ratio is the same as that occurring in polyneuropathy (Chapter III) and this agreement of the sex distribution of these two disorders is rather important. This fact should be made a point of departure for further etiological investigations.

A factor which cannot be neglected in the genesis of alcoholic Korsakoff's psychosis is the fact that among the alcoholic psychoses it shows the highest onset age. According to the statistics of Pollock (b) the average onset age for all alcoholic psychoses (first admissions to New York state hospitals, 1920–1923) was 43.7 years, but that for Korsakoff's psychosis was 51.4 years. High onset age is also reported by Meggendorfer—48.0 years, by Kauffmann (cit. Meggendorfer)—52.6 years, and by Bumke and Kant—in the fifties. This may mean that a longer period of drinking is required for Korsakoff's psychosis than for other alcoholic diseases, or that, as in the case of delirium tremens, particularly alcohol-resistant or alcohol-tolerant persons are subject to the disturbance and it is owing to their high tolerance that a longer drinking period results.

As in delirium tremens the forms of alcohol most productive of Korsakoff's psychosis are the high-proof liquors, but wine and beer drinkers are by no means immune. Kraepelin found 20 per cent beer drinkers, and Pollock (b) has, in his 1936–1937 sample, approximately 10 per cent wine and beer drinkers, while in his 1920–1923 sample the same group is approximately 14 per cent. It must be remembered that these percentages, as they are based on the statements of patients, cannot be taken at face value.

The early history of etiological theories of Korsakoff's syndrome is reflected in the changes in the designation of this disturbance. Originally Korsakoff called it "polyneuritic amnestic psychosis." Although he pointed out that the amnestic psychosis occurred in connection with nonalcoholic conditions, he assumed that polyneuropathy was always present. He emphasized that the polyneuropathy was in some cases of so slight a degree as to be completely overshadowed by the mental picture. Tibing; Regis; and Babinski [all cit. Bonhoeffer (c)], and also Gudden, showed that the disturbance described by Korsakoff occurred also in the absence of polyneuropathy. In consequence of this Korsakoff dropped his original term for the disease and called it "psychic-toxemic-cerebropathy," since he thought that all conditions in which the amnestic disturbance appeared had a toxic process in common. Jolly [cit. Bonhoeffer (*d*)], however, showed that this disturbance also occurred in conditions which had definitely no toxic involvements, as head injuries and strangulation. Jolly proposed to call this disturbance Korsakoff's syndrome since it was not a disease *sui generis* as Korsakoff had assumed. In more modern terms this means that Korsakoff's syndrome is a phenotype but not a genotype. Bonhoeffer (*d*) proposed that the alcoholic form, which is practically always connected with polyneuropathy and is distinguishable from the nonalcoholic forms, should be called Korsakoff's psychosis, while the other forms should be called Korsakoff's syndrome. This suggestion has been widely accepted, although the terms are still used interchangeably by some authors. The standpoint involved in this may be revised, however, if future researches should reveal common factors in all forms of this syndrome.

As early as 1928 Meggendorfer pointed out that there was a nutritional disturbance present in patients with the alcoholic form of Korsakoff's psychosis. However, he could not decide whether this was due to the long lasting alcohol poisoning or to some other cause. In subsequent years the etiology of alcoholic polyneuropathy was equated with the etiology of beriberi, that is, with a vitamin B_1 deficiency. This led to the treatment of Korsakoff patients with vitamin B complex and vitamin B_1. The reports of Corwin; Bowman, Goodhart and Jolliffe; Rosenbaum and Merritt; Wexberg (*b*); and Norbury, indicate that the use of thiamin chloride, particularly in connection with vitamin rich diets, is sometimes associated not only with a cure of the neuropathic symptoms but also with a partial alleviation of the mental disturbances. This has been regarded by some investigators as an indication of the vitamin deficiency origin of the Korsakoff psychosis, inasmuch as it is dependent on polyneuropathy. Askey, for example, stated that "Korsakoff psychosis is due to altered brain cell function, possibly due to thiamin lack." Wortis and Jolliffe, however, have recently stated that "the role of thiamin . . . still remains to be determined."

The Korsakoff psychosis has sometimes been called a chronic delirium tremens [e.g., Chotzen; Bonhoeffer (*d*)]. The fact that delirium tremens is of short duration when precipitated by some passing condition, but that it becomes chronic in the presence of severe polyneuropathy, and sometimes disappears with the polyneuropathy, would suggest that polyneuropathy may be a fixating factor, which is likely to turn delirium tremens into the chronic form of Korsakoff's psychosis. Since, however, not every delirium tremens in patients with polyneuropathy develops into Korsakoff's psychosis, one must assume that the combination of the two conditions is not a sufficient cause but that at least a third factor must be involved. The quest for this third factor is one of the tasks for future research in chronic alcoholism.

The treatment of Korsakoff's psychosis in the past was the same as that for polyneuropathy, namely, largely strychnine, and was naturally no more successful. As late as 1933 Korsakoff's psychosis was considered practically incurable [Siebert (b)]. Sporadic attempts with insulin were made by Klemperer and Weissmann, by Bostock and by Talkington and Cheavens. Reifenstein and Davidoff (b) used benzedrine without success. It was not until 1939 that reports on treatment with vitamin B₁ became frequent [Martimor and Neveu; Bostock; Corwin; Bowman, Goodhart and Jolliffe; Rosenbaum and Merritt; Wexberg (b); Talkington and Cheavens; Brodsky; Norbury]. Experience with this treatment of Korsakoff's psychosis has not advanced sufficiently to permit of final judgment. Wortis and Jolliffe believe that it is not specific for the mental symptoms. From the entire literature it is apparent that patients with Korsakoff's psychosis almost invariably suffer from nutritional deficiencies and their treatment with vitamins is therefore highly indicated irrespective of whether or not the mental symptoms are improved.

Fatality rates from 25 to 50 per cent have been reported (Meggendorfer; Rosenbaum and Merritt; Radu). The mortality from this disease among women seems to be greater than among men. Age appears to be one of the factors influencing prognosis as the disturbance seems to be more serious in young patients (Radu). Under the vitamin regime the prognosis *ad vitam* must be revised. There is, however, insufficient evidence at hand as yet.

V. ACUTE ALCOHOLIC HALLUCINOSIS

Acute alcoholic hallucinosis is an easily described syndrome which, however, closely resembles several other disorders, in its acute as well as in certain of its chronic phases. Largely due to its resemblance to certain onset forms of schizophrenia, in particular, catatonia, there are wide divergencies in the description of the course and the occurrence of alcoholic hallucinosis and also, to some extent, in the description of the symptoms.

Acute alcoholic hallucinosis (and it is assumed here that all schizophrenic states are excluded) occurs only in chronic alcoholics and not as a manifestation of acute intoxication. It apparently develops after a much shorter period of drinking and consequently at a lower onset age than delirium tremens [Bonhoeffer (c); Schroeder; Tetz].

It is referred to in the German literature sometimes as "acute alcoholic insanity," and in the French literature it is still sometimes referred to by the name given it in 1847 by Marcel, *folie d'ivrogne*. Kraepelin has occasionally referred to it as "acute alcoholic paranoia."

The main issues in the psychiatric literature center around (a) the relation of acute alcoholic hallucinosis to delirium tremens and (b) its relation to schizophrenia. All the aspects of this psychosis, including etiology and even its occurrence, are discussed most profitably in terms of differentials. Before entering into that part of the discussion, a brief description of the clinical picture will be given.

Clinical Picture

The onset is sometimes sudden; more frequently, however, there is a prodromal stage with general anxiety, headache, insomnia and increased sensitivity to sound. The main symptoms of the psychosis are fear, auditory hallucinations which are frequently phonemes, inclination to anxiety, misinterpretations and systematization with intact orientation and presence of mind (Bumke and Kant).

The speech is usually identified as coming from some definitely known or sometimes unknown person. At the height of the disturbance entire events are represented in the form of auditory hallucinations; for instance, a court trial of the patient may be represented in this way. In the beginning the statements made by the voices are of a simple character, such as "get along." Soon, however, they attain to reproachful and criticizing contents (Schroeder). An interesting feature is that the auditory hallucinations are usually the conversations of a number of persons talking about the patient in the third person (Kraepelin; Heilbronner). Bleuler (a) attributes diagnostic importance to this differential. Visions, although occurring in practically every patient, play a small role in the total psychotic picture of the individual. Cutaneous hallucinations also occur, such as the feeling of a cold breath or of fine rain on the skin. Suicide and suicidal attempts are frequent and are carried out with great energy. The extraordinary fear and the conviction of a terrible end make the patient choose this way out (Schroeder).

Bromberg and Schilder regard the suicide attempts as the expression of a tendency to self-castration and self-dismembering. According to these authors, homosexual tendencies appear openly or as thinly disguised symbolisms in the manifest contents of the psychosis. Davidson, on the other hand, found no overt homosexuality and only 2 patients with latent homosexuality among 30 patients with acute alcoholic hallucinosis. Curran, who studied 27 women having alcoholic hallucinosis, stated that the women showed in their hallucinations fear of removal of receptive sex organs and a general fear that their bodies might be injured. They showed great interest in their own bodies. Their sexual inferiority found expression in the hallucinosis in which they heard themselves called prostitutes. The reproach of homosexuality by voices was less frequently mentioned than in the case of men.

The bodily symptoms of chronic alcoholism are usually present but may not be marked, perhaps because of the lower age of the patients (Schroeder).

Relation to Delirium Tremens

The relationship between acute alcoholic hallucinosis and delirium tremens is assumed to be a close one by many authors. Jolly (cit. Schroeder) has called it *die systematisierende Varietät der deliranten Form des akuten Alkoholismus.* Magnan (*a*), as well as Fabre (cit. Tetz) and also Auglade (cit. Tetz), refer to it as *délire systématisé alcoolique,* and Papadaki describes it as the *délire alcoolique du type auditive.* Bonhoeffer (*c*) and Kraepelin do not go so far, but believe that delirium tremens and hallucinosis are different manifestations of the same process. In the French literature, even at present, one occasionally finds delirium tremens and acute alcoholic hallucinosis thrown together under the designation, *délire hallucinatoire aigu.* Tetz, and with him many other recent investigators, however, state that careful comparison of the symptoms yields such differences that it is impossible to accept acute hallucinosis and delirium tremens as forms of the same mental disturbance.

The essential differences between these two alcoholic psychoses, aside from the dominance of auditory hallucinations in the one and visual hallucinations in the other, will be examined here:

1. In contrast to delirium tremens, patients with acute alcoholic hallucinosis are usually well oriented; their perception and attention are not impaired and generally they are willing to talk; they are rather accessible (Schroeder).

2. While delirium tremens patients accept their hallucinations and delusions, the acute hallucinosis patients seek for explanations (Meggendorfer).

3. Generally the hallucinations of acute hallucinosis do not have the illusional coloring of those in delirium tremens; they are less dependent on sense perception and cannot be altered by suggestion (Schroeder).

4. There is motor unrest only at the very beginning in acute hallucinosis but even then much less than in delirium tremens (Schroeder).

5. Acute alcoholic hallucinosis is much less dependent upon the consumption of high-proof spirits than is delirium tremens (Kraepelin; Schroeder; Bumke and Kant), and as a matter of fact there is quite a high proportion of beer- and wine-drinkers among the former [Pollock (b)].

6. It is generally accepted that the precipitating factors of delirium tremens are never present in acute alcoholic hallucinosis and that there is also no relation to epileptic seizures [Schroeder; Pohlisch (c); Cosack; and Meggendorfer]. From the etiological standpoint this is one of the most important differentials.

7. Although few pathological differences are known, because of the low mortality and consequent lack of autopsy material in acute alcoholic hallucinosis, one difference is well established: In acute alcoholic hallucinosis, especially at the beginning, there is a definite leucopenia of 3,500 to 4,000 white blood cells, while in delirium tremens there is a leucocytosis (Streltschuk).

8. The duration of acute hallucinosis is considerably longer than that of delirium tremens.

9. Lastly there is a difference in personality and constitution in the two disturbances. The differential in the constitutional factor is definite. There is general agreement that patients with acute alcoholic hallucinosis have a high occurrence of psychosis, inebriety, psychopathy and suicide in their families, while this is not the case in delirium tremens patients [Pohlisch (c); Cosack; Meggendorfer; Kolle (b); Schroeder; Bonhoeffer (c); and Alexander].

The presence of a personality differential is not so well established. Bonhoeffer's (c) contention that patients with acute alcoholic hallucinosis came from a higher educational level than delirium tremens patients has not been accepted as a valid observation [Pohlisch (c); Tetz; Bumke and Kant; and E. Meyer (a)].

On the other hand, there is fair agreement on the point that delirium tremens patients are largely extroverts or cyclothymic normal personalities, while patients with acute alcoholic hallucinosis are introverts or frankly schizothymic personalities. Hoch found in delirium tremens patients only 12.5 per cent introverts, but in acute alcoholic hallucinosis 60.5 per cent. This is in good agreement with the findings of

Pohlisch (*c*); and even Bigelow, Lehrmann and Palmer, who do not accept the personality factor as a differential diagnostic point, admit that the delirium tremens patients are, to a greater degree, reminiscent of the manic personality.

Relation to Dementia Praecox

The similarity between acute alcoholic hallucinosis and some schizophrenic episodes, or the onset of schizophrenia, particularly of the catatonic form, is rather marked and undoubtedly such episodes have not infrequently been erroneously diagnosed as acute alcoholic hallucinosis. Some students of inebriety represent the extreme standpoint of entirely denying the existence of a clinical entity of alcoholic hallucinosis. Henderson and Gillespie regard the term as a misnomer and, without assigning alcoholic hallucinosis to any definite psychiatric entity, state that in these cases drinking is merely a symptom of an underlying instability. Karlan, too, refers to an underlying constitution without specifying any psychiatric syndrome. Bleuler (*b*) has classified acute alcoholic hallucinosis definitely with the schizophrenias. Generally, however, the standpoint is that there is an acute hallucinosis of chronic alcoholic origin, but that this is a rare condition, and that perhaps in the majority the psychoses so diagnosed belong to the schizophrenic psychoses in which drinking is merely symptomatic.

Schroeder, in 1912, pointed out that great caution must be exercised in the diagnosis of acute alcoholic hallucinosis, especially if a prodromal stage of hypochondriasis and of exaggerated self-observation precedes it. A diagnosis of dementia praecox rather than of acute alcoholic hallucinosis should also be made when alcohol indulgence shortly before the onset can be excluded, when the fear is not very pronounced and when at the onset affect is incongruous with the content of the representations. Delusions of smell and taste, independent motoric symptoms, mannerisms, negativism, indifference and bizarre ideas also contraindicate the diagnosis of acute alcoholic hallucinosis. Bumke and Kant did not believe that alcoholic hallucinosis could be segregated as an exogenous clinical entity "since latent schizophrenic drinkers constitute a large percentage of patients with alcoholic hallucinosis."

Wolfensberger reported on several patients who had originally been diagnosed as having acute alcoholic hallucinosis, but were later recognized as dementia praecox. Minski also reported on 3 patients with hallucinosis, 2 of whom were later found to be psychopathic personalities and 1 to have manic-depressive psychosis. Pohlisch (c) found a pre-dominance of schizoid individuals among the patients diagnosed as having acute alcoholic hallucinosis and suggested a possible genetic relationship with schizophrenia. All patients showed asocial behavior and less affectivity than most delirious patients. Tetz frequently found transitions into schizophrenia and said that in his patients terminal states could have been diagnosed as paranoiac dementia.

Wyrsch (a) stated as the main differentiating factor between alco-holic hallucinosis and schizophrenia the fact that in the former the patient is auto-physically well oriented and continues to live in the daily world of his normal life.

In his recent textbook, Noyes states that the "present tendency is to look upon it as a psychogenic reaction liberated by alcoholic excess rather than as a purely toxic expression. Many factors suggest a close relationship to schizophrenia and, in some cases, lead one to believe that the disorder is a schizophrenic reaction released by alcohol." Huber distinguishes two forms of alcoholic hallucinosis:

One in which the alcoholic factor is apparent and which may be consid-ered the auditory complement of delirium tremens, and another in which beside the alcoholic factor a schizophrenic component is evident. There the symptoms of hallucinosis either become schizophrenic in quality or are accompanied by an additional complex of schizophrenic symptoms. This latter form frequently results in schizophrenia. Whether alcoholic halluci-nosis is a purely alcoholic disease or a specific reaction to alcoholic intoxica-tion of a basically schizophrenic disposition can not be decided at present. It must be considered, however, that alcoholic hallucinosis is an indepen-dent syndrome and that it may indirectly cause the outbreak of a latent schizophrenia.

On the other hand, Davidson has recently expressed the opinion that "in view of the fact that in the vast majority of cases the syndrome occurs in connection with alcoholism, even if alcohol is admittedly not the sole cause, the significance of alcoholism in the problem requires investigation." This, one must agree, is a reasonable standpoint since, in an effort to arrive at a diagnostic truth, the role which alcohol plays, at least in giving a distinct coloring to a schizophrenic psychosis, has been lost from sight.

The psychoanalytic interpretation of alcoholic hallucinosis as given by Bromberg and Schilder is practically identical with that of schizo-phrenia and this strengthens the arguments of those who maintain that the majority of patients with alcoholic hallucinosis should be placed in the schizophrenic group.

Further factors which would make it appear that in a great number of instances this psychosis is of schizophrenic, rather than alcoholic nature, are the following: (a) An onset age significantly lower than the average for alcoholic psychosis in general. (b) A high incidence of psychotic heredity in these patients is found in contrast to patients with delirium tremens and Korsakoff's psychosis in whom the incidence of psychotic heredity is not greater than in the general population. (c) Acute alcoholic hallucinosis is less dependent upon the consumption of high-proof spirits than the other alcoholic psychoses.

It may be mentioned that acute alcoholic hallucinosis has also been classified with the manic-depressive psychoses [e.g., C. Schneider (cit. Davidson); Hart; and de Ponte], but these suggestions have not met with any degree of acceptance.

It would appear that in state hospitals, at least in New York, acute alcoholic hallucinosis is diagnosed more frequently than delirium tremens and, as a matter of fact, it there constitutes the largest diagnostic group among all of the alcoholic psychoses [Pollock (b)].* When, however, statistics are obtained from psychiatrists whose diagnoses tend to exclude any instance which suggests schizophrenia, acute alcoholic hallucinosis appears to be one of the rarest alcoholic diseases. Thus Kraepelin found 1 alcoholic hallucinosis for every 5 delirium tremens patients; Schroeder gives the ratio as 1:21; Heilig as 1:34 and Bleuler (b), 1:44. Wolfensberger stated that the admissions for acute alcoholic hallucinosis to Burghölzli Hospital were 1.4 per 1,000 of all alcoholic admissions.

Etiology

In 1906, Wernicke expressed the view that alcoholic hallucinosis is a symptom complex which is found in a wide range of acute and chronic disorders and from which etiologically no conclusions can be drawn.

The preceding discussion shows that the position relative to the etiology of acute alcoholic hallucinosis has hardly changed since Wernicke. There have been a few attempts at establishing disease processes as etiological factors in hallucinosis. Thus, Damaye (b) suggested an underlying septicemia and Hartman (cit. Tetz) saw the pathogenesis of hallucinosis in the mutual action between lung tissue and Koch's bacillus, especially in the early stages when the products of the impaired lung metabolism have a neurotoxic character. Korbsch thought that

---

*It must be considered that because of their physical condition fewer delirium tremens patients go to mental hospitals.

the same metabolic processes evoked by prolonged drinking were operative in delirium tremens and in acute hallucinosis and that differentiation was brought about by personality factors. However, the metabolic processes which have been fairly well established in chronic alcoholics developing delirium tremens have never been shown for patients with acute alcoholic hallucinosis. Dick and Colbert, who examined 144 patients with alcoholic hallucinosis, found that the percentage of patients with hallucinations was higher in a series of patients with sinusitis than in a series of patients without sinusitis. They admitted, however, that the difference was not so great as to permit the conclusion that chronic sinusitis may have a marked etiological significance. These etiological theories have not been supported by other observers.

In view of the somewhat obscure status of the present knowledge of acute alcoholic hallucinosis it would seem that further research is indicated. On the other hand, it is not apparent that any important contribution toward the knowledge of the alcoholic psychoses could be expected from such researches.

In view of the large percentage of schizophrenics among patients with alcoholic hallucinosis, and in view of the meager knowledge of the true alcoholic hallucinosis, little can be said about treatment. Davidson has pointed out that "the treatment of the non-alcoholic groups ought to be given on lines indicative for the respective disorders." For the alcoholic group dietary treatment, promotion of sleep, the administration of fruit juices and treatment with strychnine sulfate have been suggested. Dietary treatment is indicated inasmuch as all chronic alcoholics suffer more or less from nutritional deficiencies. The general agreement is that the prognosis for acute alcoholic hallucinosis is benign. The course of the psychosis depends on whether the patient is placed soon enough in the proper environment. Prompt hospitalization usually tends to shorten the duration according to most observers.

VI. ALCOHOLIC PARANOID CONDITION

While Bleuler (b) and Henderson and Gillespie have rejected alcoholic paranoid condition as an alcoholic mental disorder, and while their classificatory systems have found many followers, it is not possible as yet to exclude this condition quite categorically. The late onset age hardly warrants the assumption of mere incidental drinking in some schizophrenic psychoses. Either a specific alcoholic psychosis must be assumed or, and this is more likely, the late precipitation of a latent schizophrenic condition. At least the alcoholic coloring of these states must be admitted. We believe, therefore, that a brief description of the alcoholic paranoid condition is not out of place in this chapter.

Bowman (a) has described this condition as follows:

While many paranoid ideas are often found in cases of chronic deterioration due to alcohol, there is a rather specific type of paranoid reaction which warrants a brief description. Some cases of chronic alcoholism develop a paranoid attitude without the other signs of chronic deterioration. Delusions of various sorts may occur, but one particular type is so common as to be almost pathognomonic. The patient, who is usually a male, develops ideas of infidelity on the part of his consort. In the beginning these ideas may appear only when the patient is under the influence of alcohol. After he has sobered up, he may deny having expressed such ideas. Frequently he tries to gloss things over, stating that he may have said them when he was drunk but that he really has no such ideas and that he knows there is no basis to such accusations. As time goes on, these delusions become more fixed and the patient finally expresses them at all times. In cases which do not show intellectual deterioration, the history given by the patient is often so logical and reasonable that one cannot be certain as to whether or not the ideas expressed are delusions. In cases with deterioration, the reasons given are commonly so bizarre that one has no difficulty in classifying the patient as psychotic. These cases are of considerable medicolegal importance and are so difficult to prove that committing physicians will often refuse to sign commitment papers. One may feel absolutely certain that the patient has delusions and yet there is not sufficient proof to warrant legal commitment. These patients frequently attack their wives, particularly when under the effect of alcohol. For this reason it is important to see that such a case is committed in order to protect the wife and family. Case investigation by a well-trained psychiatric social worker will often enable one to make a definite diagnosis. Another device which will sometimes settle the question is to interview both the patient and his wife at the same time and have them both tell their stories. Under such conditions one will often find that it is possible to establish the true facts of the case. The diagnosis is commonly made on the history of chronic alcoholism and the characteristic set of delusions. The basis for developing such ideas is felt by some to depend upon an incipient paranoid condition or schizophrenia which is released by alcohol. In some cases impotence on the part of the husband seems to give rise to the ideas. In still other cases the wife's growing dislike of her husband because of his alcoholism seems to be a factor. Homosexuality may be considered a possible cause with the husband projecting his own desires for sex relations with other men onto his wife.

VII. CHRONIC ALCOHOLIC DETERIORATION

The "continued use of excessive amounts of alcohol over a long period of time produces certain characteristic physical and mental conditions which are best grouped under the heading of chronic deterioration" [Bowman (*a*)]. Since this condition can hardly be described in terms of a clinical entity, and since its manifestations, so far as they are not physical, are rather on the level of conduct than of symbolic functions, it has not been consistently classified as an alcoholic psychosis. It has been discussed more frequently in connection with addiction without psychosis than in connection with discussion of the alcoholic mental disorders. This may be attributed in part at least to the fact that persons with chronic alcoholic deterioration not following any definite psychosis are infrequently admitted to mental hospitals. On the other hand, chronic alcoholic deterioration, through which perhaps every chronic alcoholic goes if he survives until the picture becomes manifest, is that manifestation of abnormal drinking which gives it the character of a social disease. The condition, irrespective of whether or not it should be classified as a psychosis, is *par excellence* a matter for psychiatric consideration.

From the standpoint of research, chronic alcoholic deterioration does not offer any urgent problems. The problems involved are more of a therapeutic and administrative nature. As such these problems are important.

Bleuler (*b*) gives the following description of the mental picture in chronic alcoholic deterioration.

In the psychological field there is ethical degeneration, dulling of the finer sentiments, and brutality. This is the picture usually given, but it is not quite true. The originally decent alcoholic remains attached to his club and is very sympathetic with the misfortunes of his fellow men. He can become enthusiastic about ethical aims. He not only expresses himself with fine sentiments but may really experience them. If he is an artist he may create works which are expressions of fine sentiments, ethic and tact. Nevertheless the descriptions of his brutality and impulsive actions are not without foundation, for he does behave brutally in the presence of affects and under certain conditions. This is especially likely to occur at home, where he is subject to the overt or implied reproaches of the family; or at work, in which he cannot persist, or whenever a difference of opinion arises. The fact that these alcoholics, when the occasion arises, have at their disposal the most beautiful sentiments, and actually genuine ones, makes them especially dangerous, because they do not dissimulate these feelings.

The most important change of the affects and sentiments of the chronic alcoholics is their lability. With this is coupled a great affect tone to all experience which makes the affect master over the will and common sense. This lability of affect makes consistent goal-behavior impossible. Will power is markedly diminished. The euphoric attitude makes it possible to perceive misery as something good or, at least, not very bad. The exaggerated ego reference forms the basis of the suspiciousness of the alcoholic.

The memory is impaired. Much of the behavior is dependent on the oblique position of the alcoholic towards his surroundings. In spite of his aggressiveness it is easily seen that he is actually on the defensive in relation to those who do not indulge in alcohol. Orientation remains intact in the uncomplicated cases. Jealousy is a frequent manifestation.

The physical characteristics of chronic alcoholic deterioration are described by Bowman (a) as follows:

There is commonly dilatation of the facial capillaries, especially of the nose. This, however, may occur even in teetotalers. The heart often shows myocardial changes, although these may be the result of the alcoholic's general way of life. There is frequently a "bloated" look, and the muscles are flabby. In those who use distilled spirits there is likely to be chronic gastritis. Cirrhosis of the liver may develop, although the relationship of this to the consumption of alcohol has not yet been determined. Tremors, usually fine, appear commonly; sometimes there is twitching and choreiform movements. There is often pain in the calves of the legs, sometimes tenderness over the large nerve trunks, and peripheral neuritis. Pupillary changes are frequent, the reaction being often sluggish. The libido is oftentimes increased or unchanged while potency is diminished or absent. It is a question, however, whether the alcohol has led to impotency or impotence to alcohol indulgence. Epileptiform attacks, sometimes called "rum fits," may occur, but these are not always clearly distinguishable from true epilepsy. Physical capacity and stamina are impaired, and there is marked diminution of disease resistance.

VIII. "ALCOHOLIC EPILEPSY" AND DIPSOMANIA

The questions of dipsomania and of "alcoholic epilepsy" are so intricately interwoven in the alcohol literature that the best course appears to be to treat these questions jointly.

It has been stated in the Introduction that the present view is that neither "alcoholic epilepsy" nor dipsomania is caused by alcohol indulgence but that they are alcoholic manifestations of underlying mental or nervous disorders. Strictly speaking, neither of these disorders is an "alcoholic mental disorder." Nevertheless the position in these conditions is different from mere incidental drinking in, let us say, incipient schizophrenia. The latter may be largely neglected in the discussion of the alcoholic psychoses without detriment. Dipsomania, however, even if regarded as a secondary manifestation of some other disorder, must be considered here, since the excessive alcoholic indulgence in this case has a definite function in the course of the underlying disorder and, moreover, the periodic drinking may turn into steady drinking with a subsequent secondary addiction. On the other hand, this subject is not at present of sufficient importance to warrant such detailed discussion as accorded to the disorders dealt with in preceding sections. The presentation of this question will be restricted, therefore, largely to the tabulation of opinions, so that this section is rather in the nature of a supplement to the preceding ones.

Dipsomania has been postulated by some investigators as a disease *sui generis*, but much more frequently as a form of epilepsy or of manic-depressive psychosis. A discussion of so-called alcoholic epilepsy should, therefore, precede the discussion of dipsomania.

The problems of "alcoholic epilepsy" may be stated as follows:

1. Can alcohol provoke epilepsy in persons having no epileptic disposition?

2. Does alcohol precipitate latent epilepsy?

3. Are epileptics apt to become abnormal drinkers? The question of heredity is involved in this problem.

Naturally, these questions are not mutually exclusive although the answers have been frequently so represented by many investigators.

Data relative to the coincidence of epilepsy and abnormal drinking are presented in Table 9.

TABLE 9

Coincidence of Epilepsy and Abnormal Drinking

A. INCIDENCE OF EPILEPTICS AMONG CHRONIC ALCOHOLIC PATIENTS

Investigators	*Year*	No. of Chronic Alcoholics	Per cent Epileptics
Echeverria	1881	572	45.0
Moeli	1900	?	30.0
Witten (cit. Hoppe)	1905	?	23.0
Wassermeyer	1908	?	40.0
Pohlisch (*b*)	1927	162	27.0
Drouet (cit. Meggendorfer)	1928	526	10.0
Mignot	1933	86	27.0
Minski	1938	50	2.0

B. INCIDENCE OF ABNORMAL DRINKERS AMONG EPILEPTIC PATIENTS

Investigators	*Year*	No. of Epileptics	Per cent Abnormal Drinkers
Küffner	1927	?	8.0
Notkin	1928	40	12.5
Bratz (cit. Meggendorfer)	1928	400	20.0
Küenzi	1929	129	26.0
Lennox	1941	1,254	6.0

The standpoints relative to the role of alcohol in epilepsy as represented in the literature are given in Table 10; the role of heredity in "alcoholic epilepsy" will be dealt with in detail in a chapter on "Alcohol, Germ Damage and Heredity."*

On the whole it may be stated:

(A) Abnormal drinking is definitely greater among epileptics than in the general population.

(B) There is a high concomitance of alcohol addicts and epileptics in families with psychopathic heredity.

(C) There is an acceleration of epileptic seizures in genuine epileptics through the use of alcohol.

(D) There is some indication that alcohol may precipitate latent epilepsy.

(E) There is insufficient evidence that epilepsy is caused by alcoholic excess.

Epilepsy has been frequently postulated as the basis of dipsomania. At present there is more inclination to place this behavior disorder in the manic-depressive group. The conflicting nature of opinions is in part ascribable to the fact that frequently any drinking at irregular intervals is designated as dipsomania irrespective of whether or not it shows truly pathological aspects.

TABLE 10

Opinions on the Role of Alcohol in Epilepsy

Year	Author	Opinion
1874	Magnan (b)	Ethyl alcohol has only a precipitatory role in epilepsy but absinthe is causative of it.
1881	Echeverria	572 cases: in 257 of these, history of alcoholism and epilepsy in sequence; in 126 epilepsy resulted from alcoholic excess in conjunction with other nervous and mental diseases; in 189 drinking really caused by epilepsy and exaggerated it.
1897	Joffroy and Serveaux	Neither ethyl alcohol nor absinthe can cause epilepsy but merely precipitate it.
1897	Krafft-Ebing	Epilepsy may be caused by changes in the brain due to alcoholic excesses. Any alcoholic drink can produce it. 10 per cent of all alcoholics have epileptic incidents.
1897	Neumann	Probably 10 per cent of all epileptics owe their condition to alcohol.
1897	Wartmann	Alcohol does not cause epilepsy in persons who have no latent epilepsy due to hereditary disposition.

*To be published in a later volume of this work.

Year	Author	Opinion
1898	Reissig	Alcohol in combination with damages (brain lesions) may cause epilepsy.
1899	Bratz	51 alcoholic epileptics with epileptic attacks before alcoholism—16 some inferiority of nervous system before alcoholism—22 perfectly well before alcoholism—13
1905	Triboulet, Mathieu and Mignot	2 general groups: (a) alcoholism associated with mental disease, i.e., dipsomania, alcoholic jealousy; and (b) genuine alcoholic mental disease, i.e., hallucinosis, Korsakoff, *épilepsie alcoolique d'origine toxique*, etc.
1908	Gelma	Absinthe can make an epileptic of a sane person.
1909	Redlich	Same opinion as Wartmann.
1922	Ossipoff	Did not believe in causal relation. Similarities between epilepsy and dipsomania due to fact that alcohol promotes the appearance of epileptic states.
1927	Pohlisch (b)	162 cases of delirium tremens. 44 (27 per cent) had one or more epileptic attacks shortly before first delirium. Epilepsy and delirium tremens are etiologically similar reaction forms of the brain to chronic alcoholism.
1927	Küffner	Did not believe in low alcohol resistance of epilepsy. 100 women given 40–80 cc. alcohol in grog. No increase in number of attacks and no "pathological intoxication." On the other hand, epileptics are inclined to alcoholic excesses.
1928	Notkin	40 epileptic women: 4 with dipsomanic history and 1 who became an addict 3½ years after onset of epilepsy. Hence alcohol part of symptom complex in 1 case, in 4, the precipitating factor.
1928	Meggendorfer	Distinguished between alcoholic and genuine epilepsy, the former caused directly by alcoholic abuse and affecting young people with tainted heredity (not necessarily epileptic).
1929	Jablow	Epileptic syndromes may occur in chronic alcoholism as the belated appearance of latent epilepsy.
1930	Bregman and Gleichgewicht	"Alcoholism is regarded as a factor of first order" in the causation of epilepsy.
1935	Galant (a)	2 alcoholic patients. Epilepsy can be induced by alcoholic excess, and alcohol leads to congenital feeblemindedness, epilepsy, and epileptoid psychopathy in second generation.
1936	Henderson and Gillespie	Epileptiform episodes occur in alcoholics but do not constitute monosymptomatic disorders and should not be called "alcoholic epilepsy."
1937	Bleuler (b)	Alcoholic epilepsy is nothing but epilepsy and is not to be classed with the alcoholic mental disorders.

Year	*Author*	*Opinion*
1939	Froment, Masson and Brun	Epilepsy due more or less to alcoholism alone would not manifest itself before the age of 40. Such late epilepsy is rather rare.
1940	Lévy	In some drinkers epileptiform attacks may occur, but not true epilepsy. The former is always incomplete. The subcortical tonic element is lacking.
1941	Lennox	"Alcohol is a narcotic and when given in large amounts to animals, it produces sleep, but not seizures. Apparently in man it precipitates convulsive attacks only in those who are subject to seizures."

In Table 11, we are listing etiological theories and their supporters.

TABLE 11

Etiology of Dipsomania

Etiology	*Authors*
Hereditary disposition	Magnan (*a*); Bezzola (cit. Gaupp); Marguliès; Gaupp; Dobnigg and von Economo; Schule (cit. Gaupp); Meggendorfer; Stora and Gaultier; Enteres.
Epileptic origin	Schuster; Gaupp; Roemer; Westphal; Wirth (the latter 3 cit. Meggendorfer); Kraepelin.
Manic-depressive origin	Griesinger (cit. Gaupp); Pappenheim; Meggendorfer; Korsakoff; Rybakoff (cit. Ossipoff); Daumezon; Ossipoff; Schultze; Storch; Rieger; Grable (the latter 2 cit. Meggendorfer); Bleuler (*b*). (The latter admits also epileptic origin.)
Disturbance of mid-brain	Bonhoeffer (*b*); Hoff and Poetzl; Riebeling; Pichard and Liber.

A number of etiologies are represented by one or two investigators only. Pisk mentions postencephalitic personality; Wingfield postulates head injuries. Peserico mentions merely "sensations of thirst."

Dipsomania in women is reported to be rare and has been related to menstrual disturbances by Krafft-Ebing; Gaupp; Wingfield; and Daumezon.

In general it may be stated that at present with few exceptions (e.g., Courbon and Tusques) dipsomania is not regarded as an independent disease but largely as a manifestation of the manic-depressive type without excluding epileptic origins. The organic theories as yet suggested have not met with any wide acceptance, in spite of the fact that most investigators believe that an organic basis most likely exists. While the manic-depressive and epileptic character of most dipsomaniacs is obvious, it is an insufficient explanation. A special factor whether organic or not must be postulated. Dipsomania still remains a challenging problem.

BIBLIOGRAPHY FOR PART I

ABRAHAM, K. The psychological relation between sexuality and alcoholism. Int. J. Psycho-Anal. **7**: 2, 1926.

ACHARD, C., LÉVY, J. and WELLISCH, F. Modifications chimiques des éléments inorganiques du sang au cours du delirium tremens et chez des animaux alcoolisés. C. R. Soc. Biol., Paris **108**: 620, 1931.

ADAMS, E. W. What is addiction? Brit. J. Inebr. **33**: 1, 1935.

DE AJURIAGUERRA, J. and NEVEU, P. Traitement des troubles mentaux de l'alcoolisme. Gaz. Hôp., Paris **111**: 817, 1938.

ALCOHOLICS ANONYMOUS. New York, Works Publishing Co., 1939.

ALEXANDER, L. Alcoholism and mental disease. In: Mental Health (Amer. Ass. Advancement Sci., Publ. No. 9), p. 83. Lancaster, Science Press, 1939.

ALLEN, E. B. Alcoholism as a psychiatric medical problem. N.Y. St. J. Med. **38**: 1492, 1938.

ALZHEIMER. Das Delirium alcoholicum febrile Magnan's. Zbl. Nervenheilk. Psychiat. **27**: 437, 1904.

ANGYAL, A. Phenomena resembling lilliputian hallucinations in schizophrenia. Arch. Neurol. Psychiat., Chicago **36**: 34, 1936.

ANONYMOUS. Can the alcoholic become a moderate drinker? Ment. Hyg. **23**: 80, 1939.

ARNDT, M. Über die Glykosurie der Alkoholdeliranten. Mschr. Psychiat. Neurol. **27**: 222, 1910.

ASKEY, J. M. The use of vitamins in the treatment of alcoholic diseases. Calif. West. Med. **51**: 294, 1939.

BALDIE, A. (a) Alcoholic craving. Lancet **221**: 434, 1931.

——— (b) The causation, treatment and control of the alcohol habit. Brit. J. Inebr. **30**: 45, 1932.

BANCROFT, W. D., GUTSELL, R. S. and RUTZLER, J. E. Reversible coagulation in living tissue; XI. Proc. nat. Acad. Sci., Washington **19**: 85, 1933.

BAONVILLE, H. and TITECA, J. Le rôle de sevrage alcoolique comme cause occasionnelle de la crise de delirium tremens. J. belge Neurol. Psychiat. **37**: 135, 1937.

BARGUES, M. and BERTON, M. Le liquide céphalo-rachidien dans les psychopathies alcooliques. J. Méd., Bordeaux **115**: 134, 1938.

——— and GRIMAL. Le butyl-ethyl-barbiturate de sodium dans le traitement du delirium tremens. Ann. méd.-psychol. **94**: 439, 1936.

BARHAM, P. C. Some difficulties of the institutional treatment of alcohol and other drug addictions. Brit. J. Inebr. **28**: 1, 1930.

BARNES, F. H. The alcoholic problem. Med. Rec. **142**: 120, 1935.

BELL, R. M. and TALKINGTON, P. C. An evaluation of hydrotherapy in the treatment of delirium tremens. Amer. J. Psychiat. **95**: 161, 1938.

BENDER, L. (a) Anatomopathological data on personality function. Amer. J. Psychiat. **92**: 325, 1935.

——— (b) Gestalt function in visual motor patterns in organic disease of the brain. Arch. Neurol. Psychiat., Chicago **33**: 300, 1935.

———, CURRAN, F. J. and SCHILDER, P. Organisation of memory traces in the Korsakoff syndrome. Arch. Neurol. Psychiat., Chicago **39**: 482, 1938.

BENINDE, BONHOEFFER, K. and PARTSCH. Welchen Einfluss hat der während des Krieges innerhalb der bürgerlichen Bevölkerung verminderte Alkoholgenuss auf die geistige und körperliche Gesundheit des Volkes gehabt. Vjschr. gerichtl. Med. **59**: 1, 1920.

BENON, R. (*a*) Le delirium tremens. Bull. méd., Paris 44: 807, 1930.

———— (*b*) Alcoolisme et neuro-psychiatrie clinique. Bull. méd., Paris 52: 182, 1938.

———— (*c*) Épisode délirant alcoolique et responsabilité. Ann. Méd. lég. 17: 379, 1939.

BERINGER, K. and RUFFIN. Sensibilitätsstudien zur Frage des Funktionswandels bei Schizophrenen, Alkoholikern und Gesunden. Z. ges. Neurol. Psychiat. 140: 604, 1932.

BIGELOW, N. J. T., LEHRMANN, S. R. and PALMER, J. N. Personality in alcoholic disorders: acute hallucinosis and delirium tremens. Psychiat. Quart. 13: 732, 1939.

BILLINGS, E. C. A handbook of elementary psychobiology and psychiatry, pt. 3, p. 83. New York, The Macmillan Co., 1939.

BINDER, H. Über alkoholische Rauschzustände. Schweiz. Arch. Neurol. Psychiat. 35: 209; 36: 17, 1935.

BING, R. and SCHÖNBERG, S. Der pathologische Rausch. Schweiz. med. Wschr. 55: 157, 1925.

BINSWANGER, H. Klinische und charakterologische Untersuchungen an pathologisch Berauschten. Z. ges. Neurol. Psychiat. 152: 703, 1935.

BINSWANGER, K. Über schizoide Alkoholiker. Z. ges. Neurol. Psychiat. 60: 127, 1920.

BLEULER, E. (*a*) Dementia praecox. Leipzig, Deuticke, 1911.

———— (*b*) Lehrbuch der Psychiatrie. 6th ed. Berlin, J. Springer, 1937.

BLOOMBERG, W. Treatment of chronic alcoholism with amphetamine (benzedrine) sulfate. New Engl. J. Med. 220: 129, 1939.

BOETERS, H. Familienuntersuchungen bei einer Durchschnittsbevölkerung unter Berücksichtigung symptomatischer und deliranter Zustandsbilder. Z. ges. Neurol. Psychiat. 153: 90, 1935.

BOGEN, E. (*a*) Drunkenness; a quantitative study of acute alcoholic intoxication. J. Amer. med. Ass. 89: 1508, 1927.

———— (*b*) The human toxicology of alcohol. In: Alcohol and man (Emerson, H., ed.), p. 126. New York, The Macmillan Co., 1933.

BOLES, R. S. and CREW, R. S. Observations on chronic alcoholism and cirrhosis of the liver. Quart. J. Stud. Alc. 1: 464, 1940.

BONHOEFFER, K. (*a*) Der Geisteszustand der Alkoholdeliranten. Breslau, Trebnitz, Maretzke & Schles, 1897.

———— (*b*) Pathologisch-anatomische Untersuchungen an Alkoholdeliranten. Mschr. Psychiat. Neurol. 5: 265, 379, 1899.

———— (*c*) Die akuten Geisteskrankheiten der Gewohnheitstrinker. Jena, G. Fischer, 1901.

———— (*d*) Der Korsakowsche Symptomenkomplex in seinen Beziehungen zu den verschiedenen Krankheitsformen. Allg. Z. Psychiat. 61: 744, 1904.

BOSTOCK, J. Alcoholism and its treatment. Med. J. Aust. 26: 136, 1939.

BOSTROEM, A. Über Leberfunktionsstörung bei symptomatischen Psychosen insbesondere bei Alkoholdelirien. Z. ges. Neurol. Psychiat. 68: 48, 1921.

BOWMAN, K. M. (*a*) The practitioner's library (Blumer, G., ed.), IX, 349. New York, D. Appleton-Century Co., 1936.

———— (*b*) The treatment of acute deliria. Virginia med. Mon. 67: 724, 1940.

————, GOODHART, R. and JOLLIFFE, N. Observations on the role of vitamin B_1 in the etiology and treatment of Korsakoff psychosis. J. nerv. ment. Dis. 90: 569, 1939.

———— and KEISER, S. Treatment of disturbed patients with sodium chloride orally and intravenously in hypertonic solutions. Arch. Neurol. Psychiat., Chicago 41: 702, 1939.

————, WORTIS, H. and KEISER, S. The treatment of delirium tremens. J. Amer. med. Ass. 112: 1217, 1939.

BRATZ. Alkohol und Epilepsie. Allg. Z. Psychiat. 56: 334, 1899.

BREGMAN, L. E. and GLEICHGEWICHT, S. Contribution à l'étude de la myoclonie. J. Neurol. Psychiat. 30: 495, 1930.

BRODMAN, K. Experimenteller und klinischer Beitrag zur Psychopathologie der polyneuritischen Psychose. J. Psychol. Neurol., Leipzig 1: 225, 1902; 3: 1, 1904.

BRODSKY, M. E. Treatment of alcoholic psychoses with thiamin chloride. J. Conn. med. Soc. 2: 228, 1938.

BROMBERG, W. and SCHILDER, P. Psychologic considerations in alcoholic hallucinosis —castration and dismembering. Int. J. Psycho-Anal. 14: 206, 1933.

BROWN, W. Psychology in relation to alcohol and drug addiction. Brit. J. Inebr. 33: 61, 1935.

BRUEL, L. La lutte contre l'alcoolisme chronique; les injections intraveineuses d'alcool à 30%. Écho méd. Nord. 10: 497, 1939.

BRUGGER, C. (a) Familienuntersuchungen bei Alkoholdeliranten. Z. ges. Neurol. Psychiat. 151: 740, 1934.

——— (b) Die eugenische Bedeutung der chronischen Alkoholiker. Schweiz. med. Wschr. 17: 381, 1936.

BRUSH, N. H. The treatment of delirium tremens. Sthwest. Med. 15: 560, 1931.

BUMKE, O. Paraldehyde als Schlafmittel. Mschr. Psychiat. Neurol. 12: 489, 1902.

——— and KANT, F. Rausch- und Genussgifte; Giftsuchten. In: Handbuch der Neurologie (Bumke, O. and Foerster, O., ed.), XIII, 828. Berlin, J. Springer, 1936.

BUREAU OF THE CENSUS, U.S. Dept. Commerce. Patients in hospitals for mental disease, 1937. Washington, U.S. Govt. Ptg. Office, 1939.

BÜRGER-PRINZ, H. Über das Delirium tremens. Z. ges. Neurol. Psychiat. 131: 7, 1930.

——— and KAILA, M. Über die Struktur des amnestischen Symptomenkomplexes. Z. ges. Neurol. Psychiat. 124: 553, 1930.

BUSCH, A. Versuche über die Alkoholempfindlichkeit Hirnverletzter. J. Psychol. Neurol., Leipzig 24: 101, 1918.

CARMICHAEL, E. A. and STERN, R. O. Korsakoff's syndrome: its histopathology. Brain 54: 189, 1931.

CARROLL, R. What price alcohol? New York, The Macmillan Co., 1941.

CARVER, A. E. (a) The psychology of the alcoholist. Brit. J. med. Psychol. 11: 117, 1931.

——— (b) Psychology and management. In: Alcoholism in general practice (Carver, A. E., Hunt, T. and Wilson, W., ed.). London, Constable & Co., 1936.

CHAMBERS, F. J. A psychological approach in certain cases of alcoholism. Ment. Hyg. 21: 67, 1937.

CHOTZEN, F. Über atypische Alkoholpsychosen. Arch. Psychiat. Nervenkr. 41: 383, 1906.

CIMBAL, W. Trinkerfürsorge als Teil der Verwahrlostenfürsorge. Allg. Z. Psychiat. 84: 52, 1926.

CLARK, L. P. (a) Psychological study of some alcoholics. Psychoanal. Rev. 6: 268, 1919.

——— (b) Some psychological aspects of alcoholism. N.Y. med. J. 109: 930, 1919.

CLINE, W. B. and COLEMAN, J. V. The treatment of delirium tremens. J. Amer. med. Ass. 107: 404, 1936.

CLOUSTON, T. S. Clinical lectures on mental disease. 5th ed. Philadelphia, Lea Bros. & Co., 1898.

COBB, S. and COGGESHALL, H. C. Neuritis. J. Amer. med. Ass. 103: 1608, 1934.

COMMITTEE ON STATISTICS, American Psychiatric Association. Statistical manual for the use of hospitals for mental diseases. 5th ed. New York, National Committee for Mental Hygiene, 1931.

CORIAT, I. (a) The psycho-pathology and treatment of alcoholism. Brit. J. Inebr. 9: 138, 1911–12.

――― (b) Some statistical results of the psychoanalytic treatment of the psychoneuroses. Psychoanal. Rev. 4: 210, 1917.

CORWIN, E. M. Korsakoff's psychosis treated with vitamin B. Med. Bull. Veterans' Adm., Washington 15: 407, 1939.

COSACK, H. Kasuistischer Beitrag zur Pathogenese der Alkoholpsychosen. Mschr. Psychiat. Neurol. 92: 122, 1935.

COSSA, P., BOUGEANT, H., PUECH, M. and SASSI, P. Le traitement des complications nerveuses de l'alcoolisme par la strychnine. Ann. méd.-psychol. 96: 167, 1938.

COTLIER, I. Etilista crónico tratado por la sugestión hipnótica y la reeducación psíquica de su personalidad. Sem. méd., Buenos Aires 45: 336, 1938.

COURBON, P. and TUSQUES, J. Maladies du rythme et de l'équilibre; manie postébrieuse récidivante. Ann. méd.-psychol. 90: 51, 1932.

CRAMER, A. Über die forensische Bedeutung des normalen und pathologischen Rausches. Mschr. Psychiat. Neurol. 13: 56, 1903.

CRICHTON-MILLER, H. Etiology of alcoholism. Proc. R. Soc. Med. 21: 1356, 1927–28.

DE CRINIS, M. Über die Bedeutung der Leberfunktionsstörung für das Auftreten des Alkoholdeliriums und über eine ursächliche Behandlung desselben. Mschr. Psychiat. Neurol. 76: 1, 1930.

CROTHERS, T. D. Physical character of crimes of the alcoholic. Med.-leg. J. 33: 13, 1916.

CROWLEY, R. M. Psychoanalytic literature in drug addiction and alcoholism. Psychoanal. Rev. 76: 37, 1939.

CURRAN, F. J. (a) Personality studies in alcoholic women. J. nerv. ment. Dis. 86: 645, 1937.

――― (b) A study of fifty cases of bromide psychosis. J. nerv. ment. Dis. 88: 163, 1938.

CURTIUS, F. and WALLENBERG, M. Über die Entstehung des Pneumonie-Delirs. Dtsch. Arch. klin. Med. 176: 100, 1933.

DAMAYE, H. (a) Delirium tremens et plaies infectées. Progr. méd., Paris 1: 657, 1935.

――― (b) Delirium tremens et abcès du poumon. Progr. méd., Paris 1: 726, 1936.

――― and POIRIER, B. Delirium tremens par brulures infectées. Progr. méd., Paris 2: 1340, 1930; Les méningo-encéphalites des psychoses toxi-infectieuses. Progr. méd., Paris 2: 1374, 1931.

DAMRAU, F. The treatment of chronic alcoholism. Med. Rec. 147: 557, 1938.

DANIELS, G. E. Turning points in the analysis of a case of alcoholism. Psychoanal. Quart. 2: 123, 1933.

DAUMEZON, G. Dipsomanie réactionelle et périodique. Ann. méd.-psychol. 94: 739, 1936.

DAVIDSON, G. M. The syndrome of acute (alcoholic) hallucinosis. Psychiat. Quart. 13: 466, 1939.

DENT, J. Y. (a) Apomorphine in the treatment of anxiety states with especial reference to alcoholism. Brit. J. Inebr. 32: 65, 1934.

――― (b) The environmental factors in the causation and prevention of alcoholism. Brit. J. Inebr. 35–36: 1, 1937.

――― (c) Anxiety and its treatment. London, John Murray, 1941.

DICK, W. M. and COLBERT, C. N. Sinusitis in a series of alcoholic hallucinosis. Arch. Otolaryng., Chicago 14: 327, 1931.

DIETHELM, O. Treatment in Psychiatry. New York, The Macmillan Co., 1936.

DITTMER, A. Versuch einer Klassifizierung der Alkoholkranken. Med. Welt 6: 1256, 1932.

DOBNIGG and VON ECONOMO, C. Die hereditäre Belastung von Dipsomanen. Allg. Z. Psychiat. **76**: 382, 1920.

DÖLLKEN, A. Die körperlichen Erscheinungen des Delirium Tremens. Leipzig, von Veit & Co., 1901.

DOUGNAC, F. J. N. Le vin aux points de vue physico-chimique, physiologique, hygiénique et thérapeutique. Bordeaux thesis, 1933.

DRESEL, E. G. Sozialfürsorge. 2d ed. Berlin, S. Karger, 1922.

DROBNES, S. Zur Frage des Entziehungsdelirs. Nervenarzt **9**: 358, 1936.

DURFEE, C. H. (*a*) Re-education of the problem drinker. J. Conn. med. Soc. **2**: 486, 1938.

――――― (*b*) To drink or not to drink. New York, Longmans, Green & Co., 1938.

DYNES, J. B. Survey of alcoholic patients admitted to the Boston Psychopathic Hospital in 1937. New Engl. J. Med. **220**: 195, 1939.

EAST, W. N. Alcoholism and crime in relation to manic-depressive disorder. Lancet **230**: 161, 1936.

ECHEVERRIA, M. G. Alcoholic epilepsy. J. ment. Sci. **26**: 489, 1881.

EHRENWALD, H. Über den Zeitsinn und die gnostische Störung der Zeitauffassung beim Korsakoff. Z. ges. Neurol. Psychiat. **134**: 512, 1931.

ENDERSZ, F. Spread of alcoholism in Europe. Med. World, London **52**: 432, 1934.

ENTERES, J. L. Die Ursachen der Geisteskrankheiten; Vererbung, Keimschädigung. In: Handbuch der Geisteskrankheiten (Bumke, O., ed.), p. 50. Berlin, J. Springer, 1928.

EPSTEIN, A. L. Somatologische Studien zur Psychiatrie; die vestibulären Störungen bei den akuten Alkoholpsychosen. Z. ges. Neurol. Psychiat. **143**: 759, 1933.

ERNST, K. Klinische Beobachtungen an Alkoholikern. Klin. Wschr. **12**: 1829, 1870, 1933.

ERWIN, H. J. Oxygen in delirium tremens. J. nat. med. Ass., Tuskegee, Ala. **31**: 111, 1939.

ESQUIROL (J.) E. (D.) Mental maladies; a treatise on insanity (Hunt, E. K., tr.). Philadelphia, Lea & Blanchard, 1845.

EUZIERE, J., VIDAL, J. and ZAKHAMM, J. De quelques modifications humorales dans un cas de delirium tremens. Arch. Soc. Sci. méd. biol. Montpellier **13**: 578, 1932.

FARIS, R. and DUNHAM, H. W. Mental disorders in urban areas. Chicago, The University of Chicago Press, 1939.

FERENCZI, S. (*a*) Über die Rolle der Homosexualität in der Pathogenese der Paranoia. Jb. psychoanal. psychopath. Forsch. **3**: 106, 1911–12.

――――― (*b*) Alkohol und Neurosen. Jb. psychoanal. psychopath. Forsch. **3**: 853, 1911–12.

FLEMING, R. (*a*) A psychiatric concept of acute alcoholic intoxication. Amer. J. Psychiat. **92**: 89, 1935.

――――― (*b*) The management of chronic alcoholism in England, Scandinavia and Central Europe. New Engl. J. Med. **216**: 279, 1937.

――――― (*c*) The treatment of chronic alcoholism. New Engl. J. Med. **217**: 779, 1937.

――――― and TILLOTSON, K. Further studies on the personality and sociological factors in the prognosis and treatment of chronic alcoholism. New Engl. J. Med. **221**: 741, 1939.

FLEMMING, C. F. Über Classification der Seelenstörungen nebst einem neuen Versuche derselben, mit besonderer Rücksicht auf gerichtliche Psychologie. Allg. Z. Psychiat. **1**: 97, 1844.

FREUD, S. Der Witz und seine Beziehung zum Unbewussten. Leipzig, Deuticke, 1905.

FRIEDENWALD, W. F. The acute alcoholic. J. Mo. med. Ass. **34**: 410, 1937.

Froment, J., Masson, R. and Brun, J. Comitialité tardive et alcoolisme chronique. Lyon méd. **163**: 733, 1939.

Gabriel, E. (*a*) Über die "Ursachen" des Alkoholismus. Psychiat.-neurol. Wschr. **35**: 90, 108, 115, 1933.

——— (*b*) Die Nachkommenschaft von Alkoholikern. Arch. Psychiat. Nervenkr. **102**: 506, 1934.

——— (*c*) Worin besteht die Behandlung von Trinkern? Wien. klin. Wschr. **50**: 637, 1937.

——— (*d*) Die Behandlung von Trunksüchtigen. Wien. med. Wschr. **88**: 682, 1938.

——— and Kratzmann, E. Die Süchtigkeit. Berlin, Neuland Verlag, 1936.

———, Novotny, S. and Palisa, C. Liquoralkoholwerte bei Delirium-Tremens-Kranken. Arch. Psychiat. Nervenkr. **106**: 312, 1937.

Galant, J. S. (*a*) Über alkoholische Psycho-Epilepsie. Schweiz. med. Wschr. **16**: 603, 1935.

——— (*b*) Über die Apomorphinbehandlung der Alkoholiker. Psychiat.-neurol. Wschr. **38**: 85, 1936.

Ganser, S. Zur Behandlung des Delirium Tremens. Münch. med. Wschr. **54**: 120, 1907.

Gaupp, R. Die Dipsomanie. Jena, Fischer, 1901.

Gelma, E. Considérations sur les rapports de l'épilepsie latente avec alcoolisme. Paris thesis, 1908.

Glover, E. G. Etiology of alcoholism. Proc. R. Soc. Med. **21**: 1351, 1927–28.

Goldsmith, H. Spinal drainage in alcoholic deliria and other acute alcoholic psychoses. Amer. J. Psychiat. **10**: 255, 1930.

Graeter, K. Dementia praecox mit Alcoholismus chronicus. Leipzig, J. A. Barth, 1909.

Graf, O. Möglichkeiten und Grenzen der Heilbehandlung von Alkoholikern. Berlin, Neuland Verlag, 1929.

Gregor, A. and Roemer, H. Zur Kenntnis der Auffassung optischer Sinneseindrücke bei alkoholischen Geistesstörungen, insbesondere bei der Korsakoffschen Psychose. Neurol. Zbl. **25**: 339, 1906.

Grünthal, E. (*a*) Zur Kenntnis der Psychopathologie des Korsakowschen Symptomenkomplexes. Mschr. Psychiat. Neurol. **53**: 88, 1923.

——— (*b*) Über das Corpus mamillare und den Korsakowschen Symptomenkomplex. Conf. neurol. **2**: 64, 1939.

Gudden, H. Klinische und anatomische Beiträge zur Kenntnis der multiplen Alkoholneuritis, nebst Bemerkungen über die Regenerationsvorgänge im peripheren Nervensystem. Arch. Psychiat. Nervenkr. **28**: 643, 1896.

Guiraud, Ey, H. and Bonnafous-Serieux. Syndrome de Korsakoff alcoolique aigu. Ann. méd.-psychol. **96**: 74, 1938.

Hadlik, J. [Treatment of delirium tremens: our trials with insulin treatment.] Čas. Lék. čes. **78**: 1287, 1311, 1335, 1939.

Hagelstam, J. Das Vorkommen von Alkoholkrankheiten im Nervensystem während der Zeit des Alkohol-Totalverbotes in Finnland. Acta psychiat., Copenhagen **5**: 311, 1930.

Haggard, H. W. and Greenberg, L. A. The effects of alcohol as influenced by blood sugar. Science **85**: 608, 1937.

Hart, H. H. Personality factors in alcoholism. Arch. Neurol. Psychiat., Chicago **24**: 116, 1930.

Hartmann, H. Gedächtnis und Lustprinzip. Z. ges. Neurol. Psychiat. **126**: 496, 1930.

Heilbronner, K. Über pathologische Rauschzustände. Münch. med. Wschr. **48**: 962, 1013, 1901.

HEILIG. Über Alkoholpsychosen. Z. ges. Neurol. Psychiat. **10**: 109, 1912.

HENDERSON, D. K. (*a*) Chronic alcoholism and its treatment. Edinb. med. J. **40**: 1, 1933.

———— (*b*) Alcoholism and psychiatry. Edinb. med. J. **43**: 717, 1936.

———— (*c*) Alcoholism and psychiatry. Brit. J. Inebr. **34**: 99, 1937.

———— and GILLESPIE, R. D. A textbook of psychiatry, chap. 11, Alcoholic psychoses, p. 281. New York, Oxford University Press, 1936.

HENDERSON, J. L. Alcoholism: its psychiatric treatment. Calif. West. Med. **52**: 11, 1940.

HENRY, G. W. Essentials of psychiatry, chap. 8, Toxic psychoses, p. 144. Baltimore, Williams & Wilkins, 1938.

HERINGA, S. Over atypische Alcoholpsychosen. Psychiat. neurol. Bl., Amsterdam **41**: 47, 1937.

HERON, D. Second study of extreme alcoholism in adults. Eugen. Lab. Mem. **17**: 1, 1912.

HERTTELL, T. Exposé of the causes of intemperate drinking, and the means by which it may be obviated. New York, N.Y. Soc. for Internal Improvement, 1819.

HERTZOG, A. W. Medical jurisprudence, chap. 36, Inebriety, p. 528. Indianapolis, Bobbs-Merrill Co., 1931.

HILL, O. L. Metrazol in alcoholism with a complication of fracture of spine. Memphis med. J. **14**: 194, 1939.

HILTON, J. P. and Alderson, D. M. Sucrose solution in the treatment of alcoholism and confusional states. Rocky Mtn med. J. **35**: 227, 1938.

HOCH, P. H. Personality factors in alcoholic psychoses. Psychiat. Quart. **14**: 338, 1940.

HOFF, H. and POETZL, O. Über Anomalien der Zwischenhirntätigkeit in Trinker-familien. Psychiat.-neurol. Wschr. **33**: 373, 1931.

HOGAN, J. J. Treatment of acute alcoholic delirium. J. Amer. med. Ass. **67**: 1826, 1916.

HOPPE, H. Die Tatsachen über den Alkohol. 4th ed. Munich, E. Reinhardt, 1912.

VAN DER HORST, L. Über die Psychologie des Korsakowsyndroms. Mschr. Psychiat. Neurol. **83**: 65, 1932.

HOWARD, C. E. and Hurdum, H. M. Therapeutic problems in the alcoholic psychoses. Psychiat. Quart. **14**: 347, 1940.

HUBER, K. Über die Alkoholhalluzinose und ihre Beziehung zur Schizophrenie. Schweiz. Arch. Neurol. Psychiat. **44**: 43, 1939.

HUSS, MAGNUS. Chronische Alkoholskrankheit, oder Alcoholismus Chronicus. (Translated from the Swedish by Gerhard van dem Busch.) Stockholm, C. E. Fritze, 1852.

IMBER, I. Klinischer Beitrag zum Studium der akuten alkoholischen Angstpsychose. Z. ges. Neurol. Psychiat. **140**: 557, 1932.

JABLOW, L. Alcoolisme et epilepsie. Paris thesis, 1929.

JAHRREISS, W. Störungen des Bewusstseins. In: Handbuch der Geisteskrankheiten (Bumke, O., ed.), I, 601. Berlin, J. Springer, 1928.

JELLIFFE, S. E. and WHITE, W. A. Diseases of the Nervous System, chap. 21, The toxic psychoses, p. 1062. Philadelphia, Lea & Febiger, 1929.

JELLINEK, E. M. and McFarland, R. A. Analysis of psychological experiments on the effects of alcohol. Quart. J. Stud. Alc. **1**: 272, 1940.

JISLIN, S. G. Zur Klinik der Abstinenzerscheinungen beim alcoholismus chronicus. Z. ges. Neurol. Psychiat. **136**: 645, 1931.

JOFFROY, A. and SERVEAUX, R. Mensuration de la toxicité vraie de l'alcool éthylique; symptômes de l'intoxication aiguë et de l'intoxication chronique par l'alcool éthyli-que. Arch. Méd. exp. **9**: 681, 1897.

JOHNSON, SAMUEL. The lives of the most eminent English poets; Addison. Vol. II. London, Methuen & Co., 1896.

JOLLIFFE, N., WORTIS, H. and FEIN, H. D. The Wernicke syndrome. Arch. Neurol. Psychiat., Chicago 46: 569, 1941.

JOURNAL OF THE AMERICAN MEDICAL ASSOCIATION, Bureau of Investigation. Rx medicinal spirits; the peculiar claims for a "nonintoxicating" whisky. J. Amer. med. Ass. 112: 351, 1939.

JULIUSBURGER, O. Alkoholismus und Psychosexualität. Z. Sexualwiss. 2: 357, 1916.

KALLENBERG, K. [Hypnotic treatment of alcoholics.] Svenska Läkartidn. 35: 2149, 1938.

KANT, IMMANUEL. Anthropologie in pragmatischer Hinsicht. 1st ed. Koenigsberg, 1798.

KANT, O. Differential diagnosis of schizophrenia in the light of the concept of personality-stratification. Amer. J. Psychiat. 97: 342, 1940.

KANTOROVICH, N. [Alcohol and the excitatory and inhibitory processes in the central nervous system.] Nov. refl. fiziol. nerv. sist. 3: 210, 1929. Abstr. in: Psychol. Abstr. 4: 493, 1930.

KARLAN, S. C. Alcoholism and hallucinosis. Psychiat. Quart. 15: 64, 1941.

KAUFFMANN, M. Stoffwechseluntersuchungen bei Alkoholdeliranten. J. Psychol. Neurol., Leipzig 10: 28, 1907.

KEELEY, L. E. The non-heredity of inebriety. Chicago, S. G. Griggs & Co., 1896.

KEESER, E. and KEESER, I. Untersuchungen über chronische Alkoholvergiftung. Arch. exp. Path. Pharmak. 113: 188, 1926; 119: 285, 1926.

KEHRER, F. and KRETSCHMER, E. Die Veranlagung zu seelischen Störungen. Berlin, J. Springer, 1924.

KERR, N. Inebriety, or narcomania; its etiology, pathology, treatment and jurisprudence. 3d ed. London, H. K. Lewis, 1894.

KIELHOLZ, A. (a) Einige Betrachtungen zur psychoanalytischen Auffassung des Alkoholismus. Abstr. in: Int. Z. (ärztl.) Psychoanal. 10: 115, 1924.

—— (b) Analyseversuch bei Delirium tremens. Int. Z. (ärztl.) Psychoanal. 12: 478, 1926. Abstr. in: Psychoanal. Rev. 19: 92, 1932.

KIENE, H. E., STREITWIESER, R. J. and MILLER, H. The role of vitamin B_1 in delirium tremens. J. Amer. med. Ass. 114: 2191, 1940.

KLEMPERER, E. Die Behandlung des Delirium tremens mit Insulin. Psychiat.-neurol. Wschr. 34: 117, 134, 1932.

—— and WEISSMANN, M. Heilung einer Korsakoff'schen Psychose durch Insulin-behandlung bei einem Fall von Diabetes mellitus. Nervenarzt 3: 291, 1930.

KLOSTER, J. B_1-Vitaminbehandlung bei Delirium tremens. Nervenarzt 11: 413, 1938.

KNAPP, A. (a) Die polyneuritischen Psychosen. Wiesbaden, J. F. Bergmann, 1906.

—— (b) Epilepsie und Korsakowscher Symptomenkomplex. Mschr. Psychiat. Neurol. 44: 74, 1918.

KNIGHT, R. P. (a) The psychodynamics of chronic alcoholism. J. nerv. ment. Dis. 86: 538, 1937.

—— (b) The dynamics and treatment of alcohol addiction. Bull. Menninger Clin. 1: 233, 1937.

—— (c) The psychoanalytic treatment in a sanatorium of chronic addiction to alcohol. J. Amer. med. Ass. 111: 1443, 1938.

KOLLE, K. (a) Über Eifersucht und Eifersuchtswahn bei Trinkern. Mschr. Psychiat. Neurol. 83: 224, 1932.

—— (b) Die Unfruchtbarmachung bei Alkoholismus. Allg. Z. Psychiat. 112: 397, 1939.

KÖPPEN, M. and KUTZINSKI, A. Systematische Beobachtungen über die Wiedergabe kleiner Erzählungen durch Geisteskranke. Berlin, S. Karger, 1910.

KORBSCH, H. Im Leben erworbene körperliche äussere Ursachen. In: Handbuch der Geisteskrankheiten (Bumke, O., ed.), I, 308. Berlin, J. Springer, 1928.

KÖRNER, G. Zur Psychopathologie des amnestischen Syndroms. Mschr. Psychiat. Neurol. **90**: 177, 1935.

KÖRNYEY, S. Aufsteigende Lähmung und Korsakowsche Psychose by Lymphogranu-lomatose. Dtsch. Z. Nervenheilk. **125**: 129, 1932.

KORSAKOFF, S. Eine psychische Störung combiniert mit multipler Neuritis; psychosis polyneuritica sen cerebropathia psychica toxaemica. Allg. Z. Psychiat. **46**: 475, 1890.

KRAEPELIN, E. Psychiatrie, II, chap. 3, Der Alkoholismus, 346. 9th ed. Leipzig, J. A. Barth, 1927.

KRAFFT-EBING, R. Lehrbuch der Psychiatrie, chap. 4, p. 507. Stuttgart, Enke, 1897.

KRAL, A., POLLAK, J. and SCHIRMER, J. Zur Insulinbehandlung der Alkoholpsychosen. Nervenarzt **10**: 520, 1937.

KRAUSS, S. Untersuchungen über Aufbau und Störung der menschlichen Handlung; I. Teil: Die Korsakow'sche Störung. Arch. ges. Psychol. **77**: 649, 1930.

KRINSKY, C. M. The treatment of delirium tremens. J. nerv. ment. Dis. **91**: 647, 1940.

KRUSE. Lohnt sich die Heilbehandlung Trunksüchtiger? Bl. Volksgesundh. **32**: 8, 1932.

KÜENZI, F. Über das Wiederauftreten der Epilepsie unter den Nachkommen von Epileptikern. Mschr. Psychiat. Neurol. **72**: 245, 1929.

KÜFFNER, W. Epilepsie und Alkohol. Z. ges. Neurol. Psychiat. **111**: 145, 1927.

KULCSÁR, I. and LAJTAVÁRI, L. [The treatment of delirium tremens with insulin-dextrose shock.] Orv. Hetil. **83**: 665, 1939.

KÜNKEL, F. Zur Psychologie des Alkoholismus. Alkoholfrage **27**: 23, 1931.

KÜNZLER, H. Resultate der Trinkerheilstätte Ellikon an der Thur. Allg. Z. Psychiat. **92**: 439, 1930.

KÜRZ, E. and KRAEPELIN, E. Über die Beeinflussung psychischer Vorgänge durch regelmässigen Alkoholgenuss. Psychol. Arb. **3**: 417, 1900.

KUTNER, R. Zur Diagnostik des pathologischen Rausches (Störung der Reflexe). Dtsch. med. Wschr. **30**: 1057, 1904.

LA BARRE, W. The psychopathology of drinking songs; a study of the content of the "normal" unconscious. Psychiatry **2**: 203, 1939.

LADAME, C. Trente années d'alcoolisme à l'asile clinique psychiatrique de Bel-Air (1901–1930) à Génève. Progr. méd., Paris **1**: 995, 1935.

LADRAGUE, P. Alcoolisme et enfants. Paris thesis, 1900–1901.

LAMB, D. Inebriety: some aspects of the problem. Brit. J. Inebr. **36**: 167, 1939.

LAMBERT, A. The nursing care of patients addicted to the use of drugs or alcohol. Trained Nurse **98**: 364, 1937.

LANCEREAUX, E. Intoxication par les boissons alcooliques. Traité Méd. Thérap. **11**: 205, 1907.

LANGE, J. Heilbehandlung von Alkoholikern. Berlin, Neuland Verlag, 1929.

LEE, E. J., JR. Alcoholism from an allergic and mental viewpoint. Med. Rec. **147**: 208, 1938.

LEGRAIN, M. Hérédité et alcoolisme. Bibliothèque anthropologique (Paris) **7**: 1, 1889.

LENNOX, W. G. Alcohol and epilepsy. Quart. J. Stud. Alc. **2**: 1, 1941.

LETTSOM, J. C. Some remarks on the effect of *lignum quassiae amarae*. Mem. med. Soc. London **1**: 128, 1787.

LÉVY, F. Crises épileptiformes alcooliques et crises d'épilepsie. Gaz. Hôp., Paris **113**: 441, 1940.

LÉVY-VALENSI, J. Le traitement de l'alcoolisme. Paris méd. **29**: 401, 1939.

LEWIS, N. D. C. Personality factors in alcoholic addiction. Quart. J. Stud. Alc. **1**: 21, 1940.

LIAN, C. L'alcoolisme, cause d'hypertension artérielle. Bull. Acad. Méd. Paris 74: 225, 1915.

LIEPMANN, H. (a) Über die Delirien der Alkoholisten und über künstliche bei ihnen hervorgerufene Visionen. Arch. Psychiat. Nervenkr. 27: 172, 1895.

────── (b) Über Albuminurie, Albumosurie und andere körperliche Symptome des Delirium tremens. Arch. Psychiat. Nervenheilk. 28: 570, 1896.

LYATHAUD, A. Enquête sur la consommation de vin des 830 pensionnaires hommes de la maison départementale de retraite d'Albigny. Lyon méd. 163: 721, 1939.

McCLELLAN, H. H. Treatment of alcoholism. Med. World, Philadelphia 53: 178, 1935.

McCONNELL, W. C. Treating the problem drinker. Med. World, Philadelphia 58: 301, 1940.

McCORMICK, E. W. The diagnosis of drunkenness. Practitioner 140: 625, 1938.

MacNISH, R. The anatomy of drunkenness. New York, W. Pearson & Co., 1835.

MAGNAN, V. (a) Étude expérimentale et clinique sur l'alcoolisme. Paris, Renou & Maulde, 1871.

────── (b) De l'alcoolisme. Paris, Delahaye, 1874.

MAINZER, F. and KRAUSE, M. Nicotinic acid in the treatment of delirium tremens. Brit. med. J. 2: 331, 1939.

MANGOLD, G. B. Public treatment of drunkenness in St. Louis. Wash. Univ. Stud. Sci. Tech., St. Louis 3: 271, 1916.

MAPOTHER, E. (a) Aetiology of alcoholism. Proc. Roy. Soc. Med. 21: 1346, 1927–28.

────── (b) The physical basis of alcoholic mental disorders. Brit. J. Inebr. 36: 103, 1939.

MARCEL. De la folie causée par l'abus des boissons alcooliques. Paris thesis, 1847.

MARCET, W. On chronic alcoholic intoxication. New York, Moorhead, Simpson & Bond, 1868.

MARCHAND, L. Les lésions du système nerveux, du foie, des reins et de la rate dans le "delirium tremens" des alcooliques. Ann. Anat. path. méd.-chir. 9: 1026, 1932.

MARGULIÈS, A. Über Pseudodipsomanie. Prag. med. Wschr. 24: 307, 321, 1899.

MARKOVNIKOV, A. [Therapy by combination of persuasion with development of conditioned reflex of vomiting after swallowing alcoholic drink.] Sovetsk. vrach. gaz., p. 807, May 31, 1934.

MARTIMOR, E. and NEVEU, P. Injections intra-rachidiens de vitamine B₁ dans la psychopolynévrite de Korsakow. Ann. méd.-psychol. 96: 242, 1938.

MARTIN, E. and MARTIN, P. E. Delirium tremens. Ann. Méd. lég. 14: 49, 1934.

MASTERS, W. E. The alcohol habit and its treatment. London, H. K. Lewis & Co., 1931.

MAY, J. V. Mental diseases, a public health problem; chap. 7, The alcoholic psychoses, p. 344. Boston, Richard G. Badger, 1922.

MAZEL, P. Le delirium tremens traumatique. Ann. Méd. lég. 13: 225, 1933.

MEDICAL RESEARCH COUNCIL, ALCOHOL INVESTIGATION COMMITTEE, Privy Council, Great Britain. Alcohol: its action on the human organism. London, H. M. Stationary Office, 1938.

MEGGENDORFER, F. Intoxikationspsychosen. In: Handbuch der Geisteskrankheiten (Bumke, O., ed.), VII, Spec. pt. 3, p. 165. Berlin, J. Springer, 1928.

MENNINGER, K. A. Man against himself; chap. 3, Alcohol addiction, p. 160. New York, Harcourt, Brace & Co., 1938.

MENNINGER, W. C. The treatment of chronic alcohol addiction. Bull. Menninger Clin. 2: 101, 1938.

MEYER, A. Alcohol as a psychiatric problem. In: Alcohol and man (Emerson, H., ed.), p. 273. New York, The Macmillan Co., 1932.

MEYER, E. (*a*) Korsakowscher Symptomenkomplex nach Gehirnerschütterung. Neurol. Zbl. **23**: 710, 1904.

—— (*b*) Über akute und chronische Alkoholpsychosen und über die ätiologische Bedeutung des chronischen Alkoholmissbrauchs bei der Entstehung geistiger Störungen überhaupt. Arch. Psychiat. Nervenkr. **38**: 232, 1904.

MIGNOT, R. La prédisposition aux accidents mentaux de l'alcoolisme chronique. Ann. méd.-psychol. **91**: 300, 1933.

MILES, W. R. Psychological factors in alcoholism. Ment. Hyg. **21**: 529, 1937.

MILLER, M. M. Amphetamine (benzedrine) sulphate in treatment of chronic alcoholism and depression neuroses. Med. Rec. **151**: 211, 1940.

MINSKI, L. Psychopathy and psychoses associated with alcohol. J. ment. Sci. **84**: 985, 1938.

MOELI. Über die vorübergehenden Zustände abnormen Bewusstseins infolge von Alkoholvergiftung. Allg. Z. Psychiat. **57**: 169, 1900.

MÖLLENHOFF, F. Über den Stand der Süchtenbehandlung. Fortschr. Ther. **11**: 275, 1935.

MÖNKEMÖLLER, O. (*a*) Kasuistischer Beitrag zur sogenannten polyneuritischen Psychose. Allg. Z. Psychiat. **54**: 806, 1898.

—— (*b*) Der pathologische Rauschzustand und seine forensische Bedeutung. Arch. KrimAnthrop. **59**: 120, 193, 1914.

DE MONTMOLIN, R. À propos de l'urobilinurie chez les alcooliques. Schweiz. med. Wschr. **19**: 1165, 1938.

MOORE, M. The treatment of alcoholism. New Engl. J. Med. **221**: 489, 1939.

—— and GRAY, M. G. (*a*) Delirium tremens: study of cases at Boston City Hospital, 1915–1936. New Engl. J. Med. **220**: 953, 1939.

——, —— (*b*) Alcoholism at Boston City Hospital—conditions on hospitalization of all alcoholic patients at the Haymarket Square Relief Station. New Engl. J. Med. **221**: 49, 1939.

——, —— (*c*) Alcoholism at Boston City Hospital—conditions on hospitalization of 344 patients with delirium tremens at Haymarket Square Relief Station. New Engl. J. Med. **221**: 52, 1939.

MOREL, F. (*a*) Contribution à l'étude des hallucinations visuelles du delirium tremens. Schweiz. Arch. Neurol. Psychiat. **30**: 178, 1932.

—— (*b*) Les scotomes positifs et les hallucinations visuelles du delirium tremens. Rev. Oto-Neuro-Ophtal. **11**: 81, 1933.

MORRIS, R. T. Alcohol and narcotics. Interst. med. J. **23**: 450, 1916.

MOTT, F. W. The nervous system in chronic alcoholism. Brit. med. J. **2**: 1403, 1910

MYERSON, A. (*a*) Inheritance of mental diseases. Baltimore, Williams & Wilkins, 1925.

—— (*b*) Alcohol: a study of social ambivalence. Quart. J. Stud. Alc. **1**: 13, 1940.

—— (*c*) The social psychology of alcoholism. Dis. nerv. System **1**: 1, 1940.

NASSE. [Treatment of alcoholic diseases.] Abstr. in: Gaz. Hôp., Paris **26**: 79, 1853.

NEUMANN, M. Über die Beziehungen zwischen Alkoholismus und Epilepsie. Strassburg thesis, 1897.

NICOLLE, R. Les cures de désintoxication alcoolique. Paris thesis, 1928.

NORBURY, F. G. Application of vitamin B₁ to neuropsychiatry. Illinois med. J. **78**: 228, 1940.

NOSSEN, H. L. Twelve against alcohol. New York, Harrison Hilton Books, 1940.

NOTKIN, J. A contribution to the study of epilepsy with especial reference to the literature. J. nerv. ment. Dis. **67**: 321, 457, 567, 1928.

NOYES, A. P. Modern clinical psychiatry; chap. 13, Alcoholic psychoses, p. 218. Philadelphia, Saunders & Co., 1939.

OBERNDORF, C. P. The role of an exceptional organ in a neurosis. Int. J. Psycho-Anal. **4**: 103, 1923.

ODEGAARD, O. Zur Klinik und Ätiologie des periodischen Alkoholismus. Z. ges. Neurol. Psychiat. **153**: 629, 1935.

OPPENHEIM, M. Bemerkungen zu einem Fall von Delirium tremens. Schweiz. med. Wschr. **19**: 155, 1938.

OSSIPOFF, V. Die Stellung der Dipsomanie in der Klassifikation der Psychosen. Wiss. Med. **9**: 19, 1922.

OSTMANN. Beitrag zur Statistik der durch Alkohol hauptsächlich bedingten psychischen Erkrankungen. Allg. Z. Psychiat. **87**: 243, 1927.

PAGNIEZ, P. (*a*) Au sujet du traitement du delirium tremens. Pr. méd. **44**: 2121, 1936.

———— (*b*) Le traitement des accidents délirants alcooliques par l'acide nicotinique. Pr. méd. **47**: 1682, 1939.

PAPADAKI. Un cas de delirium tremens au cours d'une hallucinose auditive éthylique. Arch. Neurol., Paris **17**: 465, 1904.

PAPPENHEIM, M. Über Dipsomanie. Z. ges. Neurol. Psychiat. **11**: 333, 1912.

PEABODY, R. R. The common sense of drinking. Boston, Little, Brown & Co., 1931.

PEARSON, S. B. Observations on brain fever. Edinb. med. surg. J. **9**: 326, 1813.

PESERICO, M. La dipsomania e veramente un impulso? Arch. gen. Neurol. Psichiat. **17**: 247, 1936.

PICHARD, H. and LIBER, A. Éthylisme et polydipsie; lésion de la selle turcique; traumatisme ancien. Ann. méd.-psychol. **91**: 100, 1933.

PICK, A. Beitrag zur Pathologie des Denkverlaufs beim Korsakow. Z. ges. Neurol. Psychiat. **28**: 344, 1915.

PIKER, P. (*a*) On the relationship of the sudden withdrawal of alcohol to delirium tremens. Amer. J. Psychiat. **93**: 1387, 1937.

———— (*b*) The treatment of acute alcoholism. Ohio St. med. J. **33**: 1318, 1937.

———— and COHEN, J. V. The comprehensive management of delirium tremens. J. Amer. med. Ass. **108**: 345, 1937.

———— and STERN, A. M. Clinical evaluation of use of fluids in treatment of delirium tremens. Arch. Neurol. Psychiat., Chicago **39**: 62, 1938.

PISK, G. Über Dipsomanie bei Frauen. Mschr. Psychiat. Neurol. **93**: 218, 1936.

PLOTTKE, P. Le problème de l'alcoolisme considéré du point de vue de l' "Individual-psychologie" d'Alfred Adler. Hyg. ment. **29**: 250, 1934.

POHLISCH, K. (*a*) Stoffwechseluntersuchungen beim chronischen Alkoholismus, Delirium tremens und der alkoholischen Korsakow-Psychose. Mschr. Psychiat. Neurol. **62**: 211, 1926.

———— (*b*) Die pathogenetische Bedeutung der Gelegenheitsursachen für das Delirium tremens. Mschr. Psychiat. Neurol. **63**: 69, 1927.

———— (*c*) Zur Pathogenese der akuten Halluzinose der Trinker. Mschr. Psychiat. Neurol. **63**: 82, 1927.

———— (*d*) Die Persönlichkeit und das Milieu Delirium tremens Kranker der Charité aus den Jahren 1912–1925. Mschr. Psychiat. Neurol. **63**: 136, 1927.

———— (*e*) Die Nachkommenschaft Delirium tremens Kranker. Mschr. Psychiat. Neurol. **64**: 108, 1927.

———— (*f*) Die Klinik des Alkoholismus. Allg. Z. Psychiat. **99**: 193, 1933.

———— (*g*) Sociale und persönliche Bedingungen des chronischen Alkoholismus. Leipzig, Georg Thieme, 1934.

———— (*h*) Prophylaxe des Rauschgiftmissbrauchs. Z. psych. Hyg. **12**: 70, 1939.

POLLOCK, H. M. (*a*) A statistical study of 1,739 patients with alcoholic psychoses. St. Hosp. Bull., N.Y. **7**: 204, 1914.

———— (*b*) Use and effect of alcohol in relation to alcoholic mental disease before, during and after prohibition. Ment. Hyg. **24**: 113, 1940.

DE PONTE, E. Ein Fall einer Alkoholhalluzinose in der manischen Phase eines Zirkulären. Z. ges. Neurol. Psychiat. **131**: 265, 1930.

Pontoppidan, K. Delirium tremens. Bibl. Læger 6: 369, 1895.

Praetorius, H. L. Sonderbehandlung von Alkoholkranken in Heil- und Pflegeanstalten. Psychiat.-neurol. Wschr. 32: 213, 1930.

Rado, S. (a) The psychic effect of intoxicants. Int. J. Psycho-Anal. 7: 396, 1926.

—— (b) The psychoanalysis of pharmacothymia. Psychoanal. Quart. 2: 1, 1933.

Radu, D. Contribution à l'étude du syndrome de Korsakoff aigu. Paris thesis, 1933.

Read, S. C. The psycho-pathology of alcoholism and some so-called alcoholic psychoses. J. ment. Sci. 66: 233, 1920.

Redlich, E. Bemerkungen zur Alkohol-Epilepsie. Epilepsia, 1909.

Reifenstein, E. C. and Davidoff, E. (a) The treatment of alcoholic psychosis with benzedrine sulfate. J. Amer. med. Ass. 110: 1811, 1938.

——, —— (b) The use of amphetamine (benzedrine) sulfate in alcoholism with and without psychosis. N.Y. St. J. Med. 40: 247, 1940.

Reissig, H. Über den Zusammenhang zwischen Alkoholismus und Epilepsie. Berlin thesis, 1898.

Reploh, H. Beiträge zur Krebsstatistik mit besonderer Berücksichtigung der sozialen Klassen und Berufe. Alkoholfrage 28: 134, 1932.

Reynell, W. R. Treatment of alcoholism. Med. Pr. 135: 508, 1933.

Richards, G. Diplopic and triplopic hallucinations in delirium tremens. J. nerv. ment. Dis. 75: 630, 1932.

Richardson, J. L. and Blankenhorn, M.A. New clinical aspects of alcoholism. Amer. J. med. Sci. 176: 168, 1928.

Richter, C. and Campbell, K. H. Alcohol taste thresholds and concentration of solution preferred by rats. Science 91: 507, 1940.

Riebeling, C. Einige neuere Arbeiten über Intoxikationspsychosen. Med. Klinik 35. 392, 1939.

Riggall, R. Homosexuality and alcoholism. Psychoanal. Rev. 10: 157, 1923.

Robbins, B. S. A note on the significance of infantile nutritional disturbances in the development of alcoholism. Psychoanal. Rev. 22: 53, 1935.

Roberson, R. S. Cerebral edema in chronic alcoholism (alcoholic wet brain). Sth. Med. Surg. 94: 584, 1932.

Robinson, G. W. The treatment of delirium tremens with insulin in sub-shock doses. Amer. J. Psychiat. 97: 136, 1940.

Roch, M. Der Alkoholismus in der medizinischen Klinik Genf in den Jahren 1933–36. Schweiz. med. Wschr. 69: 772, 1939.

Rolleston, J. D. The folk-lore of alcoholism. Brit. J. Inebr. 39: 30, 1941.

Rosanoff, A. J. (a) Alcohol in relation to mental disease. Boston med. surg. J. 174: 611, 1916.

—— (b) Manual of psychiatry; chap. 14, Alcoholism, p. 364. New York, John Wiley & Sons, 1938.

Rosenbaum, M. and Merritt, H. H. Korsakoff's syndrome; clinical study of the alcoholic form with special regard to prognosis. Arch. Neurol. Psychiat., Chicago 41: 978, 1939.

——, Piker, P. and Lederer, H. Delirium tremens; a study of various methods of treatment. Amer. J. med. Sci. 200: 677, 1940.

Rosenfeld, M. Die exogenen Intoxikationen und Infektionen. In: Lehrbuch der Nerven- und Geisteskrankheiten (Weygandt, W., ed.), p. 511. Halle a. S., Marhold, 1935.

Rothschild, D. and Burke, E. R. Blood–cerebrospinal fluid barrier in alcoholic disorders and in schizophrenia complicated by alcoholism; distribution ratios of bromide, calcium, sugar and chlorides. Arch. Neurol. Psychiat., Chicago 30: 141, 1933.

RUGGLES, A. H. Mental health, past, present and future. Baltimore, Williams & Wilkins, 1934.

RUPP, J. R. and PUCKETT, H. L. Treatment of alcoholism. J. Mich. St. med. Soc. 29: 801, 1930.

RUSH, BENJAMIN. An inquiry into the effects of ardent-spirits upon the body and mind; with an account of the means of preventing and of the remedies for curing them. 8th ed. Brookfield, Merriam & Co., 1814.

SACHS, H. The genesis of perversion. Int. Z. (ärztl.) Psychoanal. 9: 176, 1923.

SADGER (J.) Zur Psychologie und Therapie des Tunichtguts und des Trinkers. Wien. klin. Rdsch. 28: 287, 1914.

SÄKER, G. Zur Behandlung des Delirium tremens. Nervenarzt 12: 410, 1939.

SALINGER, F. Behandlung der Trunksucht in den Irrenanstalten, ihre Erfolge und ihre Kosten. Alkoholfrage 24: 285, 1928.

SANTESSON, C. G. [Treatment of delirium tremens with vitamin B.] Svenska Läkar-tidn. 36: 926, 1939.

SCELETH, C. E. and BEIFELD, A. F. The diagnosis of delirium tremens. Interst. med. J. 23: 408, 1916.

SCHABELITZ, H. Ein die Differentialdiagnose sichernder Reflex bei Delirium tremens. Med. Welt 10: 1808, 1936.

SCHARPFF. Geniales Trinkertum und Goethe's "Ergo bibamus." Dtsch. med. Wschr. 64: 1228, 1265, 1938.

SCHILDER, P. (a) Psychotherapy of addiction. New York, W. W. Norton & Co., 1938.
———— (b) The psychogenesis of alcoholism. Quart. J. Stud. Alc. 2: 277, 1941.

SCHNEIDER, K. Die Störungen des Gedächtnisses. In: Handbuch der Geisteskrank-heiten (Bumke, O., ed.), I, 508. Berlin, J. Springer, 1928.

SCHROEDER, P. Intoxikationspsychosen. In: Handbuch der Psychiatrie (Aschaffen-burg, G., ed.), p. 180. Leipzig, Deuticke, 1912.

SCHULTZE, E. Toxische Psychosen. In: Lehrbuch der Psychiatrie (Binswanger, O. and Siemerling, E., ed.), p. 274. Jena, G. Fischer, 1923.

SCHUSTER, P. Über das Krankheitsbild der Dipsomanie. Bonn thesis, 1930.

SCHWARTE, F. Ein Beitrag zur medikamentösen Behandlung des Alkoholismus. Fortschr. Med. 56: 321, 1938.

SCHWARZ, L. M. Zur Frage der Anstaltsbehandlung asozialer Alkoholiker insbesondere der sogenannten Selbststeller. Allg. Z. Psychiat. 96: 36, 1931.

SCICLOUNOFF, F. and FLAGG, J. La vitamine B₁ dans le delirium tremens. Rev. méd. Suisse rom. 60: 715, 1940.

SEELERT, H. Zur Frage der Entwicklungsbedingungen des pathologischen Rauschs. Mschr. Psychiat. Neurol. 86: 191, 1933.

SELIGER, R. V. (a) The problem of the alcoholic in the community. Amer. J. Psychiat. 95: 701, 1938.
———— (b) Recent psychological approaches to patients with alcohol problems. Sth. med. J., Birmingham 32: 1049, 1939.
———— (c) Working with the alcoholic. Med. Rec. 149: 147, 1939.

SHALLOO, J. P. Some cultural factors in the etiology of alcoholism. Quart. J. Stud. Alc. 2: 464, 1941.

SIEBERT, H. (a) Die psychiatrische Stellung der pathologischen Rauschzustände. Neurol. Zbl. 38: 610, 1919.
———— (b) Über den nicht ungünstigen Verlauf von amnestischen und polyneuritischen Alkoholpsychosen. Allg. Z. Psychiat. 99: 219, 1933.

SILKWORTH, W. D. (a) Alcoholism as manifestation of allergy. Med. Rec. 145: 249, 1937.
———— (b) Reclamation of the alcoholic. Med. Rec. 145: 321, 1937.

———— (c) Psychological rehabilitation of alcoholics. Med. Rec. 150: 65, 1939.

———— (d) A new approach to psychotherapy in chronic alcoholism. J. Lancet 59: 321, 1939.

SILVERMAN, I. J. The treatment of delirium tremens and acute alcoholic hallucinosis. Med. Ann. D.C. 9: 291, 1940.

SIMMEL, E. Psychoanalytic treatment in a sanatorium. Int. J. Psycho-Anal. 10: 83, 1929.

SLUCHEVSKY, I. F. and FRIKEN, A. A. [Apomorphine treatment of chronic alcoholism.] Sovetsk. vrach. Gaz., p. 557, June 30, 1933.

SMALLDON, J. L. The etiology of chronic alcoholism. Psychiat. Quart. 7: 640, 1933.

STANOJEWITSCH, L. Prophylaxe des Rauschgiftmissbrauchs. Z. psych. Hyg. 12: 65, 1939.

STAPEL, F. Das Verhalten der Pupillen bei der akuten Alkoholintoxikation; Alkoholversuche mit psychisch Gesunden und Minderwertigen. Mschr. Psychiat. Neurol. 29: 216, 1911.

STECK, H. Die Statistik des Delirium tremens in der Schweiz. Schweiz. Med. Wschr. 17: 182, 1936.

STEFAN, H. Alkoholismus und Erbgesundheitsgesetz. Med. Klinik 33: 48, 85, 1937.

STEVENSON, G. H. The psychological and medical aspects of the excessive use of alcohol. Canad. med. Ass. J. 42: 57, 1940.

STEVENSON, L. D., ALLEN, A. M. and McGOWAN, L. E. A study of the brain changes in alcoholism. Trans. Amer. neurol. Ass. 65: 93, 98, 1939.

————, McGOWAN, L. E. and ALLEN, A. M. Changes in the brain in alcoholism. Arch. Neurol. Psychiat., Chicago 45: 56, 1941.

STIEFEL, F. Über einen neuen Abbaureflex bei Delirium tremens. Mschr. Psychiat. Neurol. 74: 369, 1930.

STOCKERT, F. G. Zur Frage der Disposition zum Alkoholismus chronicus. Z. ges. Neurol. Psychiat. 106: 379, 1926.

STOECKER, W. Klinischer Beitrag zur Frage der Alkoholpsychosen. Jena, G. Fischer, 1910.

STORA, R. and GAULTIER. Sidérodromomanie et dipsomanie chez un déséquilibre. Ann. méd.-psychol. 96: 197, 1938.

STORCH. [Book review of] Gaupp, R., Die Dipsomanie. Mschr. Psychiat. Neurol. 12: 407, 1902.

STRASSER, G. Die ambulante Behandlung Alkoholkranker durch den Nervenarzt. Schweiz. med. Wschr. 69: 578, 1939.

STRECKER, E. A. Some thoughts concerning the psychology and therapy of alcoholism. J. nerv. ment. Dis. 86: 191, 1937.

———— and CHAMBERS, F. T. Alcohol, one man's meat. New York, The Macmillan Co., 1939.

———— and EBAUGH, F. G. Practical clinical psychiatry; chap. 5, Delirious-hallucinatory reactions, p. 205. Philadelphia, P. Blakiston's Sons, 1935.

STRELTSCHUK, I. W. Zur Frage der Veränderungen des morphologischen Blutbildes bei Alkoholikern. Z. ges. Neurol. Psychiat. 142: 774, 1932.

STRONG, W. A. Alcoholism, its frequency, etiology and treatment. Psychiat. Quart. 14: 403, 1940.

STUNGO, E. On the withdrawal treatment of heroin and morphine addiction and alcoholism with Rossium. Brit. J. Inebr. 36: 193, 1939.

SUCKOW, H. (a) Das Blutbild beim chronischen Alkoholismus und akuten Psychosen der Gewohnheitstrinker. Mschr. Psychiat. Neurol. 62: 240, 1926.

———— (b) Flockungsreaktion des Blutplasmas und Senkungsgeschwindigkeit der roten Blutkörperchen bei chronischen Alkoholisten und akuten Psychosen der Gewohnheitstrinker. Mschr. Psychiat. Neurol. 62: 270, 1926.

SUTTON, THOMAS. Tracts on delirium tremens, on peritonitis and on some other in-
flammatory affections. London, Thomas Underwood, 1813.
TABORI, J. Über die seelischen Hintergründe des Alkoholismus. Psychoanalyt. Praxis
3: 10, 1933.
TAIT, W. D. Psychopathology of alcoholism. J. abnorm. (soc.) Psychol. 24: 482, 1930.
TALKINGTON, P. C. and CHEAVENS, T. H. Insulin shock therapy in Korsakoff's
psychosis. J. nerv. ment. Dis. 91: 175, 1940.
TAUSK, V. On the psychology of alcoholic occupational delirium. Int. Z. (ärztl.)
Psychoanal. 3: 204, 1915.
TETZ, B. Über Halluzinose der Trinker, Königsberg thesis, 1930.
THOMAS, A.-E. Contribution à l'étude des limites de certains délires alcooliques. Paris
thesis, 1933.
THOMAS, J. M., SEMRAD, E. V. and SCHWAB, R. S. (a) Studies of the blood proteins in
delirium tremens. Amer. J. med. Sci. 195: 820, 1938.
————, ————, ———— (b) Observations on the use of fluids and lumbar puncture in
the treatment of delirium tremens. Ann. intern. Med. 12: 2006, 1939.
TILLISS. Die Wahl der Behandlungsmethode nichtgeisteskranker Trinker. Psychiat.-
neurol. Wschr. 35: 130, 1933.
TILLOTSON, K. J. and FLEMING, R. Personality and sociologic factors in the prognosis
and treatment of chronic alcoholism. New Engl. J. Med. 217: 611, 1937.
TOKARSKY, B.A. [Therapy of alcoholism.] Sovetsk. vrach. Jur., p. 1033, 1938.
TOULOUSE, E., COURTOIS, A. and RUSSELL. Modifications chimiques du sang au
cours du delirium tremens alcoolique. Ann. méd.-psychol. 89: 124, 1931.
————, MARCHAND, L. and COURTOIS, A. L'encéphalite psychosique aiguë des al-
cooliques. Ann. méd.-psychol. 91: 1, 1933.
TOWNS, C. B. Drug and alcohol sickness. New York, M. M. Barbour Co., 1932.
TRAMER, M. Der Fussballenreflex und sein Wert als Differentialdiagnostikum bei
Delirium tremens. Psychiat.-neurol. Wschr. 34: 37, 1932.
TRIBOULET, H., MATHIEU, F. and MIGNOT, R. Traité de l'alcoolisme; chaps. 5 and 6,
p. 191. Paris, Masson & Co., 1905.
TROTTER, THOMAS. An essay, medical, philosophical, and chemical, on drunkenness,
and its effects on the human body. Boston, Bradford & Read; and Philadelphia,
A. Finley, 1813.
TROTTER, W. Herd instinct and its bearing on the psychology of civilized man.
Sociol. Rev. 1: 227, 1908.
TRUCHE, C. Les modifications biologiques du sang, des urines et du liquide céphalo-
rachidien dans l'alcoolisme aigu et chronique. Paris thesis, 1933.
VERSTRAETEN, P. Syndrome de Korsakoff d'origine paludéenne. J. belge Neurol.
Psychiat. 33: 275, 1933.
VIGNE, P. Le grave problème de la dépopulation de la France; la question du nombre
et celle de la qualité; l'alcool cancer social. Avenir méd. 36: 178, 1939.
VOEGTLIN, W. L. The treatment of alcoholism by establishing a conditioned reflex.
Amer. J. med. Sci. 199: 802, 1940.
————, LEMERE, F. and BROZ, W. Conditioned reflex therapy of alcoholic addiction;
III, an evaluation of present results in the light of previous experience with this
method. Quart. J. Stud. Alc. 1: 501, 1940.
VOSS. Zur Ätiologie der Dämmerzustände. Zbl. Nervenheilk. 31: 678, 1908.
WADDELL, J. A. and HAAG, H. B. Alcohol in moderation and excess. Richmond,
William Byrd Press, Inc., 1938.
WAGNER VON JAUREGG, J. Die Giftwirkung des Alkohols bei einigen nervösen und
psychischen Erkrankungen. Wien. klin. Wschr. 14: 359, 1901.
WALL, J. H. (a) A study of alcoholism in men. Amer. J. Psychiat. 92: 1389, 1936.
———— (b) A study of alcoholism in women. Amer. J. Psychiat. 93: 943, 1937.

WARTMANN, E. Alkoholismus und Epilepsie in ihren wechselseitigen Beziehungen. Arch. Psychiat. Nervenkr. **29**: 933, 1897.

WASSERMEYER. Delirium tremens. Arch. Psychiat. Nervenkr. **44**: 860, 1908.

WEBER, A. Delirium tremens und Alkoholhalluzinose im Rorschachschen Form-deutversuch. Z. ges. Neurol. Psychiat. **159**: 446, 1937.

WECHSLER, D. A study of retention in Korsakoff psychosis. Psychiat. Bull. N.Y. St. Hosp., p. 1, 1917.

WEEKS, C. C. Alcohol and human life. London, H. K. Lewis, 1938.

WEGENER, H. Der gegenwärtige Stand des Alkoholismus in den rheinischen provinzial Heil- und Pflegeanstalten. Alkoholfrage **24**: 225, 1928.

WEISS, O. L. Zur Frage der Alkoholentziehung. Psychiat.-neurol. Wschr. **35**: 85, 1933.

WERNICKE, C. Grundriss der Psychiatrie. 2d ed. Leipzig, G. Thieme, 1906.

WEXBERG, E. (*a*) Some remarks on the treatment of alcoholism. Sth. med. J., Bir-mingham **30**: 842, 1937.

———— (*b*) Metabolic deficiency as a possible factor in neuropsychiatric states. Amer. J. Psychiat. **95**: 1127, 1939.

WEYGANDT, W. Lehrbuch der Geisteskrankheiten. Halle a. S., Marhold, 1935.

WHITE, W. A. (*a*) Alcoholism, a symptom. Interst. med. J. **23**: 404, 1916.

———— (*b*) Outlines of psychiatry. Washington, Nerv. Ment. Dis. Publ. Co., 1932.

WHITNEY, J. S. Death rates by occupation. New York, National Tuberculosis Asso-ciation, 1934.

WHOLEY, C. C. Revelations of the unconscious in a toxic (alcoholic) psychosis. Amer. J. Insan. **74**: 437, 1917.

WILBUR, D. L., MacLEAN, A. R. and ALLEN, E. V. Clinical observations on effect of benzedrine sulphate. Proc. Staff Meet. Mayo Clin. **12**: 97, 1937.

WILLIAMS, I. D. The emergency treatment of the alcoholic. J. nerv. ment. Dis. **72**: 161, 1931.

WILLIAMS, T. A. The pathogenesis of alcoholism and narcotism and the treatment of their causes. Interst. med. J. **23**: 455, 1916.

WILLS, E. F. Delirium tremens: its causation, prevention and treatment. Brit. J. Inebr. **28**: 43, 1930.

WILSON, H. H. Management of alcoholism. Calif. West. Med. **45**: 349, 1936.

WINGFIELD, H. The forms of alcoholism and their treatment. London, Hodder & Houghton, 1919.

WITTMAN, P. (*a*) A controlled study of the developmental and personality characteris-tics of chronic alcoholics. Elgin Papers **3**: 77, 1939.

———— (*b*) A differential analysis of "adjustment" scores for chronic alcoholics and controls. Elgin Papers **3**: 85, 1939.

———— (*c*) Diagnosis and analysis of temperament for group of alcoholics compared with controls. Elgin Papers **3**: 94, 1939.

WLASSAK, R. (*a*) Ist der Alkohol ein primärer Degenerationsfaktor? In: Bericht über den XIII. Internat. Kongress gegen den Alkoholismus, p. 186. Utrecht, Van Boekhoven, 1912.

———— (*b*) Grundriss der Alkoholfrage. Leipzig, S. Hirzel, 1929.

WOLFENSBERGER, M. Der Alkoholwahnsinn (akute Halluzinose der Trinker) und seine Beziehungen zu den Schizophrenien. Z. ges. Neurol. Psychiat. **82**: 385, 1923.

WOLFF, H. G. and CURRAN, D. Nature of delirium tremens and allied states. Arch. Neurol. Psychiat., Chicago **33**: 1175, 1935.

WOLFF, P. Alcohol and drug addiction in Germany. Brit. J. Inebr. **31**: 141, 1933.

WORTIS, H. (*a*) Vitamins in nervous health and disease. N.Y. St. J. Med. **39**: 1178, 1939.

———— (*b*) Delirium tremens. Quart. J. Stud. Alc. **1**: 251, 1940.

—— and Jolliffe, N. Present status of vitamins in nervous health and disease. N.Y. St. J. Med. **41**: 1461, 1941.

——, Wortis, S. B., Frank, P., Jolliffe, N. and Bowman, K. M. Biochemical changes associated with alcoholic delirium. Arch. Neurol. Psychiat., Chicago **41**: 655, 1939.

——, —— and Marsh, F. I. Vitamin C studies in alcoholics. Amer. J. Psychiat. **94**: 891, 1938.

Wortis, J., Bowman, K. M. and Goldfarb, W. The use of insulin in the treatment of alcoholism. Med. Clin. N. Amer. **24**: 671, 1940.

Wuth, O. (*a*) Über psychische Krankheitserscheinungen by Hypoglykämie. Mschr. Psychiat. Neurol. **73**: 129, 1929.

—— (*b*) Zur Erbanlage der Süchtigen. Z. ges. Neurol. Psychiat. **153**: 495, 1935.

Wyrsch, J. (*a*) Über Wahnbildung bei Alkoholdeliranten. Allg. Z. Psychiat. **103**: 67, 1935.

—— (*b*) Alkoholikerbehandlung und psychiatrische Polikliniken. Schweiz. med. Wschr. **67**: 951, 1937.

Zehner, L. Über die chronischen Psychosen nach Alkoholmissbrauch. Bonn thesis, 1930.

Ziehen (G.) T. Psychiatrie für Aerzte und Studierende. 4th ed. Leipzig, S. Hirzel, 1911.

Part II

CHAPTER III

Vitamin Deficiencies in Chronic Alcoholism*

Norman Jolliffe

INTRODUCTION

ALTHOUGH the role of alcohol as the direct etiologic factor in various "alcoholic" diseases was questioned for many years, it has been only in the past decade that the concept of the "alcoholic" diseases has been importantly modified. These modifications are so radical that for the purpose of theoretical discussion this review may be limited to the recent literature. Some older publications will be utilized mainly for their descriptive value. The alcoholic psychoses will be considered only in so far as nutritional deficiency may be advanced as an etiologic factor in these conditions.

The theory that certain "alcoholic" diseases result from nutritional deficiencies rather than from the direct toxic action of alcohol meets nowadays with little resistance. This is especially true for a group of "alcoholic" neuropsychiatric syndromes. A vitamin deficiency or adequacy is the modern explanation of the axiom that heavy drinkers who consume little food are subject to "alcoholic" diseases, while those who eat well, and in whom assimilation is not impaired by gastrointestinal disorders, seldom develop these diseases. Listed in the order of the weight of evidence in their favor, the following diseases of the alcoholic are now known as vitamin-deficiency diseases: "alcoholic" or "pseudo" pellagra, "alcoholic" polyneuropathy, nicotinic acid deficiency encephalopathy, and Wernicke's disease. In addition, experimental and clinical findings point toward a nutritional deficiency in the Korsakoff psychosis, delirium tremens, acute alcoholic hallucinosis, and fatty infiltration and cirrhosis of the liver, but no conclusive evidence has been adduced. These facts suggest the possibility that any disease or syndrome which occurs more frequently in the alcoholic than in the nonalcoholic may be a deficiency disease, except those due to trauma or infection.

General recognition of the immediately causative role of nutritional

*The combined bibliography of Chapters III, IV, V and VI appears at the end of Chapter VI, pp. 310–324.

deficiencies in the "alcoholic" diseases has led to two curious developments:

1. The proalcohol group have tended to distort these findings into arguments for the essential harmlessness of alcohol (e.g., Smith and Helwig).

2. The antialcohol group have made the same error in interpretation, and hence have attempted to combat the findings themselves (e.g., Weeks).

It should be clearly stated that, although these diseases do unquestionably develop as a direct result of nutritional deficiency, it is the ingestion of too much alcohol that is responsible for the nutritional deficiency.

Before discussing these specific diseases, consideration must be given to the relation between alcohol and nutrition, as well as to the role of vitamins in general metabolism, in order to understand the metabolic changes that take place in the chronic alcoholic.

I. ALCOHOL AND NUTRITION

Vitamin deficiencies in the chronic alcoholic were originally attributed exclusively to the substitution of vitamin-free alcohol for vitamin-containing foods. The inadequacy of this explanation was soon realized and it is now believed that alcohol may contribute to the production of deficiency diseases in two main ways: (*a*) through modifications of the diet which change the actual or relative vitamin and caloric content, and (*b*) through chemical, physiological or structural changes in various organs of the body which, in turn, may lead to changes in the absorption, assimilation and excretion of vitamins.

Dietary changes. Adequacy of a diet with respect to vitamin B was first estimated by Cowgill, who showed, from careful feeding experiments with mice, rats, pigeons and dogs, that man's requirement of vitamin B_1 could be predicted by the formula

$$\frac{\text{Vitamin } B_1 \text{ Milligrams Equivalent}}{\text{Calories}} = 0.0284 \text{ Weight in Kilograms.}$$

He tested this prediction formula for man by analyzing 180 human dietaries associated and unassociated with beriberi. A close agreement was found between the adequacy of the diet, as predicted by this formula, and the presence or absence of beriberi.

From the nature of the equation, the expression

$$\frac{\text{Vitamin } B_1 \text{ Milligrams Equivalent}}{\text{Calories}}$$

(hereafter referred to as the vitamin B_1/calorie ratio) may be used as an index of the adequacy or inadequacy of a diet in vitamin B_1 by reference to Cowgill's prediction chart (Fig. 1). If, considering the

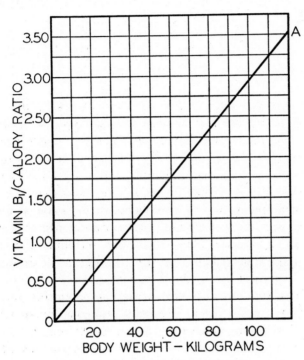

Figure 1. Cowgill's Prediction Formula.

weight of the subject, the vitamin B_1/calorie ratio is definitely above the line AO, the diet is theoretically adequate in vitamin B_1. If the vitamin B_1/calorie ratio is definitely below the line AO, the diet is theoretically inadequate in vitamin B_1. Vitamin B_1/calorie ratios falling on or near the line are considered borderline in character. In Table 1 the vitamin B_1 requirement, in international units, has been calculated on the basis of this formula for persons of various weights and caloric intakes.

Cowgill's prediction formula, which he hoped would "be correct in the sense of a reasonable first approximation," indicates that the vitamin B_1 requirement of man is directly proportional to both body

TABLE I

*Vitamin B₁ Requirement of Man Estimated from Cowgill's
Formula for Various Body Weights and Caloric Intakes*

Body Weight Kilograms	Required Vit. B_1/Cal. Ratio	I.U. Vitamin B_1 Required in Diets Containing Following Calories				
		1,500	2,000	2,500	3,000	3,500
50	1.47	110	147	184	220	257
60	1.77	134	178	222	226	311
70	2.05	154	205	256	307	359
80	2.40	180	240	300	360	420
90	2.65	200	266	332	398	464
100	2.95	221	295	369	442	516
110	3.25	244	325	406	487	569

weight and caloric intake. It is understandable that a man weighing
100 kg. should require about twice as much vitamin B₁ as a man
weighing 50 kg., since the larger person, other things being equal,
requires a higher caloric intake than the smaller. It is difficult to
explain, however, why a man weighing 100 kg. should require a larger
amount of vitamin B₁ to metabolize 1 g. of sugar than one weighing
50 kg. For example, Cowgill's formula indicates (Table 1) that a man
weighing 50 kg. and consuming a 1,500-calorie diet would require
110 I.U. while a man weighing 100 kg. and consuming a 3,000 calorie
diet would require not 220 but 440 I.U. of vitamin B₁. In questioning
this portion of the Cowgill prediction formula, Williams and Spies
have advanced some weighty criticisms. They point out that a Great
Dane weighing 72 kg. would require 63 times as much vitamin B₁
daily, in 5.25 times as much food, as a dog weighing 6 kg.; and 392
times as much vitamin B₁, in 10.9 times as much food, as a Pekingese
of 2 kg. Also, if the vitamin B₁/calorie ratio is directly proportional to
body weight there should be, in outbreaks of beriberi in prisons, ships
and asylums, a preponderance of men of above average weight developing beriberi—a supposition not substantiated by their review of
the available data in the literature. Williams and Spies concluded that
the vitamin B₁/calorie ratio appears to be independent of the weight
of the individual within the limits of experimental error.

Jolliffe, Goodhart, Gennis and Cline have presented some evidence
from experiments with normal human subjects which seems to indicate that small persons consistently excrete more thiamin in the urine
than larger ones maintained with the same caloric and vitamin B₁
intake. Symptoms of vitamin B₁ deficiency also developed earlier in
the larger than in the smaller subjects when all were maintained with

a constant, identical weighed diet containing a vitamin B_1/calorie ratio of 1.0. As only 5 subjects were studied it is too early to make, from direct experimentation, even a first approximation of the relation of weight to the vitamin B_1 requirement.

Since the relation of body weight, independent of the caloric intake, to the vitamin B_1 requirement is doubtful and in dispute, is it practical to disregard it in adults in judging the adequacy of vitamin B_1 in a diet? An analysis of 100 of Cowgill's dietaries as retabulated by Williams and Spies indicates that human beriberi is almost always associated with dietaries having a vitamin B_1/calorie ratio of less than 1.7 and almost never associated with dietaries having a ratio of 2.3 or more. Dietaries having vitamin B_1/calorie ratios between 1.7 and 2.29 are irregularly associated with beriberi. Therefore, until more is definitely known of the influence of body weight, diets having vitamin B_1/calorie ratios of 1.7 to 2.29 may be taken as borderline, and those below and above these figures as inadequate and adequate, respectively.

While there is a difference of opinion as to which calories modify the vitamin B_1 requirement, the available evidence supports the hypothesis that the vitamin B_1 requirement rises with the caloric intake, provided the increase in calories is not derived from fat. It is well known that experimental animals who fail to eat or who are maintained with water alone do not develop polyneuropathy. Animals forcibly fed a diet above their caloric needs but poor in vitamin B_1 develop deficiency earlier than animals maintained with the same type of diet in normal caloric amounts; the latter, in turn, develop deficiency earlier than those animals who eat poorly or are permitted less than their caloric needs. Wechsler, Jervis and Potts have shown that the addition of alcohol to a diet containing borderline amounts of vitamin B_1 will produce polyneuropathy in monkeys.

The customary ingestion of large quantities of alcohol may affect the vital vitamin B_1/calorie ratio in several ways:

1. The inebriate may, and frequently does, eat very little, and thus substitutes vitamin-free alcohol for vitamin-containing foods.*

2. Even if food intake is not decreased, the alcohol itself contributes a large number of calories without increasing the amount of vitamin B_1 and hence the ratio between the two is adversely affected.

3. The use of alcohol may so irritate the gastrointestinal tract as to

*Richter has shown that rats using a weak alcohol solution, instead of water, decrease their food intake in proportion to the calories obtained from alcohol.

cause considerable restriction of the diet, and this again would disturb the vitamin B_1/calorie ratio.

4. It is possible, according to Alexander (b), that such modifications in the diet may bring about an imbalance of various vitamins, which may be as important as a deficiency in one or more of them. This theory of Alexander's will be developed in detail in the discussion of Wernicke's disease (Chapter IV).

The first point requires little discussion. Reliance upon alcohol in place of a balanced diet leads inevitably to nutritional deficiency. But that alcohol calories may increase the vitamin requirement is not generally known or well understood, and is still neglected in estimating the adequacy of a diet. This role of supplementary alcohol calories has been recently reviewed [Jolliffe (c)] and can be easily illustrated.

Sherman's average American diet contains 6,847 mg. equivalent of vitamin B_1 (342 I.U. or 1.03 mg. as thiamin chloride) and 2,500 calories, which gives a vitamin B_1/calorie ratio of 2.74 and a margin of safety of 19 per cent above the upper borderline level of 2.29. An individual who supplements this diet with vitamin-B_1-free calories, such as those obtained from alcohol, adds only to the denominator of the vitamin B_1/calorie ratio, thereby lessening it. If the alcohol supplement amounts to 1,320 calories (the approximate caloric value of 16 ounces of proof whisky) the vitamin B_1 intake in absolute amounts remains the same but the vitamin B_1/calorie ratio is reduced to 1.79, a level only slightly above that usually associated with beriberi. If the alcohol supplement amounts to 660 calories (the approximate value of 8 ounces of proof whisky) the vitamin B_1/calorie ratio is 2.17, a value in the borderline range which is irregularly associated with clinical beriberi. An analysis of the effect of alcohol calories on the actual diets of inebriates, as made by Jolliffe, Colbert and Joffe, will be presented in the section on polyneuropathy.

An instance of a diet originally adequate in vitamin B_1 becoming deficient when supplemented with vitamin-free calories from a source other than alcohol, namely sucrose, was reported by Stepp and Schroeder. Their patient had beriberi, but his diet appeared adequate in vitamin B_1. It was not until a daily supplement of 500 to 1,500 g. of sugar was discovered that the cause of the beriberi became evident.

Mentally ill patients who refuse to eat when admitted to a hospital are often maintained, not with tube feedings of milk, cream, fruit juices and eggs, but with parenteral, oral or rectal feedings of glucose. With such treatment they often develop a polyneuropathy, sometimes within 7 days. For example, a 20-year-old girl was transferred to the Psychiatric Division of the Bellevue Hospital from another hospital where she had been admitted 7 days previously in an acute stupor of psychogenic origin. During those 7 days all calories had been administered by parenteral infusions of 10 per cent glucose solutions. Tube feedings were not given because of the fear of aspiration pneumonia. When brought to Bellevue, the patient had polyneuropathy as evidenced by bilateral foot drop, absent knee and ankle jerks, marked calf muscle tenderness and stocking hyperesthesia. After 7 days of thiamin therapy all polyneuropathic signs had disappeared.

As a high caloric intake often renders a diet containing a considerable absolute amount of vitamin B_1 a beriberi-producing diet, so a low caloric intake will often make a diet containing small absolute amounts of vitamin B_1 adequate to prevent the development of clinical evidence of vitamin B_1 deficiency. Clinical evidence of vitamin B deficiency diseases, in the author's experience, is practically unknown in subjects eating little or no food, provided they have not subsisted on alcohol, or on a diet of tea and toast or coffee and crackers, and have not been forcibly fed with glucose, corn syrup or other vitamin-free nourishment. For example, an 18-year-old girl, admitted to the Psychiatric Division of Bellevue Hospital with marked undernutrition, had subsisted on one-half grapefuit and two shredded wheat biscuits with added whole milk and four teaspoons of sugar daily for a period of more than three months. The vitamin B_1 intake was estimated as not more than 100 I.U. (150 cc. of milk and 20 g. of sugar were estimated as the amount used with the two shredded wheat biscuits), the caloric intake was about 500, and the vitamin B_1/calorie ratio about 4.0. During this time her weight had fallen from 107 to 68 pounds. She had never been forcibly fed or given vitamin supplements. This patient showed no clinical signs of deficiency disease.

It is clear, then, that an absolute quantity of vitamin B_1 cannot be given as the requirement of man, but that the caloric intake, whether it is low, average or high, must always be considered in evaluating the adequacy of vitamin B_1 in a diet. It seems, therefore, that calories derived from alcohol, if taken in significant amounts, should always be considered when estimating the adequacy of dietaries. Sherman, in 1924, did not include the alcohol calories in his average American diet; nor did Stiebeling and Phipard, in 1939, include them in their analysis of the diets of wage earners and clerical workers.

The extent to which alcohol enters into the American diet and the resulting modifications of the vitamin B_1/calorie ratio are of particular interest to the nutritionist, physician and public health authorities.

Alcohol (100 per cent) contained in the tax-paid beverages consumed* in the United States during the fiscal year ending June 30, 1938, amounted to 618,284,952 liters or 4.756 liters per capita per annum. This amount of alcohol would provide 9.5 liters of proof whisky per capita per year, equivalent to about 73 calories per capita *per diem*. A per capita *per diem* basis in estimating the caloric consumption from alcoholic beverages does not, however, furnish an accurate index, since these beverages are used chiefly by the adult population. Admission statistics from large hospitals in the United States as well as from European hospitals indicate that 95 per cent of the drinking population is in the age range of 25 to 64 years. Thus 95 per cent of this alcohol would be consumed by approximately 60,000,000 people in the United States. On this basis the "drinking age" population consumed an average of 157 alcohol calories per person daily.† This figure should be increased to include the legal consumption of alcohol contained in medicines of all sorts, in flavoring extracts and in homemade beverages, plus that from illicit sources. Including these, the total caloric consumption from alcohol by the "drinking age" population must amount to some 200 calories per capita *per diem*.‡

The significance of the omission of these alcohol calories in influencing our estimate of the adequacy of American dietaries can be illustrated as follows. The addition of 200 vitamin-free calories to Sherman's average American diet reduces the vitamin B_1/calorie ratio from 2.74 to 2.53, and the margin of safety from 19 per cent to 10 per cent, almost a 50 per cent reduction. The diets of families of employed

---

*Calculated from statistics on alcoholic beverages issued by the United States Treasury Department, Bureau of Internal Revenue, Alcohol Tax Unit. Tax-paid withdrawals in any one fiscal year do not represent precisely the amount that enters into consumption. Comparison of the withdrawals during recent years indicates, however, that there has not been any marked fluctuation in the quantities withdrawn annually. It is therefore safe to assume that during the period considered the tax-paid withdrawals represent a fair approximation of the amounts entering into consumption.

†This may be broken down into separate estimates for the male and female population. Assuming that males consumed 5/6 of the total amount of liquor, their average alcohol caloric intake would be 215 per day and that of the females would be 43.

‡According to Donovan and Hanke beer contains not more than 10 Sherman Units (2.5 I.U.) of vitamin B_1 per hundred cubic centimeters. Since there are sufficient non-alcohol calories in beer to cancel this small amount of vitamin B_1 in the vitamin B_1/calorie ratio, both items have been omitted from these calculations.

wage earners and clerical workers in cities, recently analyzed by Stiebeling and Phipard, contained an average of 3,051 calories and 9,745 mg. equivalent (488 I.U. or 1.46 mg. as thiamin chloride) of vitamin B_1 (prior to cooking), giving a vitamin B_1/calorie ratio of 3.32. The addition of 200 vitamin-free calories to this diet reduces the ratio to 3.13 and the margin of safety from 44 per cent to 36 per cent, an 18.2 per cent reduction in the margin of safety.

The reduction, by the average consumption of alcohol, of the margin of safety in vitamin B_1 by from 18 to 50 per cent is thus an important factor. Our dietary, without alcohol calories, already provides such a small margin of safety in the B vitamins that when any of the numerous factors that increase the vitamin requirement of the individual occur, clinical subvitaminosis is likely to develop. In this country, when vitamin B_1 deficiency occurs, the disease is not usually labeled beriberi, and its true etiology is obscured by naming it after the factor that increases the vitamin requirement, such as "diabetic," "metabolic," "infectious," "gestational," or "gastrogenous" polyneuropathy. The margin of safety of the American diet was not always so low, for the American of 1840, in order to obtain 2,500 calories from the foods then available, must incidentally have obtained 900 to 1,000 I.U. of vitamin B_1 daily, and probably an equivalent increase in the other B vitamins, or about three times the amount obtained by us. On the basis of 2,500 calories and 900 I.U. of vitamin B_1, the vitamin B_1/calorie ratio was 7.2, providing a margin of safety of 230 per cent. This diet would permit the addition of 2,625 vitamin-free calories and still remain equal, as measured by vitamin B_1/calorie ratios, to the contemporary diets reported by Stiebeling and Phipard. In other words, if all the alcohol could be metabolized, the 1840 American could use a quart of proof whisky daily and still be consuming a diet as adequate in vitamin B_1 as the average American of today. This explains in part the apparently greater immunity of our great-grandparents to certain nutritional deficiency diseases, and their traditional ability, if true, to consume large amounts of liquor without impairment of health and with survival to old age.

Finally, there is no doubt that constant ingestion of alcohol serves to irritate the gastrointestinal tract, as is evidenced by the traditional morning nausea and vomiting of the chronic alcoholic. This naturally results in further dietary restrictions and so a vicious circle is set up.

Chemical, physiologic and structural changes. Wechsler (*a*) suggested that changes in the gastrointestinal tract and the liver could impair absorption and utilization of the vitamins. This idea was seconded by Minot, Strauss and Cobb and by Strauss (a). It was not, however, until after Cowgill approximated the vitamin B_1 requirement of man and gave a method for its estimation that Jolliffe, Colbert and Joffe were able to emphasize the importance of the role played by the increased vitamin requirement in consequence of the calories furnished by alcohol. Thus by 1939 Alexander (a–d); Facquet; Gounelle; Jolliffe, Goodhart, Gennis and Cline; Langeron; McGee; and Villaret, Justin-Besançon, Klotz and Sikorav were all in virtual agreement as to the part played by these several factors in explaining the role of alcohol ingestion in producing deficiency diseases. To these, however, McGee adds the increased excretion of water-soluble vitamin B_1.

Recent experiments on the metabolism of alcohol in the presence of injuries of the liver (e.g., Clark, Morrissey, Fazekas and Welch; Mirsky and Nelson) suggest that the liver conditions frequently found in chronic alcoholics may be a cause of malutilization of vitamins. Recent acquisitions to our knowledge of the disturbed carbohydrate metabolism in chronic alcoholism (Goldfarb, Bowman and Parker; Dontcheff) indicate a connection with vitamin metabolism. We may have here a further contribution to the anomalous vitamin utilization of inebriates. These investigations, however, require much refinement before definitive conclusions can be drawn. It is clear, however, that the habitual excessive use of alcohol leads to nutritional and metabolic disturbances which must be considered in relation to the etiology of the diseases of chronic alcoholism discussed in this work.

II. POLYNEUROPATHY

Although alcoholic polyneuropathy has interested the medical profession so greatly as to give rise to a large literature, it is not the most frequent complication of chronic alcoholism. My experience, and that of my associates at Bellevue Hospital, indicates an incidence of approximately 20 per cent. Recently, however, there has been a perceptible decrease. Analysis of the literature would indicate that it may be between 15 and 20 per cent in European countries. There seems, however, to be considerable geographic variation in the incidence of polyneuropathy. For example, de Soldati states that in the Argentine it is a rare disease.

Pathology

Afflictions of the peripheral nerves have been known since Hippocrates gave a clinical description of diphtheritic paralysis. Jacob Bontius wrote of beriberi in 1642, and John Coakley Lettsom of "alcoholic" polyneuropathy in 1787. The first pathologic description of the peripheral nerves was that of Duménil, who designated the neuropathy as "paralysis périphérique due mouvement et due sentiment partout sur les quatre membres." Pathologic studies of the 1880's by Lancereaux, by Gombault, and by Joffroy* led to the term "neuritis" being firmly established in the medical literature. The work of Carmichael and Stern and of Mott showed, however, that the pathology in the peripheral nerves was not inflammatory but degenerative. Orton and Bender showed that the pathology was not limited to the peripheral nerves but involved as well tracts of the spinal cord, especially the lateral horns.

Polyneuropathy vs. polyneuritis. In consequence of these, as well as of his own findings, it has been suggested by Wechsler (*d*) that "the term multiple neuropathy, polyneuropathy or peripheral neuropathy be substituted for multiple neuritis in those cases in which both the cause and the pathologic changes point to a degenerative process, and that the designation neuritis be retained only in those cases in which there is adequate causation and in which an inflammatory condition is recognized as well as demonstrable." This distinction seems justified, and throughout this review, the term "polyneuropathy" will be used except in direct quotations. As Wechsler says, "This is not mere cavilling with words. . . . The change in nomenclature is important because it embodies a different concept and fits an actual pathologic condition." Furthermore, "It is obvious that the treatment of degenerative diseases differs from that of inflammatory states." The distinctions made here correspond to distinguishing encephalopathy and myelopathy from encephalitis and myelitis. The former terms cover degenerative changes and the latter terms refer to inflammation of the brain and the spinal cord respectively. It is noteworthy that very early Erb proposed to reserve the term "neuritis" for inflammatory processes of the nerves only, in distinction from simple degenerative changes. Apparently he did not succeed with his suggestion because of Strümpell's resistance to this idea.

The justification of Wechsler's terminology is in itself a contribution to the pathology of polyneuropathies and parts of it are given here *in extenso.*

As to the pathology one could justly conclude on theoretical grounds alone that the changes in "neuritis" from the effects of alcohol are not inflammatory in nature. To begin with, the neuron, and indeed all nerve

*All cit. Rosenheim.

tissue, being ectodermal in origin, does not easily react with an inflammatory reaction (except in poliomyelitis and some forms of encephalitis). Mesodermal structures, that is, connective tissue and blood vessels, do so react. It is the coverings of the brain and spinal cord and of the peripheral nerves that show inflammatory reactions. The nerve fibers show degeneration. Secondly, it is not likely that a substance which causes degenerative destruction of the brain or spinal cord will bring about inflammation of the peripheral nerves if it happens to affect them. It is known, for instance, that alcohol causes encephalopathy, and so does lead. Neither causes encephalitis. What passes for alcoholic polioencephalitis is not an encephalitis at all but an encephalopathy.

Aside from theoretical consideration, however, it is necessary merely to examine photomicrographs of the pathologic processes of "multiple neuritis." They show destruction of myelin, fragmentation of axis cylinders and no round cell infiltration or inflammatory changes of an exudative nature. If the nerve cell is affected in the same process, there is no clouding, swelling, and no neuronophagia, but just disappearance of the body and nucleus. In short, one sees only the changes of true degeneration. It is of interest that the pathologic changes observed in most cases of "neuritis" are precisely the same as those associated with poisoning by heavy metals and vitamin deficiency. In the latter conditions there never is any question of inflammation. The fact is that the old descriptions of "neuritis" date to the days when histologic methods were less refined and the concepts less precisely defined.

Still other evidence points to the validity of the concept of neuropathy as against that of neuritis. If it is true that in many cases of so-called multiple neuritis there is food privation, and therefore avitaminosis, there is every reason to expect a degenerative process, such as is seen, for instance, in spinal cord and root lesions of pernicious anemia. Such a process is precisely what occurs; the peripheral nerves, however, are more selectively its seat, although the spinal cord does not escape in many cases of peripheral neuropathy. Indeed, in some instances, particularly of poisoning by alcohol, lead or carbon monoxide, the brain, too, suffers. It may be repeated once more that in these cases one is dealing with an encephalopathy and not an encephalitis.

The conclusion is justified that the same degenerative process in the brain affects the peripheral nerves and leads to multiple neuropathy.

The peripheral nerves. The description of the pathology of the peripheral nerves in alcoholic polyneuropathy is surprisingly infrequently and scantily represented in the literature. It is characteristic that in the *Handbuch der Neurologie,* 1936 (Vol. XIII), by Bumke and Foerster, no description of peripheral pathology dating later than 1896 is given. The 200-page dissertation of Klotz (*a*), 1937, on alcoholic polyneuritis does not contain more than a mere mention that the peripheral nerves undergo a process of degeneration.

Table 2 lists some of the peripheral nerves, and authors who have given more or less detailed descriptions of changes in these in poly-neuropathy.

TABLE 2

Peripheral Nerves, and Authors Who Have Described Changes in Each with Polyneuropathy

Peripheral Nerve	Authors
Sciatic	Rosenheim; Vedder (*a*); Carmichael and Stern
Popliteal	Duménil; Carmichael and Stern
Superficial Peroneal	Oppenheim; Déjerine; Gudden
Radial	Oppenheim; Déjerine; Gudden; Carmichael and Stern
Tibial	Leschke; Carmichael and Stern
Median	Duménil; Carmichael and Stern
Ulnar	Duménil; Carmichael and Stern
Vagal	Rosenheim; Déjerine; Gudden
Phrenic	Campbell
Internal Cutaneous	Carmichael and Stern
Musculospiral	Carmichael and Stern
Acoustic	Halphen, Salomon and Loiseau
General description of de-generative changes in pe-ripheral nerves aside from the above	Leyden; Eichhorst; Eisenlohr; Stewart; Mueller; Oppen-heim; Vierordt; Roth; Webber; Strümpell; Pierson; Caspari; Hirt; Löwenfeld; Bernhardt; Remak; Lilien-feld; Francotte; Schulz; Steegmann; Boeck; Joffroy; and Kast (the latter 3 cit. Rosenheim)

All these authors stressed the progression of the severity of changes from the center to the periphery. They also commonly observed that there was a predilection for the peroneal nerve (!) and, to somewhat less extent, for the radial nerve. It has been also commonly found that the axis cylinders are mostly intact and that an uncharacteristic de-generation of the medullary sheath occurs. The diseased nerves shrink to a coarse gray string. Steegmann states that the fibers carrying "new" sensation ("epicritic sensation" of Head, or "neosensibility" of Brouwder) are damaged more than those carrying "old" sensation ("protopathic sensation" of Head, or "vital" or "paleosensibility" of Brouwder).

In view of the scarcity of intensive descriptions, those of Vedder, as well as of Carmichael and Stern, are presented here in some detail. The pathology of the peripheral nerves in subjects having beriberi has recently been summarized by Vedder (*b*) as follows:

Since the legs are first affected in beriberi, degeneration is most marked in the sciatic nerve and its branches, but some degree of degeneration may be found in any peripheral nerve. Degeneration of the myelin sheath is constant and affects the majority of the fibers, the myelin being broken up into balls or beads and eventually disappearing. When this occurs, the axis cylinders may show a coiled appearance and in certain cases are fragmented or atrophied. The more chronic and advanced the case, the more nerve cylinders are affected, but usually the majority appear normal even when the medullary sheath shows advanced degeneration. At the same time that such advanced changes are found in the nerves supplying the legs, the brachial nerves may show only a diffuse blackening of the myelin sheath with the Marchi stain. Similar degenerative changes have been found in the cranial nerves, particularly the phrenics and the vagi. It is especially to be noted that degeneration of the sympathetic system has been demonstrated, as in branches of the cardiac plexus, the splanchnic nerves and branches of the solar and renal plexuses.

The muscles supplied, particularly of the leg and thigh, are markedly atrophied, with loss of cross striation and shrinkage of the sarcoplasm, often combined with cloudy swelling or fatty degeneration. These changes are not characteristic of beriberi but may be found in the muscles in any variety of polyneuritis.

Most observers have not noted "naked eye" changes in the brain and spinal cord. Bentley described, however, 19 necropsies of human beriberi in which he observed congestion and softening of the brain, the spinal cord, and the meninges.

The lesions of the cord were so gross as not to require the use of the microscope to see them, for in some, only a few hours after death, the cord was soft and diffluent with hemorrhages, marked congestion and extensive edema quite sufficient in themselves to cause all the symptoms. My observations go to prove that it is a cord lesion which involves both sensory and motor functions of central origin, a subacute inflammation of the spinal cord and its membranes.

Vedder (*b*) notes that while

most observers have not found such gross changes or have attributed them to postmortem degeneration, there can be no doubt as to the microscopic changes, which have been reported by all observers. Degeneration of the medullary sheath has been demonstrated in scattered fibers in all tracts of the cord, but especially in the posterior columns as well as in both anterior and posterior nerve roots. In some cases the axis cylinder is fragmented. Degeneration of the medullary sheath is best demonstrated by the Marchi method; of the cells by Nissl or Giemsa stains. The axis cylinder is readily seen when degeneration of the medullary sheath is extensive but may be brought out more clearly by special stains, such as those of Golgi or Mallory. Wright found changes in the posterior spinal ganglion and anterior horn cells, and in the nuclei of the medulla in cases in which the fibers originating from these cells were atrophied. That is, atrophy or loss of function in the axon leads to or is concomitant with disturbances in its trophic cell. The changes found in these cells depend in intensity on the length of time the polyneuritis has existed and include swollen and dislocated nuclei and loss of the Nissl bodies, which break down into a powdery mass. In more advanced degeneration this powdery mass almost disappears and there is vacuolation of the cell with rupture of its membrane and fragmentation of its processes. Similar changes have been found in the ganglion cells of the medulla and pons. These degenerative changes in most cases are not to be regarded as complete, which would mean the death of the cell, from which there could be no recovery; but they do indicate a very complete exhaustion of the affected cells.

The work of Carmichael and Stern, and of Mott, demonstrates that the pathology of alcoholic beriberi is comparable to that of Oriental beriberi. The former have described the peripheral nerve pathology in five of their subjects as follows:

Case 1. In a small portion of the popliteal nerve no interstitial changes were seen in sections stained by haematoxylin and van Gieson; but Kernohan's modification for celloidin sections of Bielschowsky's method showed degeneration of many axis cylinders.

Case 2. The following peripheral nerves were examined: sciatic, median, ulnar, radial, internal cutaneous. The majority of the fibers were seen to be degenerating when stained by the Marchi-Busch method. An advanced stage of degeneration in many fibers was demonstrated by the Weigert-Pal method. In the sciatic nerve there was a slight perineural infiltration with small round cells. In the radial nerve early interfibrillar fibrosis was seen, but no cellular infiltration. The degenerative process appeared to be a simple parenchymatous degeneration of the nerve fibers.

Case 3. The only peripheral nerve examined was the musculospiral nerve. There was no evidence of degeneration, and no cellular infiltration or fibrosis.

Case 4. The median, ulnar, sciatic and posterior tibial nerves were examined. Early degeneration was found in all these nerves by the Marchi method, but more advanced degeneration was present in the posterior tibial than in the other nerves. In the ulnar and median nerves the perineural spaces contained a small number of lymphocytes and large mononuclear cells. In the posterior tibial nerve no infiltration with cells was observed, but there was slight proliferation of the cells of the sheath of Schwann.

Case 5. The following peripheral nerves were examined microscopically: both sciatic nerves, both internal popliteal nerves and both anterior tibial nerves. Definite degeneration of the anterior tibial and popliteal nerves was seen in sections stained with Scharlach R. The myelin sheaths, especially those of the larger nerve fibers, were broken up into globules which stained either intensely red or orange with Scharlach R. Similar sections stained by the Marchi-Busch method showed fatty changes, though these were not nearly so evident as with the Scharlach R. stain. Weigert-Pal sections showed obvious fragmentation of the myelin, but in no case complete demyelination. There was a similar degeneration, though of much lesser degree, in the sciatic nerves. In no section was there any evidence of an inflammatory reaction. No cellular infiltration of the nerves whatsoever was found.

Mott examined microscopically the brain of a large number of alcoholic cases.

In all of these where there was a pronounced neuritis, there were characteristic changes affecting the large psychomotor cells. The changes in these cells are similar to the changes in the anterior horn cells of the spinal cord, and are very evident; the nucleus is large and clear, it is dislocated to the side, sometimes extruded altogether, there is a marked cell chromatolysis. The Nissl granules may be almost entirely absent or only found at the periphery. Sometimes the cytoplasm is vacuolated or shows excess of pigment. In a few cases were found similar changes of the cells of the nucleus of the motor oculi. It may be asserted that these changes in the cerebral and spinal motor neurones indicate a toxic action upon the whole motor efferent path. The changes in the anterior horn cells and the cells of the posterior spinal ganglia are, however, similar to those produced in animals by section of the nerves—namely there is swelling of the cells, eccentric position of the nucleus, and a disappearance of the Nissl granules from within outwards (perinuclear chromatolysis); it may be, however, concluded that these changes are not solely due to a "réaction à distance" caused by destruction of the peripheral nerves, for similar changes are found in the Betz cells of the motor area. Examination of the sensory path, in severe cases, often shows profound changes in the posterior spinal ganglion cells and degeneration in the posterior roots and columns of the spinal cord. In one severe case a spinal ganglion was destroyed and only a cavity left. It was the fifth lumbar ganglion and there was glossy skin of the foot on the same side and a trophic sore on the sole.

It is seen thus that the brain and nerve pathology in alcoholic neuropathy does not differ from that found in nonalcoholic neuropathies. A full investigation and description, however, are still wanting.

Liver pathology. In a recent monograph Klotz (*a*) states that in 15 cases of alcoholic "polyneuritis" with lethal termination he found fatty degeneration of the liver, but no cirrhosis, or only in an attenuated form. This seems to him a significant fact for an etiologic theory of alcoholic neuropathy. Gouget reported similar findings in 1911 and

Pitres and Vaillard found only minimal neuritic lesions at autopsy of patients dead from cirrhosis of the liver. Whether or not a dissociation between neuropathy and cirrhosis exists can hardly be decided on these grounds. Wayburn and Guerard state in a paper published in 1940 that in 317 patients with cirrhosis of the liver (70 per cent of these with alcoholic history) they found that neuropathy occurred with a frequency of 17 per cent. They regard this as a proof of association between the two diseases and stress the importance of the fact. Naturally, some would say that an occurrence of *only* 17 per cent is indicative of dissociation. The question is of sufficient importance for further study.

The endocrines. The occurrence of anatomicopathologic changes of the endocrine glands in alcoholic neuropathy has been reported by various investigators [see Klotz (*a*)]. However, these changes are also reported in practically all other forms of chronic alcoholism. It may be possible to analyze the existing literature relative to the claim made by Klotz (*a*) that these changes are much more consistent in alcoholic neuropathy than in other alcoholic diseases. Klotz states that consistent changes occur in the thyroid and the ovary. In the thyroid he found dense interstitial sclerosis which distinctly separates the vesicles. The lesions in the ovaries consist of diffuse sclerosis; no yellow bodies in development, no adult or primordial follicles. The other endocrine glands show no consistent changes in alcoholic neuropathy, according to this investigator. The claim that endocrine changes are specifically important in neuropathy cannot be accepted without further study.

Clinical Manifestations

The classic descriptions of Lettsom in 1787 and of Jackson in 1822 leave little in 1942 to add to a general description of patients having advanced "alcoholic" polyneuropathy. Lettsom wrote:

The appetite for food vanishes but sometimes continues voracious; and, at the same time, whilst the body is costive, and no vomiting ensues, the lower extremities grow more and more emaciated; the legs become as smooth as polished ivory, and the soles of the feet even glassy and shining, and at the same time so tender, that the weight of the finger excites shrieks and moaning; and yet I have known, that in a moment's time, heavy pressure has given no uneasiness. The legs, and the whole lower extremities, lose all power of action; wherever they are placed, there they remain till moved again by the attendant; the arms and hands acquire the same *paralysis*, and render the patients incapable of feeding themselves. Thus for years they exist, with no material alteration of the size of the body, or aspect of the countenance. Whether they really undergo the agonies they appear to suffer, I much doubt, as at this period their minds appear idiotish: they often shriek out with a vehemence that may be heard at a considerable distance, but upon inquiring about the seat of pain, they have been vague and indecisive in their answers. When a cramp comes on the lower extremities, involuntary motions draw up the legs, and produce the most piercing shrieks: and the features of the face, altered by convulsive twitchings, excite pain in a spectator. For some months before they die, these shrieks are more incessant, and as violent as the strength will admit.

They talk freely in the intervals of mitigation, but of things that do not exist; they describe the presence of their friends, as if they saw realities, and reason tolerably clearly upon false premises.

Mostly before they die, they take less food; sometimes a *diarrhoea* succeeds, of a thin substance, and of a dark green colour; sometimes a vomiting of black matter; but mostly generally they gradually sink from the accumulation of pain and debility. There is rarely any fever; and after the disease is far advanced, the *menses* have continued. They do not, as in the preceding state, fall into dropsies, but usually become paralytic: the breath is not offensive, nor is there the same difficulty of breathing, or horror of suffocation: whether the imperceptible and gradual augmentation in the use of spirits, is the cause of this difference, I am not certain; but the difference is considerable, as must appear from their histories, which I have drawn from actual observation. . . .

I would not, however, infer that every spirit-drinker acquires the symptoms of disease above related.

James Jackson's description in 1822 of a peculiar disease resulting from the use of ardent spirits follows:

Among the diseases, arising from the use of ardent spirits, there is one, which is very distinctly marked, but which I have never seen described. Several instances of this disease have occurred to my notice, and I regret to say that they have been mostly among females. For want of a better name I have called this disease arthrodynia a potu; but this name may convey some false notions, as will appear in the sequel, though none better has suggested itself to me.

This arthrodynia comes on gradually. It commences with pains in the lower limbs, but especially in the feet; and afterwards extends to the hands and arms. The hands may be affected first in some instances; and in all cases in an advanced state, the pain is more severe in the feet and hands, than in the upper parts of the limbs. The pain is excruciating, but varies in degree at different times. It is accompanied by a distressing feeling of numbness. After the disease has continued a short time, there takes place some contraction of the fingers and toes, and an inability to use these parts freely. At length the hands and feet become nearly useless, the flexor muscles manifesting, as in other diseases, greater power than the extensors. The whole body diminishes in size, unless it be the abdomen, but the face does not exhibit the appearance of emaciation common to many visceral diseases.

This diminution is especially observable in the feet and hands; and at the same time the skin of these parts acquires a peculiar appearance. The same appearance is sometimes noticed, in a slighter degree, in the skin of other parts. This appearance consists in a great smoothness and shining, with a sort of fineness of the skin. The integuments look as if tight and stretched without rugae or wrinkles; somewhat as when the subjacent parts are swollen; but the skin is not discoloured. Yet in this disease there is not any effusion under the skin, and the character, which this assumes, arises from some change in the organ itself. A similar appearance may sometimes be seen, I think, in cases of paralysis. It may arise perhaps from similar causes in the two diseases; for in this arthrodynia there is a partial paralysis. But here the paralysis is to be referred to some affection of the muscles, and not to the nerves, as in common paralytic cases.

The most characteristic symptoms of this disease are manifested in the limbs; but the pain is not limited to these, and other symptoms are exhibited in other parts. The pain sometimes shoots suddenly up one or both legs, and in one case it frequently passed up the back and then forward to the pit of the stomach, taking the course of the diaphragm. The functions of the stomach are always impaired and generally very much. The appetite is lost, or is morbid, the patient craving only the most powerful stimulants; the food is often rejected, and constipation or diarrhoea take place. The mind is weakened; but it is free from delirium ordinarily, and is alive to the horrible sufferings of the disease. Sleep is prevented by pain and is procured only by opiates.

In the progress of the disease spasmodic affections often ensue, and both mind and body are liable to be disturbed and agitated by slight causes. The powers of life at length are exhausted and delirium perhaps occurs at last, as a precursor to dissolution.

I believe that this disease is always fatal, when the use of spirituous liquors is not abandoned, before the powers of the digestive organs are greatly impaired. In private practice I have not been able to control patients in respect to the use of these liquors. Several years since, I saved one patient in the almshouse, having her under entire control there; and within the last year I have had one male patient in the Massachusetts General Hospital, who after six months treatment was dismissed almost well and capable of returning to labour.

These descriptions should be compared with the following descriptions of the polyneuropathy of beriberi found in Vedder's (a) monograph on beriberi.

Beriberi frequently begins gradually, so that for several days or weeks the patient experiences an ill-defined malaise, associated with heaviness and weakness of the legs. In some cases there is a little fever, but this is by no means characteristic, and is quite possibly caused by a concomitant cold in the head, a slight attack of gastro-enteritis or other similar complication. Because of this weakness of the legs there is an indisposition to walk far. The legs are stiff and numb, particularly in the calves. There may be a little oedema of the legs or face, and the patient is quite likely to complain of pain or oppression in the epigastrium and of palpitation of the heart. The patient may continue in this condition for months or even years, with periods of slight improvement or exacerbation of these symptoms, but without material change. Such cases have been called the rudimentary, incomplete or larval type of the disease. As a matter of fact, however, it is simply a very mild case of chronic beriberi, since it differs from the more serious cases solely in the mildness of the symptoms exhibited. Every grade of intensity of the disease may exist, some of these rudimentary cases showing nothing more than a trifling anaesthesia of the skin of the legs and a little muscular weakness. Should the disease become progressively worse, however, all these symptoms become accentuated, so that what was previously only a little numbness and weakness of the legs now becomes positive pain, especially if the affected muscles are squeezed. Anaesthesia becomes almost complete, the muscles shrink and waste away and the gait becomes markedly altered as the result of the muscular weakness. The legs are almost invariably affected first, but as the disease progresses the arms become involved in the same manner until in the severest cases the patient cannot perform the movements necessary to ordinary life, such as feeding and dressing himself. In this condition the patient lies on a bed, shrunken almost to a skeleton and quite helpless. This is the picture of the atrophic form or dry beriberi.

In other cases, while there is marked loss of power in the limbs and varying grades of anaesthesia, and other symptoms indicating that peripheral neuritis exists, the patient never becomes actually bedridden. Some of these cases may develop such marked general anasarca as to resemble an advanced form of kidney disease, but if the urine is examined it will usually be found to be normal in quality, though diminished in quantity. This corresponds to what is described as dropsical, wet or hydro-atrophic beriberi. In any of these cases the cardiac symptoms may be so slight as to be unnoticed, or they may be severe and may end in sudden death directly due to cardiac insufficiency.

In such cases the cardiac and pulmonary symptoms are so accentuated as to mask the rest of the clinical picture. There is probably almost always some weakness of the muscles of the legs, loss of sensation, particularly over the tibiae, some pain in the affected muscles and a partial loss of the patellar reflexes, and frequently some oedema, but these symptoms may be overlooked because of the severe dyspnoea, palpitation and precordial distress. It is quite possible on theoretical grounds that these cases may exist without any sensory or motor disturbances in the limbs, and such cases have been reported. But it is believed that such cases are the exception, and that examination will generally reveal some evidence of neuritis of the limbs. The dyspnoea, cardiac pain and the palpitation gradually or suddenly increase until the patient is evidently suffering from such a paroxysm that even the casual observer would recognize the fact that he is in extremis. Percussion and auscultation show that the right heart is dilated. The pulse becomes small, the cervical vessels throb, the face becomes cyanosed, and the body becomes cold. Although gasping for breath and suffering the most intense precordial pain, consciousness is not lost until a few moments before death cuts the agony short. This is the usual termination of such a paroxysm. If the patient should recover from such an attack, or in those cases where such an acute paroxysm has not developed, vomiting may occur, the appetite is lost, the bowels may be constipated, the urine much diminished in amount and thirst may be added to the symptoms. But the dyspnoea and the cardiac insufficiency continue until in a few hours, a few days, or several weeks, another paroxysm occurs. These acute cardiac cases are almost always fatal, but fortunately comprise only a small proportion of the cases of beriberi. It should not be forgotten, however, that such an acute cardiac seizure is liable to occur in any case of beriberi at almost any time, and that this constitutes its main danger.

In those cases in which oedema occurs the amount and location of the oedema also varies greatly, in some cases being so slight as to be scarcely noticeable, and being limited to slight puffiness over the ankles or in the face. Between this condition and general anasarca all intermediate grades exist. In many cases in which this anasarca is pronounced the neuritic changes are slight or may be absent altogether.

The above description might lead the reader to suppose that, aside from the development of cardiac crises, the disease is quite chronic. This, indeed, is usually the method of onset, but cases which develop dropsy or paralysis very suddenly are by no means unknown. This sudden appearance of "wet" beriberi is particularly common in women during pregnancy or the puerperium, when it must be carefully distinguished from cases of renal insufficiency.

The fact that chronic cases may suddenly take on an acute aspect has been sufficiently emphasized. It should also be remembered that in certain instances the atrophic form of beriberi may be quite acute. Thus H. Wright records a case (*Brit. Med. Journ.*, 1901, i, 1611) in which loss of power in the hands and feet appeared within 15 days after the first symptom, consisting of slight numbness, was noticed, and the patient became paralyzed and died 23 days after the first symptoms appeared.

A most excellent conception of the disease is therefore gained by recognizing that beriberi is a composite of three main sets of symptoms:

1. The symptoms of peripheral neuritis.
2. Cardiac insufficiency.
3. A generalized tendency to oedema.

The type or variety of the disease as observed in a specific case depends simply upon the manner and intensity with which these sets of symptoms are blended together.

These classic descriptions of "alcoholic" polyneuropathy and of beriberi polyneuropathy which is unquestionably due to a vitamin B_1 deficiency make it hardly necessary to point out that the same disease has been described under different labels. Agreement with this point of view can be found repeatedly in contemporary medical literature [Flaig; Jolliffe and Colbert; Madden; Meiklejohn; McGee; Minot, Strauss and Cobb; Wechsler (*a*); and Weiss].

Jackson first reported that alcoholic polyneuropathy was more frequent in women than in men, and since then the same observation has been made by Wilks, by Clarke, and by Oettinger. Klotz (*a*) has recently stressed the preponderance of women in this type of patients and believes this fact to be of etiological importance. The literature on polyneuropathy has been scanned in an attempt to determine the relative incidence of this disease in the two sexes. Unfortunately, numerous papers give no numerical data at all, while others report definite numbers of cases but do not specify sex. Altogether, 29 papers on alcoholic neuropathy were found from which this datum was obtainable. For these, the aggregate number of patients is 968, of whom 490 are men and 478 are women. This is approximately an even division. But only about 20 per cent of all chronic alcoholics are women, so that if women make up 50 per cent of all of the alcoholic polyneuropathies, as this determination would suggest, there is a real excess of women suffering from this disorder. Age of onset is apparently between 30 and 45 years in both men and women.

The clinical manifestations of vitamin B_1 deficiency, whether due to the excessive consumption of polished rice or of alcohol or to a disease process preventing utilization or increasing the requirement of vitamin B_1, are not limited to the peripheral nerves alone, although polyneuropathy is the most characteristic and frequent neurological syndrome. There are frequent concurrences of other neuropsychiatric, circulatory, gastrointestinal, metabolic, and possibly endocrine manifestations of this deficiency. Furthermore, subvitaminosis in man is not usually limited to one vitamin as has been demonstrated by Spies (*b*), by Sydenstricker, Sebrell, *et al.*, and by Jolliffe (*d*), and there may also be protein or mineral deficiencies. When all of these deficiency manifestations, in all possible combinations, are added to a basic neurosis or psychosis which is likely in inebriety, or to the original symptomatology of some disease process which incidentally alters the vitamin requirement, the clinical picture becomes so confused that it is little wonder that the basic similarity in all these conditions went unrecognized for so long. Multiple vitamin deficiency is the probable explanation for the protean manifestations of "alcoholic" and beriberi polyneuropathies. The use of newly available crystalline vitamins under controlled conditions has made it possible to make considerable progress in identifying some of the more prominent clinical syndromes of multiple vitamin deficiencies. [Jolliffe (d)].

The onset of a peripheral neuropathy in the alcoholic is preceded by a period of neurasthenia which is the most common manifestation of early vitamin B_1 deficiency. This has been recently described as follows:

As in neurasthenic syndromes of any origin, the symptomatology is varied but its outstanding symptoms are anorexia, fatigue and insomnia. Completing the picture of neurasthenia are such complaints as irritability, "gas," nausea, constipation, uncomfortable sensation in the abdomen and other parts of the body, depression, backache, headache (usually of the occipital or constricting band type), sighing, palpitation, and precordial distress. For several years I have been cognizant of this group of symptoms in my patients having objective signs of a vitamin deficiency. I usually attributed it to neurasthenia on the basis of an abnormal psyche which, leading to further dietary restrictions, in turn led to the development of objective signs. Adequate treatment for the deficiency was followed, not only by disappearance of the objective signs but also, as a rule, of the neurasthenic syndrome. I then applied to subjects having the neurasthenic syndrome without objective signs of vitamin deficiency the treatment-regimen of dietary correction, vitamin supplements rich in the entire B-complex, and thiamin chloride. Many, though not all, of these patients were helped. The improvement was attributed to better nutrition plus the psychotherapy of this dietary regimen. Not until Williams, Mason, Wilder, and Smith,* in a well-controlled experiment with human subjects, reproduced this characteristic neurasthenic syndrome by inducing an isolated thiamin deficiency, have I been willing to include this syndrome as a manifestation of thiamin deficiency. It should not be inferred, however, that all neurasthenia is based on thiamin deficiency. Almost any agent causing the triad of anorexia, fatigue and insomnia, if not soon relieved, will cause, in susceptible persons, the development of other neurasthenic symptoms. Nevertheless the proportion of neurasthenia caused by vitamin deficiency may be larger than is now commonly believed. [Jolliffe (e)]

Neurologic disturbances. Following these early symptoms of neurasthenia, anorexia and fatigue, calf muscle cramps, burning of the soles of the feet, and paresthesias in the toes and fingers occur. Neurologic examination during the neurasthenic stage discloses, as a rule, no abnormal signs. Soon, however, plantar hyperesthesia and calf muscle tenderness develop, both significant objective signs. The plantar hyperesthesia is not the common sensation of ordinary tickling usually elicited by scratching the plantar surface of the foot, but definite

*This extremely interesting paper is discussed at some length in the section on etiology.

hyperesthetic pain which is manifest and unmistakable in the facial expression. A healthy calf muscle, if squeezed from behind so as not to include the tibia in the grip, can stand considerable pressure; this is not so in the presence of mild B_1 deficiency. At about this time the vibratory sensation in the toes becomes diminished. These signs, however, are suggestive only and a positive diagnosis of polyneuropathy cannot be made from them alone, as circulatory disturbances of varying etiologies may cause these or similar findings. When, however, in addition to these signs, the ankle jerks are absent, a diagnosis of mild polyneuropathy is made. By this time the plantar hyperesthesia may have extended so that there is sock dysesthesia. The vibratory sensation is usually absent in the toes and very occasionally may be absent in the malleoli or even in the tibiae. Position sense at this time, as a rule, is intact in the toes, though a few mistakes may be made in very small changes in position.

As the deficiency progresses to that of moderate polyneuropathy, absence of knee and ankle jerks is found, but the signs are still limited to the lower extremities. Definite impairment of position sense in the toes can now be generally elicited, and vibratory sensation is lost over a greater extent, even on occasion up to and including the pelvis. Some atrophy of the calf muscles may be evident. Calf tenderness and sock dysesthesia continue. Occasionally a "delayed" plantar hyperesthesia now becomes evident. Toe drop or foot drop is not usually present at this stage. The gait may be natural, but often a definite abnormality is noted. The burning soles of the feet, with some loss of position sense, make these patients walk carefully as though barefoot on a floor strewn with carpet tacks.

If the deficiency continues, the upper extremities become involved so that the biceps and triceps jerks disappear. Glove dysesthesia and loss of finger dexterity rapidly develop. Calf muscle atrophy is now usually marked, toe and foot drop are plainly evident, and wrist drop soon appears. The gait, if the patient is able to walk, is by now that of the steppage type. Walking, however, is, as a rule, impossible because of the central nervous or circulatory involvement.

The neurologic manifestations of vitamin B_1 deficiency, whether in a mild or severe form, are bilateral and symmetrical and characteristically involve first and predominantly the lower extremities. Peripheral neuropathy that involves a single nerve, or that is not bilateral and symmetric, or that does not involve first and predominantly the lower extremities, is not, in my experience, due to vitamin B_1 deficiency. Exceptions that prove the rule can probably be found for each of these dicta. For example, a man crippled by hip joint disease was confined to a wheel chair which he propelled with his arms. Polyneuropathy occurred first and predominantly in his upper extremities.

Circulatory changes. If physical effort is maintained, circulatory symptoms may become manifest. These may be restricted to "sighing respiration" in the beginning, or neurasthenic stage, but eventually dyspnea, palpitation, and tachycardia occur on exertion. Precordial pain, called pseudoangina by the Mayo group, occurs not infrequently, and because of the associated electrocardiographic changes, a diagnosis of structural coronary artery disease is often suggested. The pain is most frequently described as precordial and substernal in location without radiation, aching in character, and occurring on effort. This pain is the type produced in experimental vitamin B_1 deficient subjects by Jolliffe, Goodhart, Gennis and Cline.

Gastrointestinal manifestations. The anorexia which precedes the nervous involvements for several years is of a progressive type. Klotz contends that the gastritis in alcoholic polyneuropathy is atrophic and in this respect differs from the gastritis of all other alcoholic diseases, but final confirmation of this is lacking.

Many authors give data on the occurrence of achlorhydria and hypochlorhydria in chronic alcoholics generally, but only 4 studies specify polyneuropathy and the data from these are presented in Table 3.

TABLE 3

*The Occurrence of Achlorhydria and Hypochlorhydria
in Patients with Polyneuropathy*

Author	No. with Achlorhydria	No. with Hypochlorhydria	Normal
Minot, Strauss and Cobb	21	15	7
Perkins	31	8	3
Villaret, Moutier, Justin-Besançon and Klotz	33	12	5
Joffe and Jolliffe	15	22	15

Biochemical changes. In the vast literature on biochemical changes in alcoholism, which will be reviewed in detail elsewhere, there is usually no reference to any specific alcoholic disease. A few authors (Madsen; and O'Connell, McLeman and Stern) have noted that changes in the blood lipids and in the spinal fluid are the same in alcoholic polyneuropathy as in chronic alcoholism in general. Bueding and Wortis have noted elevated blood pyruvic acid values in patients with poly-neuropathy but not in other chronic alcoholics.

Endocrine manifestations. Some endocrine symptoms are also found in alcoholic polyneuropathies, but it is not known whether they occur with greater frequency than in other alcoholic diseases, or with any specific coloring. Klotz (*a*) found an amenorrhea preceding the syn-drome of polyneuropathy by several months in 42 of 56 women; in 6 of 8 men with alcoholic polyneuropathy, he found testicular atrophy with decreased libido or complete impotence. Klotz also believes that thyroid insufficiency is indicated by the fact that in 48 out of 60 pa-tients he found dry and even infiltrated skin and complete depilation of the axillary and pubic regions. He attaches considerable significance to this in view of corroborative anatomicopathologic findings. Depi-lation in polyneuropathy has also been reported by Laignel-Lavastine *et al.* and by Carnot *et al.* Without reference to any specific alcoholic disease, numerous observers have reported such symptoms in chronic alcoholism.

The clinical picture, as described, may be interrupted at any point in its course from the stage of neurasthenia to that of advanced poly-neuropathy by resumption of a normal diet, termination of drinking, and vitamin B supplements. Those having only neurasthenic symp-toms or mild signs will make a complete recovery rapidly if given spe-cific therapy, more slowly if only dietary measures are employed. Those with moderate degree of involvement can usually be completely cured with specific therapy. If dietary measures alone are employed, or if specific therapy is not rigorously employed, the patients are often left with absent ankle jerks and impaired vibratory sensation in the toes. Those with advanced polyneuropathy are often invalided for weeks or months, and too often, even with specific therapy, crippling defects may remain permanently.

Differential diagnosis. The diagnosis of an "alcoholic" or vitamin B_1 deficiency polyneuropathy is, as a rule, not difficult, though at times it may be impossible without laboratory aid or a therapeutic trial. Alco-holic, or B_1 deficiency, polyneuropathy is bilateral and symmetrical and begins first with, and predominantly involves, the lower extremities. This rules out lead and most other heavy metal neuropathies, single nerve neuropathies, and "ginger jake" paralysis. Arsenical polyneuritis often can only be ruled out by history and by chemical analysis for arsenic. The clinical course of the disease and spinal fluid changes in virus neuropathies, as a rule, remove this group from difficult diagnostic problems.

There is, however, a type of polyneuropathy which, in the beginning of its course, is remarkably similar to B_1 deficiency in its clinical picture. This type of polyneuropathy has been designated Lawless, after one of the first patients studied at Bellevue who had this disease, but the name is also appropriate as a common adjective. Clinically, the bilateral distribution beginning first in, and predominantly involving, the lower extremities, is similar. Pain, however, is more prominent than in the deficiency variety. Other than the failure of thiamin therapy to stop the progress of the disease, differential diagnosis by clinical means is difficult, and laboratory aid must be resorted to. In the Lawless type, the blood pyruvic acid is not elevated and the blood thiamin and cocarboxylase may not be below normal. In untreated acute polyneuropathy due to B_1 deficiency the blood pyruvic acid is almost invariably elevated, and both thiamin and cocarboxylase are low in the blood.

Etiology

Since the first descriptions of "alcoholic" polyneuropathy by Lettsom and by Jackson, a direct alcoholic etiology has been generally assumed. Lancereaux, in 1865, suggested that only high-proof liquors could cause polyneuropathy and that wine and beer were innocent in this respect, but it was soon recognized that this was not true.

As early as 1883, Pierson suggested that polyneuropathy and beriberi were the same disease, and that the European polyneuropathy was a sporadic occurrence of the Asiatic beriberi. This seems to have been the first suggestion of an identity of these two diseases. Pierson, however, like his contemporaries generally, believed them both to be of bacterial origin.

Rosenheim, in 1887, thought that the cause should not be assigned directly to bacterial action, but rather to the effect of the metabolic products resulting from bacterial action.

In 1890, Korsakoff suggested that alcohol did not act directly on the nervous system, but facilitated the development of ptomaines and leukomaines, and their action on the nervous system.

The idea of the infectious nature of polyneuropathies has not been dropped entirely, and Klotz (a), in 1937, still regarded infection as a main precipitating factor.

That a deficiency factor should have been postulated only recently is surprising in view of the fact that ever since the syndrome was first described, it has been observed that heavy drinkers who eat well are less likely to develop peripheral neuropathy than their companions who fail to eat or to assimilate a full and varied diet. It has even been suggested that the ingestion of alcohol stimulated the formation of a toxin which was neutralized by an antitoxin formed from food. When food was not eaten the antitoxin necessary for neutralization of the toxin was not formed and in consequence, neuropathy, delirium tremens, and other nervous and mental diseases developed.

In 1913, Vedder (a) showed that the peripheral polyneuropathy of beriberi was caused by a deficiency of antineuritic vitamin B, but it was some time before any association was made between these findings and alcoholic polyneuropathy.

In 1924, Pitres and Vaillard seemed to have some idea of the nutritional nature of the disorder, although they made no reference to vitamins. They noted that polyneuropathy never occurred in intoxicated animals and that it appeared in humans only in those chronic alcoholics whose health had been seriously affected by visceral lesions, caused either by alcohol itself or by concomitant diseases. Hence they inferred that "alcoholic polyneuritis may be the consequence of complex humoral changes of a *cachectic** nature rather than of the immediate contact with the nerves of alcohol or of the immediate products of its metabolism."

Shattuck is usually credited with first calling attention to the possible relationship of certain types of polyneuropathy, including the "alcoholic," to vitamin deficiency. But, in 1925, Gigon and Odermatt, in a paper on "The influence of urine constituents and alcohol free organ extracts on the fermentation of sugar by yeast" stated, "There is in clinical as well as in the pathological anatomical picture of these two forms of polyneuritis [beriberi and alcoholic] so many analogies that we thought of an etiological relationship between these two diseases. We assume, therefore, that in certain cases of chronic alcoholism the vitamin content of the organism is perhaps involved."

In 1928, Shattuck observed that various diseases are debilitating and interfere seriously with nutrition, and said that "some of the cases of polyneuritis developing with the above mentioned conditions might, perhaps, be properly regarded as true beriberi and not merely as complications or sequelae of the other diseases." The following year this concept was restated by Minot.

*Italics mine.

Wechsler (*b*) was the first, however, to conclude from clinical observations in recorded case histories that subvitaminosis played a definite, and possibly the decisive, role in the production of polyneuropathy. He called attention to the history in these patients of prolonged anorexia, diarrhea, and vomiting; to the presence of achlorhydria, gastrointestinal and hepatic disease; to the degenerative, rather than inflammatory, nature of the pathologic changes, and to their similarity to the pathologic changes seen in beriberi. He wrote:

Before validating the conclusions and justifying the change of concepts, it may be of interest to recall how the question came to be raised. At first, general doubts arose as to the true cause in cases of polyneuritis or multiple neuritis of obscure origin; that is, in the not infrequent instances in which a specific causative factor could not be found despite diligent search. In such cases recourse was generally had to the words toxic or infectious. What was specifically toxic or infectious, when neither condition was demonstrable, was never stated. It was pointed out, therefore, that the glib tendency, hitherto indulged in to invoke those explanations, was highly unsatisfactory and that the "non-specific" use of either term merely served to cover ignorance and really explained nothing at all. Based on clinical evidence and theoretical considerations, the conclusion was reached that in obscure cases in which none of the various factors hitherto regarded as the causes of multiple neuritis could be found, the condition was due to food deficiency. From the clinical point of view the condition could not be classified either as beriberi or pellagra, although these two diseases were naturally suspected.

Meyer (*b*) studied two alcoholic patients having polyneuropathy and pellagra and came to the same general conclusions.

The evidence of clinical nutritional studies. Minot, Strauss and Cobb reported on 130 cases of alcoholic polyneuropathy. Good information on the diet of 43 patients could be obtained, and of these, only 2 had adequate diets. Treatment included a diet rich in all vitamins, particularly in B, and they reported more uniform and rapid recoveries under this regimen than with other therapies. They pointed out the similarity of the manifestations of beriberi and of polyneuropathy in the alcohol addict, and suggested a common etiologic factor, namely the lack of antineuritic vitamin B.

Strauss (*b*) treated 10 patients having alcoholic polyneuropathy with daily intramuscular injections of liver extract and a diet rich in vitamin B, but without withdrawing alcohol, and reported marked improvement in every instance. He concluded that the polyneuropathy of inebriates probably results from a dietary deficiency, and not primarily from a direct neurotoxic effect of the alcohol.

Almost simultaneously with Strauss' work, Blankenhorn and Spies (*a*), after study of a series of 50 chronic alcoholics with polyneuropathy, in all but 4 patients associated with pellagra, found that the neuropathy improved with an adequate diet with or without addition of yeast or liver extract and whether or not they kept on drinking. One patient with pellagra and polyneuropathy was kept on a pellagra-producing diet, but 15 mg. B_1 *per os* were added daily, and the neuropathy improved.

At that time (1935) this type of evidence could only be said to indicate a vitamin deficiency; vitamin B_1, through the similarity of the pathologic and clinical manifestations of beriberi and "alcoholic" polyneuropathy, could only be implicated by inference. As stated by Meiklejohn,

[the] work of the pre-thiamin era was concerned with establishing the clinical and etiologic identity of nutritional neuritis occurring in beriberi, alcoholism, pregnancy and gastrointestinal disturbances. The emphasis throughout was to the effect that adequate treatment of these conditions consisted in the administration of foods rich in the vitamin B complex. When in some cases a specific etiologic relation to vitamin B_1 deficiency was suggested, this implied no more than that these conditions were caused by deficiency of the hypothetical antineuritic vitamin, and it should not now be construed to mean that the authors believed nutritional polyneuritis to be due to a deficiency of the pure chemical substance thiamin—a therapeutic agent entirely unavailable to them at the time.

Jolliffe, Colbert and Joffe made an intensive analysis of 42 patients, selected only for the reliability of their dietary histories. Vitamin/calorie ratios were calculated from Cowgill's formula, with and without the calories contributed by alcohol in each case.* Of these 42 cases, 26 had polyneuropathy and in all of these 26, the vitamin intake was unquestionably inadequate. In 18 of these, this was true even when the calories contributed by alcohol were not included (Table 4).

Of the other 16 cases, those without polyneuropathy, 8 had an adequate vitamin B_1 intake, and 8 did not (Table 5). That the latter did not develop polyneuropathy is probably due, in most instances, to the brevity of the alcoholic bout (Table 6).

The conclusions were as follows:

The vitamin B and caloric intake of 42 alcohol addicts, 26 of whom had polyneuritis, have been estimated quantitatively by Cowgill's formula.

* It appears that the body can utilize only about 1,344 alcohol calories daily, so that quantities taken in excess of this are more properly disregarded in calculating caloric intake.

TABLE 4

Summary of Observations on 26 Alcohol Addicts with Polyneuropathy
(Data from Jolliffe, Colbert and Joffe)

				ALCOHOL	FOOD: AVERAGE DAILY CONSUMPTION IN		VIT. B_1/CAL. RATIOS			NEUROLOGIC INVOLVEMENT		
Case	Sex	Age	Time	Average Daily Intake in Calories	Calories	Vit. B_1 Mg. Eq.	Without Calories from Alc.	With Up to 1,344 Calories from Alcohol	Cowgill's Predicted Requirement	Poly-neuropathy	Cord	Brain
258	M	51	1 Y	5,286	405	1,317	3.2	0.75	1.75	+	o	o
259	M	41	6 M	2,643	755	1,725	2.3	0.82	2.35	+	o	o
271	M	37	3 Y	1,322	330	923	2.8	0.56	1.80	+	+	+
273	M	50	25 Y	1,322	2,500	6,874	2.7	1.80	1.80	+	+	+
279	F	45	7 Y	1,322	833	2,286	2.7	1.06	1.25	+	+	+
280	M	57	3 M	5,286	888	1,845	2.0	0.83	2.00	+	o	o
295	M	59	10 W	1,322	673	1,020	1.5	0.51	1.70	+	o	o
297	M	38	2 M	1,322	1,250	3,423	2.7	1.33	2.00	+	o	o
300	M	53	3 M	3,965	357	978	2.7	0.57	2.15	+	+	o
324	M	48	6 M	1,322	965	3,130	3.2	1.37	1.85	+	o	+
327	M	43	2 M	5,286	0	0	0.0	0	2.20	+	o	o
333	M	40	2 M	3,717	0	0	0.0	0	1.90	+	+	+
335	M	52	2 M	661	756	1,624	2.1	1.15	1.71	+	o	o
336	M	56	33 D	3,965	863	2,431	2.8	1.10	2.35	+	o	o
339	F	45	2 Y	1,322	492	406	0.8	0.22	1.40	+	+	o
366	M	52	22 D	2,478	500	1,800	3.6	0.98	2.55	+	o	o
388	M	47	8 M	3,304	1,121	2,590	2.3	1.05	1.15	+	o	o
392	F	57	2 M	2,148	276	671	2.4	0.41	2.05	+	o	+
443	M	35	6 W	1,982	2,018	5,932	2.9	1.76	2.20	+	+	+
444	M	29	8 Y	2,643	1,809	5,774	3.2	1.83	1.80	+	+	+
457	M	38	2 M	2,643	1,102	3,825	3.5	1.56	1.70	+	o	o
458	M	54	15 D	2,643	555	1,107	2.0	0.58	2.10	+	o	o
459	M	46	20 D	2,643	726	3,355	4.6	1.62	2.10	+	o	o
467	M	45	3 W	3,695	0	0	0.0	0	1.85	+	o	+
468	F	47	10 Y	1,982	1,568	2,878	1.8	0.99	2.30	+	o	+
472	M	46	6 Y	1,982	720	3,000	4.2	1.45	1.60	+	o	o

When the first 1,344 calories contained in the alcohol, consumed by each subject, are included in the estimation of the VIT./CAL. ratio, a definite correlation is found between the inadequacy or adequacy of the vitamin B intake and the presence or absence of polyneuritis. This correlation is as follows:

1. Every alcohol addict with polyneuritis had an estimated inadequate vitamin B[B₁] intake.

TABLE 5

Summary of Observations on 16 Alcohol Addicts without Polyneuropathy
(Data from Jolliffe, Colbert and Joffe)

				ALCOHOL	FOOD: AVERAGE DAILY CONSUMPTION IN		VIT. B₁/CAL. RATIOS			NEUROLOGIC INVOLVEMENT		
Case	Sex	Age	Time	Average Daily Intake in Calories	Calories	Vit. B₁ Mg. Eq.	Without Calories from Alc.	With Up to 1,344 Calories from Alc.	Cowgill's Predicted Requirement	Polyneuropathy	Cord	Brain
With an adequate vitamin B₁ intake.												
330	M	61	40 Y	372	2,500	7,890	3.1	2.05	2.25	o	o	o
334	M	64	40 Y	1,239	2,083	10,398	5.0	3.13	2.75	o	o	o
340	F	43	6 M	1,322	3,272	9,918	3.0	2.16	1.70	o	o	o
358	M	45	18 M	620	1,901	7,100	3.7	2.19	2.60	o	o	o
403	M	35	7 Y	661	5,021	17,784	3.5	3.12	2.67	o	o	o
417	M	55	10 Y	1,322	2,457	10,466	4.3	2.77	2.25	o	o	o
455	M	34	7 Y	1,322	2,868	12,102	4.2	2.89	2.00	o	o	o
466	M	54	10 Y	1,900	3,387	13,404	3.9	2.83	1.70	o	o	o
With an inadequate vitamin B₁ intake.												
325	F	35	14 D	1,322	2,500	6,800	2.7	1.78	1.70	o	o	o
359	M	52	7 D	2,643	112	100	0.9	0.07	2.30	o	o	o
363	M	63	14 D	3,965	0	0	0.0	0	2.15	o	o	o
357	M	20	18 D	2,643	640	2,199	3.4	1.11	2.35	o	o	o
402	M	30	6 M	1,322	2,165	7,413	3.4	2.11	2.10	o	o	o
413	M	50	10 D	1,982	638	2,000	3.1	1.01	2.40	o	o	o
438	M	48	21 D	5,286	412	660	1.6	0.38	1.80	o	o	o
456	M	48	2 M	2,643	1,445	5,667	3.9	2.03	1.80	o	o	o

2. No alcohol addict with an estimated adequate vitamin B intake had polyneuritis.

3. Every alcohol addict with estimated absolute deficiency of vitamin B, for 21 days or more, had polyneuritis.

4. Polyneuritis may develop in an alcohol addict as early as the 7th day of estimated absolute deficiency of vitamin B.

Our data substantiate the hypothesis that polyneuritis in the alcohol addict is due to the lack of vitamin B by demonstrating: (1) that the diet consumed by alcohol addicts with polyneuritis failed quantitatively and over a sufficient period of time to contain adequate amounts of vitamin B as compared with the predicted requirement; and (2) that the diet consumed by alcohol addicts without polyneuritis, though the addiction was of long duration, contained quantitatively adequate amounts of vitamin B as compared with the predicted requirement.

TABLE 6

Correlation of Days of Estimated Absolute Deficiency in Vitamin B₁
and Polyneuropathy in the Alcohol Addict
(Data of Jolliffe, Colbert and Joffe)

Case	Estimated Deficiency in Per Cent	Duration of Deficiency in Days	Estimated Absolute Deficiency in Days	Polyneuropathy
325	6.0	14	0.8	o
413	63.0	10	6.3	o
459	33.0	20	6.6	+
359	96.0	7	6.7	o
402	5.0	180	9.0	o
357	57.0	18	10.2	o
458	76.0	15	11.4	+
363	100.0	14	14.0	o
366	65.0	22	14.3	+
438	83.0	21	17.4	o
336	57.0	33	19.1	+
467	100.0	21	21.0	+
297	35.0	60	21.0	+

It is therefore concluded that alcohol has no direct toxic action (chronic) on the peripheral nerves, and that polyneuritis in the alcohol addict is due to vitamin B deficiency.

Jolliffe and Colbert, in 1936, studied 28 patients with polyneuropathy, but without complications likely to increase vitamin B requirement or to prevent its absorption or utilization. These were placed in 3 groups, A having 7 cases, B, 8, and C, 13. Patients in A received a basal diet of borderline vitamin B adequacy, 3 receiving in addition 18 g. of autoclaved vegex. The patients in Group B received the same basal diet plus 18 g. of untreated vegex, which raised their vitamin/calorie ratio to double their predicted requirement. Group C received a vitamin/calorie ratio nearly double that of Group B. The results are summarized in Table 7.

TABLE 7

Summary of Changes in Objective Neurologic Signs of Peripheral
Nerve Involvement after 21 Days of Treatment
(Data of Jolliffe and Colbert)

	No. of Cases	Vit./Cal. Ratio of Diet	WORSE Motor	Sensory	UNIMPROVED Motor	Sensory	IMPROVED Motor	Sensory
Group A	7	1.7	1	3	6	4	o	o
Group B	8	3.6	o	o	3	1	3	7
Group C	13	6.8	o	o	3	2	10	11

Two patients in Group A were then given crystalline vitamin B_1; both improved, one dramatically so. The investigators stated:

Subjects treated with a vitamin B intake approximately twice their predicted requirement showed improvement, but not as rapidly or in equal degree as those receiving four times their vitamin B requirement. We have discussed the relation of alcohol to the etiology of polyneuritis, and the possibility of a fraction in the vitamin B complex other than vitamin B itself augmenting the action of vitamin B on polyneuritis in the alcohol addict. We conclude that

  1. Alcohol *per se* is not the cause of polyneuritis in the alcohol addict.
  2. Vitamin B deficiency is a cause of polyneuritis in the alcohol addict.

Romano made a study of 87 cases of chronic alcoholics with neuropathy; 61 of these gave a history of inadequate diets. All of these patients were placed on high caloric diets, supplemented daily with 4 g. dried brewers' yeast, 30–60 g. wheat germ preparation, and either B_1 or liver preparation parenterally. Table 8 gives his results.

TABLE 8

Response of Patients with Polyneuropathy to Vitamin B
(Data from Romano)

	Mild Cases	Moderate Cases	Severe Cases
No change	2	2	1
Partial improvement	14	14	19
Total improvement	17	18	0
Total	33	34	20

Romano concluded that vitamins B_1 and B_2 are of definite value in the treatment of the deficiency syndromes associated with chronic alcoholism.

Goodhart and Jolliffe (*a*), in 1938, continuing the previous work of Jolliffe and Colbert, reported a further study on uncomplicated cases of mild polyneuropathy. Their 17 patients were divided into 2 groups, their first group of 9 patients receiving a diet with a vitamin/calorie ratio of 5.5 plus 18 g. of vegex daily (as in Group C of the earlier study), and the second group (D) receiving the same, and in addition, 10 mg. of crystalline vitamin B_1* through intravenous injection. Results are summarized in Table 9.

*Natural and synthetic crystalline vitamin B_1 were used with alternate subjects. No difference in efficacy was noted.

TABLE 9

Changes in Objective Neurologic Signs of Peripheral Nerve Involvement
after 10 Days of 2 Types of Treatment
[*Data from Goodhart and Jolliffe (a)*]

		WORSE		UNIMPROVED		IMPROVED		PER CENT IMPROVED		CURED	
Group	Cases	Motor	Sen-sory	Motor	Sen-sory	Motor	Sen-sory	Motor	Sen-sory	No.	Per Cent
C	9	0	0	7	5	2	4	22.2	44.5	1	11
D	8	0	0	3	0	5	8	62.5	100.0	4	50

The more rapid and complete improvement of Group D is very definite, and must have been due primarily to increase in vitamin B in the
form of additional B_1, since that was the only factor effectively differentiating these two groups.

McGee, in 1939, reported 48 cases of male inebriates with polyneuropathy of varying degrees of severity. He treated 25 of these patients with daily subcutaneous injections of thiamin chloride; the
other 23 received only the vitamin B_1 contained in the diet, estimated
at 1–2 mg. of crystalline vitamin B_1 daily. Withdrawal of alcohol was,
in all cases, complete at the end of the third day and no sedatives or
other drugs, to control the neuropathic symptoms, were given after
that time. All cases showed improvement, and, except in the severe
cases, subjective relief was obtained in approximately the same length
of time. In the severe cases, alleviation of symptoms was obtained in
10.4 days in the treated group, as opposed to 18 days in the untreated
group. The difference is the more important since there appears to be a
close relationship, in the untreated group, between prior duration of
attack and length of time before relief; the mean duration of attack in
the treated group was about 8 weeks, and in the control, 3.

The etiological implications of these studies, and of some others, are
briefly summarized in Table 10.

Experimental evidence. This material is derived chiefly from accessory studies. It has been established that vitamin B_1 deficiency, experimentally produced in animals, results in a polyneuropathy. (Wernicke's disease has also been produced experimentally by vitamin B_1
deficiency.) Meiklejohn, however, insists that the disturbance thus
produced in animals is not a true "polyneuritis" but a disturbance of
metabolism, and that there is no experimental evidence showing that
"true anatomic polyneuritis" is curable by thiamin.

TABLE 10

Etiology of Alcoholic Polyneuropathy according to Recent Investigators

Year	Investigators	Suggested cause
1924	Pitres and Vaillard	Complex humoral changes of a cachectic nature.
1925	Gigon and Odermatt	Vitamin content of organism involved (from analogy with beriberi).
1928	Laffitte and Leblanc	Direct action of alcohol on peripheral nerves cannot be the cause since disorders may begin after cessation of alcohol habit and outside of massive intoxication.
1928	Shattuck	Cases of polyneuritis developing with chronic alcoholism may be properly regarded as true beriberi.
1930	Wechsler (*a*)	Probably vitamin deficiency, either from not eating or from inability to absorb.
1931	Lemierre, Boltanski and Justin-Besançon	Importance of infections such as tuberculosis for initiating polyneuritis.
1932	Meyer (*b*)	Alcoholism favors the occurrence of polyneuritis or B-avitaminosis, but the important factor is an unbalanced diet.
1933	Minot, Strauss and Cobb	Lack of vitamin B_1 plays an important role in the production of "alcoholic" polyneuritis. Deficiency due to state of gastrointestinal tract and presence of factors inhibiting effectiveness of nutritional elements as well as to inadequate intake.
1933	Wechsler (*b*)	Many cases of polyneuritis of obscure origin, probably neither toxic nor infectious in nature but more likely deficiency syndromes, and might be grouped with the avitaminoses (several vitamins specified as possible factors).
1935	Jolliffe and Joffe	Peripheral neuritis in the alcohol addict is the result of vitamin B_1 deficiency.
1935	Strauss (*b*)	Alcoholic polyneuritis does not result primarily from a direct neurotoxic effect of alcohol, but is probably the result of a dietary deficiency, possibly conditioned in some cases by disturbed gastrointestinal function.
1935	Villaret, Justin-Besançon and Klotz (*a*)	Polyneuritis and endocrine symptoms are found only in cases which have a long lasting anorexia and a gastro-hepatic intolerance.
1936	Jolliffe and Colbert	Alcohol has no direct toxic action (chronic) on the peripheral nerves. Polyneuritis in the alcohol addict is due to vitamin B_1 deficiency.
1936	Perkins	Dietary deficiency due to inadequate intake or inability to assimilate. More than one type of vitamin is responsible.
1936	Villaret, Justin-Besançon and Klotz (*b*)	Diet deficient in vitamins and impaired assimilation of them. Endocrine troubles depend on nutritive troubles produced by a gastric mucous membrane atrophied by constant contact with alcohol. The deficiency is very complex, and does not depend on vitamin B only.

Year	Investigators	Suggested cause
1937	Klotz (a, b)	Vitamin B_1 deficiency precipitated by thyroid and ovarian dysfunctions and by fatty liver. Predominantly female disease.
1937	Romano	Deficiency syndromes; B_1 and B_2 involved.
1937	Weiss and Wilkins	Vitamin B_1 deficiency.
1938	Bickel (a)	Chiefly B_1 deficiency. Alcohol provides nearly sufficient calories but no vitamins and gastritis and hypochlorhydria prevent vitamin absorption. Liver insufficiency does not permit storage and utilization of B_1 by the liver.
1938	van Bogaert	Vitamin B_1 deficiency.
1938	Goodhart and Jolliffe (a)	Vitamin B_1 deficiency is primary cause of polyneuritis in the alcohol addicts, but these subjects frequently have an associated multiple deficiency.
1938	Harris	"Conditioned" vitamin B_1 deficiency.
1939	Alexander (a)	Avitaminosis due to improper diet, incomplete absorption because of gastritis and intestinal changes caused by alcohol, and increased vitamin requirement due to high caloric value of alcohol. Considers avitaminotic causation proven for polyneuritis, not for other alcoholic diseases.
1939	McGee	Avitaminosis. In alcohol addicts this results from insufficient intake, insufficient absorption, and increased excretion of water-soluble B_1.
1939	Zimmerman	B_1-avitaminosis. Regards as conclusively proven.
1940	Meiklejohn	Nutritional deficiency. It is not proven that this deficiency is purely a thiamin deficiency.
1940	de Soldati	Definite vitamin B_1 deficiency.

The problem has been complicated by the fact that there is more than one factor, the lack of which can produce changes in the peripheral nerves. Starvation and various vitamin deficiencies have been designated as causes of this type of nerve degeneration.

Numerous investigators [Engel and Phillips (a); Wolbach; Vedder (b); Woollard; Williams and Spies] have reported that starvation alone, even in the presence of adequate vitamins, can result in certain changes in the myelin sheaths of the peripheral nerves. Vedder (b); Woollard; and Swank, however, have raised the question as to whether these changes are identical with those which are produced by vitamin deficiencies.

Several experiments (Mellanby; Zimmerman and Cowgill; Lee and Sure) have established the fact that deficiency in vitamin A produces changes in the peripheral as well as in the central nervous system. Zimmerman and Cowgill state that these lesions develop in rats shortly after the appearance of xerophthalmia, and Mellanby found them in rabbits at about the same time.

Before 1936, when thiamin chloride was isolated, it was practically impossible to make adequately controlled investigations of the role of the vitamin B complex, although as early as 1912, Vedder and Clark had shown that degenerative changes in the peripheral nerves of birds could be produced by a diet lacking in this.

In 1913 Vedder (a), using a relatively crude extract of rice polishings which must have contained many of the other factors in the B complex, stated that

birds affected with the form of the disease described as fulminating have been observed that appeared at the last gasp, but recovered almost completely after the administration of this extract, so that they were able to walk about within a few days. This result has not been obtained with fowls suffering with marked paralysis. If birds of this latter group are given this extract they improve in general health, but the paralysis remains, and it is usually only after several months of treatment that they recover complete control of their legs.

This has been confirmed by numerous other observers [Engel and Phillips (a); Swank; Prickett; Prickett, Salmon and Schrader] who have noted that animals who developed very acute fulminating symptoms, and who died rapidly, did not, as a rule, develop visible changes in the peripheral nerves, even after careful pathologic study. Other birds, more chronically ill, were much more likely to develop weakness of the legs; moreover, as Peters noted, there was a rather marked difference in response to treatment. He adds that in chronic cases it is easy to imagine a true polyneuropathy, though its actual existence he regarded as unproved, particularly in birds deficient in thiamin alone.

Sebrell and Elvove reported a similar phenomenon in rats: "The symptoms of polyneuritis in rats appear to be associated with shortage, rather than complete absence of the antineuritic vitamin." Since these authors used convulsive seizures as their criterion, they probably referred to the central nervous system manifestations of deficiency of the heat-labile factor, rather than to true peripheral neuropathy. Williams and Spies have made the same observation.

Phillips and Engel found that riboflavin deficiency produced a severe peripheral nerve degeneration in chicks, although their earlier experiments with rats [Engel and Phillips (b)] did not give this result.

Zimmerman, Cowgill and Fox have reported that deficiency of the whole B complex except for the heat-labile component resulted in the development of demyelinization of the peripheral nerves and degeneration of axis cylinders in dogs.

Results of recent experiments are given in Table 11.

TABLE II

Histopathologic Results in Experimental Deficiency of the Vitamin B Complex. Recent Experiments

Authors	Animals	Diets	Clinical Notes	Pathologic Changes
Lee and Sure	Albino rats	Deficient in heat-labile (h-l) factor. B complex supplied by autoclaved yeast and beef.		Constant changes in peripheral nerves, varying directly with length of experiment. Mild: swelling of fibers. Severe: degeneration of myelin and fragmentation of axis cylinders.
		Deficient in whole B complex.		Similar but milder changes over similar periods of time.
		Deficient in vitamin A.		Degeneration more pronounced in optic than in sciatic nerves (reverse of B deficiency).
Prickett, Salmon and Schrader	Rats	Severely deficient in h-l factor.	Severe neuromuscular symptoms.	Relatively slight anatomic changes of the peripheral nerves. Rather more severe changes when caloric intake limited although some h-l factor added.
		Same diet, but small amounts thiamin chloride added after acute symptoms.	Partial alleviation of symptoms but continued impairment of equilibrium, loss of vestibular righting reflexes, and convulsive attacks. New symptoms developed: ataxic walk followed by paralysis.	Peripheral nerves showed distinctive changes in myelin sheaths, axis cylinders, and interfibrillar connective tissues, not seen in other groups.
Swank	Pigeons	Inadequate in calories and in h-l factor.	After 13–34 days, leg weakness and opisthotonus.	Degenerating fibers in peripheral nerves, roughly proportional to degree of leg weakness.

Authors	Animals	Diets	Clinical Notes	Pathologic Changes
		Deficient in h-l factor until vomiting occurred. Then 50 γ thiamin daily 3–6 weeks, then discontinued.	7–12 days after discontinuance, opisthotonus developed.	Most showed no degeneration of peripheral nerves, a few had occasional degenerating fibers.
		Deficient in h-l factor *or* in B complex. After vomiting, 7–15 γ thiamin parenterally.	16–30 days later, ataxia developed, followed shortly by inability to stand.	Severe degenerative changes, found in peripheral nerves, more pronounced in distal than in proximal portions. More severe changes associated with severer leg weakness.
		15 of these birds given 50 γ thiamin daily.	Amelioration of leg weakness. 6–9 weeks required for complete rehabilitation after 7–10 days of weakness and continued deficiency.	Number of normal myelinated fibers increased.
		Inadequate amounts of food but extra 50 γ thiamin.	No paralysis after 15–33 days.	Some myelin changes but no degenerating axons.
Swank and Bessey	Pigeons	B₁-free.	Opisthotonus developed. Thiamin intramuscularly relieved this quickly.	
		Partially deficient in B₁.	Leg weakness developed. Intramuscular thiamin relieved this slowly. If thiamin discontinued severe cardiac failure and dyspnea. Only about ½ saved by thiamin.	Hydropericardium and pulmonary edema.

In the first two papers, the pathological changes were determined by a polarized light technique, while Swank used several stains, and examined various portions of the peripheral nerves. Lee and Sure stated that starvation could not be the controlling factor in their results, as there was no correlation between severity of the pathological changes and weight loss.

In his second group, Swank also reported that a number of these birds showed degeneration in what appeared to be a spinocerebellar tract. A significant number of chronically deficient birds in this study showed signs of cardiac failure, but this did not appear in any of the acutely deficient birds.

Analysis of the results presented in these four studies makes it possible to offer some conclusions. Starvation does produce changes in the peripheral nerves, but these appear to involve primarily the myelin sheath, leaving the axon untouched, and are not accompanied by any perceptible paralysis. Acute deficiency of the heat-labile factor, regardless of other factors, produces a picture of severe involvement of the central nervous system, which may be rapidly and completely relieved with thiamin chloride, and may show no histopathologic lesions on examination of the tissues. Other authors have pointed out that this is associated with a specific metabolic disturbance of carbohydrate metabolism. Chronic partial deficiency of the heat-labile factor (with or without the rest of the B complex) regularly produces a syndrome of leg weakness and paralysis, which is associated with marked histopathologic changes in the peripheral nerves, affecting axons as well as myelin. When thiamin (alone or with the rest of the B complex) is administered, slow recovery from the paralysis usually results, associated with corresponding improvement in the histopathologic changes in the peripheral nerves. But if the disorder is too far advanced, recovery may never be complete.

Further evidence is supplied by Alexander (b), who has reported that "Wernicke's disease cannot be produced in pigeons which are receiving crystalline vitamin B_1, though they may be deficient in all other vitamins or in any other vitamin for a period of over six months."

Meiklejohn has recently criticized much of the work purporting to show that thiamin is the antineuritic vitamin. Some of his objections do not apply to recent studies, but he is justified in calling attention to the fact that animals, deficient in the heat-labile factor, may, through vomiting, anorexia, and impaired absorption, lose significant quantities of other essential constituents of the diet which are necessary for the preservation of the integrity of the peripheral nerve, and that restoration of thiamin (particularly in the company of other B factors) may reverse the process by this nonspecific effect alone. It is not practicable to give an adequate diet parenterally, and variation of absorption cannot, therefore, be completely eliminated as a possible factor. There is, however, little indication that those factors which are taken are poorly absorbed, so far as the vitamin fraction is concerned. Both nicotinic acid and riboflavin, at least, seem to be adequately absorbed by patients deficient in thiamin.

At the present time, then, the evidence from animal experimentation indicates that a diet partly deficient in thiamin alone results in the appearance of weakness and ultimately of paralysis of the legs, associated with demonstrable anatomic changes in the peripheral nerves, and that administration of thiamin will reverse the process in most cases. Whether these lesions are the direct or indirect result of thiamin lack has not yet been determined. From the work of Zimmerman, Cowgill and Fox, it appears that this picture can also be produced by deficiency of other factors in the B complex.

Further evidence comes from investigations on blood pyruvic acid. Platt and Lu demonstrated that in Oriental beriberi there is an accumulation of pyruvic acid in the body fluids. Bueding and Wortis, with an improved technique, investigated the blood pyruvic acid values of 67 assorted patients. Sixteen of these were found to have abnormally high values; these included 12 chronic alcoholics with acute peripheral neuropathy, and 1 case of beriberi. The group of patients with normal blood values included 15 chronic alcoholics without polyneuropathy and in no case of a chronic alcoholic with neuropathy was a normal blood pyruvic acid value found.

A paper by Williams, Mason, Wilder and Smith is briefly reported here, because of its considerable interest, although it does not bear directly upon the etiology of polyneuropathy. These authors reproduced the neurasthenic symptoms so characteristic of the inebriate, not by alcohol, but by a diet deficient only in thiamin chloride (50 I.U. daily). Heretofore, these symptoms, both in inebriates and in temperate persons, have been attributed to an abnormal psyche. The subjects were 6 female patients at Rochester State Hospital chosen for coöperation, absence of physical defects and abnormal nutritional history, and quiescence of mental illness. The experimental period lasted 88 days. The time of onset of symptoms varied. These included

depressed mental states, generalized weakness, dizziness, backache, soreness of muscles, palpitation, dyspnea and precordial distress (pseudoangina) on exertion, insomnia, anorexia, nausea, vomiting, loss of weight, atony of muscles, very slight roughness of the skin, faint heart sounds, lowered blood pressure, and bradycardia at rest with tachycardia and sinus arrhythmia on exertion. In all cases physical activity greatly decreased. Less regularly, there were observed states of apathy, reawakening of psychotic trends, difficulty of thought and memory, photophobia, headache, abdominal distention, sensations of cold and heat, burning of the soles of the feet, numbness of the legs, fatigue of ocular muscles, tenderness of the muscles of the calves and depressed tendon reflexes. Changes in the size of the heart were not detectable in any case. Edema was not apparent in any case. Plasma proteins remained within normal limits in all cases. Values for serum calcium and serum phosphorus remained normal. Anemia did not develop, cheilosis was not seen and there was no reddening of the skin or of the tongue. In all cases the capacity for work, as measured with a calibrated chest-weight exercising machine, fell progressively during the period of restricted intake of thiamin. Electrocardiographic abnormalities developed.

Two of the six subjects placed on the diet restricted in thiamin were given thiamin chloride orally. This was done without their knowledge. In both of these subjects, an intake of less than 0.95 mg. (315 I.U.) of thiamin daily was associated with fatigue, irritability, poor appetite, insomnia, soreness of muscles and constipation. On the other hand, a feeling of unusual well-being, associated with unusual stamina and enterprise accompanied the period in which the intake of thiamin was at the level of 2 mg. (660 I.U.) daily. This was followed by a let-down when the intake of thiamin was lowered by substituting the routine hospital diet for the basal diet which had been supplemented with thiamin chloride. The change at this time was so striking that one subject begged to be returned to the basal diet.

The disease induced by the isolated restriction of thiamin resembles minutely that disorder which the discriminating psychiatrist designates as neurasthenia and differs from hysteria, from obsessive and compulsive states, from anxiety neurosis and other conditions which an undiscriminating physician commonly would lump together with neurasthenia under such designations as chronic nervous exhaustion or functional neurosis. Thus, neurasthenia, properly defined, may be less of a functional abnormality than has been supposed and it may depend on improper nutrition of neurons.

The force of this suggestion can be appreciated best by comparing the symptoms and objective evidence of abnormality which we encountered in our studies with the symptoms and abnormalities of neurasthenia as recorded by Wilson.

Not every symptom of neurasthenia was represented in every one of our subjects, but neither is this true of all patients who have neurasthenia.

At the end of the period of deprivation of thiamin, the clinical picture presented in all our cases was that of anorexia nervosa and this condition as one encounters it clinically is usually an end stage of more severe neurasthenia. We wish to make clear, however, that we are comparing the state of thiamin deficiency not with the functional neuroses in general, but with neurasthenia, when the term, "neurasthenia," is used with the discrimination that we have demanded. Nor do we mean to imply that all patients with the diagnosis neurasthenia, could be shown to be victims of thiamin deficiency, especially of a primary deficiency of this vitamin. Possibly only a small percentage of such cases are nutritional in origin, but it may be that the number is large. What we do suggest, on the basis of observations of the disease induced by withdrawal of thiamin, is that thiamin deficiency, as this exists in our part of the country where we see only a few cases of beriberi or pellagra, should be looked for principally in that large group of patients who have the infirmity to which the diagnosis, neurasthenia, has appropriately been applied.

Therapeutic evidence. Although there are still a few dissenting voices (e.g., Bolten, who states he has never seen good results with "betaxine" in polyneuropathy!), the results of studies on the effects of vitamin B therapy in polyneuropathy are very consistent. Not all patients treated with vitamin B recover completely, but many more recover than have under other forms of therapy and most show some improvement. The issue still being debated is whether the chief factor in these cures is the B_1 fraction or not. The chief opponent to the B_1 theory is Meiklejohn.

I believe that the work that my associates and I have done, as well as that of others, supports the belief that the polyneuropathy associated with alcoholism is similar to the polyneuropathy of Oriental beriberi, and that this polyneuropathy of Oriental beriberi is caused by a lack of the antineuritic vitamin B_1 (vitamin B_1 being used as pre-1936). Meiklejohn agrees, at least, with the first part of this statement. "The polyneuritis associated with alcoholism, pregnancy, and gastrointestinal disturbances is unquestionably due to nutritional deficiency, and is in every way similar to the polyneuritis of Oriental beriberi."

His criticism, that diets deficient in one member of the vitamin B complex are almost certainly deficient in others, is one that was recognized by me as far back as 1935 when I noted that "the alcohol addicts forming the basis of this study often manifested signs attributable to an avitaminosis other than B_1." The mere fact, however, that other B deficiencies may be manifest does not negate a close parallelism between vitamin B_1 and polyneuropathy. Many patients having pellagra also have polyneuropathy. This does not contraindicate that pellagrous stomatitis is a nicotinic acid deficiency. It is important to realize that vitamin B deficiencies are multiple but clinical investigation has enabled us to differentiate to some extent between the manifestations of each. In subjects who have simultaneous deficiencies of thiamin, riboflavin and nicotinic acid, the specific clinical signs of each deficiency (polyneuropathy, cheilosis and stomatitis) have been separately cleared by the administration of the specific vitamins one at a time while the patients were maintained with a diet inadequate in the entire vitamin B complex (Jolliffe, Fein and Rosenblum).

In these later studies, since the synthetic production of thiamin chloride, it has been possible to make more exact determinations and I believe that our results indicate that the improvement in the objective signs of polyneuropathy in the alcohol addict vary directly with thiamin intake up to the amount used in our study.

Meiklejohn's criticism that "the additional thiamin might have had some influence in improving digestive function and facilitating the absorption of other antineuritic factors present in vegex" does not seem the most likely explanation. It is true that diets containing a constant amount of vitamin B_r but rich in the entire vitamin B complex, apparently lead to greater improvement in objective signs of polyneuropathy than diets poor in the vitamin B complex (Jolliffe and Colbert; Goodhart and Jolliffe). On the other hand, with diets rich in the vitamin B complex, the rate and degree of improvement vary directly with the vitamin B_r intake.

Three treatment groups (Groups B and C of Jolliffe and Colbert,* and C and D of Goodhart and Jolliffe) received the same amount of vegex, and from 2 to approximately 14 times more than the predicted requirement of vitamin B_r. Since changes in objective signs varied with the vitamin B_r intake, it seems more logical to connect the increasing improvement to thiamin than to increased absorption of a hypothetical and unknown fraction possibly contained in vegex.

Meiklejohn's final criticism that "the changes in physical signs observed must have been due to improvement in the function rather than in the structure of the nerves, since they took place in the short space of 10 days, which would hardly be long enough to allow of much regeneration of degenerated nerve fibers," is surprising in 1940 when emphasis is being placed more and more on biochemical and physiologic alterations, which, in many disease processes, precede gross anatomic changes.

A new type of criticism has more recently been leveled against the theory of vitamin deficiency in the etiology of the polyneuropathy of chronic alcoholics. Brown has counted the days spent in the Boston City Hospital by patients with "alcoholic polyneuritis" who were discharged as "well, improved or relieved" during two periods. In the first period, 1920–1929, these patients were maintained with a "routine house diet," while in the second period, 1930–1938, they were given the same diet with supplements rich in vitamins and, in numerous instances, injections of liver extract or thiamin. There were 118 patients in each group. After stating, "I doubt very much that we

*Meiklejohn, in criticizing this work, refers to the "report of 3 cases by Jolliffe and Colbert." These "3 cases" in fact were 3 *groups* of cases, numbering 28 in all.

should ever have any better 'yardstick' of the effect of the therapy than the length of stay in the hospital required before the patient was able to leave on his own feet," Brown concluded as follows: "The average time spent in the hospital by patients suffering from alcoholic polyneuritis who were discharged as well, improved or relieved was the same regardless of whether the routine house diet or intensive vitamin therapy in addition was prescribed. The economic aspect of this conclusion is apparent." Accepting both the proposed "yardstick" and the conclusion based thereon, the view has been formulated in an editorial in the *American Journal of Digestive Diseases* that "alcoholic neuritis" is "apparently not due to deficiency of vitamin B_1."

Without analysis, Brown's findings seem to be in complete conflict with those of numerous investigators, cited above, who have reported, not from a counting of days in hospital but on the basis of controlled observations, that patients treated with vitamins recover more rapidly from polyneuropathy than those not so treated, and that there is also a direct relationship between the intensity of vitamin therapy and the time required for recovery. Records of the Medical Service of the Psychiatric Division of the Bellevue Hospital show, also, that patients treated with vitamins in recent years have stayed on the wards as long as those not so treated, or even longer. This, however, is not related to the time required for benefits to set in after treatment is begun, but to the fact that the vitamin-treated patients have been "study cases." They are usually carefully observed for a number of days as a control period before treatment is instituted and are often held for a few days after treatment is concluded in order to complete various control and check-up procedures. Undoubtedly the same condition prevails at other hospitals where the nutritional diseases of chronic alcoholics have been studied extensively during the past 10 years. This, in all probability, is the true explanation of the fact that the "well, improved or relieved" patients in the vitamin era, whose records were examined by Brown, stayed as long in the hospital as the group in the pre-vitamin era. This finding, however, cannot be used as a "yardstick" of the effectiveness or relative economy of the two forms of treatment. Such a yardstick is fundamentally misleading, since the essential of any standard for gauging the effectiveness of a form of therapy is, what proportion of patients are benefited. Only when two forms of therapy are equally efficacious in degree and in the proportion of patients benefited, can the administrative issue of how long each form of treatment requires become of importance. Brown's investigation ignored the question of the percentage of patients benefited under the two regimens compared, and this omission invalidates any conclusions which might be made as to their relative effectiveness.

Recapitulation of etiology. Since some of the facts pertaining to the etiology and pathogenesis of "alcoholic" polyneuropathy are, by necessity, scattered over various sections of this review, a brief restatement of the present status is given here.

The neuropathologic and clinical identity of polyneuropathy and beriberi stands today unchallenged. There is slightly less agreement relative to the etiology. No one doubts the basic nutritional deficiency in alcoholic neuropathy and the avitaminotic nature is also generally recognized. There are, however, a few dissenting voices relative to the specific vitamin involved. The vast majority of modern investigators is in agreement that the basic etiologic factor is a vitamin B_1 deficiency. The few opponents of this theory should realize that the exponents of it are fully aware of the concomitant deficiency of other vitamins and their role in the total picture and that this is reflected in the therapeutic procedures advocated. The B_1 deficiency is regarded, however, as the dominant deficiency which gives the coloring to the syndrome.

The idea of a direct causation through alcohol had to be abandoned in view of (*a*) the identity of "alcoholic" neuropathy and beriberi, (*b*) the fact that alcoholized animals did not develop neuropathy, (*c*) the fact that adequately nourished inebriates did not develop it, and (*d*) the fact that vitamin B_1-deficient diets produced experimentally the characteristic symptoms in the peripheral nerves and the clinical manifestations of neuropathy including the neurasthenic manifestations. Further support comes from the analysis of the pretreatment diets of patients with alcoholic neuropathy and from the therapeutic application of vitamin B_1.

The genesis of the vitamin deficiency is a complicated one. The original assumption that it is merely due to the poor food habits of the alcoholic is insufficient, although this is a contributing factor. More important is the relation found between caloric intake and vitamin B_1 requirement. In this sense one may speak of a relative B_1 deficiency. The deficiency is further fostered by the gastric and hepatic conditions which create a food intolerance as well as anomalies of absorption and assimilation, and possibly by increased elimination of vitamin B_1 in the urine.

The fact that women, although not forming more than 20 per cent of the alcoholic population, are predominant among patients with "alcoholic" neuropathy is perhaps a lead for further clarification of the pathogenesis of "alcoholic" neuropathy and merits attention in future researches. Precipitating factors of neuropathy, if any can be clearly distinguished, should also receive more consideration in the future since their recognition would lead to the clarification of some puzzling variations in the course of chronic alcoholism.

III. CIRCULATORY DISTURBANCES

That "drinking affects the heart" and the circulatory system was known, or assumed, even in ancient times. As a matter of fact, in the past, intemperance was regarded as affecting the circulatory system more extensively than it is today (e.g., as the cause of arteriosclerosis and kidney disease). Apparently the first description of enlarged hearts in inebriates was made by Bauer (cit. Huchard) in 1860. On the basis of observations made on 20 excessive drinkers, Bauer named this condition "alcoholic heart." The condition, however, was known for some time after that as *myodegeneratio cordis*. Since Bollinger's report of the high occurrence of what he called idiopathic hypertrophied hearts in the Munich population, which he found only in beer drinkers, the name *Bierherz* has been generally used. Aufrecht showed, in 1895, that what he called alcoholic myocarditis occurred in drinkers of alcoholic beverages other than beer just as frequently as in beer drinkers, but in spite of this the term *Bierherz* has been used until recent times, although the term "alcoholic heart" has also appeared.

After the recognition of the common etiology of polyneuropathic beriberi and alcoholic polyneuropathy, attention was naturally directed to the cardiovascular syndrome of these diseases to such an extent that the term "alcoholic" beriberi is now frequently used as a label for some of the circulatory disturbances occurring in alcoholism. These are receiving more attention now than when they were called *Bierherz*. The newer label is, in addition to being etiologically more appropriate, also more correct, for the circulatory disturbances of the inebriate are not limited to cardiac dysfunction.

The Clinical Picture

Beriberi is best defined as "a clinical syndrome which follows failure to ingest, absorb, or utilize sufficient amounts of vitamin B_1. It is, as a rule, associated with prolonged and too exclusive use of a diet rich in calories derived from refined carbohydrate or alcohol. It is characterized clinically by varying degrees of a peripheral symmetrical poly-neuritis which may occur alone or in combination with edema, serous effusions, enlarged heart and circulatory failure." (Jolliffe and Rosen-blum.) This definition indicates the clinical types, namely: (*a*) the neuritic or "dry" beriberi, in which the signs are practically limited to the nervous system; (*b*) the edematous, or "wet" type, in which the polyneuropathy, often minimal or mild (occasionally no signs) but sometimes severe, is associated with edema and serous effusions in the pericardial, pleural, and peritoneal cavities; (*c*) the "cardiac" type, in which the polyneuropathy is associated with heart failure; and (*d*) the "mixed" type, a combination of polyneuropathy, edema, and con-gestive heart failure.

Clinically the circulatory manifestations can be divided into three groups as follows:

1. Edema (and serous effusions) occurring without enlargement of the heart or other signs of congestive heart failure.

2. Edema and serous effusions occurring with supporting signs and symptoms of congestive heart failure, usually with definite roentgeno-graphic evidence of cardiac enlargement.

3. Sudden circulatory collapse.

Edema without enlargement of the heart, or other signs of congestive heart failure, is the type of circulatory disturbance most frequently seen in the inebriate. The edema is dependent, it may be mild and limited to pitting at the ankles, or it may be anasarca. The edema can-not be attributed to a failing heart as there are no other signs of heart failure, such as an elevated venous pressure, prolonged circulation time, dilated cervical veins, or enlarged heart. In these subjects the plasma proteins are above the critical level of edema; though many inebriates have edema due to low plasma proteins, these cases are not included in this group. There is no evidence of renal disease. Also, the edema in most of these patients responds to bed rest alone, and in many subjects the response is dramatic. The interne is often bewildered by admitting a patient with marked edema, possibly so extensive as to be anasarca, only to find, on presenting the subject the following day to his superior, that the anasarca now consists of moderate, or even mild, pitting of the ankles. Similarly, mild or moderate degrees of edema frequently disappear within 24 to 48 hours of bed rest.

The diagnosis of the cardiac form of beriberi should be made in the absence of definite heart enlargement only when there is evidence of congestive heart failure other than edema and serous effusions. If this rule is followed the cardiac form of beriberi will, as a rule, manifest signs of both right and left heart failure, though the signs attributed to failure of the right heart usually predominate. Consequently a patient with the cardiac form of beriberi usually shows, in addition to edema and possibly serous effusions, dilated cervical veins, a palpable liver, dyspnea, and orthopnea; and will usually complain of palpitation, breathlessness, particularly after exertion, and often of precordial pain. Pulmonary congestion is common; most patients develop pulmonary edema before exitus. The pulse is rapid and bounding, and often there is a high pulse pressure with pistol shot sounds heard over the great arteries. Cyanosis is not frequent, but generalized arteriolar dilatation is common. The velocity of the blood flow is usually normal or increased, and there is a low arteriovenous oxygen difference. As noted by Weiss, epinephrine exaggerates the symptoms while pitressin brings about temporary improvement. Teleoroentgenographic examination shows enlargement of the heart, attributed chiefly to enlargement of the right ventricle and auricle, and frequently, increase in the size of the pulmonary conus and pulmonary artery is noted. The left auricle and ventricle often contribute to the enlargement of the cardiac shadow, but as a rule to a lesser extent than their mates on the right. Though few patients present normal electrocardiographic tracings, the alterations found are not usually characteristic or diagnostic.

Circulatory collapse and sudden death are described as common in all studies of beriberi in the Orient. Some resemble shock, with rapid thready pulse and low or unobtainable blood pressure; others resemble the syndrome produced by a hyperactive carotid sinus reflex of the vagotonic type. These manifestations may occur without previous warning, or only after other circulatory manifestations are well established. They occur most frequently in ambulatory patients and particularly in those engaged in physical labor.

There is still some controversy over the essential identity of the cardiovascular disturbances in chronic alcoholism and in beriberi. But the apparent discrepancies can be easily reconciled, as will appear below, and leave the identity in no doubt. Opinions on this point are summarized in Table 12.

As can be seen, agreement is general with the exception of Doumer. Doumer's opinion is based, in part, upon a misconception and, in part, upon inadequate evidence.

That the heart is enlarged only to the right in beriberi is an idea widely held among workers in Oriental beriberi and appears to be

TABLE 12

Opinions on the Relation of Circulatory Disturbances
in Chronic Alcoholism and in Beriberi

Author	*Year*	*Opinion*
Weiss and Wilkins	1937	Beriberi cardiovascular disease is of common occurrence in the United States. "We attribute to alcohol a secondary predisposing role in the precipitation of beriberi."
Desrochers and Larue	1937	The clinical manifestations and the anatomopathological lesions in beriberi are evidently the same as those in alcoholic beriberi.
Goodhart and Jolliffe (b)	1938	The similarity between the manifestations of cardiovascular dysfunction in endemic beriberi and those in alcohol addicts is striking.
Bickel (a, c)	1938 and 1939	The large heart of the alcoholic is identical with the *fruste* beriberi heart. In beriberi and chronic alcoholism the same signs and symptoms are found: tachycardia; dyspnea; cardiac irritability; arrhythmia; edema; increase in heart volume; arterial hypertension; increased pulse volume; normal blood velocity; nonspecific electrocardiographic changes of the ventricle complex, mainly of the T-wave; precordial anxiety.
Doumer	1939	Differences between beriberi and alcoholic heart: In beriberi only the right side is dilated; adrenalin test is always positive; edema is late; improvement after B_1 therapy very fast and electrocardiogram shows shortening of P–R interval and right preponderance. In the alcoholic heart, the entire heart is involved and more often the left than the right; adrenalin test is negative (von Gogaert); edema is precocious; improvement after B_1 therapy is slow and electrocardiograms show other changes.
Facquet	1939	The particular symptoms of the beriberi heart are identical with myocardial insufficiency in alcoholics.
Gounelle	1939	Heart symptoms in beriberi and chronic alcoholism are similar, namely: right insufficiency, cyanosis, jugular dilatation, dyspnea, gallop rhythm, tricuspidal insufficiency with murmur, large heart with right side dilatation, high pulse pressure, hepatomegaly, peripheral and serous edema, low voltage and anomalies of T-wave in electrocardiogram; relative inefficacy of usual cardiotonics; special efficacy of vitamin B_1.
Jolliffe and Rosenblum	1939	Same as Goodhart and Jolliffe.
Langeron	1939	Anatomical and functional changes in beriberi and alcoholism are identical.
Merle and Larpent	1939	The two conditions are essentially identical.
de Soldati	1940	The two conditions are essentially identical.

based entirely on the finding of percussion dullness to the right of the sternum. This, however, is not correct, as is best shown by recent roentgenographic studies (Keefer) which demonstrated that the heart may not be enlarged at all, or that it may be enlarged to the right, to the left, or in all diameters. Nor is this finding entirely new. As early as 1889, Yamagiwa found that the entire heart was enlarged; that the right ventricle was more frequently dilated and hypertrophied, or simply dilated, but the left ventricle was also dilated. Wenckebach (a) denied this, but de Soldati has recently affirmed that the left heart is also dilated, but less obtrusively, than the right heart.

Doumer based his statement regarding the adrenalin test on one case; Weiss found it frequently positive. His distinction of the two by their response to thiamin therapy is based on two cases of alcoholic beriberi. A larger series would undoubtedly have shown that in these cases the speed of improvement following B_1 therapy is extremely variable.

We may, then, state that the consensus is that cardiovascular disturbances in alcoholic and cardiac beriberi are essentially the same. These are described by Weiss and Wilkins thus:

The most common cardiovascular symptoms of beriberi, in our experience, are dyspnoea on exertion associated with palpitation, tachycardia and embryocardia. During improvement the tachycardia may change to bradycardia. Gallop rhythm, prominent cardiac and epigastric pulsations and bounding peripheral pulses with sounds ("pistol shots") are also frequently present. The heart may be normal in size or enlarged, and systolic and rarely diastolic murmurs may be heard. In the severe cases the dyspnoea is intense and can appear with unexpected severity. Cardiac asthma (paroxysmal dyspnoea) has also been observed. Signs of pulmonary congestion are frequently present, and cloudiness of the lung fields is seen on roentgenologic examination. The arterial pressure is usually normal, with a tendency to increased pulse pressure. In some cases the systolic pressure is moderately elevated during the acute stage of circulatory failure, but it returns to normal when the patient's condition improves. The veins of the neck are normal or engorged, as is confirmed by the normal or elevated venous pressures. The skin is usually warm and of normal color; at times it is cyanotic. Edema is frequently present, either diffuse or dependent, and it may be of extreme degree. The patients with severe cardiovascular manifestations are prone to develop fever and this, in turn, aggravates failure of the circulation.

Patients incapable of exertion because of severe polyneuritis, like those described in the Orient, are less liable to have advanced circulatory failure. Contrariwise, those with mild cardiovascular symptoms may be made to have pronounced symptoms by moderate exercise.

To these symptoms de Soldati would add intense visceral congestion, especially in the liver, which is palpable and painful, diminished lung capacity, diminished oxygen consumption, and increased velocity of the blood stream.

Very few laboratory reports are available and only one study reports determination of vitamin B_I in the blood. Konstam and Sinclair found this very low in two cases, i.e., 1.5 μg. per 100 cc. in one and 2.5 μg. per 100 cc. in the other.

Goodhart and Jolliffe (b) studied 83 alcohol addicts, aged 27 to 51 years, who did not have, and never had had as far as could be ascertained, chronic cardiovascular or acute or chronic kidney disease. Eighteen of these patients were alcohol addicts without complications of any sort. In the remaining 65, various complications were present: 94.0 per cent had polyneuropathy, 32.3 per cent had clinical evidence of cardiovascular disturbance, 47.0 per cent gave electrocardiographic evidence of it, and in addition, 10 patients had large palpable livers, but no other evidence of circulatory failure. These patients were studied very extensively and some of the findings are summarized in Table 13.

It is immediately evident that the "uncomplicated" group was

TABLE 13

Findings on the Cardiovascular Status of a "Complicated" and an "Uncomplicated" Group of Chronic Alcoholic Patients
[Data of Goodhart and Jolliffe (b)]

	Occurrence in 65 "Complicated" Cases, Per cent	Occurrence in 18 "Uncomplicated" Cases, Per cent
T-wave changes in the electrocardiogram tracings	47.7	22.0
Palpable liver (for any reason)	40.0	0.0
Edema	30.7	0.0
Axis deviation in the electrocardiogram tracings	29.2	5.5
Enlarged heart by x-ray	25.4	0.0
Systolic hypertension (over 150)	23.0	13.0
Dyspnea	18.4	0.0
Diastolic hypertension (over 100)	13.8	0.0
Palpitation	12.3	0.0
Cyanosis	4.6	0.0
Angina	4.6	0.0

without symptoms, except for a small incidence of systolic hypertension and of T-wave changes, and had no clinical signs of circulatory anomalies, while almost half of the patients presenting clinical evidence of a deficiency disease had some circulatory abnormality.

In 1934 Wenckebach (b) reported no, or very slight, electrocardiographic changes, but Keefer, as well as Dassen (cit. de Soldati), found modifications of the T-waves, and increased Q–T interval. Other studies have added weight to the T-wave changes reported by Goodhart and Jolliffe. Jolliffe, Goodhart, Gennis and Cline induced, experimentally, an isolated thiamin deficiency in a group of 4 subjects; T-wave changes appeared in 2 of these, but disappeared rapidly when thiamin was returned to the diet. Williams, Mason, Wilder and Smith found T-wave changes in each of 6 subjects in whom experimental B_1 deficiency was induced. These changes consisted of diminution of magnitude, particularly of the T-waves of the chest leads, and they disappeared rapidly upon administration of thiamin in the diet. A similar phenomenon is reported in several animal studies (Weiss, Haynes and Zoll; de Soldati). The occasional occurrence of electrocardiographic disturbances in "normal" controls is possibly due to the fact that not all "normals" have an optimum diet.

The incidence of cardiovascular disturbances in chronic alcoholics is not well established. Münzinger and Aufrecht have both remarked on the high incidence of heart disease in inebriate populations. Goodhart and Jolliffe (b) stated, "Our studies indicate, however, that approximately one-third of the alcohol addicts who show vitamin B_1 deficiency in the form of peripheral neuritis present clinical evidence of some degree of cardiovascular dysfunction secondary to this deficiency." Bickel (c) stated that more than 20 per cent of patients with moderate chronic alcoholism are suffering from "myocardie éthylique." Konstam and Sinclair, however, report that cardiac beriberi is very rare in England. The characteristic diagnostic features of these circulatory manifestations of beriberi, as they occur in the chronic alcoholic, are:

   1. Dependence on vitamin B_1 deficiency.
   2. Mild degree, as a rule, of the polyneuropathy.
   3. Increased or normal velocity of the blood flow in the presence of congestive heart failure.
   4. Definite response to specific therapy with complete reversibility of the circulatory manifestations.

Before arriving at a presumptive diagnosis preceding therapy a number of observations must be evaluated. First, the more conventional etiologic factors for circulatory failure must be eliminated. These include rheumatic fever, syphilis, hypertension, arteriosclerosis, thyroid heart disease, and constrictive pericarditis. Second, the nutritional history of the patient must be appraised. The mere fact that a patient consumes alcohol daily does not necessarily presuppose the presence of a vitamin deficiency. Third, the presence of noncirculatory manifestations of deficiency diseases should be sought. The most important is a peripheral symmetric polyneuropathy involving first and predominantly the lower extremities. It is not sufficient to test the knee jerks and to look for muscle atrophy, paralysis, and foot and wrist drop. These are the signs of advanced polyneuropathy. Just as heart disease exists without heart failure, polyneuropathy may exist without nerve failure. It is therefore necessary to examine carefully for mild polyneuropathy as evidenced by calf muscle tenderness, plantar hyperesthesia, and diminished vibratory sensation in the toes. If these signs exist, one may strongly suspect polyneuropathy, and if present simultaneously with absent ankle jerks, the diagnosis of polyneuropathy can definitely be made. However, the absence of a definite polyneuropathy does not rule out the diagnosis of circulatory failure due to vitamin B_1 deficiency. I have seen undoubted cases in which a diagnosis of polyneuropathy could not be made. Clinical evidence of deficiency in other vitamins, as shown by a stomatitis, glossitis, cheilosis, pellagrous dermatosis, should always make one look for signs of B_1 deficiency and, if circulatory signs are present, suspect that the patient has a thiamin deficiency.

Pathology

Although the literature contains a number of reports of cases of alcoholic beriberi under one name or another, the pathology has not been extensively studied. Aufrecht, in 1895, reported that microscopically he found consistent alterations and enlargement of the muscular fibers and interstitials of the heart, an increase in the volume of the nuclei, thickening of the arterioles with increased number of nuclei, and occasionally fragmentation of the myocardium.

Mönckeberg studied the hearts of Tübingen inebriates. He always found hyaline sclerosis of the arterioles.

Vaquez stated that aside from dilatation, hypertrophy, and fatty overlayers, the anatomic lesions were inconsistent and nonspecific.

Weiss and Wilkins examined a series of hearts and reported that the gross changes were not so marked nor so frequent as, but the histo-logic changes were identical with, those described by Aalsmeer and Wenckebach in hearts of Javanese with beriberi. These consisted of interstitial edema and histologic changes characterized by hydropic degeneration of the myocardial fibers and the conductive bundles. Most of these hearts also exhibited considerable dilatation of the right ventricle. Weiss and Wilkins' data, however, indicated that the micro-scopic changes were neither specific nor characteristic and were present in other diseases. Their measurements of the water content of the skeletal and cardiac muscles of patients with beriberi and with heart failure of known etiology, other than beriberi, and of control groups without heart failure, disclosed no essential differences.

Etiology and Pathogenesis

As early as 1877, Münzinger attributed the high incidence of this condition among the vineyard workers in Tübingen to their poor diet, which consisted mainly of potatoes and flour pastes. He felt that the very hard labor which these people performed required a "well-nourished heart." Bollinger believed that the idiopathic heart atro-phies he observed should be attributed to the habitual overindulgence in beer and the concomitant occurrence of plethora. Aufrecht pointed out that any alcoholic beverage could be concerned. Until the analogy between these disorders and beriberi and the relation between beriberi and vitamin B_1 deficiency became apparent, most workers ignored the nutritional aspect, and attributed the disease directly to alcohol in-dulgence.

"That alcohol *per se* is not the primary factor responsible for changes described" was pointed out by Weiss and Wilkins, who ad-duced as evidence that:

1. Chronic alcoholism is an exceedingly common condition, in comparison with which beriberi is relatively rare. 2. Pharmacologic studies do not indi-cate that alcohol *per se* causes polyneuritis or cardiovascular disease. 3. Symptoms of dietary deficiency may appear long after the consumption of alcohol, particularly if prolonged gastrointestinal disturbances follow the alcoholic debauch. 4. It is known that patients with alcoholism are predis-posed also to pellagra, and that they frequently have low cevitamic acid content of the blood. It is improbable that a substance through "toxic action" should produce manifestations similar to those known to be caused by deficiency of vitamins B_1, B_2 and C. 5. Finally, polyneuritis, pellagroid lesions and cardiovascular dysfunctions disappear on continuous alcohol intake provided vitamin B is administered simultaneously.

On the other hand, we attribute to alcohol a secondary predisposing role in the precipitation of beriberi. Alcohol is a food substance par excellence in its capacity to supply the body with necessary calories but with a minimum of vitamin B. This is an ideal combination for beriberi, as high caloric and low vitamin B_1 intake, rather than general inanition, precipitates the clinical vitamin deficiency. The gastro-intestinal changes often present in chronic alcoholism may well interfere with the absorption or utilization of the available vitamin B_1, while alcohol itself, a freely diffusible substance, is absorbed readily. There is also a possibility that a high intake of alcohol plays an additional predisposing role, similar to that of a diet rich in carbohydrate, as is common among the rice eaters. It is known that if B_1 avitaminotic animals are kept on a diet that is rich in fatty acids instead of carbohydrates, the manifestations of B_1 deficiency may be prevented.

The origin of the "beer heart" cannot be explained on the basis of increased intake of alcoholic fluids. This condition was described before the use of the sphygmomanometer and it has "disappeared" since the recognition of the clinical significance of arterial hypertension; hence it is probable that these instances of cardiac hypertrophy represent unrecognized cases of hypertensive heart disease. Such a careful investigator as Hirsch observed as early as 1899 that patients with "beer hearts" suffer from nephritis, and he suggested that beer drinking causes nephritis and this, in turn, cardiac hypertrophy.

Bickel (*a*); Goodhart and Jolliffe (*b*); Price; Gounelle; Merle and Larpent; Konstam and Sinclair; and others, concur in attributing the true cause of this condition to a deficiency of vitamin B_1. But there are a few dissenters, whose opinions have not been published. The only questions of importance in the etiology and pathogenesis of this disease concern the physiological mechanisms by which the characteristic clinical manifestations are produced.

The pathogenesis of these circulatory disturbances, except that they are dependent upon a deficiency of vitamin B_1, is still largely conjectural. The most obvious explanation for the edema and serous effusions in the "wet" type of beriberi would be right heart failure, but edema and serous effusions alone, as pointed out by Keefer, are insufficient to justify the diagnosis of right heart failure. To what, then, should be attributed the edema and serous effusions when, in addition to lack of supporting evidence for right heart failure, there is no elevated capillary pressure, lowering of the plasma proteins, damage to the walls of the capillaries, lymphatic obstruction, high salt intake or sodium chloride retention, or a high fluid intake or warm environment? Weiss and Wilkins call attention to the generalized arteriolar dilatation; Platt and Lu emphasize the high excretion of creatinine in the urine, muscle cramps, and accumulation of pyruvic acid in the blood; and

Thompson points out that the kidney is the only organ, other than the brain, in which the oxygen uptake is lowered as a specific effect of the lack of vitamin B_1. Unless these observations provide the explanation, it would seem that the edema and serous effusions may be attributed to a specific action of vitamin B_1 deficiency, the dynamics of which are not at present understood.

Wenckebach (b) believes that vitamin B_1 is a factor regulating humoral osmotic pressure and that the simple edematous infiltration of the cardiac fiber is the cause of its hypodynamics. This would explain the regression of the anasarca, the cardiac hypertrophy and the functional troubles under the influence of vitamin treatments. Merle and Larpent, however, believe that the process is actually much more complex than this. Vitamin B certainly plays an important role in the metabolism of glucides and, on the other hand, it is well established that in beriberi the myocardium shows an impoverishment of glycogen and is encumbered by such intermediary products as lactic acid and pyruvic acid. The importance of the processes of anaerobic disintegration of muscular glycogen with the temporary formation of lactic acid followed by the resynthesis of the lactic acid to glycogen in the contraction of striated fibers is well known. Thus the disturbance which a lack of vitamin B may bring about in this physicochemical interplay may be applicable to the cardiac trouble of beriberi.

The mechanism of the congestive heart failure, when it develops, has been variously explained. That the heart failure in these subjects is due to neuritis of the vagus nerve is untenable, since vagal paralysis does not cause enlargement of the heart (Hodges and Eyster). Furthermore, there is no evidence that vagal neuritis can cause the picture of heart failure seen in beriberi, and many patients have beriberi without evidence of vagal involvement (Keefer). That heart failure in beriberi is a result of respiratory paralysis is even more untenable. By this theory, dilatation of the right side of the heart and subsequent failure is due to the retraction of the lungs and elevation of the diaphragm that follow hydrothorax. This explanation fails to account for the presence of heart failure without hydrothorax or diaphragmatic paralysis, or the lack of heart failure in the many subjects with tuberculosis treated by collapse therapy. Aalsmeer and Wenckebach attributed the heart failure to a disturbance of water metabolism, which results in edema of the heart muscle with consequent loss in contractility. Without discussing the pros and cons of this theory, which has much to support it, the observations of Weiss and Wilkins that the beriberi heart has an unaltered water content, as compared with normal hearts, or hearts of patients dying of heart failure from other causes, are especially significant. To explain the loss of contractile power of the heart, several observations of different investigators must be correlated. The first of these is that vitamin B_1 is necessary in complete oxidation of carbohydrates, the lack of which decreases the contractile power of the heart muscle. The second is the observation of Harrison and Pilcher that edema *per se* increases the work of the heart and thus would secondarily contribute to the production of heart failure. The third is the frequent observation that subjects with beriberi, who have polyneuropathy of a degree still permitting physical effort, are the most likely to develop heart failure. This is in agreement with Barr's study demonstrating the importance of physical exercise in the production of heart failure from any cause. These three factors are all present in most patients with beriberi who develop congestive heart failure.

Further evidence in regard to the etiology of these disorders comes from various studies of experimentally induced vitamin B_1 deficiency which are summarized in Table 14.

While there are gaps in our knowledge of the pathogenesis of cardiac beriberi, and while the filling in of these gaps is of more than academic interest, research in this field has little bearing on the problems of alcoholism. The question, however, of what factors determine whether an alcoholic will acquire the predominantly polyneuropathic or pre-

TABLE 14

Cardiovascular Disturbances in Experimentally Induced Vitamin B_1 Deficiency

Year	Author	Animal	Diet	Results
1928	McCarrison	Pigeons	Diet "similar to that used in India"	Edema and dilatation of heart
1929	Carter and Drury	Pigeons	Polished rice	Bradycardia and cardiac blocking
1930	Drury and Harris	Rats	Diet deficient in B_1	Diminishing heart frequency in proportion to advancing deficiency
1930	Drury, Harris and Maudsley	Rats	Diet deficient in B_1	The bradycardia was cured through administration of vitamin B concentrate
1941	Swank and Bessey	Pigeons	B_1-free diets	Opisthotonus and cardiac failure: hydropericardium and pulmonary edema frequent

dominantly cardiac type of beriberi, is of definite interest to the student of alcoholism. Studies in differential causation would contribute to the understanding of the makeup of alcoholics. Such investigations require more detailed medical and nutritional histories of the patients than those ordinarily obtained. The emphasis on pathologic process has probably led to a neglect of the unit in which the process takes place. Advance in the knowledge of the process should now permit a shift in emphasis.

IV. PELLAGRA*

Pellagra itself was originally described by the Spanish physician, Casal, whose succinct discussion of what he called *mal de la rosa* was written about 1735, though not published until 1762. In addition to an account of the symptoms of the disease, Casal remarked that the principal article of diet of the affected population was corn bread, and he suggested that a more varied diet would be of some therapeutic benefit. "I have regularly observed that to vary the customary diet with other more substantial and more nutritious foods is helpful in alleviating the disease." He was convinced, however, that the illness was a combination of leprosy and scurvy.

The first available published description of the disease, under the name of *mal de la rosa* was that of Thieri, whose account is dated 1755; Garrison, however, stated that Thieri based his account on facts obtained from Casal. The name pellagra first appeared in the literature in the Animadversiones of Franciscus Frapolli, in 1771, from which it appears that the word was then in general use in Italy.

Klauder and Winkelman mention several interesting historical points in their discussion of this disease: Casal is said to have mentioned the role of alcohol in his description of pellagra. During the nineteenth century there were a number of studies which associated alcohol with pellagra. Nobili, in 1841, attributed pellagrous episodes in Italy to abuse of wine. In Spain, Calmarza, in 1870, advocated the view that pellagra was a disease produced by misery and alcohol, and a number of authors in Spain, Italy, and France expressed similar views.

Until recently, the clinical descriptions of pellagra have been in substantial agreement with those of older authors. The recent discovery of the role of nicotinic acid in the prevention of pellagra, however, has demonstrated the fact that some of the symptoms associated with the disease are due to related deficiencies, rather than to nicotinic acid

*Dr. Martin Stein collaborated in the preparation of this Section.

deficiency itself, and distinctions are beginning to appear in the description of pellagrous symptomatology on the basis of etiologic considerations.

Clinical Manifestations

Incidence. Pellagra is endemic in the north of Spain, in Italy, Rumania, Egypt, and in the United States, and occurs sporadically in other countries. In the United States, Stepp and Voit quote Robertson as stating that from 1906 to 1920 there were 500,000 cases of pellagra, of which 50,000 were fatal. The Bureau of the Census (*b*) reported for 1938 a total of 3,205 deaths from pellagra in this country.*

Relative to pellagra in alcoholics, there are no accurate estimates of the present day frequency or geographic distribution. It is certain, however, that it is fairly common, and a statistical study would be desirable. Some idea of its frequency may be inferred from analyses of the larger series reported during the last few years, which have been chiefly from areas where pellagra does not occur in the mass of the nonalcoholic population. Bickel (*b*) stated, in 1938, that all the cases of pellagra reported in Switzerland had been on an alcoholic basis.

In 1928, Klauder and Winkelman reported a series of 100 cases, 97 of which were alcoholic. A year later, Maloney and Tulipan reported the admission of 21 cases of alcoholic pellagra, most of them mild, to the dermatologic clinic of the New York University College of Medicine between June and October. In a series of 73 pellagrins from Cincinnati, Spies and De Wolf found that 90 per cent were on an alcoholic basis, and in 1936, Blankenhorn and Spies (*b*) reported 200 cases of chronic alcoholism and pellagra.

It is common knowledge that there is a seasonal variation in incidence. For example, Spies and De Wolf found that the largest number of their cases occurred between June and September. Even in 1771, Frapolli noticed such a variation: "When upon the approach of spring the peasantry—men and women, boys and girls—settle down with more determination all day long to farming and each one shares in the heavy and light work according to his age and strength, it often hap-

*This figure is probably not accurate since under the present system for computing statistics of causes of death, deaths reported as "alcoholic" pellagra are included in deaths due to alcoholism. If, however, a death is reported as due to pellagra with alcoholism listed as secondary cause, it is included among deaths due to pellagra. In 1938, 26 deaths from pellagra were reported for New York State; 16 of these were in cities with populations above 100,000. It may safely be assumed that at least some of these were alcoholic.

pens that the color of their skin changes suddenly to red. . . . When the summer time has passed every affected part is restored to its former condition; the natural constitution of the skin returns and unless there is a change for the worse, the peasants do not trouble themselves about pellagra and for the time being they suffer no further ill."

Endemic and "alcoholic" pellagra. The clinical manifestations of "alcoholic" pellagra are essentially those of endemic pellagra, plus the effects of alcohol and other factors present in the chronic alcoholic. The number of severe and fatal cases is higher in the "alcoholic" than in the endemic type, since the inebriate is likely to consume a great number of calories *completely* free not only of nicotinic acid but also of other vitamins and other nutritive essentials. However, it is probable that a considerable proportion of the cases represented as endemic are also subject to alcohol addiction, as well as to the regional, economic, and social influences which result in food habits leading to a pellagra-producing diet.

"Alcoholic" pellagra has often been called pseudopellagra or, in the French literature, the *pellagroïde* of alcoholics. While some investigators have endeavored to demonstrate morphologic and clinical differences [e.g., Maloney and Tulipan; Kleiminger; MacKee (the latter 2 cit. Jadassohn)] it is now conceded that there is a morphologic identity between the "alcoholic" and idiopathic forms [Finnerud; Hein and Merrill; Jadassohn; Spies; Littmann; Oliver (the latter 2 cit. Jadassohn)]. All the characteristic symptoms and signs of endemic pellagra have been reported in cases of the alcoholic variety and the response to specific treatment is identical.

Symptomatology. The *dermatitis* is a common finding in "alcoholic" pellagra. It is, however, less characteristically a part of this picture than of the endemic variety. This difference can probably be accounted for by differences in exposure to the sun, trauma, and to the more completely deficient diet of the inebriate. This often leads to the development of encephalopathy before the dermatitis has had time to appear (Jolliffe, Bowman, *et al.*). The dermatitis is otherwise similar to that of endemic pellagra (Heller; Klauder and Winkelman; Maloney and Tulipan; Mills; Roncoroni; Spearman and Smith; Zimmerman, Cohen and Gildea). It is described as a symmetric dermatitis on the dorsal aspects of wrists and hands, with pigmentation, eroded areas and crusts (Maloney and Tulipan). Like the lesions of the endemic variety, it is apparently brought out by exposure to the sun (Heller) and by trauma. It is important to note, however, that severe nicotinic acid deficiency may occur *without* the appearance of dermatitis or of the characteristic stomatitis (Jolliffe, Bowman, *et al.*). This is true, in general, of all the symptoms of "alcoholic" pellagra—as in endemic pellagra the manifestations may appear singly or in any order or combination.

Stomatitis is a very characteristic symptom of "alcoholic" pellagra, often the earliest to appear [Bickel (*b*); Blankenhorn and Spies (*b*); Klauder and Winkelman; May; Zimmerman, Cohen and Gildea]. In a series of 200 patients with alcoholism and pellagra, approximately 60 per cent were found to have specific lesions of the mouth and tongue [Blankenhorn and Spies (*b*)]. The tongue, lips, buccal membranes, gums, and palate may be involved in a scarlet red process which is followed by ulceration. Secondary infection by anaerobic organisms of Vincent's group is not infrequent, responding promptly to nicotinic acid, but not to cleansing and antiseptic measures. The possibility of pellagrous stomatitis should always be considered in cases of Vincent's infection in chronic alcoholics or in others liable to dietary deficiency. The stomatitis may further contribute to dietary inadequacy by making it impossible to take solid food.

Gastrointestinal disturbances, particularly diarrhea, are also rather frequent. In chronic alcoholics, the appearance of diarrhea is serious; it indicates the necessity for immediate and vigorous treatment with nicotinic acid preparations, preferably by a parenteral route.

Mental changes may occur in every severe case of pellagra, and probably there is some blunting of intellect in the milder cases. The specific nicotinic acid deficiency encephalopathy (Jolliffe, Bowman, *et al.*) will be described in Chapter IV. In typical "alcoholic" pellagra the patient is confused and disoriented, often hallucinating and fearful, even when the complete encephalopathic picture has not developed. Hypochondria, ideas of persecution, and cataleptic symptoms have also been noted. This type of disturbance, however, is not specific for pellagra, as it may result from any severe nutritional disturbance. Generally the mental picture in "alcoholic" pellagra does not differ materially from that in endemic pellagra.

As in endemic pellagra, most of the other symptoms which have been associated with pellagra in chronic alcoholics are in large part the result of factors other than the deficiency of nicotinic acid. *Peripheral neuropathy* is one of the conditions most frequently associated with the pellagra of chronic alcoholics [Bianco and Jolliffe; Blankenhorn and Spies (*a*); Carroll; Jolliffe, Fein and Rosenblum; Leschke; May;

Meyer; Spies and De Wolf; Strauss; Villaret, Justin-Besançon, Klotz and Sikorav; Wexberg; Zimmerman, Cohen and Gildea] and is of the same variety as that previously described as primarily the result of thiamin deficiency. In this condition, too, there is evidence that the neuropathy is primarily dependent upon a disorder of metabolism resulting from a deficiency of vitamin B_1. Blankenhorn and Spies (*a*) were able to demonstrate improvement in the peripheral neuropathy of a pellagrous patient treated with vitamin B_1 and a pellagra-producing diet. The development of neuropathy in pellagrins who were receiving autoclaved yeast was reported by Spies and De Wolf. The same phenomenon has been observed on the medical service of the Psychiatric Division of the Bellevue Hospital. This does not imply that the conditions are unrelated.

Some of the lesions of face and lips which have been described as part of the picture of "alcoholic" pellagra have been identified as a manifestation of riboflavin deficiency (Jolliffe, Fein and Rosenblum) which, again, is a frequent accompaniment of nicotinic acid deficiency. This same phenomenon occurs in endemic pellagra.

The *anemia* of alcoholic pellagrins is frequent, occurring in over half of the patients studied (Bianco and Jolliffe; Spies and Chinn; Mills). It is macrocytic in type and has been found to be essentially independent of the presence of achlorhydria or the severity of liver damage (Bianco and Jolliffe). It was rarely found in alcohol addicts who were otherwise free of the manifestations of nutritional deficiency. It was concluded, therefore, that the anemia was the result of a deficient intake of some necessary hemopoietic substance (other than iron).

Porphyrinuria was for a time believed to be part of the picture of pellagra (Beckh, Ellinger and Spies; Spies, Gross and Sasaki; Boulin, Justin-Besançon and Geffroy). Watson, however, has shown that the red pigment described by Beckh, Ellinger and Spies was not a porphyrin, but some unidentified substance, possibly an indigo derivative. Dobriner, Strain and Localio suggested that porphyrinuria may be associated with hepatic insufficiency rather than with pellagra itself.

Emaciation is rather common, but not an invariable finding (Mills).

"Alcohol" amblyopia has also been reported in pellagrous alcohol addicts (Carroll).

In summary, then, the symptomatology of "alcoholic" pellagra is that of endemic pellagra modified by the direct and indirect effects of chronic alcoholism. It should be emphasized that any one symptom of pellagra, mental changes, the dermatitis, the stomatitis, or the gastrointestinal disturbances, may be the *only* symptom present. It will be pointed out in Chapter IV that oftentimes the neuropsychiatric disturbance may be the *only* discoverable indication of a grave nicotinic acid deficiency. Certain other symptoms, such as the anemia and the polyneuropathy, while common enough to be considered part of the complete picture of pellagra, are nevertheless the direct result of factors other than a deficiency of nicotinic acid. All cases of pellagra, however, represent a multiple deficiency of the B group of vitamins, as well as of other vitamins, in which nicotinic acid deficiency is most prominent. In peripheral neuropathy of inebriates, and in Wernicke's disease, there is again a deficiency which involves the whole B complex; but here the thiamin deficiency is the most prominent, and clinical manifestations of nicotinic acid deficiency may or may not be present. In each, therefore, partial, sometimes dramatic, relief may be obtained by the use of a pure vitamin; but it is incomplete and likely to result in relapse if the whole B complex, other vitamins, and a good diet are not soon supplied.

Pathology

There has been a persistent difficulty in describing the pathologic lesions of "alcoholic" pellagra inherent in the nature of the problem. This disease practically never occurs in pure form, being invariably accompanied by various associated lesions. The inebriate who dies with pellagra always bears the evidences of a number of other diseases. He practically always suffers from other vitamin deficiencies (Jolliffe, Bowman, *et al.*), including thiamin, riboflavin and ascorbic acid, any of which may produce visible and significant lesions. Cirrhosis of the liver is a very frequent finding, and secondary infections are almost inevitable. Moreover, there may be present the still undefined lesions which are due to the action of alcohol directly, and cerebral lesions in chronic alcoholism may be indistinguishable from those ascribed to pellagra. Not only are these present as incidental findings, but a number of them doubtless contribute to the development of the pellagrous picture by increasing the need for the vitamin, and reducing the capacity to store it. In addition, it is probable that the deficiency of thiamin and riboflavin may also interfere with the utilization of nicotinic acid. To some extent the same factors operate in endemic pellagra (particularly, associated deficiency of other vitamins), so that a similar difficulty in defining the pathologic changes exists.

Relatively few pathologic studies of "alcoholic" pellagra are available. Zimmerman, Cohen and Gildea have reported necropsy studies of two chronic alcoholics who died with evidence of pellagra. One had glossitis, the other the characteristic triad of dermatitis, dementia and diarrhea. Both patients died with pneumonia. The central nervous system lesions were similar in both, but were more severe in the second. The nerve cells of the cortex showed distinct changes in the Nissl preparations, most marked in the frontal lobes. These consisted of rounding and swelling of the cell bodies; the cytoplasm had a turbid appearance and was indistinct. The tigroid substance in most of the cells was absent, and the nuclei were small and eccentrically placed. In the giant cells of Betz, and in the motor cells of the anterior horn of the spinal cord, the cytoplasm had a hyaline-like appearance, and the nuclear eccentration was marked. The appearance of these cells was identical with that seen in the axonal type of reaction. Areas of degeneration were found to be scattered, partly in the pyramidal and partly in the sensory tracts of the spinal cord. In the second of the two patients, extensive destruction of the medullary sheaths of the peripheral nerves was found. The latter finding was probably the result of thiamin deficiency, primarily, rather than an integral part of the pellagrous picture.

Cobb and Coggeshall noted, in 1934, that the cerebral changes in inebriates who died with Korsakoff's psychosis (a condition which is very frequently found in association with nicotinic acid deficiency, but probably has no direct relation to it) were very similar to those of endemic pellagra, the essential lesions consisting of nerve cell degeneration in the cerebral cortex.

Kennedy described the autopsy findings in one patient who died of alcoholism with pellagra and Korsakoff's psychosis. The brain showed multiple pial hemorrhages. There was pellagrous pigmentation of the hands and wrists. The viscera showed various changes, including thickening of the rugae of the stomach, passive congestion of the liver and spleen, and a nutmeg liver. In this case, too, a considerable portion of the picture cannot be ascribed to pellagra (nicotinic acid deficiency) as such.

In general, the neuropathologic changes are not specific, and may be the result of any of a number of factors.

The Role of Alcohol in the Production of Pellagra

Precise reasoning in this field has, of necessity, been hampered until recently by a lack of information concerning the essential nature of pellagra. For a time it was assumed that pellagra was caused by a hypothetical ptomaine *pellagrazeine*, derived from diseased maize. The demonstration, by Goldberger and others, of the deficiency nature of the disease cleared the matter somewhat. Nevertheless, in spite of some very accurate speculations by a number of investigators (Cobb and Coggeshall; Heller; Spies (*a*); Meyer; Rutledge; Spies and De Wolf; Strauss), the particular deficiency involved and the identity of alcoholic and endemic pellagra remained uncertain until the recent identification of nicotinic acid as a specific curative factor (Elvehjem, *et al.*); and as a coenzyme essential for carbohydrate metabolism.

There is still considerable question, however, as to the exact role of alcohol in the production of "alcoholic" pellagra. The most plausible explanation has been that based on the part alcohol plays as a vitamin free food of high caloric content. The inebriate who subsists for several weeks on liquor alone is unique in his ability to obtain a diet high in calories, and completely free of vitamins. There seems little doubt that this is a most important factor in the production of "alcoholic" pellagra.

It is likely that alcohol is of importance in other respects. The chronic alcoholic is subject to infections, and to acute delirious episodes which increase his metabolic needs considerably and may precipitate a clinical vitamin deficiency [Wortis (*b*)].

Many chronic alcoholics have chronic gastritis and other changes in the gastrointestinal tract which may interfere with the efficient absorption and utilization of nicotinic acid (Cobb and Coggeshall; Minot; Heller). This mechanism is difficult to evaluate because vitamin deficiency itself may be a cause, as well as a result, of gastrointestinal changes. Moreover, it is a matter of common clinical observation that nicotinic acid is absorbed with great rapidity, even by severe chronic alcoholics with gastric symptoms, as manifested by the prompt appearance of the typical vasomotor reaction. More important, probably, is the reduction of food intake due to anorexia, nausea, and vomiting, which frequently precede pellagrous manifestations (Gaté, Tiran and Thévenon; Spies and De Wolf). It has also been suggested that lesions of the liver and endocrine glands may interfere with utilization of vitamins (Villaret, *et al.*), but the importance of this in "alcoholic" pellagra is somewhat uncertain. Boggs and Padget thought that either alcohol destroyed the P-P factor in the gastrointestinal tract, or the tract underwent such changes, as a result of alcohol, that it was not able to assimilate the P-P factor. Jadassohn stated that the combination of inebriety and undernourishment cannot suffice to explain the onset of pellagra, for in that case alcoholic pellagra would be much more frequent than it is.

Many attempts have been made to implicate alcohol, or specific types of alcoholic beverages (particularly corn whisky), as specific toxins in the production of pellagra (Chick; Maloney and Tulipan; Silberman). Several experiments have been performed, however, which tend to discredit this concept. Spies and De Wolf treated 10 alcoholic pellagrins by administering a well-balanced diet, 75 g. of autoclaved yeast and 900 cc. of corn whisky daily. All recovered from their pellagra, although 8 of the 10 developed signs of peripheral neuropathy subsequent to their admission to the hospital. By giving large amounts of the whole B complex, with alcohol, Strauss demonstrated relief in patients with neuropathy. That the continued consumption of alcohol would not cause relapse in cured pellagrins, when the diet was adequate in B complex, was shown by Blankenhorn and Spies (a).

Alcohol is most important, therefore, in its role as a source of vitamin free calories. Less important, but probably contributory, are its effects on appetite and gastrointestinal function, on total metabolic rate, hepatic damage, and associated vitamin deficiencies. Its direct toxic action in producing pellagra is very questionable. "Alcoholic" pellagra may then be considered to be a disease resulting from the deficiency of the vitamin B complex, predominantly nicotinic acid, occurring in alcohol addicts.

From the standpoint of the student of alcoholism, there is one question in connection with pellagra which calls for research. The insufficient vitamin intake attendant upon inebriety, the changes in vitamin assimilation and utilization resulting from liver damage and gastric anomalies in chronic alcoholics are a necessary cause for any deficiency disease. What, then, are the factors which bring about one type of vitamin deficiency rather than another? Is this an individual response, or are ecologic factors responsible? Physiologic, as well as statistical, studies are required to clarify this point which is relevant to prevention as well as to general theory.

CHAPTER IV

Alcoholic Encephalopathies and Nutrition*

NORMAN JOLLIFFE, HERMAN WORTIS *and* MARTIN H. STEIN

THE role of vitamin deficiencies in the etiology of some of the mental disorders of chronic alcoholism has been established quite recently. These are (*a*) Wernicke's syndrome and (*b*) nicotinic acid deficiency encephalopathy [Jolliffe (*b*); Jolliffe, Bowman, *et al.*]. In addition, the dependence of delirium tremens, the Korsakoff psychosis and perhaps Marchiafava's disease on a nutritional deficiency has been suggested by some investigators. The latter three will not be discussed in this chapter since delirium tremens and Korsakoff's psychosis have been dealt with in detail in Chapter II, while Marchiafava's disease is treated in Chapter V.

I. THE WERNICKE SYNDROME

In 1881 Carl Wernicke, on the basis of a careful study of 3 patients during life and at the autopsy table, delineated a clinical syndrome characterized by clouding of consciousness, varying ophthalmoplegias, and ataxia. The author did not state that alcohol was the causative agent but suggested that various toxins, including alcohol, might produce the clinicopathologic picture of acute hemorrhagic polioencephalitis superior. Nonetheless, most subsequent cases were reported in inebriates, and the excessive use of alcohol gradually came to be accepted as the etiologic basis of this condition. It is therefore important to emphasize that his first observations were not made on an inebriate.

The Clinical Picture

Wernicke's first patient was a 20-year-old seamstress who was admitted at the Berlin Charité, following a suicidal attempt by sulfuric acid. She left the hospital after several days, but soon thereafter persistent and intractable vomiting set in, probably as the result of pyloric stenosis. The vomiting continued and after 1 month she became stuporous and developed ophthalmoplegia and ataxia. In addition,

*The combined bibliography of Chapters III, IV, V and VI appears at the end of Chapter VI, pp. 310–324.

there was moderate swelling of the optic discs with associated retinal hemorrhages. Her condition gradually became worse and she died 1 week after the onset of these complications. His other 2 patients, however, were chronic alcoholics who were admitted in delirium.

The association between delirium tremens and the Korsakoff psychosis and the Wernicke syndrome has frequently been commented on (e.g., Bonhoeffer; Bumke and Kant; Wechsler (c); Wortis (b); Jolliffe, Wortis and Fein). Bumke and Kant mentioned the frequency with which delirium preceded the syndrome and noted that those cases which did not end fatally were frequently left with a residual Korsakoff psychosis.

Wechsler gave an excellent clinical description of the syndrome and reaffirmed its frequent association with delirium. He intimated that the ataxia might result from involvement of the brachium conjunctivum and nucleus ruber, which are in close proximity to the usual site of pathologic involvement. He mentions that, as in other forms of encephalopathy, there may occur rigidities, catatonias, abnormal movements, disturbances of consciousness and various grades of polyneuropathy. Mental symptoms ranging from simple psychotic phenomena to the Korsakoff syndrome may also be present. The author states that the disease often terminates fatally in 1 to 2 weeks or that recovery may be complete. In incomplete recoveries, residual ocular palsies, mental symptoms, general weakness and ataxia may remain.

As will be noted later, Jolliffe, Wortis and Fein have presented evidence indicating that the Wernicke syndrome is probably a combination of several nutritional deficiencies. The resulting clinical picture may therefore vary with the nature of the nutritional deficiencies, the presence or absence of complicating factors and the personality of the patient.

The clinical picture of this syndrome is not clear cut. As a matter of fact, psychiatric textbooks usually do not discuss it but refer to works on pathology. The central features of this syndrome are clouding of consciousness, ophthalmoplegia and ataxia. However, the ataxia and ophthalmoplegia need not necessarily coexist in the same patient (Jolliffe, Wortis and Fein).

Pathology

The essential pathology was described by Wernicke and has been further elaborated by others. In general, the lesions are confined to the periventricular gray matter and are characterized by small foci of degeneration and varicose deformities of the blood vessels. There is subacute necrosis of the adjoining parenchyma, and small petechial hemorrhages are frequently but not always found throughout the lesions. The areas most constantly involved are the paramedian and periventricular nuclei of the thalamus and hypothalamus, the mammillary bodies and periaqueductal regions of the midbrain (3d and 4th nerve nuclei), the abducens nuclei, the nuclei triangularis and Bechterew of the vestibular nerve and the dorsal vagus nuclei.

In his original report, Wernicke pointed out that the levator palpebrae superioris muscle and the sphincter of the iris might be spared, indicating nuclear rather than peripheral involvement of the nerve supply to the eye muscles. He also raised the question whether the delirium, which was a complicating factor in 2 of his patients, was a part of the polioencephalitic syndrome or whether it was merely a coincidental complication.

Jacobäus, in 1894, reported similar findings on an inebriate, but observed that the polioencephalitic changes were complicated by involvement of the peripheral nerves and the spinal cord. He stressed the fact that the central changes resulting from the habitual ingestion of alcohol are often overlooked and that they are frequently so marked as to be the actual cause of death.

That the pathology was different from that usually associated with inflammatory lesions was pointed out by Bonhoeffer in 1899. This has been re-emphasized in the most recent edition of Bing's textbook.

In 1906, Hunt reported an excellent clinical case and described the pathologic findings in 22 others. He pointed out that the lesion was usually, but not invariably, confined to the gray matter and suggested that those cases with involvement of both gray and white matter formed a pathologic bond of union between polioencephalitis of the Wernicke type, the so-called Strümpell-Leichtenstern type and encephalitis in general.

Creutzfeld confirmed the pathologic findings in 2 patients with Wernicke's disease, but noted additionally that cellular rarefaction and glial proliferation occurred in the cortex and more particularly in the frontal lobe.

Gamper's description of the pathologic anatomy can hardly be improved upon. Interestingly, he associated the changes in the mammillary bodies with the Korsakoff features which were so frequently observed as a complication.

Bender and Schilder, in their excellent contribution, claimed that many atypical pictures are seen and that one should not adhere too closely to Wernicke's original description. They indicated that the syndrome was frequently complicated by other alcoholic mental disorders (delirium tremens, Korsakoff's psychosis, catatonic syndrome) and confirmed Jacobäus' observation that the spinal cord and peripheral nerves did not escape damage. In addition to the more usual brain pathology, they reported changes in the cortex and neocerebellum.

In 1934, Lauretta Bender (a) again contributed to the knowledge of the problem and described involvement of the spinal cord in 5 patients.* Changes were most marked in the periventricular gray matter, the dorsal and lateral columns, the vegetative centers in the lateral horn and in Clarke's column. She justly pointed out that it is often impossible to differentiate sharply the symptoms resulting from lesions, "because one knows that the pathologic process in alcoholism involves all parts of the central and peripheral nervous systems."

The frequency of pathologic findings in Wernicke's syndrome has been, perhaps, well approximated in the report of Campbell and Biggart on 12 patients of whom only 1 was a chronic alcoholic. Four of these patients had polyneuropathy.† The findings are given in Table 1. The optic nerves were examined in only 2 patients (lesions found in 1 patient) and, therefore, are not included in the table.

A brief remark of Myerson in his discussion of a paper by Alexander, Pijoan and Myerson brought out one of the most interesting observations on the pathology of Wernicke's syndrome. He pointed out that the mineral content of the involved cells remained intact, indicating viability and potential reversibility. In Tay-Sachs' disease, on the other hand, the minerals disappear quite early and the condition is irreversible. In view of the therapeutic results to be reported, this finding assumes the utmost importance.

On the whole, the pathology of this syndrome is fairly definite and of great relevance to the clinical picture. This is not true of any other type of alcoholic encephalopathy. On the other hand, it must be pointed out that the pathology of the alcoholic Wernicke syndrome does not differ in any way from the pathology of the nonalcoholic forms.

Etiology and Pathogenesis

As mentioned above, Wernicke did not insist on an alcoholic etiology

* Her paper contains an excellent bibliography referring to similar findings by others.
† It must be pointed out that the authors did not examine the patients personally.

TABLE I

Order of Frequency of Lesions in 12 Patients with Wernicke's Disease
(After Campbell and Biggart)

Cerebrum
Corpora mammillaria 12
Other parts of hypothalamus 9
Fornix 2
Thalamus (juxtaventricular zone) 7
Habenular nuclei 2
Corpus striatum (ant. part including caudate and putamen) . 3
Substantia nigra 1

Midbrain
Periaqueductal gray matter 8
Anterior colliculi 2
Posterior colliculi 9

Hindbrain
Floor of 4th ventricle 3
Cerebellar cortex 2

but, since the mass of experience with this syndrome came from observations on inebriate patients, there was a tendency to restrict the etiology to alcohol. This in spite of the fairly frequent occurrence of the disease in nonalcoholics. Such cases were reported by Wernicke; Okhuma; Neubürger (*b*); Tanaka; Ecker and Woltman; Campbell and Biggart; Alexander (*b*); Jolliffe, Wortis and Fein.

Clinical and therapeutic evidence. Okhuma suggested that alcohol was responsible only insofar as it facilitated the production of some intermediary toxin, which in turn acted on the nervous system to produce the representative pathology and clinical symptomatology. As a result of his own experiences, he concluded that one cannot always correlate the clinical picture with the pathologic findings in cases of chronic alcoholism and that the pathologic process may produce a clinical picture of Wernicke's disease, Korsakoff's syndrome or delirium tremens. This very important observation has never been sufficiently stressed and the author himself did not emphasize the fact that these pictures frequently merge.

The idea that alcohol was not a primary etiologic factor was further elaborated by Neubürger (*c*), who reported on 3 old women who had died with signs of severe gastrointestinal disturbances. Necropsy in all revealed evidences of severe chronic atrophic gastritis and a "hemorrhagic encephalitis," with characteristic distribution of the lesions. The author suggested that the severe chronic gastritis caused the cerebral changes, probably through the formation of intestinal poisons.

Tanaka reported an unusual case of the Wernicke syndrome in a 5½-month-old breast-fed infant. The mother had no definite signs of beri-beri, but was pale, anemic and nephritic. He mentioned several cases in infants nursed by mothers having beriberi and stated that the symptoms were alleviated or cured when artificial feedings or wet nurses were substituted for the mother's milk. The clinical picture and brain pathology after death in the reported case were typical of the Wernicke syndrome.

Because the lesions in the Wernicke syndrome were most marked in those portions of the nervous system adjacent to the cerebrospinal fluid, Bender and Schilder felt that a noxious agent carried in the spinal fluid was responsible for the observable pathology. They mentioned, however, the possibility of vitamin deficiency and suggested that the cerebral changes might well be secondary to some generalized metabolic disease.

Brain reaffirmed previous descriptions of the clinical pathology and apparently accepted alcohol as the etiologic agent.

Neubürger (b) reported on this syndrome in 14 nonalcoholic patients. Ten of these patients had malignancies of the gastrointestinal tract and 7 of these were located in the stomach. The author again implicated an intermediary toxin and suggested that in chronic alcoholism a similar mechanism was at play.

In 1937, Neubürger (c) reported on 3 elderly women (nonalcoholic) with chronic atrophic gastritis who developed the condition terminally. He suggested that this condition would probably be encountered very frequently if patients with carcinoma or generalized cachexia were examined more carefully prior to death. He justly pointed out that since such persons are considered incurable, careful physical and neurologic examinations are not done when they lapse into terminal stupor.

In the same year, Környey published two similar cases in abstainers. One had a gastrointestinal malignancy and the other a carcinoma of the cervix. It is noteworthy that in both reports persistent vomiting characterized the picture prior to the onset of the encephalopathic signs. In both, there was definite evidence of peripheral neuropathy in addition to the more centrally located lesions.

Wagener and Weir reported that acute optic atrophy, hemorrhages in the retina, paralyses of the ocular muscles and nystagmus might all be caused by dietary or nutritional deficiency and also commented on the frequency with which such complications followed persistent vomiting with resultant lack of food absorption.

Campbell and Biggart remarked that the pathogenesis is not entirely clear, but that of the pathogenic factors which appear singly or in combination, vitamin deficiency and more especially a deficiency of thiamin seems most likely.

Ecker and Woltman reported a case following cholecystectomy. The onset of the syndrome was preceded by vomiting, and the authors suggested that Wernicke's disease might result from nutritional deficiency. They stated that large doses of vitamins B and C affected the recovery in some of their cases.

Wortis (b) again noted that the Wernicke syndrome was frequently preceded by delirium tremens and suggested that the increased psychomotor activity which so frequently accompanied the alcoholic delirious state might so increase the metabolic requirements of the individual as to make clinically evident any latent deficiency states. A similar statement was made by Jolliffe, Wortis and Fein. It was therefore suggested that to prevent the development of the Wernicke syndrome in patients with alcoholic delirium, large amounts of the vitamins, particularly thiamin, should be given.

In the same year, Jolliffe, Wortis and Fein reported their results on patients with Wernicke's disease treated with differential dietary regimens. Their results may be summarized as follows:

1. Of their 27 reported patients, 3 were nonalcoholics (2 depressed individuals who refused to eat and 1 patient with pulmonary tuberculosis with associated vomiting). These 3 abstainers were offered as additional evidence that the Wernicke syndrome is of nutritional rather than of toxic or alcoholic origin.

2. Twenty-five of 26 (1 chart was incomplete) had peripheral neuropathy and in every instance this syndrome preceded or accompanied the ophthalmoplegia. In no instance did the ophthalmoplegia precede the development of peripheral neuropathy. The latter syndrome in chronic alcoholism, and in other conditions leading to disturbed nutrition, is now generally accepted as clinical evidence of thiamin deficiency. The fact that the neuropathy antedates or accompanies the ophthalmoplegia in every instance tends to confirm Alexander's contention that smaller amounts of thiamin hydrochloride are required to prevent angiodegeneration than are necessary to preserve the functional integrity of the peripheral nerves.

3. In addition to peripheral neuropathy, the following deficiency states were observed:

(*a*) Nicotinic acid deficiency encephalopathy: 9 patients
(*b*) Nicotinic acid deficiency stomatitis: 9 patients
(*c*) Nicotinic acid deficiency dermatosis: 3 patients
(*d*) Riboflavin deficiency: 1 patient

Whenever appropriate specific therapy was given early enough, improvement or cure resulted. The authors doubted whether this represented a complete list of the various deficiency syndromes which complicate the Wernicke picture. They pointed out that the clinical awareness of the deficiency states had increased markedly during the past few years and that many of their early charts were obviously deficient in this respect.

4. Regarding the ophthalmoplegia, 8 patients were unimproved or grew worse during their hospital stay. Of this number only 2 received thiamin hydrochloride supplements. In 1 patient, the thiamin hydrochloride was given by mouth and may not have been properly absorbed or utilized, and in another, the thiamin hydrochloride was given with the patient *in extremis*. The 19 patients in whom the ophthalmoplegia improved, or more usually cleared entirely, had all been treated with thiamin hydrochloride in adequate amounts. As a matter of fact, the ophthalmoplegia usually cleared more rapidly in those to whom thiamin hydrochloride was given parenterally in concentrated form. Nicotinic acid was tried in 9 patients without any appreciable effect on the ophthalmoplegia. To 1 patient, pyridoxine was given parenterally, again without effect.

5. Nineteen patients entered the hospital in delirium or developed delirium at some time during their hospital stay. With regard to the delirium itself, the authors were unable to relate this type of encephalopathy to any of the known vitamin deficiencies and felt that their results indicated clearly that delirium tremens was not related to a deficiency of thiamin or nicotinic acid.

6. Fourteen patients entered the hospital in a stuporous condition or developed such a condition while under observation. This stuporous condition in patients with Wernicke's syndrome is usually attributed to changes in the periventricular gray matter surrounding the third ventricle and the hypothalamic region. The authors do not deny this contention but point out that this hypothesis takes no account of the cortex in the genesis of consciousness and that it bridges too many gaps in our knowledge to become completely acceptable in evidence. They further note that cortical changes have been described in polio-encephalitis hemorrhagica superior and that thiamin deficiency will interfere with cortical metabolism (and therefore function) even though no histopathologic changes are demonstrable. They noted that the brain is dependent for its normal functioning on a carbohydrate substrate, an adequate supply of oxygen and various enzyme and coenzyme systems. Among the more important of these latter are cocarboxylase (thiamin pyrophosphate), nicotinic acid and riboflavin. Furthermore, Himwich *et al.* have already demonstrated that in patients with thiamin deficiency there is a marked reduction in the total oxygen uptake of the brain. In addition, they note that there are various other enzymes and vitamins whose exact identity and function are still under observation and that a disturbance in any of these might conceivably be concerned with a disturbance in cerebral functioning and consciousness.

Relative to the effect of therapy on the stupor of the 14 patients who were admitted in this condition, no definite conclusions could be reached. In some cases, thiamin hydrochloride seemed to help, in others nicotinic acid, and in others neither. While thiamin hydrochloride seemed to offer the best therapeutic results, the authors felt that their conflicting results emphasized the importance of controlled observations in this field.

7. Ataxia of movement or speech (dysarthria) was present in 10 patients and except in 1 showed little or no response to the various forms of therapy employed. It was pointed out that ataxia may occur more often, but that it is frequently impossible to obtain the coöperation of such mentally ill patients for the necessary tests; and that the patients are almost invariably too sick for testing of their gait. They noted, additionally, that ataxia as a sign has no localizing value and may be the result of peripheral nerve, spinal cord, cerebellar, extra-cerebellar nuclei or even frontal lobe involvement. However, they definitely state that ataxia and ophthalmoplegia need not necessarily co-exist in the same patient and that the ataxia certainly does not show the same dramatic response to thiamin hydrochloride as does the ophthalmoplegia. They remark that Pappenheimer and Goettsch produced a cerebellar syndrome in vitamin E deficient chicks, but none of their patients received this form of treatment. Finally, they noted that their patients invariably had nystagmus, usually most marked after the ophthalmoplegia had cleared. This sign was not appreciably af-

fected by any one specific therapy, but usually disappeared gradually.

8. Fourteen of their patients eventually died, 7 because of associated infections which in themselves were sufficient cause for death (2 pneumococcus pneumonia, 1 pulmonary tuberculosis, 1 erysipelas, 2 bronchopneumonia, 1 toxic hepatitis). The other 7 deaths occurred in patients who were inadequately treated in the previtamin era. There were no deaths in patients who were treated adequately from the nutritional standpoint. Of the 13 patients so treated, 12 were left with a residual Korsakoff syndrome. This condition did not show a specific therapeutic response to thiamin hydrochloride, as has frequently been claimed.

The investigators concluded that the syndrome, as described by Wernicke, is probably a combination of several nutritional deficiencies affecting the nervous system and that it need not necessarily be complete in any single case. Their results indicate that (*a*) the ophthalmoplegia responds to thiamin therapy, (*b*) the clouding of consciousness may be related to anything which interferes with proper brain metabolism. Among these are lack of carbohydrate, lack of oxygen, lack of thiamin, nicotinic acid or riboflavin or of all three and probably a lack of many other substances now under investigation. (*c*) The ataxia is difficult to evaluate and its response to therapy has not as yet been worked out.

Wortis, Bueding, *et al.* have since treated 4 additional patients suffering from Wernicke's syndrome with essentially similar results. All recovered but were left with a residual Korsakoff syndrome. It was found that the blood pyruvate which is elevated in peripheral neuropathy is also abnormally elevated in patients with Wernicke's disease and that treatment with thiamin promptly results in a reduction of the fasting pyruvate to normal levels.

More recently, Vonderahe has noted that the pathologic lesions characteristic of Wernicke's syndrome may occur with many forms of severe disease of the abdominal viscera and that chronic damage to the autonomic and metabolic areas in the hypothalamic region may persist. He offers convincing case material to illustrate the fact that such damage may be reflected in conditions variously diagnosed as psychoneurosis, neurasthenia, autonomic imbalance or neurocirculatory asthenia. The treatment of these patients is based on the psychotherapeutic procedure of permitting the patient to recognize an organic handicap, on a program of regulated rest and activity and on symptomatic treatment of metabolic disturbances and subvitaminosis. It must, however, be noted that in none of his patients were eye muscle changes observed, nor indeed did pathologic examination reveal evidences of any damage in the region of the eye muscle nuclei. This work is of the utmost importance, but Jolliffe, in the discussion of Vonderahe's report, pointed out that the tendency to group cases without ophthalmoplegia into the Wernicke classification must eventually lead to hopeless confusion.

In a personal communication, Alexander writes that changes in the peripheral nerves are present in almost all cases and that these changes consist of advanced Marchi and Weigert degeneration characteristic of peripheral neuropathy. The changes in the spinal cord, except for axonal changes incidental to peripheral neuropathy, were rather rare and he suggested that they were more apt to be present when the condition was complicated by advanced nicotinic acid deficiency. Definite cortical changes in his cases were rare and consisted of neuronal changes. Here, too, Alexander suggested the possibility that a deficiency of nicotinic acid might be responsible for the complications. Involvement of the optic nerves and optic tracts by direct extension from the hypothalamus were, however, noted. Changes in the cerebellar cortex were again unusual and he, too, suggested that they might be related to a deficiency in vitamin E.

Experimental evidence. In 1934, Prickett described hemorrhagic lesions in the floor of the fourth ventricle in thiamin deficient rats. He did not, however, investigate the underlying vascular disease and apparently did not recognize its similarity to the pathology described by Wernicke.

Pappenheimer and Goettsch had previously described similar lesions in the cerebellum in chicks fed on a vitamin E deficient diet. They did not, however, definitely exclude the possibility of a coexisting thiamin deficiency.

In 1938, the eminent contribution of Alexander, Pijoan and Myerson appeared. Their results may be briefly summarized as follows:

1. Wernicke's hemorrhagic polioencephalitis can be produced with significant regularity in pigeons deficient in thiamin hydrochloride as a complication of beriberi, if large amounts of other vitamins (A, B$_2$, C and D) are fed.

2. If the pigeons are kept on an entirely vitamin free diet, the resulting beriberi will only rarely be complicated by lesions of the Wernicke type.

3. Wernicke's disease cannot be produced in pigeons receiving crystalline thiamin hydrochloride although they may be deprived of all other vitamins, or of any one other vitamin for a period of over 6 months.

4. Their observations suggested that thiamin hydrochloride possesses antiangiodegenerative properties, in addition to antineuritic properties; and that a smaller amount of thiamin hydrochloride is sufficient to act as an antiangiodegenerative agent than is necessary for its antineuritic action.

5. The administration of large doses of vitamins A, B_2, C or D in thiamin deficiency probably raises the thiamin requirements of the tissues and angiodegeneration manifests itself soon after the onset of the neuronal degeneration.

Following the appearance of this important paper, Zimmerman reviewed some of his studies on thiamin deficient pigeons and dogs; these confirmed Alexander's work in every detail. Prickett reached a similar conclusion after reviewing his studies on thiamin deficient rats.

In 1940, Alexander (*d*) amplified his original report. He apparently showed conclusively that the lesions of Wernicke's polioencephalitis occurring in man, and the disease which he produced experimentally in thiamin deficient pigeons, were identical in their topographic distribution and in their morphologic and histologic characteristics. He also reported his pathologic findings on 12 alcoholic and 4 nonalcoholic patients (2 associated with scurvy, 1 with pernicious anemia and 1 with a marked depression and cachexia).

Recapitulation

A review of the literature to date therefore reveals the following essential points:

The syndrome, as originally described by Wernicke, is probably a combination of several nutritional disturbances affecting the nervous system and need not necessarily be complete in any one patient. The clinical picture is not clear cut, but in general consists of clouding of consciousness, varying ophthalmoplegias, and ataxia. Furthermore, the syndrome is frequently preceded or accompanied by a delirious episode and in those individuals who recover, a residual Korsakoff syndrome is seen.

Pathologically, the lesions have been adequately described, but on occasions, additional cortical and cerebellar changes have been noted. There is also reason to believe that the spinal cord and the peripheral nerves do not escape. Moreover, the pathologic changes are not those usually associated with an inflammatory lesion.

Although the syndrome is most usually associated with chronic alcoholism, there is good evidence that alcohol, *per se*, is not responsible for the clinical picture. Of the pathogenic factors which appear singly or in combination, a nutritional deficiency and, more especially, a deficiency in thiamin hydrochloride, seem to be the most obvious common factors. This is further stressed by the fact that a similar pathologic picture has been reproduced in thiamin deficient animals (dogs, pigeons, rats). Finally, it is evident that the clinical picture is the result of multiple deficiencies. Thiamin hydrochloride therapy is successful in reversing the ophthalmoplegia and frequently helps in altering the disturbed state of consciousness. Other nutritional factors, however, which contribute to the production of the varying clinical picture should be noted and optimum therapy in any individual patient must not disregard these other factors.

II. NICOTINIC ACID DEFICIENCY ENCEPHALOPATHY

References to mental changes occupy a prominent place in early descriptions of pellagra. Casal, who is credited with the first description of this disease, noted the lachrymose mood and Thiery, in 1755, spoke of the "maniacal melancholia" of patients afflicted with the *mal de la rosa*. Thiery thought that the mental disturbances of pellagra were "produced by metastasis to the brain of the acrid and malign humor which produced this malady."

Clinical Picture and Etiology

The mental disturbances associated with deficiencies of nicotinic acid are of many types. Any case of pellagra, in temperate or inebriate persons, reveals neuropsychiatric disturbances, varying from simple memory gaps and mood changes to stupor or coma of a fatal nature. Since nicotinic acid is an essential factor in the completion of the enzyme system necessary for carbohydrate metabolism, it is probable that the neuropsychiatric changes are directly related to metabolic disturbances in the brain.

It is difficult at this time to separate sharply, on a clinical basis, those specific encephalopathies which are associated with vitamin deficiency from other types which occur in the alcohol addict. However, certain types of neuropsychiatric disturbance have recently been described which respond specifically to nicotinic acid.

Aside from the "neurasthenic" syndromes which occur in the pellagrin, and which have been shown to respond specifically to nicotinic acid (Spies, Aring, *et al.*), more obvious manifestations of cerebral dysfunction occur. Various organic psychoses occur as part of the well-recognized clinical picture of pellagra in chronic alcoholism and other conditions associated with disturbances of nutrition. These are discussed elsewhere in this work.

There is, however, an important group of encephalopathies which only recently has been shown to be associated with nicotinic acid deficiency.

In 1933, before modern specific therapy was available, Bender and Schilder, on clinical grounds, classified a large number of major alcoholic encephalopathies into five groups, as follows:

1. In this group changing rigidities were in the foreground. Sucking and grasping reflexes were present, and there were clouding of consciousness, sleep disturbances and asynergia. Pellagrous changes in the skin were frequent.

2. In this group, cerebellar symptomatology was the dominant feature.

3. This group was characterized by an acute catatonic picture with rigidities and grasping and groping reflexes.

4. The patients in this group showed delirium as a more prominent feature, while neurologic changes were less marked.

5. In these patients polyneuritic signs were associated with the encephalopathic features.

Jolliffe, in a discussion of Stevenson's paper, suggested modification of this classification on the basis of response to treatment with vitamins. Groups *1* and *5* were responsive to therapy with nicotinic acid, while groups *2, 3* and *4* failed to respond to such therapy.

Cleckley, Sydenstricker and Geeslin reported a series of 19 patients in stupor who responded dramatically to nicotinic acid therapy. Two of these were inebriates, while most were elderly individuals with advanced arteriosclerosis. It is noteworthy that the usual criteria for the diagnosis of pellagra were largely absent. Four patients had glossitis, while 2 had vaginitis. None showed dermatitis or diarrhea. The authors pointed out that hebetude, grading into profound stupor, may be the only sign of severe acute pellagra. They suggested, therefore, that therapeutic trial with nicotinic acid is justifiable as the only method at present available for the accurate diagnosis of such cases.

Jolliffe, Bowman, *et al.* have recently reported 150 cases of an encephalopathic syndrome in chronic alcoholics, heretofore almost invariably fatal, which they believe to be caused by nicotinic acid deficiency. It may occur as the only manifestation of vitamin deficiency or it may occur in association with typical pellagra, peripheral neuropathy or with the ophthalmoplegia characteristic of Wernicke's disease.

The clinical picture of this syndrome is more or less well-defined and consists of clouding of consciousness, cog-wheel rigidities of the extremities and uncontrollable sucking and grasping reflexes.* To be excluded are the encephalopathic manifestations of groping, grasping and sucking which may occur during the course of delirium tremens, infectious diseases with delirium, expanding intracranial lesions, advanced cerebral arteriosclerosis and other diseases.

Patients manifesting this syndrome treated by hydration or hydration plus thiamin hydrochloride, with the house diet, almost invariably died (95 per cent). In a group of patients who received a vitamin-rich diet, hydration and vitamin B complex, the mortality fell to 52 per cent. When a group of these patients was treated with nicotinic acid, a vitamin-poor diet and fluids, the mortality was reduced to 14 per cent.

Since not all of the patients showing this syndrome presented the usual skin and mouth lesions associated with pellagra, it was suggested that this encephalopathic syndrome represented an acute *complete nicotinic acid deficiency* which develops so rapidly that the structural changes in the skin and mouth, characteristic of pellagra, do not always have time to develop.

Since the nutritional deficiency accompanying the development of this type of alcoholic encephalopathy is generally multiple, treatment should consist not only of the administration of nicotinic acid in large amounts (300 to 1,000 mg. per day), but should include the rest of the B complex as well. The presence of diarrhea, or of concomitant delirium tremens, requires especially energetic and prompt therapy by a parenteral route, as well as by mouth.

Pathology

Since nicotinic acid deficiency encephalopathy is probably the largest clinically defined group of the encephalopathies, which is often immediately fatal in outcome, it might be assumed to be most suitable for histopathologic study. Due to the short period of time which has

*Some of the cases described by Spies, Aring, *et al.*, by Cleckley and his associates and by Sydenstricker and Cleckley may have belonged to this group.

elapsed since its description, however, and for other reasons to be noted below, it can not yet be considered a pathologic entity. These remarks on the pathology of alcoholic encephalopathy associated with nicotinic acid deficiency apply to the whole group of fatal encephalopathies, although further research may clarify this matter. Nicotinic acid deficiency encephalopathy can be considered only a more or less discrete but pathologically undefined subgroup of the fatal encephalopathies of the chronic alcoholic.

The nervous system is capable of reacting only in a limited way to various noxious agents and metabolic disturbances and for this reason a variety of etiologic factors may produce identical histopathologic pictures. Moreover, it is likely that no inebriate dies of a single pure metabolic deficiency, as vitamin deficiencies are generally multiple. Also, we must add to these factors the numerous complications which affect the chronic alcoholic. Pneumonia, hepatic disease, head trauma and syphilis all may leave their mark. Finally, there is the effect of alcohol itself, a powerful drug, yet one which is seldom directly responsible for the death of the inebriate. Death from alcoholic encephalopathy occurs as a rule after all the alcohol has been oxidized or excreted. It is still impossible to separate pathologically those changes which may be the result of long continued alcohol ingestion itself from those caused by vitamin deficiency or other generalized disease. Descriptions of post-mortem pathology of the alcoholic encephalopathies must therefore be interpreted as the end result of multiple, poorly defined influences, varying in importance from case to case.

Following Wernicke's classic description, Meyer (a) described the condition of "central neuritis," which was found in a variety of pathologic states, including alcoholism.

In 1913, Singer and Pollock described similar changes in pellagrins. Gamper's contribution to the problem has already been discussed.

Creutzfeld, in a post-mortem study of the brains of 9 chronic alcoholics (Korsakoff's psychosis, polyneuropathy, delirium tremens, Wernicke's disease, and simple alcoholic delirium), noted a proliferation of vessels in the tectum and in the subependymal tissue about the aqueduct of Sylvius and the third ventricle. In all, it was possible to demonstrate changes in the cells of the central nervous system particularly marked in the frontal lobes.

Pearson studied the brains in 1,000 consecutive autopsies of patients dying of all causes and found 31 cases of "central neuritis." This condition was characterized by disease of the large and medium sized pyramidal cells of the cerebral cortex, consisting of swelling of the cell body, displacement of the nucleus and dissolution of the Nissl substance. Of the 31 cases, 4 occurred in chronic alcoholics and 9 in pellagrins. The author emphasized that only in cases of pellagra were the cerebral changes constant, while they might or might not be found in alcoholism and other conditions. He suggested that some subtle disturbance of metabolism was at fault.

Okhuma, in 1930, reported necropsy studies on 4 chronic alcoholics, and noted signs of a diffuse, chronic, progressive parenchymatous degeneration in many sections of the central nervous system with capillary hemorrhages and glial proliferation. Vascular lesions were very marked in the mammillary bodies. He emphasized, however, that it was impossible to establish a clear relation between the clinical signs and the anatomic picture.

Carmichael and Stern, in 1931, presented the findings on 5 patients with Korsakoff's psychosis. All were chronic alcoholics, who died in delirium or stupor, but the authors pointed out that the syndrome is not peculiar to inebriates. All had evidence of peripheral neuropathy. The constant findings in the cerebral cortex were deposition of extensive amounts of lipochrome in all the nerve cells, in the neuroglial cells and around the blood vessels in the prefrontal and motor cortex. There were acute chromatolytic changes in the larger nerve cells in those areas, particularly the Betz cells. They emphasized the similarity of the histopathologic appearances of these cases to those of pellagra and suggested that a common factor of deficiency may be present.

Necropsy studies of 7 cases of alcoholic encephalopathy were reported by Bender and Schilder. They observed that the pathology was most pronounced in those portions of the nervous system closest to spinal fluid spaces and was accentuated at points where the spinal fluid flow is relatively slow. Gliosis was observed in the first cortical layer, and "cytoplastic gliosis" in the second and third layers. A marked ependymal reaction was noted. Capillary budding and hemorrhages were regarded as characteristic. Vascular changes were found to some extent on all surfaces of the brain and cord. Severe lesions were also found in the floor of the fourth ventricle, including the nuclei of the 8th to 12th cranial nerves, and about the oculomotor nuclei. They indicated that there was considerable correlation between clinical and pathologic pictures.

Warner studied 7 chronic alcoholics, all of whom may be considered to have presented a picture of encephalopathy. One had Wernicke's syndrome, 2 had Korsakoff's psychosis and the remaining 4 were described as alcoholism with delirium. No correlation was found between the severity of the classical symptoms and the degree of brain damage. He concluded that the histopathologic changes in chronic alcoholism showed a great variation both in variety and distribution. His findings indicated that the clinical and histopathologic findings do not necessarily correspond.

Zimmerman, Cohen and Gildea found marked changes in the nerve cells of the cortex of 2 chronic alcoholics who died of pellagra.

Bumke and Kant noted that there were reports of many histologic changes in chronic alcoholism, but none was specific. The changes in Korsakoff's syndrome correspond to those of chronic alcoholism in general. They observed that reports concerning rarefaction in the cells of the cerebral cortex were contradictory.

Alexander (b) has discussed the causes of death in acute alcoholic intoxication and chronic alcoholism. In the former, the patient dies of acute poisoning due to the alcohol itself. The drug causes rapid dilatation of the vascular beds, including that of the brain, and in excess, leads to stasis, hemorrhages and serous transudation. The pathologic changes are hyperemia, sometimes associated with edema and flattening of the convolutions. After a time, perivascular histiocytic infiltration may occur. None of these changes is specific for alcohol. Only chemical analysis can confirm its presence. Causes of death in chronic alcoholism can be divided into three groups:

1. Trauma.
2. Intercurrent infections.
3. Death in the course of one of the chronic diseases of the central nervous system related to inebriety.

He asserts that the damage which occurs is due to avitaminosis rather than to the primary toxic injury of alcohol itself. Alexander implicates deficiency of the members of the vitamin B complex primarily.

In the light of recent clinical studies of encephalopathy, which have tended to establish the nutritional origin of a large group of cases, Stevenson, Allen and McGowan have attempted to correlate symptomatology and post-mortem pathology. Their report deals particularly with those syndromes which have been clinically related to vitamin deficiencies, especially that classed as nicotinic acid deficiency encephalopathy by Jolliffe (b) and Jolliffe, Bowman, et al.

Forty-four chronic alcoholics of various types were studied. Of these,

22 were classified, clinically, as having alcoholic encephalopathy. Eight patients in this group were considered as having nicotinic acid deficiency encephalopathy. In 3, the diagnosis was alcoholic psychosis with somatic disease; in 6, alcoholic psychosis with delirium; in 2, Korsakoff's psychosis; in 8, acute and chronic alcoholism; in 2, the diagnosis was unclassified psychosis due to alcohol. In 1, the condition was originally diagnosed as acute encephalitis, but was subsequently discovered to be an alcoholic encephalopathy.

Some alteration of consciousness, apathy, dullness, confusion or semicoma was present in all cases. Sixteen patients were described as confused, and 15 were disoriented. Fifteen had hallucinations, and 10 had tremors. Only 2 had delirium and only 2 presented catatonic features. Excitement or agitation was uncommon.

Fourteen patients presented the grasping reflex; 13, the sucking reflex. In 9 patients, there were changing rigidities. In 18 patients, change in the pupillary reflexes, inequality of the pupils or paralysis of ocular muscles occurred. Nystagmus was noted in 8. In 13, there were signs of peripheral neuropathy. Obviously many of these patients must have belonged to the Wernicke group.

The most consistent pathologic finding outside the central nervous system was a fatty liver, which was present in almost every case.

Fibrous thickening of the arachnoid was noted in 20 cases and edema was present in 18. Petechial hemorrhages occurred in 16 cases, but were generally insignificant in number and size. Increase of lipochrome in the nerve cells was present in only 2 cases.

The authors were unable to confirm previous observations of other investigators with regard to the frequency and severity of lesions in the optic nerves, medulla and cerebellum, or in the blood vessels, or with regard to the marginal location of lesions. They concluded, therefore, that there was little correlation between the clinical picture and the anatomic distribution of lesions, except in cases of Wernicke's syndrome.

Since the pathologic alterations demonstrated were so slight, as compared with the severe and fatal illness of the patients, they concluded that the changes were not demonstrable by present histopathologic methods and were probably due to vitamin deficiency rather than to alcohol itself.

In summary, then, it may be said that the post-mortem pathology of alcoholic encephalopathy is, except in the case of Wernicke's syndrome, an inadequate reflection of the actual disturbance of the central nervous system which is responsible for the symptoms. Even in Wernicke's syndrome this is true to some extent. This suggests, rather, what Peters has called a "biochemical lesion," a disturbance of function of cells resulting from a disorder in their chemical processes, which need not be reflected under the microscope. A familiar analogy is the coma of diabetic acidosis, resulting from disordered metabolism, which is capable of causing death without producing significant visible changes in cell structure. An analogous state of affairs is almost certainly present in acute encephalopathies due to nicotinic acid or thiamin deficiency. They, too, are frequently equally reversible by correction of the biochemical defect.

Wortis (b) has pointed out that the same principles are, to some extent, applicable to cases of delirium tremens, in which histopathologic studies have also been inconsistent and have thrown little light on the distinctive symptomatology.

Finally, it is evident that if pathology is to contribute appreciably to the problem of alcoholic encephalopathy, a closer correlation with the clinic is necessary.

Discussion

As noted above, the brain is dependent for its normal functioning on a carbohydrate substrate, an adequate supply of oxygen and various enzyme and coenzyme systems. Among the more important of these latter are thiamin, nicotinic acid and riboflavin. Since all of these substances are of great importance in the catabolism of carbohydrate, it is conceivable that a deficiency in any of them may interfere with proper brain functioning by interfering with the proper utilization of dextrose, the essential foodstuff of the brain. It is therefore pertinent that we have never seen a case of acute peripheral neuropathy that did not simultaneously show some evidence of cortical dysfunction. The relationship of these changes to thiamin, or other nutritive factors, is indicated and this problem is now under investigation.

The more obvious manifestations of alcoholic pellagra are the various organic psychoses which complete the diagnostic triad of diarrhea, dermatosis and dementia. The most common is perhaps that in which loss of memory, disorientation, confusion and confabulation are present. There are also types in which excitement, depression, mania and delirium may occur. In our experience, a paranoid condition is common in alcoholic pellagrins, as in many other organic psychiatric pictures. Spies, Aring, et al. report that all their psychotic patients recovered, but the psychosis in most of their cases was only of 1 to 2 weeks' duration. Wortis and Jolliffe have confirmed these findings at Bellevue Hospital. They have, however, emphasized the fact that careful psychiatric examination reveals that these patients are frequently left with residual organic memory defects. In the psychoses of longer duration associated with chronic alcoholism and pellagra, the response to nicotinic acid is not spectacular and specific therapy may not help at all. This does not mean that a lack of nicotinic acid was not important in the genesis of the mental picture. It does, however, accentuate the fact that these metabolic disturbances may finally proceed to structural changes. When this stage is reached, the process may become irreversible. It must similarly be stressed that many of the acute excitements and deliriums associated with pellagra frequently clear up without nicotinic acid therapy. Finally, pellagrins usually lack other factors contained in the well-balanced diet, which are probably necessary for normal brain metabolism. It is therefore suggested that adequate amounts of other vitamins be given to pellagrins with encephalopathic manifestations in order to insure maximal therapeutic results.

Post-mortem studies, as already pointed out, have done relatively little to clarify the problem, except, perhaps, in the case of the Wernicke syndrome. As noted above, similar pathologic findings are often associated with markedly dissimilar clinical pictures. Furthermore, it is fairly obvious that many identical clinical pictures have been described under varying terms owing to the present confusion in terminology. Finally, it seems necessary to advance to newer pathologic concepts, particularly chemical and electrophysiologic, if we are to advance our knowledge of the essential nature of these diseases.

A brief statement regarding personality factors in the evolution of the final clinical picture is appropriate here. Jellinek and Jolliffe have pointed out that chronic alcoholics do not form a homogeneous group, but are heterogeneous with regard to etiology, reaction and course of disease. Wortis (b), in commenting on personality factors in the alcoholic psychoses, corroborates this statement and points out that the difficulties in evaluating such personality factors are even greater. With regard to the particular type of alcoholic psychosis which an individual develops, there are certain groups (Wernicke's syndrome, nicotinic acid deficiency encephalopathy) in which the physiologic variant is dominant, and others (alcoholic hallucinosis) in which our present knowledge indicates that psychologic variants are of paramount importance in evaluating the final clinical picture. Nonetheless, it is certain that within every psychosis individual variations are conditioned by personality factors. Personal characteristics, dominant interests, past experience, age, sex and intellectual experience, all unmistakably mold and individualize the personal reaction. It is plain that the evidence at hand makes it likely that a pluralistic psychosomatic approach to this problem will prove most fertile.

Regarding the manifestations of *encephalopathia alcoholica*, it is recommended that each patient should be classified according to the clinical signs or syndromes presented and the response of these phenomena to specific therapeutic agents should be recorded. Personality factors should be noted. Finally, some attempt should be made to correlate the clinical features with the specific metabolic disturbances during life as well as with the post-mortem findings. It seems certain that studies of this type will lead to a much better understanding of the personality, nutritional, pathologic and metabolic disorders which frequently complicate the long continued abuse of alcohol and thereby interfere with the functional economy of the nervous system.

CHAPTER V

Marchiafava's Disease*

Giorgio Lolli

IN 1897 two Italian pathologists, Marchiafava and Bignami, described (not published until 1903) some definite lesions of the central nervous system accompanied by and probably related to a complex of psychotic symptoms.† Subsequently this condition became known as Marchiafava's disease. It has been recorded in about 50 patients, all but one of whom were Italians and, with one possible exception, suffered from chronic alcoholism. The descriptive literature on Marchiafava's disease, except for two American reports (King and Meehan; Bohrod), has been contributed by Italian observers. Nevertheless, German as well as English and American students of alcoholism have taken cognizance of this disease. The larger handbooks (e.g., Bumke and Foerster) have incorporated it in their classifications of alcoholic encephalopathies and occasionally surmises relative to its etiology have been made outside of the Italian literature (e.g., Moore).

In spite of its apparent localization to Italy and its apparent rarity, Marchiafava's disease merits at least a brief review because of the definiteness of the pathologic picture which it presents. This is a distinction which this disease shares with only a few other alcoholic diseases.

The description which follows is based chiefly on the papers of Marchiafava and his pupils (Marchiafava and Bignami; Marchiafava; Bignami; Marchiafava, Bignami and Nazari; Bignami and Nazari). The few observations (Rossi; Guccione; Fittipaldi; de Albertis; Mariconda) recorded subsequently do not add any important detail to the original findings. Almost all the observations were recorded at the Pathological Institute of Rome and the necropsies were performed on patients admitted to the Santo Spirito Hospital, which is a large general hospital not limited to the care of insane patients or chronic alcoholics.

The aim of the present review is only to call attention to some of the

---

*The combined bibliography of Chapters III, IV, V and VI appears at the end of Chapter VI, pp. 310–324.

†One of the first three cases observed by Marchiafava and Bignami was described by Carducci in a doctor's thesis (1898).

lesions which probably are much more frequent than is supposed and which, because of their localization, may furnish an explanation for some of the symptoms and signs of chronic alcoholic encephalopathies.

The Clinical Picture

The age range found in this disease was from 35 to over 80 years. Syphilis was present in a few cases, but certainly nonexistent in the majority of the subjects who were all heavy drinkers, some since childhood. Many were sons of chronic alcoholics. The disease lasts from 3 to 6 years; perhaps even for a longer period, since, because of the slow evolution of the symptomatology, the first manifestations may escape notice.

While the psychiatric pictures of Wernicke's syndrome and nicotinic acid deficiency encephalopathy are colorless and the neurologic symptoms are dominant, in the encephalopathy designated as Marchiafava's disease, the psychologic manifestations are outstandingly marked. The symptomatology does not suggest a definite psychiatric syndrome but contains elements of various alcoholic mental disorders, particularly of chronic alcoholic deterioration, with the general affect tone of delirium tremens. There are also some symptoms similar to those occasionally found in Wernicke's syndrome.

The dominant features of the clinical picture are: a marked and abnormal excitability, peculiar disposition toward wrath and acts of violence, modifications of affection, moral and sexual perversions, progressive mental decadence until mental confusion and finally dementia set in. But almost constant, too, are the physical disturbances, dominant among which are: epileptiform and apoplectiform attacks, transient hemiparesis (preceded by the common phenomenon of ictus), clonic-tonic convulsions followed generally by rise in body temperature, tremors, disturbances of speech, vertigo, frequent fainting, sudden and transient weakness of the lower limbs, and ataxia. Headache is not uncommon, but other disturbances of sensitivity are lacking. Notwithstanding this picture, which appears very rich in its symptomatology, the patients are frequently able to carry on their usual daily life up to the very end, when the final phase of the disease sets in. This phase usually starts with an apoplectiform or an epileptiform ictus from which the patient does not recover. Ictus is followed by denutrition, growing weakness of the lower limbs, sopor and coma.

Necropsy in some cases showed that death was due to some intercurrent sickness as frequently happens in many other diseases of the nervous system. In other cases only the cerebral lesions characteristic of the Marchiafava disease were observed. In the field of the brain lesions the occasional findings of an hemorrhagic pachymeningitis, of an hyperemic and thickened pia mater also have to be considered as accompanying lesions which do not have any connection with the disease which we are describing. Because many cases arrived at the hospital in a critical condition, neither a detailed past history could be recorded nor a careful neurologic examination performed.

Clinical report of a case observed by Bignami and Nazari. A man, aged 70, a streetcleaner, was admitted to the hospital on April 30, and died on May 1, 1913. From the history given by his wife, it seemed that the father and 2 sisters of the patient had died from pulmonary diseases. When he was 24 years old he married. He had 7 children, 5 of whom were still living in good health at that time. At 50 years of age he was infected with gonorrhea. He was always a heavy drinker of wine and liquors and at least once a week he was intoxicated. He was also a heavy smoker. When he was drunk, he became violent. In 1907 he started to feel a general weakness, particularly of the lower limbs, which grew progressively worse and to which was added, in the last year, a tremor of the upper limbs so strong as to compel his wife to feed him like a child. Walking, especially during bad weather, became difficult. Nights were usually restless. Sleep was intermittent. His mental condition became worse and he attempted many times to escape from his home. He was seized by attacks of tremor, frequently 3 or 4 times a day, during which he fell gradually to the ground and asked with self-pity to be assisted to his feet. He was religious, of good character, not talkative and clean. He showed no incontinence. For about 20 years he did not have any sexual intercourse. He asked many times to be taken to an insane asylum. On April 29, 1913 he left his home with the help of a boy while his wife was ill. As soon as the wife discovered this, she called from her window trying to restrain him, but to no avail. He was soon brought home, almost unconscious, and wounded on the face from a fall. From his home he was transferred to the hospital where he remained in a comatose state until death, which occurred on May 1, 1913. Necropsy showed: grayish red degeneration of the anterior or frontal part of the corpus callosum, of the commissura anterior and of the white substance of the cerebral circumvolutions, aortic arteriosclerosis of moderate degree, cardiac hypertrophy, pulmonary emphysema, chronic nephritis, interstitial fibrous orchitis and cyst of the right epididymis.

Pathology

The main pathologic finding which is constant in all cases and which, even if observed alone, gives sufficient evidence for a definite diagnosis, consists of a primary grayish degeneration, localized in the corpus callosum and in the commissura anterior, not affecting the whole of these formations, but involving only their median layers, leaving intact 2 layers of normal white substance, respectively upper and lower (see Fig. 1). Because of this location it is impossible to see

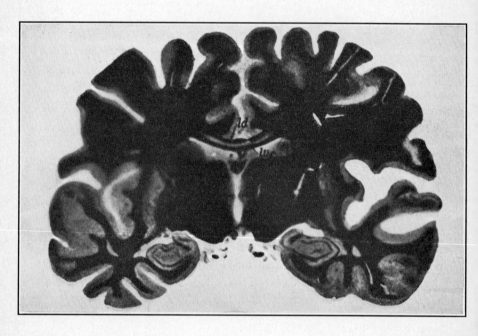

Figure 1. Frontal section through both the cerebral hemispheres at the level of the anterior third of the thalamus. Marked degeneration of the middle layer of the corpus callosum.

the area of degeneration on inspection of the corpus callosum from above; while, when frontal sections are performed, the marked difference of color makes the abnormal condition easily recognizable. On the other hand, when a horizontal section, passing through the corpus callosum, is performed, the lesion may escape notice. In frontal sections of the brain stained by the Weigert-Pal method the median, degenerated layer has a pale appearance which markedly contrasts with the dark blue color of the 2 normal layers, upper and lower, and of the remaining normal parts of the white substance of the brain. Sometimes Weigert-Pal's method shows that the raphe of the corpus callosum is not affected and consequently has a dark blue color while 2 longitudinal areas of degeneration are evident on either side of the raphe itself. The degenerative process usually extends throughout all of the length of the corpus callosum from the genu to the splenium, laterally reaching the foot of the corona radiata. Usually the intensity of the degeneration is less marked in the middle and posterior third of the corpus callosum and there, just as in the raphe, some intact nervous fibers may be found when stained by the Weigert-Pal method. The limits of the degeneration are always very marked on both the upper and lower edges of the median layer and laterally on the borders of the median layer and the white substance of the centrum ovale. Sometimes in the region of the splenium there are many degenerated spots which tend to converge. These are the most important macroscopic lesions of Marchiafava's disease, necessary and sufficient for a correct diagnosis, but frequently accompanied by other findings which will be described later.

From the histologic standpoint, the tissue in the degenerated areas is less compact and more vascularized. There is a hyaline degeneration of the walls of the blood vessels with a narrowing of the lumen. Some vessels appear obliterated; others have a wavy appearance. In the perivascular spaces there is occasionally a slight lymphocytoid infiltration; plasma cells are absent. There are no signs of truly proliferative or inflammatory alterations of the blood vessels. In the zones where the rarefaction of the nervous tissue is very marked, the fibers of the neuroglia are sometimes swollen. Occasionally, but not always, it is possible to find an increased number of neurogliar cells whose nuclei may be swollen.

The degeneration of the nerve fibers is very marked. Their myelin sheaths disappear and this condition explains the gray color of the degenerated areas in the fresh sections and the absence of the dark blue color in those sections which are stained with the Weigert-Pal method. Their axis-cylinders, chiefly in the cases in which the disease is presumably of recent date, often persist. Sometimes they are irregularly swollen. The persistence of the axis-cylinders is more frequently found in the region of the raphe and in the median and posterior third of the corpus callosum.

Lesions quite similar to those observed in the corpus callosum and in the commissura anterior may be found in the middle cerebellar peduncles (see Fig. 2) and in the white substance of the hemispheres (see Fig. 3). Both in the commissura anterior and in the middle cerebellar peduncles degenerated areas have the same location as in the corpus callosum; that is to say, they occupy a median layer which is in contact with one upper and one lower layer of normal white substance. The degenerated areas of the white substance have a peculiar aspect which makes easy their differentiation from the more frequent lesions

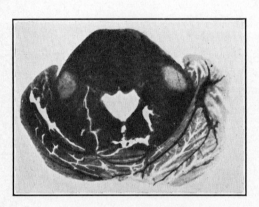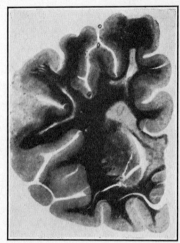

Figure 2 (left). Two symmetrical areas of degeneration in the middle cerebellar peduncles.

Figure 3 (right). Frontal section of one cerebral hemisphere at the level of the genu of corpus callosum. Marked degeneration of the middle layer of the corpus callosum extended as far as the foot of the corona radiata in the centrum ovale. The upper and lower layers are normal. Two areas of subcortical degeneration (subarcuate) are also evident.

of vascular or inflammatory origin. However, these degenerated areas of the white substance are not sufficient for the identification of Marchiafava's disease, the diagnosis of which always requires the presence of a degenerated area in the corpus callosum. The histologic picture is the same as in the corpus callosum. The preservation of many axis-cylinders is especially important in cases where large areas, and consequently main nervous pathways, are affected. These degenerations of the white substance may be easily distinguished by their characteristics from the spots of simple softening of the brain or of hemorrhagic softening of vascular origin. They may be distinguished very easily, too, from the different kinds of nonsuppurative encephalitis. These degenerations, which may be called subcortical, have not the mark of systemic character which is peculiar to the lesions observed in the corpus callosum. However, their position is quite constant. Sometimes their extension is so great as to allow the pathologist to speak of a true "alcoholic phthisis of the brain." They usually leave unaffected the short fibers of association (arcuate fibers) and for this reason they may also be called subarcuate areas. They are always symmetrical and are never followed by secondary degeneration in the internal capsule and in the pes of the crura cerebri. The most frequent location is in the white substance of the second and third frontal gyri, especially in the foot of these gyri, and in the median third of the frontal and parietal ascendant gyri. The degenerated areas never reach the foot of the corona radiata and the fibers of the internal capsule. Thus, only the white substance of the centrum ovale is affected, while the short association fibers, and all the fibers of the internal capsule, are unaffected. No alteration can be found in the external and extreme capsules. All the connections from the brain to the pons are unaffected. It is quite evident that these degenerated areas, even though they have a fairly constant location, cannot be considered as truly systemic. Through the degenerated areas pass fibers of the most varied origin and significance.

One of the chief characteristics of Marchiafava's disease is that mainly nervous fibers are involved which have an identical functional significance, that is to say, fibers which connect the two cerebral hemispheres. In fact, here a "system" of fibers is affected, as in tabes dorsalis. This pecularity allows us to include Marchiafava's disease among the systemic nervous diseases, even though frequently, besides the degeneration of the middle layer of the corpus callosum, other degenerated areas may be found.

While from the standpoint of clinical symptomatology the disease does not offer signs characteristic enough to permit a correct diagnosis *in vivo*, the pathologic picture is so definite, even on a macroscopic examination, as to justify the diagnosis of chronic alcoholism, even though nothing is known about the past history of the subject. Because of this peculiarity Marchiafava's disease has a unique place among the alcoholic encephalopathies.

In summation of the above description it is possible to say that the general characteristics of the degenerations of the brain, with which we have to deal in Marchiafava's disease, are the following: *1*. Alteration which, at least in the beginning, is localized in the medullary

sheaths of the nerve fibers; notwithstanding the presence of degenerated substance the secondary proliferation of the neuroglia is usually
scanty. *2.* Absence of proliferation of cells pertaining to the connective
tissue. *3.* Absence of proliferation of the blood vessels. *4.* Absence, or
very scanty presence, of lymphocytoid cells. *5.* Presence of granular
cells and of cells loaded with lipoid substance. *6.* Persistence of many
axis-cylinders, which is common to other primary degenerations as, for
instance, alcoholic polyneuropathy (see Chapter III) and lead intoxication; this persistence explains why, also, when very large areas of
subcortical degeneration are present, secondary degenerations in the
systems of the internal capsule and in the pes of the crura cerebri are
lacking. *7.* Symmetry of the lesions in both hemispheres; this noteworthy symmetry is also present when the degeneration is localized in
the subcortical areas and in the middle cerebellar peduncles.

Correlation between Clinical Symptomatology and Pathologic Findings

In this field, little may be said because of the lack of definite knowledge about the physiology and pathology of the corpus callosum. It is
very probable that at least part of the psychiatric symptomatology of
Marchiafava's disease may result from the degeneration of the com-
missural ways. The experimental data on the physiology of the corpus
callosum are still insufficient. The data taken from pathology do not
give sufficient evidence of a clinical syndrome definitely characteristic
of the corpus callosum. Aside from Marchiafava's disease almost all
the other pathologic lesions which affect the corpus callosum, tumors,
hemorrhages, cysts, softenings, affect other sections of the brain, too,
and also in Marchiafava's disease the frequent concomitance of lesions
of the white substance makes it impossible to establish a definite correlation between symptoms and lesions. However, the previous asser-
tion that the psychiatric symptomatology may be referred to the anatomic and functional impairment of the corpus callosum finds
support in the common observation that in all the cases in which the
corpus callosum was found affected by pathologic lesions (tumors,
softenings, etc.) the psychiatric symptomatology was dominant.

It must be stated, also, that the histologic work done by Marchiafava and his pupils is relatively old. The use of more modern histologic
techniques may reveal, in this disease, lesions at present wholly
unknown.

It is also not easy to give a definite interpretation, on the basis of the
pathologic findings, to the disorders of motility. Disorders of this kind

were observed in many lesions of the corpus callosum, but they may be caused also by the subcortical degenerations which, as we have seen, are found frequently together with the degeneration of the corpus callosum. The apoplectiform and epileptiform ictus are symptoms which occur frequently in many intoxications and infections. The ataxia may be explained with the frequent finding of a degenerated area in the middle cerebellar peduncle. (It is worth while to remember that a so-called "callosal" ataxia is sometimes mentioned.)

Etiology

Some diseases, considered at first as limited to one nationality, have been found later to be diffused among peoples of different origins, e.g., Buerger's disease. Thus the fact that until 1942 all cases were described in Italy with but one exception recorded in the United States and this, too, on a man of Italian abstraction (King and Meehan) cannot be regarded as evidence that Marchiafava's disease is specifically Italian. The racial limitation must be regarded as hypothetic and provisional. Nevertheless, the apparent limitation is a matter which must be considered in the etiology, since nutritional and perhaps even social elements may be involved which are, or were at least, predominant in Italy.

The lesions of Marchiafava's disease have been reproduced experimentally in dogs in more recent years. Testa observed, in dogs intoxicated with large doses of alcohol over a long period, an area of degeneration in the corpus callosum which is similar to the lesions observed in men. Similar findings were observed by Stanquitz-Cambilargiu.

The fact that Marchiafava's disease was observed only in Italy, and that in Italy almost all the cases were observed in Rome, suggested to the first observers that this peculiarity was due only to technical reasons, i.e., to the way of performing the sections of the brain. This explanation seems insufficient. Frontal sections of the brain are performed by the majority of pathologists and the lesions, when present, are so marked as to be unlikely to escape careful examination. The kinds of alcoholic beverages used in Italy are the same as those of many other countries. Only one hypothesis may be set forth concerning a peculiar custom, very frequent in the poorer classes of central and southern Italy, especially at the time of Marchiafava's first observations, i.e., the custom of giving small amounts of wine to very young children. It may be that alcohol given during the growth period may act with a peculiar selectivity on the median layer of fibers of the corpus callosum which, according to some histologic research [Mingazzini (a, b)], seems to become myelinated later than the upper and lower layers. This may be the explanation but it is now only an hypothesis not yet substantiated by evidence. It seems reasonable to assume that some factors other than alcohol may intervene, but nothing is known about them.

Histologically a striking resemblance exists between Marchiafava's disease and the picture of peripheral polyneuropathy, and it is possible that the degenerative changes of the corpus callosum may be due to a vitamin deficiency secondary to the chronic alcoholic intoxication rather than to a direct action of the poison on the nerve fibers. This has also been suggested by Moore. Furthermore, it is important to point out the fact that the disease has been seen, up to now, only in poor persons of the lowest social classes, who presumably had, since their childhood, an insufficient and unbalanced daily diet. In the clinical histories recorded by Italian authors there is no clear reference to a concomitant involvement of the peripheral nerves, and in the necropsies performed by them the peripheral nerves were not examined.

Since the first publication of this review, Bohrod has reported the second American case of Marchiafava's disease. The patient, a 67-year-old man with a long history of inebriety, was admitted to a Florida hospital in a comatose state which had persisted for a week previously. His wife had first noted marked personality changes about 3 weeks before that. It is noteworthy that this patient was American born of Swiss parentage and without known Italian ancestry. He died within 48 hours after his hospitalization. Due to the marked personality changes and the absence of localizing signs, a clinical diagnosis of probable brain tumor, possibly of the frontal lobe, was made. The necropsy, described by Bohrod in detail, showed the characteristic features of Marchiafava's disease. The author suggested that, in common with other alcoholic encephalopathies, this condition may be related etiologically to deficiency of some member of the vitamin B complex.

CHAPTER VI

Cirrhosis of the Liver

NORMAN JOLLIFFE *and* E. M. JELLINEK

THE problem of the relationship of alcohol and cirrhosis of the liver has occupied a paramount place in research in alcoholism. Nevertheless it is still the most misunderstood issue in alcohol literature. The following review shall be limited to the clinical, statistical and experimental aspects of this question and to an exposition of the prevailing etiologic theories. It does not seem indicated to go into pathologic description except for establishing criteria. The question of liver functions in chronic alcoholism is also not touched upon here, since this subject will be discussed in one of the chapters on physiology in a later volume of this work in much greater detail than would be possible in the present one.

Diseases of the liver, resembling the condition which is now generally designated as cirrhosis, have been described perhaps as early as the second century B.C. and there may have been also in early Greek medical literature some surmises on the effects of hard drinking on this organ. Liver damage and inebriety were associated in the sixteenth century by Fernel and Vesalius. The first definite statement on the prevailing occurrence in inebriates of a condition which undoubtedly was cirrhosis was made near the end of the eighteenth century by Matthew Baillie. Since this statement made a deep impression on medical science and has governed etiologic theories for many decades, it is interesting to note exactly what he said:

This disease is hardly ever met with in a very young person, but frequently takes place in persons of middle or advanced age: it is likewise more common in men than women. This would seem to depend upon the habit of drinking being more common in the one sex than in the other; for this disease is most frequently found in hard drinkers, although we cannot see any necessary connection between that mode of life and this particular disease in the liver. It happens, however, very commonly, that we can see little connection between cause and effect in changes which are going on in every other part of the body.

This cautious statement was misinterpreted and misquoted as meaning that this condition was exclusively of alcoholic origin. After 1826, when Laënnec described the atrophic nodular liver to which he gave the name cirrhosis, this latter type, named after him, was identified specifically as the alcoholic form of cirrhosis. Peculiarly enough this identification persisted even after this type of cirrhosis was found also in abstinent and temperate persons. From the many classificatory systems of liver cirrhosis not one type has emerged which can be regarded specifically as of alcoholic origin. In 1911 Mallory (a) suggested that in alcoholic liver cirrhosis there occurs a peculiar form of necrosis of the liver cells. As the characteristic of this disease he regarded the presence of a hyaline acidophilic reticulum in the regenerating cells. This claim of specificity has been variously refuted (e.g., Rössle). Likewise, the contention of Hall and Morgan relative to the importance of fat as a differential etiologic criterion cannot be accepted, although it must be admitted that fatty cirrhosis is much more frequent in chronic alcoholism than in any other condition. The absence of specific pathology, however, does not weaken the possibility of a contingency between alcohol and cirrhosis of the liver. The evidence for this contingency is presented in the following sections.

The Clinical Evidence

The clinical evidence which is based largely on autopsy data and to some extent on clinical diagnoses has been used both in confirmation as well as in refutation of an association between inebriety and cirrhosis of the liver. All too frequently the use of these data was not particularly cogent for either aspect of the controversy.

The occurrence of cirrhosis of the liver in children, and reports of its occurrence among children and among natives of countries in which the consumption of alcohol is supposedly absent or at least negligible, has been put forward as evidence against the association.

Irrespective of other factors invalidating these arguments, and assuming that the reports may be accepted without qualification, the idea itself constitutes a confusion of the issue. The question is not whether inebriety is the exclusive etiology of liver cirrhosis but whether or not this disease occurs so frequently in chronic alcoholics that in these particular cases alcoholic etiology must be postulated. To students of the question of alcoholic liver cirrhosis this must seem practically a truism, but the reiteration of the statement is necessary in view of the fact that the data relative to cirrhosis in children and in abstinent nations are still used as indicative of a nonassociation between inebriety and cirrhosis of the liver.

Aside from the logical issue the data themselves do not seem particularly appropriate for refutation of the association with inebriety. It is surprising how frequently excessive use of alcohol appears in the history of children suffering from cirrhosis of the liver. In 1887 Mogh (cit. Rössle) described 35 instances of cirrhosis in children, 9 of whom were heavy drinkers. Other cases of liver cirrhosis in connection with drinking in children were described by Vix; Kaufmann; Rössle; and, more recently, by Caussade, Karlin and Roussel. These latter investigators estimated that in France 16 per cent of the children with cirrhosis were excessive users of fruit wines.

Relative to the occurrence of cirrhosis among abstaining Mohammedans it must be considered that (a) the abstention from alcohol is only an assumption, although it must be admitted that the use of alcoholic beverages among Mohammedans is perhaps negligible; and that (b), what is more important, oriental liver cirrhosis is highly associated with parasitic and bacterial diseases and should therefore not be compared with the type of cirrhosis around which the etiologic argument actually centers. Tirumurti and Radhakrishna Rao report from one medical college in India 535 autopsies in which 50 cases of cirrhosis of the liver were found, that is, an incidence of 9.3 per cent. This is by far greater than in any European population and the high frequency itself would indicate some relation to parasitosis in a country where this condition is of great frequency. The fact that 56 per cent of the cirrhoses found by these investigators are described as portal cirrhosis is no indication against this assumption since even in coccidiosis portal obstruction may occur. Yenikomshian, who described the occurrence of cirrhosis of the liver in the Lebanon and Syria, said that alcohol is not used by these people but mentions that dysentery and infestation with intestinal parasites are frequent. It is to be noted that the cirrhosis in these patients was nearly always of the hypertrophic type and that the liver remained large to the end.

This aspect of the controversy scarcely merits more discussion and the more common clinical evidence will now be considered. In view of the fact that data relative to the occurrence of cirrhosis of the liver in chronic alcoholics are not lacking, and that these estimates can be compared with the occurrence in the general population, it is surprising that these statistics are not frequently used in discussing the problem, but that preference is shown for a much inferior type of statistics. By this we mean statements relative to the proportion of "alcoholic cirrhosis" in a certain number of cirrhoses found in autopsies. As Rössle has remarked, much counting but little statistical work has been done. In Table 1 are presented the proportions reported by various investigators.

TABLE 1

Per cent Incidence of Alcoholics among Subjects Found with Cirrhosis of the Liver at Autopsy

Investigators	Year	No. of Cases of Cirrhosis	Percentage of Alcoholics in Those with Cirrhosis
Brule and Barbat	1931	53	86.0
Hoppe	1912	78	79.4
Hall and Morgan	1939	68	75.0
Naunyn	1904	135	61.5
Weber	1884	69	60.9
Simmonds (cit. Rössle)	1904	—	60.0
Price (cit. Rössle)		142	56.3
Chvostek (cit. Rössle)	1922	—	50.0
Boles and Crew*	1940	88	45.5
Lubarsch	1907	50	38.0
Boles and Clark*	1936	150	30.0
Coronini	1934	80	27.5

*Only the data on degenerative cirrhosis are considered here.

It is seen that the estimates of "alcoholic" cirrhosis occurring among all cirrhoses in autopsies vary from 86.0 per cent down to 27.5 per cent. Accordingly, statements have been made that cirrhosis is "more frequent" among inebriates than among temperate persons, that it is "equally frequent," and that it is "less frequent" in alcoholics than in nonalcoholics. Correspondingly, conclusions have been drawn relative to high and middling association or absence of association between inebriety and cirrhosis of the liver. To speak of these figures in terms of frequency of cirrhosis among inebriates is entirely illegitimate. These figures do not reflect such frequency. The frequency of this disease among inebriates can be determined only by stating the number of chronic alcoholics observed and the number of cirrhotic livers found among them. The statistics of Table 1 are not only unsuitable for expressing frequency in these terms but they are entirely meaningless relative to the question of association or nonassociation since their variation is dependent upon an artifact. The proportion of "alcoholic cirrhosis" to nonalcoholic cirrhosis depends largely on the proportion of inebriates in the admissions and consequently in the autopsies. Let us assume that the true incidence of liver cirrhosis in chronic alcoholics is 5 per cent and in nonalcoholics 1 per cent. If, then, in a certain autopsy experience 300 nonalcoholics and 100 alcoholics are represented, 5 cases of cirrhosis will be found in the alcoholics and 3 in the nonalcoholics; the proportion of alcoholic cirrhosis in the sample will thus be 62.5 per cent. If, however, there are 500 nonalcoholics and 100 alcoholics the cirrhosis will be distributed 5 and 5, and the alcoholic cirrhosis will be 50 per cent. If the proportion were 1,000 nonalcoholics and 100 alcoholics the distribution would be 10 for the nonalcoholics and 5 for the alcoholics; the alcoholics would then represent only 33 per cent of the sample. Whether the incidence of alcoholic cirrhosis in the total cirrhosis is small or large depends entirely on whether or not the hospital in question has a small or large proportion of alcoholic patients in its admissions. If one were to take, instead of a sample, the whole universe then by the sheer numerical superiority of nonalcoholics the incidence of "alcoholic liver cirrhosis" among all liver cirrhosis in the universe would be small. This would have no bearing whatever on the question of association between inebriety and liver cirrhosis. We must therefore dismiss the discussion of this type of statistics as entirely irrelevant.

The straightforward statistical approach to the question would be to divide the total autopsy experience into chronic alcoholics and non-alcoholics and enumerate the presence and absence of cirrhosis in both of these groups. Whether the chronic alcoholic group contributes to liver cirrhosis significantly more than its share or not can be determined from such enumeration. Not only do investigators omit to state their findings in this form but only in the rarest instances is it possible to reconstruct a dichotomy on the basis of the data published. It must be admitted that in the case of a large autopsy experience, going into the thousands, it may be difficult and in many instances even impossible to obtain evidence on the negativity or positivity of inebriety for the entire sample, while it is easier to obtain these data for the much smaller sample of liver cirrhosis. While the most useful dichotomous classifications are lacking, a number of investigators have stated their total autopsy experience with chronic alcoholics and have given the incidence of liver cirrhosis in such samples. On the other hand data from other investigators give the number or percentage of liver cirrhosis in large autopsy samples of the general population. A comparison of these two types of experience permits an estimate of whether or not the incidence of liver cirrhosis is relatively larger in the population of chronic alcoholics. Table 2 lists the number of autopsies of chronic alcoholics reported by various investigators and the number and percentage of cirrhosis found by them in these samples.

TABLE 2

*Occurrence of Cirrhosis of the Liver in Chronic Alcoholics as Determined by Autopsy**

Investigators	Year	No. of Autopsies of Chronic Alcoholics	Cirrhosis No.	Per cent
Boles and Clark†	1936	228	45	19.8
Kern	1913	—	—	16.0
Dickinson (cit. Rössle)‡		149	22	14.8
Jagié	1906	151	22	14.6
Kayser	1888	155	21	13.5
Wegelin	1935	106	12	11.3
Delore and Devant	1939	140	14	10.0
Barbier and Jacquis	1939	231	17	7.4
Fahr	1911	309	11	3.5
Lafont	1908	242	7	2.8
Formad (cit. Rössle)		250	6	2.4
Binswanger (b)§	1933	84	1	1.2

*The findings do not imply death from liver cirrhosis.
†Only the data on degenerative cirrhosis are considered here.
‡All employees of the brandy trade.
§Psychotic patients.

The variation in this table, too, is not inconsiderable but on the other hand it is not as obtrusive as the variation of the data in Table 1. Probably, to the largest part, the differences in the reports of percentages are due to varying standards in establishing the diagnosis of cirrhosis of the liver. Some investigators would probably include milder degrees of fibrosis which would be excluded by others and, in some instances, the diagnostic criteria might be unjustifiably rigorous. Another factor which may enter into the variation is the nature of the chronic alcoholics included in the samples. Thus, for example, Dickinson's sample with an incidence of 14.8 per cent and Binswanger's sample with 1.2 per cent incidence are both highly selected samples. Dickinson's 149 autopsies were all performed on employees of the brandy trade. These are men perhaps consuming nearly exclusively a high-proof liquor and probably more constantly exposed and thus having a longer time of alcohol consumption than the inebriates of the other samples. Binswanger's sample was constituted entirely of patients with alcoholic psychoses. It is a well-known fact [e.g., A. Meyer (c)] that in the alcoholic psychoses the incidence of cirrhosis of the liver is low, partly, perhaps, because of their prolonged stay in institutions where they are cut off from alcoholic beverages and partly owing to the fact that among patients with alcoholic psychosis there are many who are rather occasional spectacular drinkers than actually steady excessive drinkers. That the incidence of liver cirrhosis in the alcoholic psychoses is low not only after a long stay in the hospital but even on admission is indicated by the clinical diagnoses on 1,739 patients with alcoholic psychosis admitted to the New York state hospitals for the first time between 1910 and 1912. The diagnosis of cirrhosis of the liver was made on only 30 patients, that is, 1.7 per cent of the admissions (Pollock). Binswanger's sample is thus not representative of the incidence of liver cirrhosis in chronic alcoholism in general but rather in that part of the inebriate population which is marked by alcoholic psychosis. The incidence of the alcoholic psychoses among all chronic alcoholics may be estimated at 10 per cent and in some of the samples listed in Table 2 the incidence of alcoholic psychosis may have been actually larger than it is in the alcoholic population, thus lowering the relative incidence of cirrhosis of the liver in the sample.

Under the given circumstances we must assume that too liberal as well as too rigid diagnostic standards cancel their effects in the aggregate of the samples. Relative to the overrepresentation and underrepresentation of various types of chronic alcoholics in these samples equalization cannot be expected, since in some of the clinics from which these samples were obtained the alcoholic psychoses were not represented at all. Excluding Binswanger's sample, there are 1,961 autopsies in chronic alcoholics represented in Table 2, in 177 of which liver cirrhosis was found, that is, 9 per cent of the total. This we may regard as a fairly representative datum for chronic alcoholics excluding the alcoholic psychoses, while for the latter a relative incidence of 1 per cent of cirrhosis of the liver seems to be a fair estimate. Since, as mentioned before, 10 per cent of all chronic alcoholics have an alcoholic psychosis the relative incidence of liver cirrhosis in all chronic alcoholics, including the psychotics, would be 8.2 per cent, or roughly 8 per cent. In the absence of any facility for analyzing the original data of the listed reports in any further detail this 8 per cent incidence must serve as the best estimate of the occurrence of cirrhosis of the liver in chronic alcoholics which can be constructed from available data. That this may be regarded as characterizing the occurrence of cirrhosis of the liver in the chronic alcoholic population rather than death from this disease is evident from closer analysis of the reports, which show that probably not more than 10 per cent of those found with liver cirrhosis at autopsy had died from this cause. Nevertheless, various authors (e.g., Hoppe; Wlassak; Rössle) have pointed out that autopsy samples may be biased samples and that, therefore, the percentage of occurrence derived from these samples may be too high. This has been made as a general statement only and no one has pointed out what the nature of the bias may be. Frequently in the literature on alcoholism the statement is encountered that the incidence of cirrhosis of the liver in chronic alcoholics is probably 5 per cent. It does not appear that this statement is based on any statistical consideration but rather on an impression. It furthermore appears that it is an estimate which can no longer be traced to its original author but has been generally taken over and repeated by numerous writers to whom it appealed as fairly probable. Our estimate of 8 per cent represents a lowering from the apparent relative incidence from the rough figures but the reduction is based on certain numerical considerations. Any further reduction can be arbitrary only.

For comparative purposes the relative incidence of cirrhosis of the liver in a temperate population would be the desideratum. Instead of this, samples must be considered which are drawn from a general rather than from a temperate population. A general population naturally includes inebriates, too. It is most probable that in these samples which are represented by autopsies in general hospitals the incidence of inebriates is by far greater than in the actual general population. Nevertheless, with all its weaknesses, this is the best material available. The autopsy findings in samples from quasi-general populations are given in Table 3. Each of the samples is rather large; the total of autopsies amounts to over 110,000 and the total number of cases of cirrhosis amounts to over 2,600. Numerically, therefore, this experience would appear to be adequate. There are, however, numerous flaws inherent in the data which seriously detract from the advantage of numerical adequacy. First, it is certain that the samples of total autopsies include a not inconsiderable proportion of children in whom the occurrence of cirrhosis is practically negligible. Only very few investigators state the number of children in their samples and thus the table can not be corrected for this factor, especially as according to the nature of the hospital the proportion of children may be large, small, or near zero. On the other hand, the samples of inebriates naturally refer to adult population only and as a matter of fact to a population largely above 35 years of age. The age

TABLE 3

*Occurrence of Liver Cirrhosis in General Populations Determined
from Autopsy Material (including Inebriates)*

Investigators	Place and Year		No. of Autopsies	Cirrhosis No.	Cirrhosis Per cent
Mallory (b)	Boston	1932	9,364*	550	5.9
Ophüls (b)	California	1926	3,000	166	5.5
Askanazy (cit. Rössle)	Geneva	1916–20	7,809	284	4.0
Boles and Clark†	Philadelphia	1933–35	4,000	150	3.75
Rössle	Basel	1923–26	3,022	90	3.0‡
Birch-Hirschfeld	Leipzig	1901	—	—	3.0§
Schloss	Lucerne	1919–39	7,836	174	2.2
Boles and Crew†	Philadelphia	1938–39	4,000	88	2.2
Kühn (cit. Rössle)	Düsseldorf	1907–13	2,900	62	2.1
Kühn (cit. Rössle)	Posen	1900–04	1,808	37	2.0
Kachi and Midorikawa	Japan	1925	18,813	380	2.0
Kern	Vienna	1913	4,130	73	1.7
Blumenau	Frankfurt	1909–18	12,761	198	1.6
Paraf and Klotz	France	1933	2,341	30	1.3
Rössle	Kiel	1905	1,003	12	1.2‖
Evans and Gray	Los Angeles	1918–37	17,874	217	1.2
Gruber	Mainz	1917–22	3,134	39	1.2
Rössle	Jena	1912–14	1,300	15	1.1
Förster (cit. Rössle)	Berlin	1868	3,200	31	1.0
Kühn (cit. Rössle)	Kiel	1914–18	3,395¶	29	0.9
TOTALS			110,970	2,625	Av. 2.4

*Includes 2,066 children.
†Only the data on degenerative cirrhosis considered here.
‡3.7 per cent of 2,445 adults.
§Males only.
‖2.2 per cent of 540 adults.
¶Many children included.

factor, then, would bring about an underestimate of the incidence of
liver cirrhosis in this so-called general population. There is, however,
also a factor which tends toward an overestimate of the incidence of
liver cirrhosis in these samples of so-called general population. As we
have mentioned before, the samples in Table 3 include inebriates and,
while the proportion is entirely unknown, it is practically certain that
in autopsy samples, at least in certain hospitals, the proportion of
inebriates included is much greater than their proportion in the actual
general population. At the Bellevue Hospital in New York City, for
example, the patients admitted with some alcoholic complaint in
recent years form on the average 20 per cent of all patients admitted.
This is obviously far above the incidence of inebriates in the general

population in New York City. In some hospitals, according to the nature and the policy of the hospital the proportion of inebriates admitted may be somewhat smaller or very much smaller. On the whole, the excess in the proportion of inebriates in Table 3 over the proportion of inebriates in the general population must have the effect of exaggerating considerably the estimate of occurrence of cirrhosis of the liver obtained from this table for the general population.

From a few instances an idea may be formed of the effect of the inclusion of inebriates on the estimate of the incidence of cirrhosis of the liver for the general population obtained from this table. There is one report in Table 3, namely that of Boles and Clark, in which it is possible to separate the inebriates from the temperate and abstaining patients. For the entire sample of 4,000 the incidence of liver cirrhosis was 3.75 per cent. In this sample of 4,000 the proportion of inebriates was 5.7 per cent. When these are excluded the incidence of liver cirrhosis drops to 2.78 per cent. In another sample (unpublished data from Bellevue Hospital, not included in Table 3) in 600 autopsies a 10 per cent incidence of liver cirrhosis was found. The 600 autopsied subjects included 100, that is 16.7 per cent, inebriates. On excluding these the incidence of liver cirrhosis drops to 5 per cent, that is, the rate is actually halved. From the totals of Table 3, an estimate of the incidence of liver cirrhosis of roughly 2.4 per cent is obtained. In order to derive from this an estimate of the incidence of liver cirrhosis in a temperate and abstinent population it would seem reasonable to halve this, that is, to place it at 1.2 per cent. Since our estimate for inebriates was 8 per cent, this would mean that the relative incidence of cirrhosis of the liver in inebriates is approximately 6.7 times as great as in temperate or abstinent persons. This agrees well with the data from the sample of Boles and Clark in which the cirrhosis rate of inebriate patients is 7.1 times as great as that for the temperate and abstinent ones. In the unpublished data from Bellevue Hospital, too, the ratio was exactly 7 to 1. It would seem thus that the estimates of a liver cirrhosis rate of 8 per cent in inebriates and of 1.2 per cent in a temperate and abstinent population are fair first approximations to the actual numerical values. With respect to the ratio of the incidence rate in inebriates to the incidence rate in temperate and abstinent persons, the estimate may be considered as of more definite nature. True that the incidence of 8 per cent found in inebriates shows that it is not very common. This does not, however, preclude an association, since it is relatively much more frequent in the inebriates than in temperate and abstinent persons. The association is thus definitely indicated. On the other hand, one must agree with Boles and Crew that it is entirely unjustifiable to use the terms portal and alcoholic cirrhosis interchangeably.

Another type of data may be taken into consideration for further verification of this point. We are referring to the large volume of official statistics on death from cirrhosis of the liver. Death statistics naturally cannot indicate the extent of any disease, since some diseases may have no fatality rate at all but may be very prevalent while in another disease the fatality rate may reach 75 per cent or more. It must be considered also that while in two groups the incidence of a disease may be of equal proportions, death from that disease in the two groups may be at entirely different rates. Nevertheless if the official mortality statistics should give some indication of association between death from cirrhosis and inebriety it could be regarded as bearing out the experience of the clinical statistics discussed above.

Statistics of Death from Cirrhosis of the Liver

Official statistics for death from cirrhosis of the liver of various countries have been frequently invoked in arguments centering around the question of association between cirrhosis of the liver and inebriety. While these statistics have been frequently used incorrectly and even abused, employed judiciously they are the most potent argument in the clarification of the question. Unfortunately the misuses and erroneous techniques have left many students of the problem of alcohol and liver cirrhosis with a bitter taste and suspicion toward this approach; and even more unfortunately those who did not see through the errors were more impressed with the illegitimate than with the legitimate use of the statistics. Much of the antagonism to the use of vital statistics in this field has come, however, not so much from statistical abuses as from an overvaluation of some weaknesses which are inherent in official statistics. It devolves, therefore, upon a critical review of the present position of the problem of alcohol and liver cirrhosis to clarify also the statistical aspect of the question. We shall endeavor to show what the legitimate and what the illegitimate uses of statistics are in connection with the problem in question.

First, some methodologic errors should be pointed out. Not infrequently as an index of death from liver cirrhosis its percentage occurrence among all deaths has been used for comparison of death from liver cirrhosis during various periods in the same location or between various locations at the same time. This is a poor index, as we shall show. It has only a limited utility and cannot be interpreted, as has been done, as indicating frequency of a disease. Whether a cause of death is frequent or not can be expressed only in terms of the total living population or of the total living population of a particular age group affected by it. This is done by stating the number of deaths from a given cause per hundred thousand of people alive. Occasionally it is referred to a basis of 10,000 or 1,000,000.

It will be shown first on a hypothetical example what fallacious conclusions may arise from regarding the percentage from all deaths as an indication of the frequency of a cause of death. In Table 4 data for a hypothetical country of 2,000,000 are given relating to total deaths and deaths from liver cirrhosis in that country in 2 different years. It is assumed that because of an epidemic the total mortality was greatly increased during the second year.

The last column in Table 4 seems to show that in terms of percentage

TABLE 4

General Mortality and Death from Liver Cirrhosis in a Hypothetical Country during 2 Years

Year	Total Population	Total Deaths from All Causes	Total Deaths from Liver Cirrhosis	Deaths from Liver Cirrhosis per 100,000 Population	Deaths from Liver Cirrhosis as Percentage of All Deaths
1	2,000,000	20,000	200	10.0	1.0
2	2,040,000	24,448	204	10.0	0.7

of all deaths liver cirrhosis has decreased from 1.0 per cent of all deaths to 0.7 per cent, that is, there was a decrease of 30.0 per cent. Some would say, therefore, that death from liver cirrhosis had decreased in that country; and they would probably go even further and say that alcoholism had decreased. This would be entirely erroneous since in both years death from liver cirrhosis was 10 per hundred thousand of the population, that is, it was equally frequent in both years. It can be seen, thus, that if death from liver cirrhosis is compared in 2 countries in which the death from this cause per hundred thousand is exactly the same but in which the total death is absolutely or proportionately larger in one due to the operation of a particular disease factor, then the use of the index "death from cirrhosis as percentage of total deaths" would lead to entirely fallacious conclusions relative to the frequency of liver cirrhosis as a cause of death in these two countries.

To give a concrete example, the death rate from cirrhosis of the liver in 1935 in California was 15.7 per hundred thousand population and in 1937 it was 19.1; that is, the frequency of death from this cause increased 21 per cent. If we take, however, for this state, death from liver cirrhosis as a percentage of all deaths, 1.3 per cent is obtained for 1935 and 1.4 per cent for 1937. This would indicate an increase of 7.7 per cent only, and would probably be regarded as insignificant.

The practice of giving absolute numbers of death from liver cirrhosis for different years as a "proof" of the rise of death from this cause is naturally entirely meaningless, since the total population will have increased during the interval by an unknown amount and it is possible that the numbers presented to indicate a rise would actually indicate a decrease when referred to the total population as a basis.

The use of the per hundred thousand rate in itself does not assure correct use or correct interpretation of the statistics. Thus the comparison of per hundred thousand rates for death from cirrhosis in 2 countries may or may not be legitimate. Comparison may be invalid in spite of both being in terms of per hundred thousand population, because of different death classifications in the two countries. In one country a much larger complex of liver diseases may be covered in the term "cirrhosis of the liver" than in the other. It is therefore not permissible without very close analysis of the underlying facts to conclude from a higher cirrhosis death rate in one country a greater rate of inebriety in that country. Generally speaking it is safe to compare death rates from cirrhosis at different times within the same country unless changes in classification have taken place there. While it is not safe to compare actual cirrhosis mortality rates in 2 countries, it is safe to do so in order to compare the trends of these rates in 2 countries for some given circumstances, such as years of war, depression, etc. For such trends are much less influenced by classificatory differences than the actual rates themselves.

The worst feature of statistical investigation of death from cirrhosis of the liver is that some investigators have gone far beyond the permissible conclusion that there is association between inebriety and death from liver cirrhosis and have equated explicitly or implicitly death from liver cirrhosis with death from alcoholism (e.g., Schloss; Weeks; Wilson). Schloss in his Lucerne (Switzerland) statistics actually counted each and every death from liver cirrhosis as death from alcoholism without any further reference to the history of the deceased. Such practices have greatly contributed toward discrediting the use of vital statistics in the study of cirrhosis of the liver.

In contrast to this indiscriminate use of statistics is the entire rejection of this method on the basis of some imperfections which are present in even the best official statistics. Against the use of vital statistics such reasons have been put forward as, for instance, the reasonable surmises that statistics relative to death from cirrhosis do not include all the actual deaths from this disease and that not all the deaths recorded as from this cause are necessarily actually death from cirrhosis. Furthermore, when the cirrhosis death rates have been brought into connection with alcohol consumption rates flaws in these latter have been pointed out as invalidating factors. But from the consistency of trends shown in Figures 1 and 2 and Table 5 the only reasonable conclusion seems to be that the objections enumerated demand caution in the interpretation of the material but not rejection of the use of these methods. Briefly, the death rates may not be taken at face value but trends may be generally relied upon, assuming that they emanate from sufficiently large experience.

This discussion of principles furnishes the basis for our analysis of the data. As has been said before, trends may be the most appropriate means for exploring statistically the question of inebriety and cirrhosis of the liver. In the United States there was a period, from 1916 to 1920, of passage from state prohibitions to national prohibition, during which alcoholic beverages became more and more inaccessible until, in 1920, their supply had become practically negligible. After that followed a period, up to 1933, during which the illicit liquor trade furnished a constantly increasing supply of alcoholic beverages but without ever reaching the proportions of the legal trade. Mainly, however, during this period alcoholic beverages were accessible to a much smaller part of the population than previously. Lastly, the period from 1933 to the present represents the reinstitution of the alcoholic beverage industry in this country; and recently one year's consumption has reached more than 134,000,000 gallons of distilled spirits, 76,000,000 gallons of wine and 1,700,000,000 gallons of beer. These changing conditions should furnish an appropriate basis for testing the trend of death from liver cirrhosis in relation to relatively alcohol-free periods and periods of increasing consumption. This type of analysis has been performed repeatedly but, with the exception of Dublin, most investigators have produced rather perfunctory analyses. The conclusions drawn from such analyses, whether purporting to support or to refute the theory of alcoholic origin of cirrhosis of the liver, were hardly justified in view of the superficiality of the analyses.

The trend of the death rate from any cause must be viewed in the light of the trend of the total death rate, since, in the absence of such comparison, specific interpretation may be attached to a particular death rate although the character of the trend may not differ from the general mortality. Furthermore, it is desirable to include in the comparison the trend of the death rate from some other cause of death which is known to be different from the trend of the general mortality. Such additional comparison will guard against undue interpretation of the specific trend in question. In Figure 1 are shown the death rates

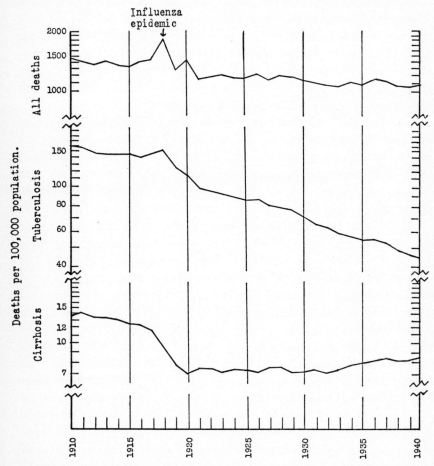

Figure 1. General mortality rates, death rate from tuberculosis and death rate from cirrhosis per hundred thousand population, U.S. expanding registration area, 1910–1940.

for total mortality, from cirrhosis of the liver and from tuberculosis for the period 1910 to 1940.* These are plotted on a logarithmic scale which makes direct comparisons possible in spite of great differences in levels.

It is seen that general mortality was on the decline between 1910 and 1915, that is, before at least partial prohibition had reached important proportions. The death rate from liver cirrhosis as well as from tuberculosis closely followed this trend with the same rate of decrease. As Table 5 shows, the average annual rate of decrease was 1.88 per cent

TABLE 5

Changes in General Mortality and in Deaths from Cirrhosis of the Liver and from Tuberculosis, per Hundred Thousand Population, during 3 Periods between 1910 and 1940

	Per cent Change for Entire Period	Per cent Average Annual Change
	1910–1915	
General mortality	−9.4	−1.88
Cirrhosis of the liver	−9.4	−1.88
Tuberculosis	−8.7	−1.74
	1916–1920	
General mortality	−7.1	−1.78
Cirrhosis of the liver	−42.2	−10.55
Tuberculosis	−19.7	−4.93
	1932–1940	
General mortality	−1.0	−0.13
Cirrhosis of the liver	+19.4	+2.43
Tuberculosis	−26.6	−3.33

for general mortality as well as for cirrhosis of the liver, while for tuberculosis it was just slightly less. During the period of the most effective state and wartime prohibition, including the beginning of the Eighteenth Amendment, i.e., 1916–1920, the decrease of the general mortality rate continued at approximately the same annual average percentage as in the preceding 5-year period. The great influenza epidemic of 1918 caused a high peak in the trend and since from the following year on the trend shows a continuation of the 1916–1917 line the impression is given that a steep decline had taken place. This steep decline is merely the effect of returning from the high point of epidemic to the normal trend. For the entire period 1916–1920 the

*Since cirrhosis of the liver occurs generally in the population above 30 years of age, death rates for this disease should properly be computed per hundred thousand of the population of that age. This has not been done here and, thus, the graph reflects only rough trends.

general mortality shows a decrease of 7.1 per cent, or an annual average of 1.78 per cent. In contrast to this the death rate from cirrhosis of the liver decreased during this period 42.2 per cent, or on the average 10.55 per cent per year. The part of this dramatic decrease which is over and above the general mortality rate would seem attributable to the effect of the practically vanishing alcohol consumption. However, the death rate from tuberculosis also showed a decrease far in excess of that of the general mortality, although considerably below that of cirrhosis, namely 19.7 per cent for the period, or an average decrease of nearly 5 per cent per year. In view of this it would seem that either the effect of reduced alcohol use must be granted for the tuberculosis death rate, too, or that the great decrease in death rate from cirrhosis should not be ascribed entirely to this effect. That the decrease in the death rate from cirrhosis of the liver and the decrease in the death rate from tuberculosis are differently determined becomes evident when the period after 1920, particularly the period 1932–1940, is scanned. In the latter 8-year period, in which repeal became effective, the general mortality rate decreased 1.0 per cent only, or on the average 0.13 per cent per year. On the other hand the great decrease of the tuberculosis death rate continued, although at a somewhat slower rate, namely, at an average of 3.33 per cent per year, while the death rate from cirrhosis showed an increase of 19.4 per cent, or an average annual increase of 2.43 per cent. Not alone are the trends of the death rates from tuberculosis and cirrhosis of the liver opposite in direction during the period of repeal, but the decrease in trend of tuberculosis is twice as great as in prohibition days. The highly accelerated decrease of the tuberculosis death rate during the period 1916–1920 can therefore hardly be ascribed to the prohibition conditions but rather to a concentrated effort centering around the combating of this disease, an effect which is still continuing but which naturally cannot make itself felt over an indefinite period at the same rate of decrease.

In view of this analysis it seems safe to conclude that a significant association exists between changes in the death rate from cirrhosis of the liver and changes in the consumption of alcoholic beverages. This conclusion, reached on the basis of American data, is borne out by European experiences. During the years of the first World War and well up to 1920 the production of alcoholic beverages in European countries was greatly reduced in favor of the production of alcohol for war industries. The prices of alcoholic beverages rose to a high level and in most countries some restrictions were placed on sales, so that alcoholic beverages became practically inaccessible to a large part of the population. These conditions held not only for the warring nations but also for the neutrals. Since a large proportion of the male population of the warring countries was on the battlefields the mortality statistics of those years cannot be utilized.* In the female population of most European countries the incidence of alcoholism is too small to be considered. An exception to this was the female population of England and Wales, where the ratio of alcoholic men to alcoholic women is less than 2 to 1. In Table 6 death rates from cirrhosis of the

TABLE 6

Death Rate from Cirrhosis of the Liver in 3 Nonwarring European Countries and in the Female Population of England and Wales during the Period 1914–1920

Year	England and Wales (Women)	Sweden	Denmark	Holland (Men)
1914	9.4	3.4	5.8	6.4
1915	8.0	2.4	6.9	5.5
1916	6.1	2.4	7.7	6.1
1917	4.2	2.0	6.1	5.9
1918	2.9	2.3	3.8	6.0
1919		2.2	3.8	4.8
1920		1.7	3.5	4.7

liver are given for some of the neutral countries and for the female population of England and Wales for the years 1914–1920.

The tabulated rates are so eloquent that nothing more needs to be said than that they parallel the American experience of the wartime prohibition years. The consistency of these phenomena definitely indicates that a certain portion of deaths from cirrhosis of the liver is related to alcoholic habits. From the American statistics presented here it may be attempted to obtain a first approximation of the contribution of inebriety to deaths from cirrhosis of the liver. Considering that between 1916 and 1920 the general mortality rate in the United States decreased 7.1 per cent and the death rate from cirrhosis of the liver decreased 42.2 per cent, and taking increases in population

*Relative to the effect of war on the death statistics in the United States it may be pointed out that (a) the first expeditionary forces went overseas only in the last year of the war; (b) the proportion of men in military service to the total population was small compared to the proportion in Europe; and (c) while in Europe men from 18 to 50 years were in the army, here only the men of young age served, who bear a relatively small part in the cirrhosis death rate.

during this time into consideration, we compute that the participation of inebriety in deaths from liver cirrhosis was approximately 35 per cent. This corresponds to the most conservative estimates made by students of cirrhosis of the liver on the basis of their clinical experience.*

Recalling the evidence of clinical statistics, it appeared that cirrhosis of the liver was 7 times as frequent among inebriates as among the temperate population. It would now seem that not only the frequency of cirrhosis is greater in inebriates but that they are also much more likely to die from this cause than temperate persons who suffer from cirrhosis. Since, however, the temperate and abstinent part of the population is numerically far superior to the chronic alcoholic population, in spite of the great difference in relative occurrence a much larger number of cases of death from liver cirrhosis is produced by the temperate and abstinent population.

Drastic changes in the death rate from cirrhosis of the liver occurring in a large population may be taken as indicative of changes in the excessive use of alcoholic beverages, but this does not mean that all deaths from liver cirrhosis or even the larger part may be ascribed to inebriety. The words "in a large population" are important since in a small population the per hundred thousand rate of a minor cause of death such as cirrhosis of the liver may be influenced to an apparently high degree by chance factors. In Table 7 death rates from cirrhosis of the liver for the 2 most populous and the 2 least populous states in the United States are given for the years 1934, 1935 and 1936. It is evident from this table that the death rate from cirrhosis of the liver is extremely unstable in the 2 least populous states and that the changes occur in a random fashion. It is not advisable therefore to draw conclusions from these statistics relative to changes in chronic alcoholism in small populations.

The association between the incidence of death from liver cirrhosis and alcohol consumption has been shown here in the broadest terms only, mainly in connection with a great scarcity and a normal abun-

---

*In a report by the Bureau of the Census (a), Division of Vital Statistics, entitled *Deaths from Alcoholism, United States: 1936*, it was estimated that 9.5 per cent of the deaths from cirrhosis of the liver were alcoholic cirrhosis. This estimate was arrived at without consideration of the trends described here but was based on a death certification of "alcoholic liver cirrhosis" which was put into practice in 1921 and which by its trend evidently shows that physicians were only slowly getting accustomed to this new classification and that it was practically an illusory statistic. The present authors have criticized this aspect of the census report in a previous publication (Jellinek and Jolliffe).

TABLE 7

Death Rates from Cirrhosis of the Liver in the 2 Most Populous and the 2 Least Populous States of the U.S. for the Years 1934, 1935 and 1936

State, Population	DEATH FROM CIRRHOSIS OF THE LIVER PER 100,000 POPULATION				
	1934	*1935*	Per cent Change *1934–1935*	*1936*	Per cent Change *1935–1936*
New York (13,479,152)	10.2	10.6	+3.9	10.4	−1.9
Pennsylvania (9,900,180)	8.9	8.7	−2.2	8.8	+1.1
Wyoming (250,742)	4.3	9.9	+137.2	6.9	−30.3
Nevada (110,247)	14.3	11.1	−22.4	17.0	+53.6

dance of alcoholic beverages. It is therefore of interest to investigate the relationship in better defined units, that is, in connection with quantitative expressions of alcohol consumption. To perform this type of analysis by taking the cirrhosis death rates and the per capita consumption of various European countries is a hopeless undertaking, if for nothing else, because of the differences in classifying and recording death as well as possible differences in computing the consumption values. Heterogeneous as the United States may be in constitution of racial as well as other social and biologic factors the statistical elements entering into procedure are by far more homogeneous than in the case of welding the data of European nations. The cirrhosis death rates and per capita consumption figures in terms of absolute alcohol consumed for the 45 "wet" states* of the Union are utilized here in a correlation analysis. In order to interpret any results the following points must be kept in mind. (a) There might be a difference from state to state in the readiness to diagnose cirrhosis of the liver. This factor is one of the minor ones involved. (b) The per capita consumption values are not of equal validity for all states since in states with a low average income and in states where local option for prohibition is exercised over parts of the state to a considerable degree there might be a fairly large consumption of illicit liquor which naturally would not enter into the per capita consumption figures. This is a more disturbing factor than the previous one. (c) The high per capita consumption may result in one state from the fact that it contains a large number of abnormal drinkers while in another state the same

*The "dry" states are Kansas, Mississippi and Oklahoma but these are not "dry" for beer, however.

per capita consumption may be brought about by a much larger
number of moderate users, that is, by the use of alcoholic beverages in
much wider circles than in the other state. This imposes definite
limitations on the interpretation of any results which may emanate
from a correlation analysis. For one thing, the results of such an
analysis cannot be interpreted in any way to apply to the incidence of
death from liver cirrhosis in individuals who drink little, medium or
excessive amounts. The type of analysis presented here is only a
rough first approximation to the problem.

In Figure 2 the death rate from cirrhosis of the liver for 45 states is
plotted against per capita consumption in terms of absolute alcohol.
It is seen that for the observed range a straight line relationship
develops. The words "for the observed range" must be emphasized
since outside of the observed range almost any change in the nature of
the relation may occur. Also, the straight line relationship might
obtain only when the two factors involved are measured in such gross

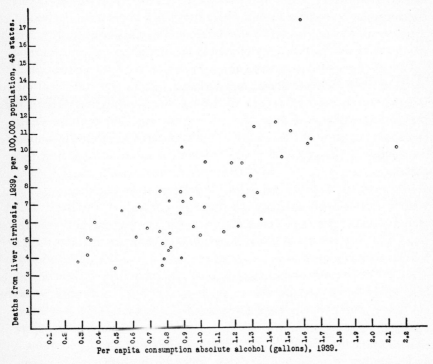

Figure 2. The relation of death from cirrhosis of the liver per hundred thousand
1939 population of 45 states of the Union to the 1939 per capita consumption of
absolute alcohol in the same states.

terms as the case in question. The scatter around the straight line is less than would be expected in such rough data. The correlation coefficient computed from these data is .61, which for a sample of 45 is highly significant. But the significance is to be understood only in the sense that the correlation has not resulted from the operation of chance factors. As far as the potency of the correlation is concerned we may say that the correlation of .61 indicates in this case that the variation in the per capita consumption accounts for 20.5 per cent of the variation of the death rates from liver cirrhosis; that is, about 80 per cent of the variation would be accounted for by other factors than the per capita consumption. Since this correlation results from admittedly rough data it is reasonable to assume that the true correlation may be much higher. This correlation should not be used as an argument that individuals who drink much are liable to die from cirrhosis of the liver. The only permissible formulation is that in territories in which the consumption of alcoholic beverages is high a greater probability obtains for a high rate of death from liver cirrhosis than in territories of smaller average consumption.

The utilization of straightforward vital statistics bears out the inferences drawn from clinical statistics, namely that a definite association between inebriety and cirrhosis of the liver exists. Since it is feasible to demonstrate this relationship on the basis of simple statistics it seems supererogation to try to prove the point through the use of statistics which contain much more serious flaws than the ones utilized here. We are referring to the frequent use of occupational statistics (e.g., Hoppe; Wlassak; Weeks; Wilson; Bandel; Kopf). It appears that many investigators feel that the association between inebriety and liver cirrhosis must be shown over and over again by drawing in irrelevant data from all available sources. The literature of this subject consists of bringing in another example and still another one, and the examples become increasingly weaker. As a net result these investigators have achieved the opposite of their aims, namely, they have brought about mistrust of the statistical approach. The literature pertaining to this type of statistics will be reviewed and evaluated in detail elsewhere.* In the present chapter those statistics bearing on this problem which do not meet the standards of applicability outlined earlier in this section are simply left out of consideration since no conclusions can be drawn from them which would help in clarifying the problem.

*In Volume III of this work.

Even the most valid statistics, vital or clinical, cannot go beyond the point of indicating the association or nonassociation between cirrhosis of the liver and inebriety. These investigations in no way answer the question whether or not there is direct causation of cirrhosis of the liver by alcohol. Even statistics of 100 per cent validity showing the association could not be interpreted in the terms that cirrhosis is caused by alcohol. The statistics merely indicate that among chronic alcoholics the occurrence of, as well as the death from, liver cirrhosis is significantly greater than among temperate persons. Etiologic theories must be based on physiologic experiment and physiologic reasoning. The statistical sidelights aid etiologic research only inasmuch as they show that a connection between inebriety and cirrhosis of the liver cannot be rejected and that, therefore, etiologic investigations of the question are not vain undertakings.

Experimental Cirrhosis of the Liver

When the authority of Baillie became shaken through clinical experience with cirrhosis of the liver in various conditions not related to inebriety, experiment was invoked to decide the question of alcoholic causation of this disease. Apparently the first investigator to administer alcohol to animals for the production of cirrhosis was Dahlström (cit. Rössle), who used dogs, in 1852. Since then more than 40 investigators have attempted to induce alcoholic cirrhosis of the liver experimentally. The number of those who have used other substances than alcohol is even greater. In the case of these other substances, as Rössle has pointed out, the experimentation frequently was far removed from the original question of etiology but was rather directed toward the clarification of some side issue in the pathogenesis.

While the consensus at present is that the experimental administration of alcohol to animals has not produced cirrhosis of the liver, some reviewers felt constrained to make some concessions at least to the claims of a few investigators. Generally there was a lack of criteria for the verification of experimental results and without such criteria the matter can hardly be discussed. Moon (a, b), in his masterly review of the data extant, employed an efficient yardstick, the validity of which we shall recognize here. Moon's criterion of portal cirrhosis is destruction of the architectural pattern. "How closely experimental cirrhosis approximated alcoholic cirrhosis in man was judged by this criterion."

In justice to the investigators it must be said that only a few of them claimed to have produced cirrhosis by the experimental administration of alcohol. These claims, however, did not conform to the requirements set up by Moon. An instance of this is Grover's statement and Moon's critique as shown in our Table 8. Another critical reviewer of the problem, Rössle, also pointed out that "wish and interpretation were stronger than the evidence" and that "some produced 'cirrhoses' which do not stand up to even mild criticism."

In Table 8 are presented reports on liver pathology in experimentally induced alcoholism. Data pertaining to acute alcoholic intoxication in animals are not presented but will be referred to inasmuch as they may contribute to the full understanding of the problem. Following Moon's procedure the early experiments* which were negative by statements of the investigators or did not furnish sufficient detail for evaluation of their findings are not considered here. Of the 20 investigators whose work is tabulated in Table 8, 16 have also been discussed by Moon (a, b) and, in the case of these 16, the entries in the column "pathologic findings" are mainly Moon's comments.

While fatty infiltration of the liver is frequently evident in these reports, and minor tissue changes also are common, the occurrence of fully established cirrhosis of the liver is not more frequent than would be expected under normal conditions. The statement frequently made that alcoholic liver cirrhosis has not been produced experimentally is well substantiated. On the other hand the negativity of these experiments can by no means be regarded as proof that alcohol or inebriety are not etiologic factors in the production of cirrhosis of the liver. One must agree with Connor (c) that the dosages used in these experiments were in some cases so large as to cause early death of the animals, so that on the whole alcoholization of insufficient duration resulted. Similar objections have been raised also by Rössle. Connor (c) believed that alcohol to be effective in such experiments must be given at least every 4 to 6 hours.

Examination of Table 8 shows that the conduct of the experiments was generally such that neither an acceptance nor a rejection of the alcoholic etiology is permissible. While the number of animals used may give the impression of numerical adequacy a closer study shows

*These include the work of Dahlström; Duchek; Joffroy; Serveaux; von Baumgarten; Reiter; Kremiansky; Ruge; Challand; Pupier; Strassmann; Afanassijew; Kublin; Magnan; Mairet and Combemale; Tobaldo; von Kahlden; Inghilleri; Jovine; d'Amata; Lafitte; Dujardin-Beaumetz and Audige; and Grandmaison [all cit. Moon (a)]. Rabbits, mainly, were used by these experimenters.

TABLE 8

Experimental Investigations of Cirrhosis of the Liver in Alcoholized Animals

Author	Animal Used; Number	Substance Used; Method	Amount Alcohol Daily	Duration	Pathologic Findings in Liver
Strauss and Blocq 1887 (cit. Moon)	24 rabbits	Mixture of ethyl and amyl alcohol through stomach tube.		Most died within 3 mos. 1 lived 7½ and 1, 12 mos.	The 2 long-lived animals showed marked perilobular lymphocytic infiltration and proliferation of young connective tissue, interpreted as early cirrhosis. (No distortion of pattern.)
de Rechter 1892 (cit. Moon)	10 rabbits, 3 dogs	Ethyl alcohol, 25%; amyl alcohol, 2.5%; water, 75%; stomach tube.		Report based on 2 rabbits living 5½ and 9 mos.; and 1 dog living 20 wks.	Livers of rabbits firm, fibrotic and granular, with perilobular increase in connective tissue. Periportal fibrosis in dog's liver. (No distortion of lobular pattern; evidence of cirrhosis inconclusive.)
Mertens 1895 (cit. Moon)	12 rabbits	Alcohol by evaporation.		25 days to 11 mos.	Ascites in 5, often with parasitic lesions in liver. Production of cirrhosis not claimed; found varying degrees of cellular degeneration and some inflammatory reaction with leucocytes and proliferating fibrous tissue in the periportal areas.
Friedenwald 1905	±20 rabbits	Absolute alcohol, diluted; whisky, diluted; by stomach tube.	5–8 cc. in 15–130 cc. water; 10–20 cc. in 10–20 cc. water.	To 4 yrs.	Temporary fatty changes frequent; only 1 cirrhosis.
Saltykow 1910	3 young rabbits	Alcohol diluted with saline.	3–15 drops in 1–1½ cc. saline.	1 animal, 2 yrs. and 7 wks.	2 died soon, nothing significant. 1 animal: marked cirrhosis and arteriosclerosis.
Fahr 1911	3 rabbits 2 guinea pigs	Alcohol in food.		To 3 yrs.	Marked fatty infiltration of liver; in 1 animal, fibrosis but no cirrhosis.
Bischoff 1912	Young rabbits	Whisky by stomach tube.	10–20 cc.	5 to 7 wks.	Marked fatty infiltration, especially in the central portions of lobules.
Schafir 1913	22 rabbits	Whisky by stomach tube.	3–4 g. per kg.	7 days to 8 mos.	Degenerative changes and fatty infiltration.

TABLE 8 (*continued*)

Author	Animal Used; Number	Substance Used; Method	Amount Alcohol Daily	Duration	Pathologic Findings in Liver
Schafir 1913	9 rabbits	Weekly intravenous injection 0.1–1 cc. absolute alcohol diluted.		7 days to 8 mos.	Ditto, more marked.
Schafir 1913	10 rabbits	Whisky by stomach tube and egg-yolk and milk in diet.	3 g. per kg.	7 days to 8 mos.	Fatty infiltration. (In all 3 experiments: Only general statements, no description of individual animals. Fatty changes and increase in stroma similar to those found in liver in alcoholism are described.)
Lissauer 1913	6 rabbits	Brandy or 50% alcohol intravenously.	5 cc. 1–8 days apart.	36 to 181 days.	In 1, liver firm and nodular; 5, infiltration and fibrosis about the markings of the lobules.
Kryle and Schopper 1914	34 rabbits	50% alcohol intravenously, subcutaneously and by mouth.	Probably 9.5 cc.	1 day to 13 wks.	Generally, parenchymatous degeneration. In 10, marked fatty degeneration. In 7, slight infiltration by small cells; in 6 this was outstanding and accompanied by proliferation of connective tissue interpreted as "beginning cirrhosis." In 3, chronic inflammation interpreted as "genuine cirrhosis." (Moon believes the drawings which illustrate this cirrhosis indicate degenerative changes and varying degrees of chronic perilobular inflammation.)
Isobe 1914	80 rabbits, 7 dogs	Alcohol and potassium sulfate, singly and in combination.	8–10 cc. per kg. 4 cc. per kg.	1 to 20 mos.	In many, severe parenchymatous degeneration and fatty infiltration; in a few, round cell infiltration and moderate fibrosis of Glisson's capsule.
Grover 1916	12 rabbits	34% alcohol by mouth.	15 cc., except Sundays.	3 to 12 mos.	Cirrhosis in varying degree in 6. (Moon states description and microphotos suggest infiltration and fibrous proliferation about the portal canals and moderate perilobular fibrosis such as is often seen in old rabbits. No distortion of lobular pattern.)
Ogata 1919	9 rabbits	40% alcohol intravenously.	Portal vein, 3–7 cc. Ear vein, 11–20 cc.	72 to 121 days. 43 to 76 days.	In some, perilobular fibrosis with degeneration of hepatic cells; no conclusions drawn.

TABLE 8 (concluded)

Author	Animal Used; Number	Substance Used; Method	Amount Alcohol Daily	Duration	Pathologic Findings in Liver
Andrianoff and Ansbacher 1930	Rats	20–50% alcohol with food.		9 to 15 mos.	No evidence of cirrhosis.
Hanzlik 1931	6 pigeons and 2 controls	Alcohol diluted in food, 2–4%.	1.3–10.2 g. per kg.	13 mos. to 2 yrs.	No demonstrable histologic changes; slight fatty infiltration of liver in both experimental and control animals.
Van der Schueren 1932	5 guinea pigs	50% alcohol.	2 cc.	14 to 20 mos.	In 2, fatty degeneration of liver; in 1, increased connective tissue and mononuclear infiltration about the portal structures.
Bucco 1935	10 rabbits	Absinth and grappa by esophageal tube.	2–4 cc. and 40 cc. water.	30 to 70 days.	Some elements of connective tissue among the liver cells; no cirrhosis.
Wechsler, Jervis and Potts 1936	14 cats; 20 monkeys	50% alcohol; 40% alcohol; stomach tube.	4–8 cc. per kg. 4–20 cc. per kg.	9 to 720 days. 40 to 630 days.	Cats: Marked fatty degeneration in all. Monkeys: Slight to severe fatty degeneration in nearly all.
Lhermitte, Ajuriaguerra and Garnier 1938	6 rabbits	Absinth	2.5 cc. absinth and 2 cc. water.	At least 40 days.	Many necrotic spots, marked hyperemia, no fatty degeneration.
Connor and Chaikoff (b) 1939	16 dogs	22.5% alcohol (after fatty liver produced by high-fat diet).	10 cc. per kg. twice daily.	70 days to 10 mos. of 4 to 7 day periods, alternate alcohol and fat feeding.	Excessive fatty livers in all resembling those in chronic alcoholism in man; in 4, definite cirrhosis, moderate, but resembling that in man.
Daft, Sebrell and Lillie 1941	20 rats	20% alcohol in place of drinking water, with low-fat, low-protein diet plus cystine.		46 to 111 days (average 83).	"All showed marked liver cirrhosis on gross and histological examination." Control rats given same diet and alcohol plus choline or methionine or casein developed no liver pathology. Other controls given same diet with water but no alcohol "died with an indistinguishable liver pathology" so that "diet is here the essential factor."

that only a small percentage of the animals was utilized in the final reporting. Thus of Strauss and Blocq's 24 rabbits only 2 are reported on and, also, only 2 out of de Rechter's 10 rabbits. Even Frieden-wald, who evidently handled his experimental animals most efficiently, had in the first month a 25 per cent loss and in the first 6 months 40 per cent loss of animals. With few exceptions the duration of the experiments was from a few weeks to a few months. The curtailment of the experimental period was probably largely due to excessive dosages which, no doubt, were given with the intention of achieving maximum effects. Daily dosages frequently reached 8 to 10 cc. abso-lute alcohol for rabbits, which for the average weight of this animal would mean 4 to 5 cc. per kg.

More than 90 per cent of the animals utilized were rabbits. Rabbits are notoriously subject to coccidiosis. Ophüls (a) reported that only 6 normal livers were found in 50 untreated rabbits. The rest showed various stages of coccidial infection with more or less cirrhosis and sometimes cirrhotic processes in cases in which coccidia could not be demonstrated. The food of laboratory rabbits is usually cabbage and this vegetable is often sprayed with arsenic or other heavy metal insecticides. An animal subsisting mainly on food thus treated may consume sufficient quantities of heavy metals to cause some of the liver damage reported in these experiments. Smetana, also, reported frequent spontaneous coccidiosis in rabbits, with diffuse cirrhosis. Gye and Purdy, however, pointed out that the frequency of coccidio-sis in rabbits depends on the amount of care in housing and feeding and that with proper measures the incidence can be reduced to insig-nificant proportions. In view of the liability of rabbits to these diseases it is amazing that control animals were not employed in these experi-ments.

While the answer emanating from these investigations to the ques-tion of the alcoholic etiology of cirrhosis is rather indeterminate than negative, some experiments in which organic as well as inorganic poisons have been used in combination with alcohol have thrown some light on the possible role of alcohol, or preferably of inebriety, in the genesis of cirrhosis of the liver. Moon (a) came to the following conclusion:

Combination of alcohol with other agents has greatly increased their toxic effects on the liver. Fischler's experiments with alcohol and phosphorus, Scagliosi's results with alcohol plus bacteria, Wallace's results with alcohol plus chloroform and the results of Lamson, Wing, Mann and others with alcohol plus carbon tetrachloride are instances of the contributory effects of alcohol. It is probable that such influence as alcohol exerts in causing human cirrhosis results from its action in reenforcing or accentuating the effects of other agents or in producing degenerative changes in the hepatic cells, thereby rendering them more susceptible to injury. . . . It is significant that combinations of agents have been found more effective than either of the agents alone. . . . The results in such instances suggest the importance of combinations of agents in the etiology of human cirrhosis.

The general discussion of Table 8 does not in any way reflect upon the experiments of Connor and Chaikoff (*a, b*) which are so different in conception and execution from the other experiments that they must be considered separately. These investigators produced fatty livers, through dietary measures, in 16 dogs. Only after fatty livers had been produced was alcoholization begun (for details of method see Table 8). The alcohol administration lasted from 70 days to 10 months and in 4 dogs a moderate but definite cirrhosis resembling that in man was found. This is a significant contribution to the pathogenesis of liver cirrhosis in chronic alcoholism and bears out some surmises on the possible transition from fatty liver to cirrhosis. On the other hand it does not throw any light on the question of direct or indirect causation of cirrhosis of the liver through chronic alcoholic excess.

It is our opinion that this question cannot be answered by the scheme of animal experiments that has been followed up to now. Even the highest incidence of liver cirrhosis in experimental chronic alcoholism, obtained with satisfactory doses, sufficient duration and adequate control series, would have no greater significance than bearing out clinical experience. On the other hand, even total absence of cirrhosis of the liver in rigorous experimentation would not refute the significant association found clinically between inebriety and cirrhosis of the liver. That such association exists cannot be explained away. No clinical statistical investigation, however, can show of what nature this association is. Animal experiments can go beyond the scope of clinical statistical investigations only if the past and present procedure of merely feeding alcohol and enumerating the liver pathology found is replaced by entirely new schemes. These new procedures, apart from observing suitable dosage, duration and control requirements, must keep adequate records on nutritional and activity changes in the experimental animals. In addition this must be supplemented by general metabolic studies and, mainly, by the introduction of factors which make it possible to distinguish between the origins of pathologic processes. This latter procedure was approached by

Wechsler, Jervis and Potts in whose investigation, however, the question of liver cirrhosis was only incidental. These investigators compared groups subjected to acute alcoholic intoxication with animals fed on diets either low in or depleted of vitamin B and with animals in which alcohol intoxication and diets low in vitamin B were combined. A more recent investigation by Daft, Sebrell and Lillie was also managed so that the effects of diet could be distinguished from the effects of alcohol and, in this case, it may be said that the use of alcohol was incidental and not the main object. The preliminary report of the authors is not sufficiently detailed to permit a full evaluation of the results.

It is important to emphasize that those who desire to approach the problem of the etiology of cirrhosis of the liver in alcohol addicts experimentally should disabuse their minds of the idea that successful experimentation can now be done merely by avoiding the errors and pitfalls of the earlier investigators. Better care of the animals, appropriate alcohol dosage and suitable duration of the procedures with sufficient numbers of animals will not yield valuable results unless the experiments are conducted generally along the lines suggested above.

Etiologic Theories

After overcoming the initial extreme view of the direct causation of cirrhosis of the liver by alcohol and a subsequent reaction toward the other extreme that cirrhosis was not related to inebriety at all, there has gradually developed the present position of etiologic views which generally acknowledge an association between inebriety and cirrhosis of the liver in which an indirect effect is assigned to the excessive use of alcoholic beverages. Sporadically even at present the association is entirely negated or, on the other hand, direct causation is still adhered to. In Table 9 the views expressed by various authors during the past decade on this problem are listed.

The viewpoint of indirect causation is by no means an achievement of modern research. Theories suggesting various indirect processes contingent upon the excessive use of alcohol were advanced fairly early. Thus Budd in 1846 thought that the cirrhosis of the liver in chronic alcoholics was brought about through disturbances of the circulation in the lung and heart. In 1896 Scagliosi said that excessive drinking did not cause cirrhosis in people with normal livers but only in people in whom previous infectious diseases had lowered the resistance of the liver. White in 1903 subscribed to this theory and we

TABLE 9

Recent Etiologic Views on Cirrhosis of the Liver (1930–1941)

Year	Author	Suggested Etiology
1930	de Crinis	Alcohol poisoning causes anatomic and functional injury to the liver which makes it susceptible to cirrhosis.
1930	Rössle	Association between alcoholism and cirrhosis definite, but causation indirect. No evidence whether the gastrointestinal troubles of chronic alcoholics are cause or effect of cirrhosis.
1931	Brule and Barbat	The alcoholic factor "is always present in cirrhosis"; the luetic factor not demonstrated.
1931	Laignel-Lavastine, Troisier and Boquien	Obscure statement on simultaneous effect of alcohol on thyroid function, gonads and liver.
1931	Mallory, Parker and Nye	Copper contained in food or drink is an important cause of hemochromatosis and alcohol may accentuate the effects of copper.
1932, 1933	Mallory (*b, c*)	Phosphorus suggested as cirrhogenic poison in alcoholic beverages but presence admittedly not demonstrated in wines and spirits.
1932	Leschke	Relation between alcohol and cirrhosis not demonstrated.
1933	Kennedy	In the genesis of cirrhosis alcohol appears to act more as a factor contributing to dietary deficiency than as a toxic substance.
1933	Radhakrishna Rao	Cirrhosis found in East India in nonalcoholics to some part due to diets deficient in vitamins A, C and D.
1934	Coronini	Although not caused directly by alcohol, alcoholic beverages, mainly brandy, are important factors in the etiology. There is no proof of causation by way of gastrointestinal troubles.
1934	Moon (*a, b*)	There is evidence that metabolic disturbances may be contributory factors, e.g., the frequently found simultaneous occurrence of exophthalmic goiter and cirrhosis.
1935	Gerlach	Suggested factors: goiter, "drinking of wine before meals," age of wine or brandy.
1937	Patek	From therapeutic success with vitamin B complex suggested, implicitly rather than explicitly, that vitamin deficiency may play a role in liver cirrhosis.
1938	Goodhart and Jolliffe (*a*)	From some therapeutic success with vitamin B_1, no conclusions drawn but suggested that the role of vitamin B_1 may be of some significance in those enlarged livers which are due to congestive heart failure.

Year	*Author*	*Suggested Etiology*
1938	Evans and Gray	Excessive consumption of alcoholic beverages seems to be a contributory factor to cirrhosis of the liver.
1938	Connor (*a*)	On the basis of experiments by Chaikoff, Connor and Biskind and by Connor and Chaikoff (*a, b*) suggested that the mechanism of production of cirrhosis of the liver in chronic alcoholism is a graduation from fatty liver to cirrhosis.
1938	Seymour	Alcohol is the cause of "fibro-fatty" liver.
1939, 1940	Connor (*b, c*)	Alcohol plus starvation, or alcohol and protein-fat diet, cause accumulation of unoxidizable fat in the liver; there is complete depletion of glycogen, the absence of which renders the liver more susceptible to all poisons.
1939	Hall and Morgan	The liver must be in a state of altered carbohydrate and fat metabolism before cirrhosis will result. Fatty liver may pass over into cirrhosis. Lowered food intake and deficiency in certain vitamins may be contributory factors.
1939	György and Goldblatt	Fibrotic changes and fatty infiltration produced experimentally in rat livers by diet which presumably lacked the filtrate factors of the vitamin B complex.
1939	Maranon, Richet, Pergola and Lesueur	A polyvitaminic insufficiency is involved in alcoholic cirrhosis of the liver, which is connected with endocrine dysfunctions.
1939	Richet	Alcoholic cirrhosis is equal to alcoholic gastritis plus symptoms of multiple alimentary insufficiency and especially an avitaminosis E.
1939	Chevalier, Olmer and Vague	Deficiency of vitamin A plays a role in cirrhosis of the liver of chronic alcoholics.
1939	Brodin	Implies that the vitamin deficiencies of chronic alcoholics are responsible for their liver cirrhosis.
1939	Nonnenbruch	Alcohol does not produce liver cirrhosis directly but by means of gastroenteritis.
1939	Levy, Greenstein and Leighton	The cause is undetermined, but relation to previous inflammation, such as appendicitis and bronchopneumonia, possible.
1939	Friedman	"In order for cirrhosis of the liver to occur in an alcoholic he must be born with what Neusser called the thymolymphatic constitution" (with hypoplasia of the entire circulatory system).
1940	Loeb	Etiology still debated but alcoholism is the most common clinical factor.
1941	Cates	For alcoholic and nonalcoholic liver cirrhosis a common predisposing factor is present, namely, failure of alimentary absorption.

find this view still represented in 1939 by Levy, Greenstein and Leighton. On the other hand Brauer in 1903 thought he had established definitely the direct causation of cirrhosis of the liver by alcohol since he found that alcohol goes over into the bile in much larger proportions than into the urine and that after large dosages coagulated albumin was always present in the bile. In 1912 Hoppe reiterated the original primitive view that proliferation of the connective tissue, ultimately leading to degeneration of the liver cells, is caused through constant irritation from the alcohol circulating in the blood.

The etiologic theories of the occurrence of cirrhosis of the liver in chronic alcoholics may be largely classified as involving (a) exogenous poisons other than alcohol contained in alcoholic beverages; (b) gastric disturbances; (c) general metabolic disturbances; (d) vitamin deficiences; and (e) transition from fatty liver to cirrhosis.

Probably the first proponent of the theory that diseases consequent upon the abuse of distilled spirits were due to exogenous poisoning was Ploucquet who, in 1780, warned the public against the ill effects of the copper salts which he believed entered into brandy from the copper distilling apparatus. By the middle of the nineteenth century, however, Magnus Huss pointed out that with the improvement in distillation, especially the tin lining of the copper vessels, copper had disappeared entirely from brandy, or was present only in negligible quantities, and nevertheless excessive drinkers were still suffering from the same diseases. In view of this background, the relatively recent revival of this etiologic issue is highly interesting.

In 1865 Lancereaux suggested that wines which had been cleared with calcium sulfate were more productive of cirrhosis than other liquors. Vallin and Rendu [both cit. Moon (a)] refuted this. In 1900 Askanazy (cit. Rössle) suggested that wine contained copper and that the deposition of this caused cirrhosis. This same factor was suggested by Mallory, Parker and Nye in 1931 and it was further suggested that copper entered the alcoholic beverages through copper vessels used in their manufacture. Previously to that Hall and Butt found that alcohol given with copper acetate did not hasten or increase the deposit of pigment. In 1935 Gerlach stated that copper is not an etiologic factor but is stored in the cirrhotic liver which is not able to dispose of this substance.

Somewhat earlier Mallory (c) thought that phosphorus was the cirrhogenic poison in alcoholic liver cirrhosis but said that he did not see how these poisons could enter into these beverages and their presence in wine and spirits has never been demonstrated. In the conclusion to his review of experimental liver cirrhosis Moon (a, b) expressed the opinion that inorganic poisons, with the possible exception of arsenical compounds, did not constitute an important factor in the etiology of cirrhosis of the liver.

Theories involving gastric disturbances merit greater attention. In 1902 von Hoppe-Seyler expressed the opinion that gastric disturbances produce toxic substances which foster cirrhosis of the liver and Lubarsch in 1907 regarded the absorption of toxic substances from the stomach and the intestines as the basis of liver cirrhosis in general, irrespective of inebriety, but thought that alcohol facilitates the absorption of toxic substances. Von Bergmann in 1927 believed that any cirrhotic process was initiated through achylia gastrica and the gastroenteritis frequent in chronic alcoholism forms the basis of the recent etiologic theories of Richet as well as of Nonnenbruch (see Table 9). Rössle, however, thought that no evidence had been adduced to show whether the gastrointestinal troubles of chronic alcoholics are cause or effect of cirrhosis. It would seem that gastric disturbances in chronic alcoholics could be initiated by liver dysfunctions not involving cirrhosis and that in their turn the gastric disturbances contribute toward the initiation of the cirrhotic process which, on the other hand, may aggravate the gastric malfunctions. Briefly, cirrhosis and gastric disturbances may form a vicious circle. Thus, investigators who postulate nutritional disturbances in general or vitamin deficiencies specifically as well as the proponents of some other etiologies do not, in fact, contradict the role of gastric disturbance in cirrhosis. These latter disturbances are explicitly or implicitly assigned at least a subsidiary role in various theories involving nutritional deficiencies or postulating transitions from fatty liver to cirrhosis.

Etiologic theories based on general metabolic disturbances of a toxic nature are much more numerous than would appear from explicit statements. The idea is implicit in all reports on positive findings pertaining to liver function tests in chronic alcoholism.*

Metabolic disturbances of endocrine origin have also been suggested. Moon (a, b) pointed out the frequently observed simultaneous occurrence of exophthalmic goiter and cirrhosis. Thyroid dysfunctions and

*E.g., Binswanger (a, b); Bostroem; Chiray and Deparis; Euziere, Vidal and Zakhamm; Heath and King; Markovitz; de Montmolin; MacNider and Donnelly; Toulouse, Courtois and Russell; Truche; and Wichels and Brinck.

other endocrinopathies have been stressed mainly by French investigators (see Table 9). The presence of gynecomastia in cirrhosis of the liver has been pointed out repeatedly. In view of the fact that only a relatively small proportion of chronic alcoholics develop cirrhosis of the liver the presence of endocrinopathies must be regarded as a possible differentiating factor and merits further research.

Nutritional deficiencies as a basis of cirrhosis of the liver were suggested even before vitamin deficiencies had received consideration. Klieneberger in 1923 attributed the severe forms of cirrhosis to poor nutrition irrespective of inebriety and Kennedy in 1933 submitted that, relative to the genesis of cirrhosis, alcohol acted more as a factor contributing to dietary deficiency than as a toxic substance. Etiologic theories involving vitamin deficiencies are listed in Table 9. Not alone vitamin B deficiencies but also deficiency of vitamin A and, with less emphasis, deficiency of vitamin E have been suggested. It is not entirely clear from these theories whether the vitamin deficiencies are to be regarded as cause or effect of the cirrhosis. Apparently there are serious disturbances of the vitamin A level in cirrhosis of the liver, as shown by tests of dark adaptation in chronic alcoholics by Patek and Haig as well as Wohl and Feldman. Connor (c) was not inclined to attach much importance to theories of avitaminotic origin of cirrhosis of the liver and expressed the opinion that "much work must be done before vitamin deficiency can be involved or ruled out" in the production of this disease.

That etiologic theories involving a transition from fatty infiltration to a cirrhotic process are of most recent origin only is rather surprising in view of the fact that it is an old observation that fatty liver is one of the most common occurrences in chronic alcoholics. In 1887 Orth (cit. Hoppe) pointed out that the typical liver condition of chronic alcoholics is fatty liver. This observation has been made since then in practically every description of the physical condition in chronic alcoholism. It would swell the bibliography to unnecessary proportions to cite references. From the combined data of numerous authors we compute that fatty infiltration of the liver is present in probably 75 per cent of patients with chronic alcoholism. Furthermore, and this is most important, the sources of the statistics given in Tables 1 and 2 show that there is a great overlap between fatty infiltration and cirrhosis, that is, that the two conditions have been frequently observed simultaneously. Generally, from the beginning of this century the abnormal fat deposition in the liver of inebriates has been attributed to the deficient utilization of carbohydrates and fats in the presence of large alcohol intake, although Kraus (*a*, *b*) believed that fatty infiltration is not dependent on the general state of the nutrition but that the cause was chronic intracranial pressure on the hypophyso-diencephalic system. This theory has not found any followers. In 1938 and 1939 Connor and Chaikoff (*a*, *b*) reported on the production of fatty livers in depancreatized dogs and the development of cirrhosis on administering alcohol to dogs in which a fatty liver had been previously produced.* Connor (*b*) used the terms toxic cirrhosis, biliary cirrhosis, pigment cirrhosis and fatty cirrhosis. This last is "caused most commonly by, or is associated with, long-continued alcohol poisoning and diabetes mellitus with which there has been a preceding fatty infiltration of the liver. . . . Fatty infiltration and occasionally cirrhosis may occur in cases of hypothyroidism or lesions of the pituitary and midbrain, as in cases of progressive lenticular degeneration (Wilson's disease). . . . There can be little doubt now that alcohol and the habits induced by the consumption of large amounts of alcohol are the most important factors in the production of fatty liver, which passes on in some cases to cirrhosis." Connor stated also that the factor next in importance to alcohol is the abnormal diet which invariably accompanies severe chronic alcoholism. He indicted a specific lack of carbohydrates and by this explained the occasional cirrhosis seen in diabetes mellitus. Connor pointed out that if two factors are operating together, as alcohol and starvation, or alcohol plus protein-fat diet, all of which cause a marked lowering of the respiratory quotient, the liver will accumulate unoxidizable fat and liver cells will be deprived of oxygen and nutrition. "The liver becomes an unnatural storehouse of fat and approaches, so far as oxygen-carbon dioxide exchange is concerned, the normal fat storage tissues of the body, in which this is very low. There is then a complete depletion of glycogen from the liver, the absence of which renders it more susceptible to all poisons of this nature." The production of cirrhosis of the liver is thus explained by this author as an enhancement of processes which take place in all tissues, i.e., slow atrophy of cells, necrosis and development of fibrous tissue. This is attributed to alcoholic poisoning and restriction or inhibition of carbohydrate metabolism.

*Fatty infiltration of the liver through the use of alcohol or other substances has been produced repeatedly since 1870 [Moon (*a*, *b*)]. The novum in the experiments of Connor and his associates is the production of cirrhosis after the production of fatty liver.

The investigations of Connor and his associates appear to be among the most important advances in the knowledge of the pathogenesis of cirrhosis of the liver in chronic alcoholism. This theory does not exclude vitamin deficiencies as contributory factors. Furthermore the predisposing role of endocrinopathies becomes plausible as fatty infiltration may be brought about also by pituitary lesions.

It is to be hoped that in future research fatty liver in chronic alcoholics will receive more attention than in the past not only in its relation to the development of cirrhosis of the liver but also for the role which it may play in the entire physiologic economy of the inebriate.

While the association between inebriety and cirrhosis of the liver is definitely established and a direct causation through alcohol is ruled out, none of the numerous etiologic theories of indirect causation can be accepted at present as sufficiently documented. On the other hand, diversity of the etiologies is not to be taken as a sign of confusion or of lack of knowledge, since most of these theories are not mutually exclusive but can be integrated into a common theory.

Lastly, the investigations of Connor and his associates have shown the possibility of progressing from theoretical surmises to etiologic research in the best sense of the word.

BIBLIOGRAPHY FOR PART II

AALSMEER, W. C. and WENCKEBACH, K. F. Herz und Kreislauf bei der Beriberi-Krankheit. Wien. Arch. inn. Med. **16**: 193, 1929.

DE ALBERTIS, D. Contributo alla conoscenza delle alterazioni istopatologiche con-comitanti alle degenerazioni secondo Marchiafava e Bignami delle commessure encefaliche negli alcoolisti cronici. Riv. ital. Neurop. **13**: 69, 1920.

ALEXANDER, L. (*a*) Alcoholism and mental disease. In: Mental Health (Amer. Ass. Advancement Sci., Publ. No. 9), p. 83. Lancaster, Science Press, 1939.

—— (*b*) The neuropathology of alcoholism. J. nerv. ment. Dis. **90**: 385, 1939.

—— (*c*) Topographic and histologic identity of the experimental (avitominotic) lesions of Wernicke with lesions of hemorrhagic polioencephalitis occurring in chronic alcoholism in men. Arch. Neurol. Psychiat. **42**: 1172, 1939.

—— (*d*) Identity of lesions produced experimentally by B_1 avitaminosis in pigeons with hemorrhagic polioencephalitis occurring in chronic alcoholism in man. Amer. J. Path. **16**: 61, 1940.

——, PIJOAN, M. and MYERSON, A. Beri-beri and scurvy; an experimental study. Trans. Amer. neurol. Ass. **64**: 135, 1938.

——, ——, SCHUBE, P. J. and MOORE, M. Cevitamic acid content of blood plasma in alcoholic psychoses. Arch. Neurol. Psychiat., Chicago **40**: 58, 1938.

AMERICAN JOURNAL OF DIGESTIVE DISEASES (Editorial). Alcoholic neuritis apparently not due to deficiency of vitamin B_1. Amer. J. digest. Dis. **8**: 359, 1941.

ANDRIANOFF, N. and ANSBACHER, S. Leber und Kupfer. Dtsch. med. Wschr. **56**: 357, 1930.

ARING, C. D. and SPIES, T. D. Vitamin B deficiency and nervous disease; a critical review. J. Neurol. Psychiat. **2**: 335, 1939.

AUFRECHT. Die alkoholische Myocarditis mit nachfolgender Lebererkrankung und zeitweiliger Albuminurie. Dtsch. Arch. klin. Med. **54**: 615, 1895.

BAILLIE, M. The morbid anatomy of some of the most important parts of the human body. 1st Amer. ed. Albany, N.Y., T. Spencer, 1795.

BANDEL, R. (*a*) Sterbstatistik zur Alkoholfrage in der "Tageszeitung für Brauerei." Alkoholfrage **24**: 237, 1928.

—— (*b*) Über Alkoholverbrauch und Alkoholschädigung im Zusammenhang mit Rasse, Beruf, Lebensalter und Jahreszeiten. Med. Klinik **32**: 559, 1936.

BANGA, I. L., OCHOA, S. and PETERS, R. A. Pyruvate oxidation in the brain; active form of vitamin B_1 and role of C_4 dicarboxylic acids. Bio-chem. J. **33**: 1109, 1939.

BARBIER and JACQUIS. Alcoolisme a l'hôpital. Lyon méd. **163**: 719, 1909.

BARR, D. P. Exercise in cardiac disease. J. Amer. med. Ass. **91**: 1354, 1928.

BECKH, W., ELLINGER, P. and SPIES, T. D. Porphyrinuria in pellagra. Quart. J. Med. **6**: 305, 1937.

BENDER, L. (*a*) Myelopathia alcoholica associated with encephalopathia alcoholica. Arch. Neurol. Psychiat., Chicago **31**: 310, 1934.

—— (*b*) Anatomopathological data on personality. Amer. J. Psychiat. **92**: 325, 1935.

—— and SCHILDER, P. Encephalopathia alcoholica. Arch. Neurol. Psychiat., Chicago **29**: 990, 1933.

BENTLEY, F. J. Beriberi, its etiology, symptoms and pathology. Edinburgh, Y. J. Pentland, 1934.

VON BERGMANN, G. Zur funktionellen Pathologie der Leber, insbesondere der Alkohol-Aetiologie der Cirrhose. Klin. Wschr. **6**: 776, 1927.

BERNHARDT, M. Über die multiple Neuritis der Alkoholisten. Z. klin. Med. **11**: 363, 1886.

BIANCO, A. and JOLLIFFE, N. The anemia of alcohol addicts; observations as to the role of liver disease, achlorhydria, nutritional factors and alcohol on its production. Amer. J. med. Sci. **196**: 414, 1938.

BICKEL, G. (*a*) Les myocardies par carence. Pr. méd. **46**: 1916, 1938.

⸻ (*b*) Alcoolisme chronique et pellagra révélée par une insolation accidentelle. Schweiz. med. Wschr. **19**: 1159, 1938.

⸻ (*c*) Hypovitaminose B₁ et cardiopathies. Arch. Mal. Coeur **32**: 657, 1939.

BIGNAMI, A. Sulle alterazioni del corpo calloso e della commissura anteriore ritrovate in un alcoolista. Policlinico (sez. Prat.) **14**: 460, 1907.

⸻ and NAZARI, A. Sulla degenerazione delle commissure encefaliche e degli emisferi nell'alcoolismo cronico. Riv. sper. Freniat. **41**: 81, 1915.

BING, R. Textbook of nervous diseases. (Tr. and ed. by W. Haymaker.) 5th ed. St. Louis, C. V. Mosby, 1939.

BINSWANGER, H. (*a*) Zur funktionellen Pathologie der Leber beim Delirium tremens alcoholicum. Klin. Wschr. **11**: 1339, 1932.

⸻ (*b*) Leberfunktionsproben bei Alkoholkranken. Allg. Z. Psychiat. **99**: 220, 1933.

BIRCH-HIRSCHFELD, A. Experimentelle Untersuchungen über die Pathogenese der Methylalkohol Amblyopie. v. Graefes Arch. Ophthal. **52**: 358, 1901.

BISCHOFF, M. Neue Beiträge zur experimentellen Alkoholforschung mit besonderer Berücksichtigung der Herz- und Leberveränderungen. Z. exp. Path. Ther. **11**: 445, 1912.

BLANKENHORN, M. A. and SPIES, T. D. (*a*) Prevention, treatment and possible nature of the peripheral neuritis associated with pellagra and chronic alcoholism. Trans. Ass. Amer. Phys. **50**: 164, 1935.

⸻, ⸻ (*b*) Oral complications of chronic alcoholism. J. Amer. med. Ass. **107**: 641, 1936.

BLUMENAU, E. Ueber Todesursache bei Lebercirrhose. Arch. VerdauKr. **27**: 1, 1920.

BOEDEKER, J. Über einen akuten (Polioencephalitis superior haemorrhagica) und einen chronischen Fall von Korsakow'scher Psychose. Arch. Psychiat. Nervenkr. **40**: 304, 1905.

VAN BOGAERT, A. Béribéri alcoolique. Arch. Mal. Coeur **31**: 1195, 1938.

BOGART, C. N. Nicotinic acid in the treatment of pellagra. J. Amer. med. Ass. **111**: 613, 1938.

BOGGS, T. R. and PADGET, P. Pellagra; analysis of 102 cases. Johns Hopk. Hosp. Bull. **50**: 21, 1932.

BOHROD, M. G. Primary degeneration of the corpus callosum (Marchiafava's disease); report of the second American case. Arch. Neurol. Psychiat., Chicago **47**: 465, 1942.

BOLES, R. S. and CLARK, J. H. The role of alcohol in cirrhosis of the liver. J. Amer. med. Ass. **107**: 1200, 1936.

⸻ and CREW, R. S. Observations on chronic alcoholism and cirrhosis of the liver. Quart. J. Stud. Alc. **1**: 464, 1940.

BOLLINGER. Über die Häufigkeit und Ursachen der idiopathischen Herzhypertrophie in München. Dtsch. med. Wschr. **10**: 180, 1884.

BOLTEN, G. C. Een bejzonder geval van polyneuritis. Geneesk. Gids. **17**: 644, 1939

BONHOEFFER, K. Pathologisch-anatomische Untersuchungen an Alkoholdeliranten. Mschr. Psychiat. Neurol. **5**: 265, 379, 1899.

BONTIUS, JACOBUS. De medicina indorum; Lib. III, Cap. I, De paralyseos quadam specie, quam indigenae Beriberii vocant, p. 115. Leyden, F. Hackius, 1642.

⸻ An account of the diseases, natural history, and medicines of the East Indies. (Translated from the Latin of James Bontius.) London, T. Noteman, 1769.

BOSTROEM, A. Über Leberfunktionsstörung bei symptomatischen Psychosen insbeson-dere bei Alkoholdelirien. Z. ges. Neurol. Psychiat. 68: 48, 1921.

BOULIN, R., JUSTIN-BESANÇON, L. and GEFFROY. Les porphyrinuries à propos de trois observations récentes. Médecine, Paris 20: 509, 1939.

BRAIN, R. Diseases of the nervous system. London, Oxford University Press, 1933.

BRAUER, L. Untersuchungen über die Leber. Hoppe-Seyl. Z. 40: 182, 1903.

BRODIN, P. Ce qu'il faut savoir des cirrhoses. Bull. Soc. Méd. Paris 143: 186, 1939.

BROWN, M. R. Alcoholic polyneuritis; an evaluation of the treatment at the Boston City Hospital from 1920 through 1938. J. Amer. med. Ass. 116: 1615, 1941.

BRULE, M. and BARBAT, R. O. Alcool et syphilis dans la genèse des cirrhoses. Pr. méd. 39: 1903, 1931.

BUCCO, G. Alterazioni del fegato da bevande alcooliche; ricerche sperimentali. Gazz. int. med.-chir. 45: 9, 1935.

BUDD, G. On diseases of the liver. Philadelphia, Lea & Blanchard, 1846.

BUEDING, E. and WORTIS, H. Pyruvic acid in blood and cerebrospinal fluid. Proc. Soc. exp. Biol., N.Y. 44: 245, 1940.

BUMKE, O. and FOERSTER, O. Handbuch der Neurologie, vol. XIII. Berlin, J. Springer, 1936.

——— and KANT, F. Rausch- und Genussgifte; Giftsuchten. In: Handbuch der Neurologie (Bumke, O. and Foerster, O., ed.), XIII, 828. Berlin, J. Springer, 1936.

BUREAU OF THE CENSUS, U.S. Dept. Commerce. (a) Death from alcoholism, United States: 1936. Vital Statistics Spec. Rep. 7: 667, 1939.

——— (b) Deaths from each cause. Vital Statistics Spec. Rep. 9: 621, 1940.

CAMPBELL. Ein Beitrag zur pathologischen Anatomie der sogenannten Polyneuritis alcoholica. Z. Heilk. 14: 11, 1893.

CAMPBELL, A. C. P. and BIGGART, J. H. Wernicke's encephalopathy (polioencephalitis haemorrhagica superior): its alcoholic and non-alcoholic incidence. J. Path. Bact. 48: 245, 1939.

CARMICHAEL, E. A. and STERN, R. O. Korsakoff's syndrome: its pathology. Brain 54: 189, 1931.

CARNOT, P., BARIÉTY and BOLTANSKY, E. Crises de tétanie au cours d'une poly-névrite éthylique. Bull. Soc. méd. Hôp. Paris 51: 568, 1927.

CARROLL, F. D. "Alcohol" amblyopia, pellagra, polyneuritis; report of ten cases. Arch. Ophthal., N.Y. 16: 919, 1936.

CARTER, C. W. and DRURY, A. N. Heart block in rice-fed pigeons. J. Physiol. 68: i (Proc.), 1929.

CASAL, G. Historia natural del principado de Asturias: de affectione quae vulgo in hac regione *mal de la Rosa* noncupatur. Madrid, 1762.

CASPARI, A. Zur Casuistik der Neuritiden. Z. klin. Med. 5: 537, 1882.

CATES, H. B. Relation of liver function to cirrhosis of the liver and to alcoholism. Arch. intern. Med. 67: 383, 1941.

CAUSSADE, L., KARLIN and ROUSSEL. Un cas de cirrhose alcoolique hypertrophique chez une fillette. Rev. méd. Est. 67: 602, 1939.

CHAIKOFF, I. L., CONNOR, C. L. and BISKIND, G. R. Fatty infiltration and cirrhosis of the liver in depancreatized dogs maintained with insulin. Amer. J. Path. 14: 101, 1938.

CHEVALIER, A., OLMER, J. and VAGUE, J. Sur la valeur diagnostique du taux de l'hémovitamine au cours des hépatites. Bull. Soc. méd. Hôp. Paris 55: 928, 1939.

CHICK, H. Current theories of the aetiology of pellagra. Lancet 225: 341, 1933.

CHIRAY, A. G. and DEPARIS, M. Le dépistage des hépatites diffuses aiguës dans l'alcoolisme chronique par l'épreuve des concentrations galactosuriques provo-quées. Arch. Mal. Appar. dig. 26: 481, 1936.

CLARK, B. B., MORRISSEY, R. W., FAZEKAS, J. F. and WELCH, C. S. The relation of the liver and insulin to alcohol metabolism. Amer. J. Physiol. 126: 463, 1939.

CLARKE, J. L. Alcoholic paresis and paraplegia. Lancet 102: 427, 1872.

CLECKLEY, H. M., SYDENSTRICKER, V. P. and GEESLIN, L. E. Nicotinic acid in the treatment of atypical psychotic states. J. Amer. med. Ass. 112: 2107, 1939.

COBB, S. and COGGESHALL, H. C. Neuritis. J. Amer. med. Ass. 103: 1608, 1934.

CONNOR, C. L. (a) Fatty infiltration of the liver and the development of cirrhosis in diabetes and chronic alcoholism. Amer. J. Path. 14: 347, 1938.

—— (b) Etiology and pathogenesis of alcoholic cirrhosis of the liver. J. Amer. med. Ass. 112: 387, 1939.

—— (c) Cirrhosis of the liver. Quart. J. Stud. Alc. 1: 95, 1940.

—— and CHAIKOFF, F. L. (a) Development of cirrhosis in fatty livers. Arch. Path. 25: 761, 1938.

——, —— (b) Production of cirrhosis in fatty livers with alcohol. Proc. Soc. exp. Biol., N.Y. 39: 356, 1938.

CORONINI. Pathologische Anatomie der Leberzirrhose. Wien. med. Wschr. 84: 231, 1934.

COWGILL, G. R. The vitamin B requirement of man. New Haven, Yale University Press, 1934.

CREUTZFELD, R. Hirnveränderungen bei Gewohnheitstrinkern. Zbl. ges. Neurol. Psychiat. 50: 321, 1928.

DE CRINIS, M. Über die Bedeutung der Leberfunktionsstörung für das Auftreten des Alkoholdeliriums und über eine ursächliche Behandlung desselben. Mschr. Psychiat. Neurol. 76: 1, 1930.

DAFT, F. S., SEBRELL, W. H. and LILLIE, R. D. Production and apparent prevention of a dietary liver cirrhosis in rats. Proc. Soc. exp. Biol., N.Y. 48: 228, 1941.

DÉJERINE. Paralysies musculaires dans le tabes dorsalis. Gaz. Hôp., Paris 57: 971, 1884.

DELORE, P. and DEVANT. Sur la proportion des cas d'alcoolisme chez les malades d'un service hôpitalier. Lyon méd. 163: 713, 1939.

DESROCHERS, G. and LARUE, G.-H. Acquisitions récentes sur le traitement des poly-névrites alcooliques. Laval méd. 2: 81, 1937.

DIXON, T. F. and MEYER, A. Respiration of the brain. Bio-chem. J. 30: 1577, 1936.

DOBRINER, K., STRAIN, W. H. and LOCALIO, S. A. The excretion of porphyrin in pellagra. Proc. Soc. exp. Biol., N.Y. 38: 748, 1938.

DONOVAN, P. B. and HANKE, M. E. The vitamin-B and -G content of commercial beer. Proc. Soc. exp. Biol., N.Y. 33: 538, 1936.

DONTCHEFF, L. (a) Évolution de la vitesse d'oxydation de l'alcool éthylique au cours du jeûne chez le rat blanc. C. R. Soc. Biol. 126: 462, 1937.

—— (b) Influence des divers types d'aliments sur la vitesse d'oxydation de l'alcool éthylique chez l'homéotherme inanitié (rat blanc). C. R. Soc. Biol. 126: 465, 1937.

DOUMER, E. Les formes cardiaques du béribéri. Bull. méd., Paris 53: 425, 1939.

DRURY, A. N. and HARRIS, L. J. Vitamin B deficiency in the rat; bradycardia as a distinctive feature. Chem. Ind. 49: 851, 1930.

——, —— and MAUDSLEY, C. Vitamin B deficiency in the rat; bradycardia as a distinctive feature. Bio-chem. J. 24: 1632, 1930.

DUBLIN, L. I. General mortality rates, 1900–1931, and death rates from alcoholism and cirrhosis of liver. In: Alcohol and man (Emerson, H., ed.), p. 373. New York, The Macmillan Co., 1933.

DUMÉNIL, L. Paralysie périphérique du mouvement et du sentiment portant sur les quatres membres; atrophie des rameaux nerveux des parties paralysées. Gaz. hebd. Méd. Chir. 1: 203, 1864.

ECKER, A. D. and WOLTMAN, H. W. Is nutritional deficiency the basis of Wernicke's disease? J. Amer. med. Ass. 112: 1794, 1939.

EICHHORST, H. Neuritis acuta progressiva. Virchows Arch. 69: 265, 1877.

EISENLOHR, C. Über einige Lähmungsformen spinalen und peripheren Ursprungs. Dtsch. Arch. klin. Med. 26: 543, 1880.

ELVEHJEM, C. A., MADDEN, R. J., STRONG, F. M. and WOOLLEY, D. W. The isolation and identification of the anti-black tongue factor. J. biol. Chem. 123: 137, 1938.

ENGEL, R. W. and PHILLIPS, P. H. (a) The lack of nerve degeneration in uncomplicated vitamin B₁ deficiency in the chick and the rat. J. Nutrit. 16: 585, 1938.

———, ——— (b) Effect of riboflavin-low diets upon nerves, growth and reproduction in the rat. Proc. Soc. exp. Biol., N.Y. 40: 597, 1939.

ERB, W. H. Handbuch der Elektrotherapie. Leipzig, F. C. W. Vogel, 1882.

EUZIERE, J., VIDAL, J. and ZAKHAMM, J. De quelques modifications humorales dans un cas de delirium tremens. Arch. Soc. Sci. méd. biol. Montpellier 13: 578, 1932.

EVANS, N. and GRAY, P. A. Laënnec's cirrhosis; report of 217 cases. J. Amer. med. Ass. 110: 1159, 1938.

FACQUET, J. Une nouvelle variété d'insuffisance cardiaque: l'insuffisance myocardique alcoolique par avitaminose B₁. J. Méd. Chir. prat. 110: 304, 1939.

FAHR. Beiträge zur Frage des chronischen Alkoholismus. Virchows Arch. 205: 397, 1911.

FINNERUD, C. W. Pseudopellagra. Med. Clin. N. Amer. 13: 448, 1929.

FITTIPALDI, C. Sul morbo di Marchiafava (degenerazione primitiva sistematizzata delle vie commessurali dell'encefalo). Riv. Patol. nerv. ment. 50: 427, 1937.

FLAIG, J. "Alkoholische Polyneuritis" und gewisse andere Nervenstörungen als Folge falscher Ernährung. Med. Klinik 35: 687, 1939.

FOUTS, P. J., HELMER, O. M., LEPKOVSKY, S. and JUKES, T. H. Treatment of human pellagra with nicotinic acid. Proc. Soc. exp. Biol., N.Y. 37: 405, 1937.

FRANCOTTE. Contribution à l'étude de la névrite multiple. Rev. Médecine 6: 377, 1886.

FRAPOLLI, F. Animadversiones in morbum, vulgo pelagram. Milan, 1771.

FRIEDENWALD, J. The pathologic effects of alcohol on rabbits. J. Amer. med. Ass. 45: 780, 1905.

FRIEDMAN, E. D. Discussion of Stevenson, L. D., Allen, A. M. and McGowan, L. E. A study of the brain changes in alcoholism. Trans. Amer. neurol. Ass. 65: 94, 1939.

GAMPER, E. Zur Frage der Polioencephalitis haemorrhagica der chronischen Alkoholiker; anatomische Befunde beim alkoholischen Korsakoff und ihre Beziehungen zum klinischen Bild. Dtsch. Z. Nervenheilk. 102: 122, 1928.

GARRISON, F. H. An introduction to the history of medicine. 4th ed. Philadelphia, Saunders Co., 1929.

GATÉ, J., TIRAN, P. and THÉVENON, J.-A. Érythème pellagroïde chez une éthylique non carencée. Bull. Soc. franç. Derm. Syph. 39: 775, 1932.

GERLACH, W. Alkohol, Kupfer, Leberzirrhose. Schweiz. med. Wschr. 65: 194, 1935.

GIGON, A. and ODERMATT, H. Die Beeinflussung der Hefegärung des Zuckers durch Harnbestandteile und alkoholfreie Organextrakte. Z. ges. exp. Med. 47: 294, 1925.

GOLDBERGER, J., WARING, C. H. and TANNER, W. F. Pellagra prevention by diet among institutional inmates. Publ. Hlth. Rep., Washington 38: 2361, 1923.

GOLDFARB, W., BOWMAN, K. M. and PARKER, S. The treatment of acute alcoholism with glucose and insulin. J. clin. Invest. 18: 581, 1939.

GOLDSMITH, H. Spinal drainage in alcoholic deliria and other acute alcoholic psychoses. Amer. J. Psychiat. 10: 255, 1930.

GOODHART, R. and JOLLIFFE, N. (a) Effects of vitamin B (B₁) therapy on the polyneuritis of alcohol addicts. J. Amer. med. Ass. 110: 414, 1938.

———, ——— (b) The role of nutritional deficiencies in the production of cardiovascular disturbances in the alcohol addict. Amer. Heart J. 15: 569, 1938.

Gouget, A. Insuffisance hépatique et névrite périphérique. Rev. Médecine 17: 537, 1897.

Gounelle, H. Les myocardies de carence B₁, alcoolique, béribérique, etc. Bull. Soc. méd. Hôp. Paris 55: 1048, 1939.

Grover, A. L. Experimental alcoholic cirrhosis of the liver. Arch. intern. Med. 17: 193, 1916.

Gruber, G. B. Pathologie in Mainz. Virchows Arch. 247: 187, 1923.

Guccione, F. Su un caso di degenerazione primaria del corpo calloso tipo Marchiafava. Riv. Patol. nerv. ment. 34: 722, 1929.

Gudden, H. Klinische und anatomische Beiträge zur Kenntnis der multiplen Alkoholneuritis, nebst Bemerkungen über die Regenerationsvorgänge im peripheren Nervensystem. Arch. Psychiat. Nervenkr. 28: 643, 1896.

Gye, W. E. and Purdy, W. J. The poisonous properties of colloidal silicia. Brit. J. exp. Path. 3: 86, 1922.

György, P. and Goldblatt, H. Hepatic injury on nutritional basis in rats. J. exp. Med. 70: 185, 1939.

Hall, E. M. and Butt, E. M. Experimental pigment cirrhosis due to copper poisoning; its relation to hemochromatosis. Arch. Path. 6: 1, 1928.

—— and Morgan, W. A. Progressive alcoholic cirrhosis. Arch. Path. 27: 672, 1939.

Halphen, Salomon and Loiseau. Surdité bilatérale apoplectiforme par névrite et lésion nucléaire chez un tuberculeux pulmonaire. Lyon méd. 154: 706, 1934.

Hanzlik, P. J. Continued drinking of alcohol in low concentrations: some experimental results. J. Pharmacol. 43: 339, 1931.

Harris, L. J. Vitamins and vitamin deficiencies; introductory and historical; vitamin B₁ and beriberi, vol. I. Philadelphia, P. Blakiston's Sons & Co., 1938.

Harrison, T. R. and Pilcher, C. Studies in congestive heart failure; I, The effect of edema on oxygen utilization. J. clin. Invest. 8: 259, 1930.

Heath, C. W. and King, E. F. The Takata-Ara test in the diagnosis of liver disease. New Engl. J. Med. 211: 1077, 1934.

Hein, G. E. and Merrill, J. Pellagra. Calif. West. Med. 30: 334, 1929.

Heller, N. B. Alcoholic pseudo-pellagra; report of cases, with notations on the etiology. J. med. Soc., N.J. 28: 467, 1931.

Himwich, H. E., Spies, T. D., Fazekas, J. F. and Nesin, S. Cerebral carbohydrate metabolism during deficiency of various members of the vitamin B complex. Amer. J. med. Sci. 199: 849, 1940.

Hirt, L. Beitrag zur Pathologie der multiplen Neuritis. Neurol. Zbl. 3: 480, 1884.

Hodges, P. C. and Eyster, J. A. E. Estimation of cardiac area in man. Amer. J. Roentgenol. 12: 252, 1924.

Hoppe, H. Die Tatsachen über den Alkohol. 4th ed. Munich, E. Reinhardt, 1912.

von Hoppe-Seyler, G. Zur Pathogenese der vorübergehenden Glykosurie. Wien. klin. Wschr. 15: 591, 1902.

Huchard, H. Le coeur alcoolique. In: Consultations médicales, vol. II, Maladies du coeur, p. 137. Paris, Baillière et fils, 1910.

Hunt, J. R. A contribution to our knowledge of the polioencephalitis superior (Wernicke type). N.Y. med. J. 83: 289, 1906.

Huss, Magnus. Chronische Alkoholskrankheit, oder Alcoholismus Chronicus. (Translated from the Swedish by Gerhard van dem Busch.) Stockholm, C. E. Fritze, 1852.

Isobe, K. Experimenteller Beitrag zur Entstehung der Lebercirrhose. Mitt. Grenzgeb. Med. Chir. 27: 750, 1914.

Jackson, J. On a peculiar disease resulting from the use of ardent spirits. New Engl. J. Med. 11: 351, 1822.

Jacobäus, H. Über einen Fall von Polioencephalitis haemorrhagica superior (Wernicke). Dtsch. Z. Nervenheilk. 5: 334, 1894.

JADASSOHN, J. Der gegenwärtige Stand der Pellagralehre. In: Handbuch der Haut-und Geschlechtskrankheiten, vol. IV, pt. 2. Berlin, J. Springer, 1933.

JAGIÉ, N. Klinische Beiträge zur Aetiologie und Pathogenese der Lebercirrhosen. Wien. klin. Wschr. **19**: 1058, 1906.

JELLINEK, E. M. and JOLLIFFE, N. Effects of alcohol on the individual: review of the literature of 1939. Quart. J. Stud. Alc. **1**: 110, 1940.

JOFFE, P. M. and JOLLIFFE, N. The gastric acidity in alcohol addicts. Amer. J. med. Sci. **193**: 501, 1937.

JOLLIFFE, N. (a) Discussion of Stevenson, L. D., Allen, A. M. and McGowan, L. E. A study of the brain changes in alcoholism. Trans. Amer. neurol. Ass. **98**: 95, 1939.

—— (b) Effects of vitamin deficiency on mental and emotional processes. Res. Publ. Ass. nerv. ment. Dis. **19**: 144, 1939.

—— (c) The influence of alcohol on the adequacy of the B vitamins in the American diet. Quart. J. Stud. Alc. **1**: 74, 1940.

—— (d) Clinical aspects of vitamin B deficiencies. Minn. Med. **23**: 542, 1940.

—— (e) The neuro-psychiatric manifestations of vitamin deficiencies. J. Mt. Sinai Hosp. **8**: 658, 1942.

——, BOWMAN, K. M., ROSENBLUM, L. A. and FEIN, H. D. Nicotinic acid deficiency encephalopathy. J. Amer. med. Ass. **114**: 307, 1940.

—— and COLBERT, C. N. The etiology of polyneuritis in the alcohol addict. J. Amer. med. Ass. **107**: 642, 1936.

——, —— and JOFFE, P. M. Observations on the etiologic relationship of vitamin B (B_1) to polyneuritis in the alcoholic addict. Amer. J. med. Sci. **191**: 515, 1936.

——, FEIN, H. D. and ROSENBLUM, L. A. Riboflavin deficiency in man. New Engl. J. Med. **221**: 921, 1939.

——, GOODHART, R., GENNIS, J. and CLINE, J. K. The experimental production of vitamin B_1 deficiency in normal subjects; the dependence of the urinary excretion of thiamin on the dietary intake of vitamin B_1. Amer. J. med. Sci. **198**: 198, 1939.

—— and JOFFE, P. M. Relation of vitamin B (B_1) intake to neurological changes in the alcohol addict. Proc. Soc. exp. Biol., N.Y. **32**: 1161, 1935.

—— and ROSENBLUM, L. A. Circulatory manifestations of vitamin deficiency: diagnosis, treatment and prevention. Med. Clin. N. Amer. **23**: 759, 1939.

——, WORTIS, H. and FEIN, H. D. The Wernicke syndrome. J. nerv. ment. Dis. **93**: 214, 1941; Arch. Neurol. Psychiat., Chicago **46**: 569, 1941.

KACHI, G. and MIDORIKAWA, B. Statistische Betrachtung über die atropische Leberzirrhose in Japan; III, Über das Volum der Leber und Milz. Trans. Jap. path. Soc. **15**: 97, 1925.

KAUFMANN, E. Lehrbuch der speziellen pathologischen Anatomie für Studierende und Aerzte. 3d ed. Berlin, G. Reimer, 1904.

KAYSER, O. Beiträge zur Alkoholfrage. Kiel thesis, 1888.

KEEFER, C. S. The beriberi heart. Arch. intern. Med. **45**: 1, 1930.

KENNEDY, J. A. Psychosis with alcoholic pellagra. Med. Bull. Veterans' Adm., Washington **10**: 155, 1933.

KERN, W. Über Leberveränderungen bei chronischem Alkoholismus. Z. Hyg. InfektKr. **73**: 143, 1913.

KIENE, H. E., STREITWEISER, R. and MILLER, H. J. The role of vitamin B_1 in delirium tremens. J. Amer. med. Ass. **114**: 2191, 1940.

KING, L. S. and MEEHAN, M. C. Primary degeneration of the corpus callosum (Marchiafava's disease). Arch. Neurol. Psychiat., Chicago **36**: 547, 1936.

KLAUDER, J. V. and WINKELMAN, N. W. Pellagra among chronic alcoholic addicts (a clinical and laboratory study). J. Amer. med. Ass. **90**: 364, 1928.

KLIENEBERGER, C. Abdominaltyphus und Lebercirrhose. Zbl. inn. Med. **44**: 129, 1923.

KLOSTER, J. B_1-Vitaminbehandlung bei Delirium tremens. Nervenarzt **11**: 413, 1938.

Klotz, P. (a) La polynévrite alcoolique; étude pathogénique et thérapeutique. Paris thesis, 1937.

——— (b) Existe-t-il un traitement pathogénique de la polynévrite alcoolique? Bull. gén. Thér., Paris 188: 249, 1937.

Konstam, G. and Sinclair, H. M. Cardiovascular disturbances caused by deficiency of vitamin B₁. Brit. Heart J. 2: 231, 1940.

Koogerdal, E. L'action de l'alcool sur les vaisseaux du cerveau. Arch. int. Neurol. 46: 10, 1927.

Kopf, E. W. Review of recent literature on alcohol as a community health problem. In: Alcohol and man (Emerson, H., ed.), p. 396. New York, The Macmillan Co., 1933.

Környey, K. Wernicke-Korsakow-Process als Komplikation bösartiger extraneuraler Geschwühle. Dtsch. Z. Nervenkr. 144: 241, 1937.

Korsakoff, S. S. Über eine besondere Form psychischer Störung combiniert mit multipler Neuritis. Arch. Psychiat. Nervenkr. 21: 669, 1890.

Kraus, E. J. (a) Über Leberverfettung bei zerstörenden Prozessen im Hypophysen-zwischenhirnsystem und bei Morbus Cushing. Frankfurt. Z. Path. 50: 429, 1937.

——— (b) Chronischer Hirndruck und Leberverfettung. Virchows Arch. 300: 617, 1937.

Kryle, J. and Schopper, K. J. Untersuchungen über den Einfluss des Alkohols auf Leber und Hoden des Kaninchen. Virchows Arch. 215: 309, 1914.

Laënnec, R. T. H. Traité de l'auscultation médiate, et des maladies des poumons et du coeur, vol. II, 4th ed. Paris, J. S. Chaudé, 1857.

Lafont. Contribution à l'étude de l'alcoolisme chez les adults dans les hôpitaux de Paris. Paris thesis, 1908.

Laffitte, A. and Leblanc, A. L'Alcoolisme; Nouveau traité de pathologie interne. Paris, Doin, 1928.

Laignel-Lavastine, Troisier, J. and Boquien, Y. Association de la cirrhose du foie à une dépilation plus ou moins complète et à une insuffisance thyro-ovarienne. Bull. Soc. méd. Hôp. Paris 47: 829, 1931.

Lanceraux. Études sur les altérations produites par l'abus des boissons alcooliques. Gaz. hebd. Méd. Chir. 2: 435, 1865.

Langeron, L. Avitaminose B₁ et insuffisance cardiaque. Pr. méd. 47: 1189, 1939.

Langworthy, O. R. Lesions of the central nervous system characteristic of pellagra. Brain 54: 291, 1931.

Lee, J. and Sure, B. Avitaminosis; XIX, Nerve degeneration in albino rats as studied by the freezing-drying method and polarized light with deficiency of vitamin A or of vitamin B. Arch. Path. 24: 430, 1937.

Lemierre, A., Boltanski, E. and Justin-Besançon, L. Les polynévrites alcoolo-tuberculeuses. Bull. Acad. Méd. Paris 105: 676, 1931.

Leschke, E. Fortschritte in der Erkennung und Behandlung der wichtigsten Ver-giftungen; chronische Alkoholvergiftung. Münch. med. Wschr. 79: 917, 1932.

Lettsom, J. C. Some remarks on the effect of lignum quassiae amarae. Mem. med. Soc. Lond. 1: 128, 1787.

Levy, W., Greenstein, N. M. and Leighton, B. Portal cirrhosis in childhood. J. Pediat. 15: 91, 1939.

Leyden, E. Ein Fall von multipler Neuritis. Charité-Ann. 7: 267, 1880.

Lhermitte, J., Ajuriaguerra and Garnier. Les lésions du système nerveux dans l'intoxication alcoolique expérimentale. C. R. Soc. Biol., Paris 128: 386, 1938.

Lilienfeld. Zur Lehre von der multiplen Neuritis. Berl. klin. Wschr. 22: 727, 1885.

Lissauer, M. Experimentelle Leberzirrhose nach chronischer Alkoholvergiftung. Dtsch. med. Wschr. 39: 18, 1913.

Loeb, W. A. Alcoholism and its effect upon body systems. Med. Bull. Veterans' Adm., Washington 16: 258, 1940.

Löwenfeld, L. Ein Fall multipler Neuritis mit Athetosis. Neurol. Zbl. 4: 169, 1885.

Lubarsch. Über Pathogenese und Aetiologie der Lebercirrhose. Dtsch. med. Wschr. 33: 1029, 1907.

McCarrison, R. Beriberi columbarum. Indian J. med. Res. (Memoir No. 10), p. 146, 1928.

McGee, A. J. Vitamin B₁ in alcoholic polyneuritis. Illinois med. J. 75: 470, 1939.

MacNider, W. de B. and Donnelly, G. L. Relationship between liver injury induced by alcohol and elimination of phenolsulphonephthalein. Proc. Soc. exp. Biol., N.Y. 29: 586, 1932.

Madden, A. B. Vitamin B₁ in peripheral neuritis. Med. Bull. Veterans' Adm., Washington 16: 16, 1939.

Madsen, J. Rapport du liquide céphalo-rachidien dans les polynévrites. Acta psychiat., Copenhagen 10: 357, 1935.

Mainzer, F. and Krause, M. Nicotinic acid in the treatment of delirium tremens. Brit. med. J. 2: 331, 1939.

Mallory, F. B. (a) Cirrhosis of the liver; five different types of lesions from which it may arise. Johns Hopk. Hosp. Bull. 22: 69, 1911.

—— (b) Cirrhosis of the liver. New Engl. J. Med. 206: 1231, 1932.

—— (c) Phosphorus and alcoholic cirrhosis. Amer. J. Path. 9: 557, 1933.

——, Parker, F., Jr. and Nye, R. N. Experimental pigment cirrhosis due to copper and its relation to hemochromatosis. J. med. Res. 42: 461, 1921.

Maloney, E. R. and Tulipan, L. Alcoholic pseudo-pellagra. N.Y. St. J. Med. 29: 1063, 1929.

Maranon, Richet, C., Pergola, A. and Lesueur, J. Cirrhoses et carences alimentaires. Rev. méd.-chir. Mal. Foie 14: 5, 1939.

Marchiafava, E. Degeneration of the brain in chronic alcoholism. Proc. R. Soc. Med. 26: 1151, 1933.

—— and Bignami, A. Sopra un'alterazione del corpo calloso osservata in soggetti alcoolisti. Riv. Patol. nerv. ment. 8: 544, 1903.

——, —— and Nazari, A. Ueber System-Degeneration der Kommissurbahnen des Gehirns bei chronischem Alkoholismus. Mschr. Psychiat. Neurol. 29: 181, 315, 1911.

Mariconda, P. Contributo alla conoscenza della malattia del Marchiafava (degenerazione del corpo calloso). Policlinico (sez Prat.) 30: 860, 1923.

Markovitz, G. Leberfunktionsprüfungen mit Iodtetragnost bei Alkoholisten. Mschr. Psychiat. Neurol. 86: 101, 1933.

May, A. M. The use of nicotinic acid in vitamin deficiency psychoses associated with alcoholism. Med. Rec., N.Y. 150: 124, 162, 1939.

Meiklejohn, A. P. Is thiamin the antineuritic vitamin? New Engl. J. Med. 223: 265, 1940.

Mellanby, E. Lesions of the central and peripheral nervous systems produced in young rabbits by vitamin A deficiency and a high cereal intake. Brain 58: 141, 1935.

Merle, E. and Larpent. Béri-béri cardiaque alcoolique. Bull. Soc. méd. Hôp. Paris 55: 1098, 1939.

Meyer, A. (a) On parenchymatous systemic degenerations mainly in the central nervous system. Brain 24: 47, 1901.

—— (b) Ueber das Vorkommen von A-Avitaminosen unter den hiesigen Lebensbedingungen. Schweiz. med. Wschr. 13: 1243, 1932.

—— (c) Alcohol as a psychiatric problem. In: Alcohol and man (Emerson, H., ed.), p. 273. New York, The Macmillan Co., 1933.

MILLS, S. R. Alcoholism and pellagra. Nav. med. Bull., Washington 32: 493, 1934.

MINGAZZINI, G. (a) Lezioni di anatomia clinica dei centri nervosi. Turin, Unione Tipografico-Editrice, 1918.

—— (b) Der Balken. Berlin, J. Springer, 1922.

MINOT, G. R. Some fundamental clinical aspects of deficiencies. Ann. intern. Med. 3: 216, 1929.

——, STRAUSS, M. B. and COBB, S. "Alcoholic" polyneuritis; dietary deficiency as a factor in its production. New Engl. J. Med. 208: 1244, 1933.

MIRSKY, A. and NELSON, N. (a) The role of the liver in ethyl alcohol oxidation. Amer. J. Physiol. 126: 587, 1939.

——, —— (b) The influence of the pancreas and the liver on the oxidation of ethyl alcohol. Amer. J. Physiol. 127: 308, 1939.

MÖNCKEBERG, J. G. Zur Genese des "Tübinger Herzens." Zbl. Herz.-Gefässkr. 12: 247, 1920.

DE MONTMOLIN, R. À propos de l'urobilinurie chez les alcooliques. Schweiz. med. Wschr. 19: 1165, 1938.

MOON, V. H. (a) Experimental cirrhosis in relation to human cirrhosis. Arch. Path. 18: 381, 1934.

—— (b) Experimentelle Lebercirrhose und ihre Beziehungen zur Aetiologie der menschlichen Cirrhose. Klin. Wschr. 13: 1489, 1521, 1934.

MOORE, M. The treatment of alcoholism. New Engl. J. Med. 221: 489, 1939.

MOTT, F. W. Discussion on alcohol and insanity. Brit. med. J. 1: 1380, 1911.

MUELLER, C. W. Zwei Fälle von Trigeminus-Lähmung. Arch. Psychiat. Nervenkr. 14: 263, 513, 1883.

MÜNZINGER, W. Das Tübinger Herz. Dtsch. Arch. klin. Med. 19: 449, 1877.

NAUNYN, [B]. Lebercirrhose. Verh. dtsch. path. Ges. 8: 59, 1904.

NEUBÜRGER, K. (a) Über Hirnveränderungen nach Alkoholmissbrauch (unter Berück-sichtigung einiger Fälle von Wernickescher Krankheit mit anderer Aetiologie). Z. ges. Neurol. Psychiat. 135: 159, 1931.

—— (b) Über die nichtalkoholische Wernickesche Krankheit, insbesondere über ihr Vorkommen beim Krebsleiden. Virchows Arch. 298: 68, 1936.

—— (c) Wernickesche Krankheit bei chronischer Gastritis; ein Beitrag zu den Beziehungen zwischen Magen und Gehirn. Z. ges. Neurol. Psychiat. 160: 208, 1937.

NONNENBRUCH, W. Die Therapie der Lebercirrhose. Med. Welt 13: 691, 1939.

O'CONNELL, D. J., McLEMAN, J. and STERN, R. O. Cranial nerve palsies as a mani-festation of peripheral neuritis in alcoholic insanity. J. ment. Sci. 80: 103, 1934.

OETTINGER. Étude sur les paralisies alcooliques. Paris, Le Mans, 1885.

OGATA, S. Studies on cirrhosis of the liver following intraportal injection of toxic substances. J. med. Res. 40: 103, 1919.

OKHUMA, T. Zur pathologischen Anatomie des chronischen Alkoholismus. Z. ges. Neurol. Psychiat. 126: 94, 1930.

OPHÜLS, W. (a) Occurrence of spontaneous lesions in kidneys and livers of rabbits and guinea pigs. Proc. Soc. exp. Biol., N.Y. 8: 75, 1910.

—— (b) A statistical survey of three thousand autopsies from the department of pathology of the Stanford University Medical School. Stanford Univ. Publ. med. Sci. 1: 127, 1926.

OPPENHEIM. Beiträge zur Pathologie der "multiplen Neuritis" und Alkohol-Lähmung. Z. klin. Med. 11: 232, 1886.

ORTON, S. T. and BENDER, L. Lesions in lateral horns of the spinal cord in acrodynia, pellagra and pernicious anemia. Bull. neurol. Inst. N.Y. 1: 506, 1931.

PAGNIEZ, P. Anorexie mentale et hypophyse. Pr. méd. 47: 668, 1939.

PAPPENHEIMER, A. M. and GOETTSCH, M. A cerebellar disorder in chicks, apparently of nutritional origin. J. exp. Med. **53**: 11, 1931.

PARAF, J. and KLOTZ, H. P. Fréquence actuelle plus grande des manifestations alcooliques chez la femme que chez l'homme. Bull. Soc. méd. Hôp. Paris **49**: 1373, 1933.

PATEK, A. J., JR. Treatment of alcoholic cirrhosis of the liver with high vitamin therapy. Proc. Soc. exp. Biol., N.Y. **37**: 329, 1937.

—— and HAIG, C. The occurrence of abnormal dark adaptation and its relation to vitamin A metabolism in patients with cirrhosis of the liver. J. clin. Invest. **18**: 609, 1939.

PEARSON, G. H. J. Central neuritis; its etiology and symptomatology. Arch. Neurol. Psychiat., Chicago **20**: 366, 1928.

PERKINS, O. C. Dietary deficiencies as the etiological factor in certain neurological syndromes. J. nerv. ment. Dis. **83**: 505, 1936.

PETERS, R. A. The biochemical lesion in vitamin B_1 deficiency. Lancet **230**: 1161, 1936.

PHILLIPS, P. H. and ENGEL, R. W. The histopathology of neuromalacia and "curled toe" paralysis in the chick fed low riboflavin diets. J. Nutrit. **16**: 451, 1938.

PIERSON, R. H. Über Polyneuritis acuta. Samml. klin. Vortr., No. 229, p. 2083, 1883.

PITRES, J. A. and VAILLARD, L. Maladies des nerfs périphériques. Paris, Baillière et fils, 1924.

PLATT, B. S. and LU, G. D. Chemical and clinical findings in beriberi with special reference to vitamin B_1 deficiency. Quart. J. Med. **5**: 355, 1936.

PLOUCQUET, W. G. Warnung an das Publikum für einem in manchen Branntweinen enthaltenen Gift samt den Mitteln es zu entdeken und auszuscheiden. Tübingen, J. F. Heerbrandt, 1780.

POLLOCK, H. M. A statistical study of 1,739 patients with alcoholic psychoses. Bull. N.Y. St. Hosps. **7**: 204, 1914.

PRICE, N. L. "Alcoholic" beriberi. Lancet **234**: 831, 1938.

PRICKETT, C. O. The effect of a deficiency of vitamin B_1 upon the central and peripheral nervous systems of the rat. Amer. J. Physiol. **107**: 458, 1934.

——, SALMON, W. D. and SCHRADER, G. A. Histopathology of the peripheral nerves in acute and chronic vitamin B_1 deficiency in the rat. Amer. J. Path. **15**: 251, 1939.

RADHAKRISHNA RAO, M. V. An investigation into decompensated portal cirrhosis. Indian J. med. Res. **21**: 389, 1933.

REMAK, B. Drei Fälle von Tabes im Kindesalter. Neurol. Zbl. **4**: 373, 1885.

RICHET, C. Carences alimentaires et pathologie interne. Pr. méd. **46**: 1777, 1939.

RICHTER, C. P. A study of the effect of moderate doses of alcohol on the growth and behavior of the rat. J. exp. Zoöl. **44**: 397, 1926.

ROBERSON, R. S. Cerebral edema in chronic alcoholism (alcoholic wet brain). Sth. Med. Surg. **94**: 584, 1932.

ROGER, H., PAILLAS, J. and LAVAL, P. Polioencéphalite de Wernicke avec délire hallucinatoire d'origine éthylique. Ann. méd.-psychol. **95**: 694, 1937.

ROMANO, J. Deficiency syndromes associated with chronic alcoholism. Amer. J. med. Sci. **194**: 645, 1937.

RONCORONI, C. Sindromi pellagroidi in casi cronici di colite dissenteriforme e di gastrite etilica. G. Clin. med. **19**: 761, 1938.

ROSENBAUM, M., PIKER, P. and LEDERER, H. Delirium tremens; a study of various methods of treatment. Amer. J. med. Sci. **200**: 677, 1940.

ROSENHEIM, T. Zur Kenntniss der acuten infectiösen multiplen Neuritis. Arch. Psychiat. Nervenkr. **18**: 782, 1887.

ROSSI, O. Sull'istologia patologica di una speciale alterazione descritta da Marchiafava nel corpo calloso degli alcoolisti. Riv. Patol. nerv. ment. **15**: 346, 1910.

RÖSSLE, R. Entzündungen der Leber; die experimentelle Leberzirrhose. In: Handbuch der speziellen pathologischen Anatomie und Histologie (Henke, F. and Lubarsch, O., ed.), vol. V, pt. 1, p. 243. Berlin, J. Springer, 1930.

ROTH, M. Neuritis disseminata acutissima. KorrespBl. schweiz. Ärz. 13: 317, 1883.

ROWNTREE, L. G. Discussion of Boles, R. S. and Clark, J. H. The role of alcohol in cirrhosis of the liver; a clinical and pathologic study based on 4,000 autopsies. J. Amer. med. Ass. 107: 1203, 1936.

RUTLEDGE, W. U. Pellagra in chronic alcoholics. Kentucky med. J. 29: 294, 1931.

SALTYKOW, S. Beitrag zur Kenntnis der durch Alkohol hervorgerufenen Organverän-derungen. Verh. dtsch. path. Ges. 14: 228, 1910.

SANTESSON, C. G. [Treatment of delirium tremens with vitamin B.] Svenska Läkar-tidn. 36: 926, 1939.

SCAGLIOSI, G. Die Rolle des Alkohols und der acuten Infectionskrankheiten in der Entstehung der interstitiellen Hepatitis. Virchows Arch. 145: 546, 1896.

SCHAFIR, M. Zur Lehre von der alkoholischen Leberzirrhose. Virchows Arch. 213: 41, 1913.

SCHLOSS, G. Pathologisch-anatomische Befunde als Alkoholschädigung am Sektions-material der kantonalen Krankenanstalt Lüzern in den Jahren 1919–1939. Ge-sundh. u. Wohlfahrt 20: 60, 1940.

SCHULZ, R. Beitrag zur Lehre von der multiplen Neuritis bei Potatoren. Neurol. Zbl. 4: 433, 1885.

SEBRELL, W. H. and ELVOVE, E. Observations on the assay of the antineuritic vita-min. Publ. Hlth. Rep., Washington 46: 917, 1931.

SEYMOUR, S. L. Fibro-fatty liver. Med. J. Aust. 1: 388, 1938.

SHATTUCK, G. C. The relation of beri-beri to polyneuritis from other causes. Amer. J. trop. Med. 8: 539, 1928.

SHERMAN, H. C. Chemistry of Food and Nutrition. New York, The Macmillan Co., 1924.

SILBERMAN, M. K. Pseudo-pellagra or post-alcoholic dermatitis. J. Amer. Inst. Homoeop. 24: 235, 1931.

SINGER, H. D. and POLLOCK, L. J. The histopathology of the nervous system in pellagra. Arch. intern. Med. 11: 565, 1913.

SMETANA, H. Coccidiosis of the liver in rabbits. Arch. Path. 15: 175, 330, 516, 1933.

SMITH, D. T., RUFFIN, J. M. and SMITH, S. G. Pellagra successfully treated with nicotinic acid; a case report. J. Amer. med. Ass. 109: 2054, 1937.

SMITH, W. H. and HELWIG, F. C. Liquor: the servant of man. Boston, Little, Brown & Co., 1939.

DE SOLDATI, L. Los Trastornos Circulatorios de la Avitaminosis B₁. Buenos Aires, El Ateneo, 1940.

SPEARMAN, M. and SMITH, L. M. Alcoholic pellagra. Sthwest. Med. 20: 9, 1936.

SPIES, T. D. (a) Observations on the relationship of alcoholic pellagra to endemic pellagra. J. Med., Cleveland, O. 17: 130, 1936.

——— (b) Discussion of Goodhart, R. and Jolliffe, N. Effects of vitamin B (B₁) therapy on the polyneuritis of alcohol addicts. J. Amer. med. Ass. 110: 419, 1938.

———, ARING, C. D., GELPERIN, J. and BEAN, W. B. Mental symptoms of pellagra; their relief with nicotinic acid. Amer. J. med. Sci. 196: 461, 1938.

——— and CHINN, A. B. Studies on the anemia of pellagra. J. clin. Invest. 14: 941, 1935.

———, COOPER, C. and BLANKENHORN, M. A. The use of nicotinic acid in the treat-ment of pellagra. J. Amer. med. Ass. 110: 622, 1938.

——— and DE WOLF, H. F. Observations on the etiological relationship of severe alcoholism to pellagra. Amer. J. med. Sci. 186: 521, 1933.

――――, Gross, E. S. and Sasaki, Y. Effect of yeast and nicotinic acid on porphy-rinuria. Proc. Soc. exp. Biol., N.Y. **38**: 178, 1938.

Stanquitz-Cambilargiu, M. Degenerazione delle vie commissurali dell'encefalo nei cani alcoolizzati. Arch. Fisiol. **23**: 318, 1925.

Steegmann, A. T. The symptomatology and treatment of alcoholic peripheral poly-neuritis. Physio-ther. Rev. **11**: 2, 1931.

Stepp, W. and Schroeder, H. Beriberierkrankung beim Menschen hervorgerufen durch übermässigen Zuckergenuss. Münch. med. Wschr. **83**: 763, 1936.

―――― and Voit, K. Pellagra. Neue dtsch. Klin. **11**: (Ergänz. Bd. 1) 97, 1933.

Stevenson, L. D. A study of the changes in the brain in alcoholism. Arch. Path. **30**: 642, 1940.

――――, Allen, A. M. and McGowan, L. E. A study of the brain changes in alco-holism. Trans. Amer. neurol. Ass. **65**: 93, 1939.

Stewart, T. G. On paralysis of hands and feet from disease of nerves. Edinb. med. J. **26**: 865, 1881.

Stiebeling, H. F. and Phipard, E. F. Diets of families of employed wage earners and clerical workers in cities. U.S. Dept. Agric., Circ. No. 5. Washington, 1939.

Strauss, M. B. (*a*) The role of the gastro-intestinal tract in conditioning deficiency disease. J. Amer. med. Ass. **103**: 1, 1934.

―――― (*b*) The etiology of "alcoholic" polyneuritis. Amer. J. med. Sci. **189**: 378, 1935.

Strümpell, A. Zur Kenntniss der multiplen degenerativen Neuritis. Arch. Psychiat. Nervenkr. **14**: 339, 1883.

Swank, R. L. Avian thiamin deficiency. J. exp. Med. **71**: 683, 1940.

―――― and Bessey, O. A. Avian vitamin B₁ deficiency; characteristic symptoms and their pathogenesis. J. Nutrit. **22**: 77, 1941.

Sydenstricker, V. P. and Cleckley, H. M. Effect of nicotinic acid in stupor, lethargy and various other psychiatric disorders. Amer. J. Psychiat. **98**: 83, 1941.

――――, Sebrell, W. H., Cleckley, H. M. and Kruse, H. D. Ocular manifestations of ariboflavinosis; progress note. J. Amer. med. Ass. **114**: 2437, 1940.

Tanaka, T. So-called breast milk intoxication. Amer. J. Dis. Child. **47**: 1286, 1934.

Testa, U. Lesioni del corpo calloso nell'alcoolismo subacuto sperimentale. Riv. sper. Freniat. **52**: 559, 1929.

Thieri. Recueil périodique d'observations de médecine de chirurgie et de pharmacie. J. Méd. Chir. Pharm. **2**: 337, 1755.

Thompson, R. H. S. The action of crystalline vitamin B₁ on the respiration of poly-neuritis tissues *in vitro*. Bio-chem. J. **28**: 909, 1934.

Tirumurti, T. S. and Radhakrishna Rao, M. V. The incidence of portal cirrhosis of the liver in Vizagapatam, based on a critical study of autopsy records and observa-tion. Indian med. Gaz. **69**: 74, 1934.

Toulouse, E., Courtois, A. and Russell. Modifications chimique du sang au cours du delirium tremens alcoolique. Ann. méd.-psychol. **89**: 124, 1931.

Truche, C. Les modifications biologiques du sang, des urines et du liquide céphalo-rachidien dans l'alcoolisme aigu et chronique. Paris thesis, 1933.

Vacquez, H. Myocardite alcoolique subaiguë; maladies du coeur. Paris, Baillère et fils, 1921.

Van der Schueren, G. Essai de production expérimentale de cirrhose à l'aide de divers agents. C. R. Soc. Biol., Paris **109**: 982, 1932.

Vedder, E. B. (*a*) Beriberi. New York, Wm. Wood & Co., 1913.

―――― (*b*) The pathology of beriberi. J. Amer. med. Ass. **110**: 893, 1938.

―――― and Clark, E. A study of polyneuritis gallinarum; a fifth contribution to the etiology of beriberi. Philipp. J. Sci. **7**: 423, 1912.

VIERORDT, O. Beitrag zum Studium der multiplen degenerativen Neuritis. Arch. Psychiat. Nervenkr. **14**: 678, 1883.

VILLARET, M., JUSTIN-BESANÇON, L. and KLOTZ, H. P. (*a*) Fréquence des alterations endocriniennes dans l'alcoolisme chronique; pathogénie de ces accidents et des manifestations névritiques. Sem. Hôp. Paris **11**: 451, 1935.

——, ——, —— (*b*) Le foie dans la polynévrite alcoolique. Bull. Soc. méd. Hôp. Paris **52**: 1159, 1936.

——, ——, —— and SIKORAV. Pellagre chez un alcoolique révélée par un essai d'héliothérapie d'une polynévrite. Bull. Soc. méd. Hôp. Paris **55**: 367, 1939.

——, MOUTIER, F., JUSTIN-BESANÇON, L. and KLOTZ, H. P. Caractère spécial des troubles gastriques (ana- ou hypochlorhydrie) au cours de la polynévrite alcoolique. Bull. Soc. méd. Hôp. Paris **52**: 1155, 1936.

VIX, W. Beitrag zur Kenntnis der Leberzirrhose im Kindesalter. Virchows Arch. **19**: 266, 1908.

VONDERAHE, A. R. Sequelae of severe disease of the abdominal viscera. J. Amer. med. Ass. **116**: 390, 1941.

WAGENER, H. P. and WEIR, J. F. Ocular lesions associated with postoperative and gestational nutritional deficiency. Amer. J. Ophthal. **20**: 253, 1937.

WARNER, F. J. The brain changes in chronic alcoholism and Korsakow's psychosis. J. nerv. ment. Dis. **80**: 629, 1934.

WATSON, C. J. The urinary pigments in four cases of alcoholic pellagra. Proc. Soc. exp. Biol., N.Y. **39**: 514, 1938.

WAYBURN, E. and GUERARD, C. R. Relation between multiple peripheral neuropathy and cirrhosis of the liver. Arch. intern. Med. **66**: 161, 1940.

WEBBER, S. G. Multiple neuritis. Arch. Med. **12**: 33, 1885.

WEBER, R. Zur Pathologie der Leberzirrhose. Breslau thesis, 1884.

WECHSLER, I. S. (*a*) Unrecognized cases of deficiency polyneuritis (avitaminosis?). Med. J. Rec. **131**: 441, 1930.

—— (*b*) Etiology of polyneuritis. Arch. Neurol. Psychiat., Chicago **29**: 813, 1933.

—— (*c*) A textbook of neurology. 3d ed. Philadelphia, W. B. Saunders & Co., 1935.

—— (*d*) Multiple peripheral neuropathy versus multiple neuritis. J. Amer. med. Ass. **110**: 1910, 1938.

——, JERVIS, G. A. and POTTS, H. D. Experimental study of alcoholism and vitamin B deficiency in monkeys. Bull. neurol. Inst. N.Y. **5**: 453, 1936.

WEEKS, C. C. Alcohol and human life. 2d ed. London, H. K. Lewis, 1938.

WEGELIN, C. Schrumpfniere und Alkoholismus. Schweiz. med. Wschr. **49**: 1181, 1935.

WEISS, S. Occidental beriberi with cardiovascular manifestations. J. Amer. med. Ass. **115**: 832, 1940.

——, HAYNES, F. W. and ZOLL, P. M. Electrocardiographic manifestations and the cardiac effect of drugs in vitamin B₁ deficiency in rats. Amer. Heart J. **15**: 206, 1938.

—— and WILKINS, R. W. Disturbance of the cardiovascular system in nutritional deficiency. J. Amer. med. Ass. **109**: 786, 1937.

WENCKEBACH, K. F. (*a*) Heart and circulation in a tropical avitaminosis (beriberi). Lancet **215**: 265, 1928.

—— (*b*) Das Beriberi Herz. Berlin, J. Springer, 1931.

WERNICKE, C. Lehrbuch der Gehirnkrankheiten fur Ärzte und Studierende. Leipzig, G. Thieme, 1881.

WEXBERG, E. Some remarks on the treatment of alcoholism. Sth. med. J., Birmingham **30**: 842, 1937.

WHITE, W. H. On some misconceptions with regard to diseases of the liver. Brit. med. J. **1**: 533, 1903.

WICHELS and BRINCK. Beiträge zur Pathogenese der Gastritis; III, Lebergifte und Gastritis. Z. klin. Med. **123**: 319, 1933.

WILKS, S. Alcoholic paraplegia. Lancet **102**: 320, 1872.

WILLIAMS, R. D., MASON, H. L., WILDER, R. M. and SMITH, B. F. Observations on induced thiamine (vitamin B_1) deficiency. Arch. intern. Med. **66**: 785, 1940.

WILLIAMS, R. R. and SPIES, T. D. Vitamin B_1 and its use in medicine. New York, The Macmillan Co., 1938.

WILSON, G. B. Alcohol and the nation. London, Nicholson & Watson, 1940.

WLASSAK, R. Grundriss der Alkoholfrage. Leipzig, S. Hirzel, 1929.

WOHL, M. G. and FELDMAN, J. B. Vitamin A deficiency in diseases of the liver: its detection by dark-adaptation method. J. Lab. clin. Med. **25**: 485, 1940.

WOLBACH, S. B. The pathologic changes resulting from vitamin deficiency. J. Amer. med. Ass. **108**: 7, 1937.

WOOLLARD, H. H. The nature of the structural changes in nerve endings in starvation and in beriberi. J. Anat., London **61**: 283, 1927.

WORTIS, H. (*a*) Vitamins in nervous health and disease. N.Y. St. J. Med. **39**: 1178, 1939.

———— (*b*) Delirium tremens. Quart. J. Stud. Alc. **1**: 251, 1940.

————, BUEDING, E., STEIN, M. H. and JOLLIFFE, N. Pyruvic acid studies in the Wernicke syndrome. Arch. neurol. psychiat. **47**: 215, 1942.

———— and JOLLIFFE, N. Present status of vitamins in nervous health and disease. N.Y. St. J. Med. **41**: 1461, 1941.

YAMAGIWA, J. Beiträge zur Kenntnis der Kakke (Beriberi). Virchows Arch. **156**: 451, 1899.

YENIKOMSHIAN, H. A. Nonalcoholic cirrhosis of the liver in the Lebanon and Syria. J. Amer. med. Ass. **103**: 660, 1934.

ZIMMERMAN, H. M. The pathology of the nervous system in vitamin deficiencies. Yale J. Biol. Med. **12**: 23, 1939.

————, COHEN, L. H. and GILDEA, E. F. Pellagra in association with chronic alcoholism. Arch. Neurol. Psychiat., Chicago **31**: 290, 1934.

———— and COWGILL, G. R. Lesions of the nervous system in vitamin deficiency; IV, The effect of carotene in the treatment of the nervous disorder in rats fed a diet low in vitamin A. J. Nutrit. **11**: 411, 1936.

————, ———— and Fox, J. C., JR. Neurologic manifestations in vitamin G (B_2) deficiency. Arch. Neurol. Psychiat., Chicago **37**: 286, 1937.

SUBJECT INDEX

ABNORMAL drinkers, 10, 12
Abnormal drinking, xvi; definition, 9
Absinthe in alcoholic mental disorders, 110–111
Abstinence, total, goal in treatment, 55
Abstinence delirium, 111–112
Acetonuria, 105, 107, 132
Achlorhydria, 197
Acidosis, 117
Acute alcoholic hallucinosis (see Hallucinosis)
Acute alcoholic intoxication (see Intoxication)
Addicts, 10, 12, 14–15 (see also Alcohol addiction; Drinker types); case histories, 17; classification of, 18; epileptic, 41; neurotic, 30, 43; parents, relation to, 23–24, 30; personality of, 10; potential, 9; secondary, 9, 25, 38, 43; true, definition, 38; unitary personality of, 17
Adrenalin reaction in "wet" beriberi, 223–224
Age:
  in acute alcoholic hallucinosis, 138–139, 143; in alcoholic paranoid conditions, 144; of drinking population, 180; in Korsakoff's psychosis, 135; in Marchiafava's disease, 264; in pathological intoxication, 92
Agraphia, 128
Albumin, blood, 106–107
Albuminuria, 105–106, 132
Alcohol:
  amount consumed, as criterion, 5; caloric value, 180; concentration in blood, 89, 91; as condiment, 11; consumption of, United States, 180; effect on society, xvi; function of, 11–14; and genius, 12; habit-forming drug, 28; immediate effect of, xvi, xxii, 3; and literary creation, 11
    literature on, xiii–xiv; coverage of, xvii
  and nutrition, 174–181; pseudo-stimulant, 11; taste threshold of, 15; tolerance (see Tolerance, alcohol)
Alcohol addiction: (see also Addicts)
  allergic theory, 15; criteria, 5–7, 9;

definitions, 7–10; differentiation from chronic alcoholism, 5, 10; differentiation from other drug addictions, 27–28; and economic depression, 40, 47
  etiologic factors, xvi, 10–49; constitution, 10; cultural theory, 49; environment, 10; heredity, 10, 20; living conditions, 47; occupation, 10; personality, 10; physiologic processes, 10, 14; psychopathy, 10; social mores, 10; tolerance, 10
  form of suicide, 31–32; as mass phenomenon, 39–40, 47, 50; medical nature of problem, 50; as poverty disease, fallacies of, 47–48; secondary, 14; social factors in, xvi, 46–48; as symptom of mental disease, 82–83; treatment, xvi, 49–80 (see Treatment of alcohol addiction)
Alcohol problem:
  addiction, central position in, 3; industrial problems, xxi; knowledge of, xx; medical issue, xi; obscuring factors, xx; social issue, xi
Alcoholic beverages, kinds, related to:
  acute alcoholic hallucinosis, 140; acute alcoholic intoxication, 91; circulatory disturbances, 228; delirium tremens, 110–111; Korsakoff's psychosis, 135; pellagra, 240; polyneuropathy, 199
Alcoholic paranoid condition (see Paranoid condition, alcoholic)
Alcoholic pellagra (see Pellagra)
Alcoholic personality, 17
Alcoholics Anonymous, 62–65
Alcoholism, term not used in present work, 7
Allergy, 15
Amblyopia, 236
Anasarca, 221, 230
Anemia, 215, 236–237
Angina, 225
Anorexia, 93, 189, 191, 195, 197, 201, 213, 239
Anxiety, 11, 93, 98–99, 138
Aphasia, 128
Apomorphine, 58
Aqueduct of Sylvius, 256
Arteriolar dilatation, 222

Associative functions, 130–131
Ataxia, 89, 241–242, 264
Axis cylinders, 184–186, 211, 270

BARBITURATES, 71
Beer, 11; role in alcoholic mental disorders, 111, 135, 140; role in circulatory disturbances, 228; role in polyneuropathy, 199
Beer heart, 229
Benzedrine, 59, 126, 137
Beriberi, 176–178, 181, 186, 194, 199, 201
    "alcoholic," 220; etiologic theories, 228–232; pathology, 227–228; use of term, 220
    "cardiac" type, 221–222, 231–232; cause of death in, 222; diagnosis, 221–222
    clinical picture, 191–193; clinical types, 221; "dry," 221; early discription of pathology, 183; experimental, 251; "mixed" type, 221
    "wet," 221; adrenalin reaction, 223–224; liver condition, 225; thiamin content of blood, 225; treatment, 224
Bierherz, 220
Bile pigments, 105–106
Biochemical changes:
    in acute alcoholic intoxication, 107; in delirium tremens, 104–107, 114; in Korsakoff's psychosis, 132–133; in polyneuropathy, 197–198
"Biochemical lesion," 260
Blood, constituents of (*see under specific constituents*)
Blood picture:
    in chronic alcoholics, 110; in delirium tremens, 110
Blood pressure, 90, 104, 222–224; diastolic, 225; systolic, 224–226; venous, 224
Blood velocity, 221–222, 225–226
Brachium conjunctivum, 242
Bradycardia, 224
Brain changes:
    in beriberi, 186; in chronic alcoholism, 258; in delirium tremens, 108–110; in Korsakoff's psychosis, 133–134; in Marchiafava's disease, 265–271; in nicotinic acid deficiency encephalopathy, 255–260; in pellagra, 237–238
    in Wernicke's syndrome, 242–244; statistics of, 245

Brain chemistry, 118
Brain injuries:
    in dipsomania, 151; and pathological intoxication, 96
Brain metabolism, 230, 249, 260
Brain stem, 109
Bromides, 71

CALCIUM, blood, 106
Calories:
    in alcoholic beverages, per capita, 180; in diet of wage earners, 181; thiamin, relation to, 174–177
Carbohydrate metabolism:
    in chronic alcoholism, 182; in delirium tremens, 116–117, 120; in experimental B-complex deficiency, 213; in liver cirrhosis, 308; role of thiamin, 231
Cardiac plexus, 186
Carnegie Corporation, xiii
Carotid sinus reflex, 222
Castration fear, 30, 139
Cellular paresis, 15
Cerebellum, 109
Cerebrine, 57
Child labor, 47
Cholesterol, 106
Chronic alcoholic deterioration, 145–147
Chronic alcoholic psychosis, 86
Chronic alcoholics, not homogeneous, 22; psychologic characteristics of, 22–24
Chronic alcoholism, 5, 22–23, 51, 60, 86, 127, 182, 226, 228, 274, 276, 307; definition, 4, 6–7; differentiation from addiction, 5, 10
Circulation time, 221–222, 225–226
Circulatory disturbances:
    alcoholic, identity with beriberi, 222–224; role of beverages consumed, 228; treatment, 226
    in beriberi, 193; in chronic alcoholic deterioration, 147; clinical picture, 220–227; in delirium tremens, 104, 120; diagnosis, 227; in experimental thiamin deficiency, 231; frequency, 226; physical activity, relation to, 224, 231; statistics on symptoms, 225; thiamin deficiency in, 226
Circulatory failure, 221–222, 224–225; conventional etiologic factors, 227
Circulatory system, effect of alcohol on, 220

Personality studies, 21–29, 119; deficiencies of, 21; naturalistic, 17; psychoanalytic, 18, 29–32; statistical, 17; psychometric, 17, 22–24

Pharmacothymia, 28, 32

Physical activity, role in circulatory disturbances, 224, 231

Physiological theories of addiction, 10, 14–16

Pia mater, 108–109, 134, 265

Pituitary lesions, 309

Plasma proteins, 221, 229

Pneumonia in delirium tremens, 104, 113

Polioencephalitis hemorrhagica superior (see Wernicke's syndrome)

Polyneuritis (see Polyneuropathy)

Polyneuropathy, 173, 178–179, 181–221, 224–225, 227–228, 240, 259, 270, 272; alternative terms, 183; axis cylinders, 184; beriberi, definite identification with, 201; beverages consumed, 199; case histories, 187–188; circulatory changes, 197; clinical picture, 189–199; in delirium tremens, 103–104

diagnosis, 196; differential, 198–199 electrocardiographic changes, 197; endocrines in, 189; etiologic theories, 199–220; experimental, 207–209; frequency, 182; in Korsakoff's psychosis, 127–128, 132–133, 135; liver in, 188–189; nerve fibers, 184; neurasthenia, 195; neurologic disturbances, 195–197; in nicotinic acid deficiency encephalopathy, 255; pathology, 182–189; in pellagra, 235, 237; peripheral nerves, 183, 185–188; precipitating factors, 198, 220; of pregnancy, 216; prognosis, 198; sex ratio in, 194; treatment, 179, 201–202, 205–207, 216–220; in Wernicke's syndrome, 242, 247

Popliteal nerve, 185, 187

Porphyrinuria, 236

Potassium, blood, 106

Poverty drinkers, 38–39, 47

P-P factor, effect of alcohol on, 239

Precipitating factors, xxiii; absent in acute alcoholic hallucinosis, 140

in delirium tremens, 112–114, 117–118; statistics of, 113

in polyneuropathy, 198, 220

Precordial pain, 222

Prognosis:
of acute alcoholic hallucinosis, 144; and age, 73; of delirium tremens, 97, 120; and heredity, 73; of impassioned drinkers, 26; in inebriates with brain changes, 73; of Korsakoff's psychosis, 126, 137; of nicotinic acid deficiency encephalopathy, 255; of occupational drinkers, 73; of polyneuropathy, 198; of schizoid drinkers, 73; of self-aggrandizing drinkers, 27; of symptomatic drinkers, 72; in Wernicke's syndrome, 242

Protein metabolism in delirium tremens, 106, 114–115, 117

Pseudodipsomania, 41

Pseudoparesis, alcoholic, 86

Pseudopellagra (see Pellagra)

Psychiatry, role of in alcohol research, xxiii

Psychoanalysis, 16, 18

Psychoanalytic treatment of addicts, 53, 68–70; statistics of success, 69

Psychoanalytic views:
of acute alcoholic hallucinosis, 142; of alcohol addiction, 29–32

Psychologic theories, 16

Psychometric studies, 17; of personality, 22–24

Psychopathy, 19; role in etiologic theories of addiction, 10; role in etiologic theories of pathological intoxication, 95

Psychotherapy of addiction, 52, 59–72; Adlerian methods, 62, 67; basic principles of, 66

causative, 61, 64–72, 79; differences in, 64, 79; difficulties of, 64–65; rationale of, 64

emotional, 61; emotional maturity as goal of, 67; role of ex-addict in, 65; incidental to drug treatment, 60; in large institutions, 68; personality analysis in, 66–67; rationale of, 59–60; reëducation, 64, 67; role of relatives in, 65; religious conversion, 62–64, 79; role of Salvation Army in, 68; of secondary addicts, 64; selective criteria for, 71; substitutive, 61–64; role of transference in, 65

Pulmonary congestion, 222

Pulse, 222; pressure, 222, 224; thready, 222